INVISIBLE WORLDS

Annie Besant and C. W. Leadbeater, 1900.

INVISIBLE WORLDS

Annie Besant on Psychic and Spiritual Development

Essays compiled by Kurt Leland

QUEST BOOKS

Theosophical Publishing House
Wheaton, Illinois * Chennai, India

First Quest Edition 2013

Quest Books
Theosophical Publishing House
PO Box 270
Wheaton, IL 60187-0270

www.questbooks.com

Cover design by Kirsten Hansen Pott

Library of Congress Cataloging-in-Publication Data

Besant, Annie, 1847–1933.
Invisible worlds: Annie Besant on psychic and spiritual development / essays compiled by Kurt Leland.
pages cm
Includes bibliographical references and index.
ISBN 978-0-8356-0910-4
1. Besant, Annie, 1847–1933. 2. Theosophy—Doctrines.
I. Leland, Kurt, editor of compilation. II. Title.
BP563.I64 2013
288′.934—dc23 2013014188

6 5 4 3 2 * 18 19 20 21 22

Printed in the United States of America

Where there is not calm self-mastery, indifference to personal matters, serene devotion to work for others, there is no true occultism, no really spiritual life.

—Annie Besant

Contents

Acknowledgments

I would like to thank the librarians who helped in the research required to assemble and annotate this book: Erika DeCarlo and Pablo Sender of the H. S. Olcott Memorial Library, Wheaton, IL; Michael Gomes of the Emily Sellon Memorial Library, New York, NY; Gloria Korsman of the Andover-Harvard Theological Library, Cambridge, MA; Nancy Lehwalder at the Theosophical Library, Seattle, WA; and Lakshmi Narayan at the Krotona Library, Ojai, CA.

I owe a debt of gratitude to Dorothy Bell, Joy Mills, Shirley Nicholson, and Maria Parisen of the Krotona School of Theosophy, Ojai, CA, for their enthusiasm and support of my researches into the writings of Annie Besant, and to the Kern Foundation for a scholarship that allowed me to attend "Annie Besant: A Voice that Calls Us Onward," which they team taught in September 2009—and especially to Shirley for inviting me.

I am also grateful for several e-mail correspondents, ever ready to provide insight, assistance, and alternative perspectives on Theosophical questions, in particular those related to the writings of Madame H. P. Blavatsky, Annie Besant, and William Quan Judge: Dara Eklund, Gerry Hejka-Ekins, William Doss McDavid, Pablo Sender (who read the manuscript and provided useful comments), and Nicholas Weeks.

Finally, I am deeply appreciative of the kind, considerate, respectful treatment I have received from the editorial staff at the Theosophical Publishing House in Wheaton, IL, especially from Sharron Dorr (always available for wise counsel on matters of style and presentation), Richard Smoley (who suggested that I compile the book and provided useful guidelines in matters of scholarship), and freelance copy editor Martha Woolverton (ever patient with details as Sharron and I worked out how best to modernize Besant's texts without losing her voice as orator and writer). If the publishing world has a Devachan for authors, TPH would be it.

ABBREVIATIONS

1. Books

CW — *Collected Writings*, vols. 1–15 (Blavatsky)

EW — *The Esoteric World of Madame Blavatsky* (Caldwell)

IGT — *The Inner Group Teachings of H. P. Blavatsky* (Spierenburg)

IU — *Isis Unveiled*, vols. 1–2 (Blavatsky)

KT — *The Key to Theosophy* (Blavatsky)

LMW — *Letters from the Masters of the Wisdom*, series 1–2 (Jinarajadasa)

LP — *Light on the Path* (Collins)

ML — *The Mahatma Letters to A. P. Sinnett from the Mahatmas M. and K.H.* (Barker or Chin). References are not to letter numbers, but to page numbers in the thematic edition (Barker) and/or the chronological edition (Chin).

SD — *The Secret Doctrine*, vols. 1–3 (Blavatsky)

TBL — *Transactions of the Blavatsky Lodge* (Blavatsky)

TG — *The Theosophical Glossary* (Blavatsky)

VS — *The Voice of the Silence, being Extracts from the Book of the Golden Precepts* (Blavatsky)

2. Organizations

ES — The Esoteric School of Theosophy (originally called the Esoteric Section of the Theosophical Society, and later the Eastern School of Theosophy)

TS — The Theosophical Society

3. Persons

AWB — Annie Wood Besant (1847–1933)

CWL — Charles Webster Leadbeater (1847/52–1934)

HPB — Helen Petrovna Blavatsky (1831–91)

HSO — Henry Steel Olcott (1832–1907)

Master KH — Koot Humi (various spellings), one of the Masters of the Ancient Wisdom behind the founding of the TS

Master M — Morya, the other Master behind the founding of the TS

Introduction

One of the three objects of the Theosophical Society is "to investigate unexplained laws of nature and the powers latent in humanity." Annie Besant (1847–1933)—outspoken feminist, political activist, advocate for the independence of India from the British Raj, and longtime president of the TS—was an ardent advocate of this object. Her many books, pamphlets, and articles on psychic and spiritual development provide guidelines and examples for their pursuit, which she felt should be available to all.

However, Madame H. P. Blavatsky (1831–91), the Russian occultist who founded the TS in 1875, was an equally ardent democrat in all things *but* the teaching of psychic and spiritual development. She believed that some aspects of occult knowledge were too dangerous to place in the hands of an ignorant populace, so she made a careful distinction between *exoteric* teachings designed to educate the masses on basic principles of religion and morality and *esoteric* teachings passed on secretly to a select group of students.

Toward the end of her life, HPB assembled such a group of students and Besant was among them. After HPB's death, Besant published these secret teachings and spent many years explaining them, making use of them, and encouraging others to explore them.[1] HPB's warnings of the dangers of such pursuits were so explicit that we must wonder at Besant's audacity in publishing the secret teachings—though she claimed to have HPB's sanction to do so.[2]

Ever since HPB's death, TS members have felt ambivalent about which voice to listen to—HPB's voice of warning or Besant's voice of encouragement. Yet HPB was just as encouraging to her personal students as Besant was to the general public, provided all reasonable precautions were taken and her students properly understood and followed all instructions.

Besant's teachings on psychic and spiritual development, which she also referred to as "occult training," must be understood in this light. She was determined to educate people about the precautions *and* the instructions—though only within a very limited and relatively safe range. Rather than advocate exploration of the whole world of occult wisdom opened up by HPB in *Isis Unveiled* (1877), *The Secret Doctrine* (1888), and numerous articles for Theosophical journals, Besant focused on the goal of developing our dense and subtle bodies. First, we should explore and master their faculties for action, feeling, and thought, each of which is well within our reach; according to Besant, these faculties correspond to our physical, astral, and mental bodies. Then we should explore and master the inner senses, specialized for perception on the higher planes on which our subtle bodies operate as vehicles of consciousness.

Aside from a personal fascination with the notion of bodies and planes that preoccupied Besant at least until 1912, when she published a definitive diagram of the relations between them,[3] her reasons for focusing on this area of occult development were derived from various passages in HPB's writings. For example, the following excerpt from a communication to HPB's private students implies a procedure and a rationale for occult development: to get in touch with Masters of the Wisdom—teachers of an ancient occult tradition who instructed HPB and who inspired her to found the TS. For emphasis, I have added a number at the end of each step in this procedure:

> It is, however, right that each member, once he believes in the existence of such Masters [1], should try to understand what their nature and powers are [2], to reverence Them in his heart [3], to draw near to Them, as much as in him lies [4], and to open up for himself conscious communication with the guru to whose bidding he has devoted his life [5]. THIS CAN ONLY BE DONE BY RISING TO THE SPIRITUAL PLANE WHERE THE MASTERS ARE, AND NOT BY ATTEMPTING TO DRAW THEM DOWN TO OURS [6].
>
> Inasmuch as growth in spiritual life comes from within, members must not expect to receive any other communications than those through H.P.B. The additional help, instruction, and enlightenment,

> will come from the inner planes of being, and will, as said, always be given when deserved [7]. (*CW* 12:492; original capitalized emphasis)

Thus the goal of occult training, as taught by Besant, was to develop the bodies as vehicles of consciousness so that students could rise to the spiritual plane, where they might be further educated by the Masters. Besant believed she had accomplished this goal for herself, that it changed her life in positive ways, and that with a proper understanding of the process, others could achieve the same goal.

In this, she had the sanction of various statements published by HPB, such as the following: "Subjective, purely spiritual 'Mediumship' is the only harmless kind, and is often an elevating gift that might be cultivated by every one" (*CW* 6:329). By the words *subjective, purely spiritual,* and *mediumship,* HPB meant an internal focus of consciousness that aspired to communication with high spiritual teachers. We might now call it "receiving internal guidance."

Such "harmless" mediumship was directly opposed to that practiced by contemporary spiritualists, which involved objectively perceived phenomena (such as levitating tables) and the delivery of inspiring messages from the recent or famous dead. HPB claimed that the forces performing such phenomena were not only *not* spiritually enlightened beings, but also often not even human. Her many pronouncements on the dangers of mediumship specifically refer to the practices of contemporary spiritualists.

The following passage from an 1885 article entitled "Spiritual Progress" further clarifies HPB's position on psychic and spiritual development—making several distinctions that Besant carried forward into all she lectured about and wrote on these subjects. The first paragraph refers to spiritual development, the second to psychic development:

> The goal of the aspirant for spiritual wisdom is entrance upon a higher plane of existence; he is to become a new man, more perfect in every way than he is at present, and if he succeeds, his capabilities and faculties will receive a corresponding increase of range and power, just as in the visible world we find that each stage in the evolutionary scale is marked by increase of capacity. This is how it is that the Adept

> becomes endowed with marvellous powers that have been so often described, but the main point to be remembered is, *that these powers are the natural accompaniments of existence on a higher plane of evolution, just as the ordinary human faculties are the natural accompaniments of existence on the ordinary human plane.*
>
> Many persons seem to think that adeptship is not so much the result of radical development as of additional construction; they seem to imagine that an Adept is a man who, by going through a certain plainly defined course of training, consisting of minute attention to a set of arbitrary rules, acquires first one power and then another; and when he has attained a certain number of these powers is forthwith dubbed an adept. Acting on this mistaken idea they fancy that the first thing to be done towards attaining adeptship is to acquire "powers"—clairvoyance and the power of leaving the physical body and travelling to a distance, are among those which fascinate the most. (*CW* 6:332–33; italics mine)

In reading what follows, we must keep in mind what Besant aims to teach—the development not of supernormal powers but of communication skills that would allow for the "additional help, instruction, and enlightenment" that would come with direct contact with the Masters. She laid out this vision in a lecture given shortly after her election as president of the TS in 1907. Her hope was

> that we may permit the Great Ones to be sufficiently in touch with our little selves to send their forces through us, and that their life shall become the life of the Society; that . . . a greater spirituality shall circulate in every vein and vessel of the Society, and it shall become again truly a vehicle for the Masters of the Wisdom.[4]

Such a vehicle would be "more truly a Brotherhood [the first object of the TS], more full of knowledge, more really linked to the higher worlds by a center of wise occultism" whose purpose would be to bring about "the birth of a more spiritual humanity." Besant saw the membership of the TS as the "builders," the "forerunners," and the "heralds" of this "next civilization."[5] She was supported in doing so by another passage from HPB's writings, in which she found her sanction for teaching psychic and spiritual development more publicly. This passage occurred in HPB's "Letter to the Fifth

Annual Convention of the American Section of the TS," which HPB had commissioned Besant to read at that convention, held in Boston in late April 1891. HPB died on May 8, while Besant was away.

To understand this passage, we need to know that HPB spoke of our current civilization as the fifth *root race* (or cyclical phase) of human evolution since the advent of humanity on earth and that each root race passed through seven stages of development called subraces. Each root race and subrace involved the development of certain aspects of consciousness called principles. The fifth subrace of the fifth root race emphasized the development of the fifth principle, which HPB called *manas* (Sanskrit for "mind"; hence *manasic*—"of the mind"). The sixth subrace would initiate the development of the illuminative or intuitional principle, *buddhi*. That development would only be completed many thousands of years hence, during the evolution of the sixth root race. HPB taught that the beginnings of the sixth subrace of the fifth root race were beginning to appear in America.

Here is what HPB wrote to the convention:

> Your position as the fore-runners of the sixth subrace of the fifth root-race has its own special perils as well as its special advantages. Psychism, with all its allurements, and all its dangers, is necessarily developing among you, and you must beware lest the Psychic outruns the Manasic and Spiritual development. Psychic capacities held perfectly under control, checked and directed by the Manasic principle, are valuable aids in development. But these capacities running riot, controlling instead of controlled, using instead of being used, lead the Student into the most dangerous delusions and the certainty of moral destruction. Watch therefore carefully this development, inevitable in your race and evolution-period so that it may finally work for good and not for evil; and receive, in advance, the sincere and potent blessings of Those whose good-will will never fail you, if you do not fail yourselves. (*CW* 13:173)

By *psychism*, HPB meant what we ordinarily think of as psychic abilities: seeing or communicating with apparitions of the dead; experiencing precognitive hunches, dreams, and visions; and sending or receiving telepathic messages. She also included mediumship in this category, when it was experienced passively (i.e., in deep or unconscious trance) in connection with unknown sources of information, as well as spiritualistic phenomena supposedly effected by the souls of the departed. By contrast, what she meant by the phrase "Manasic and Spiritual development" is hinted at in the previous citation from her writings: the process of getting into direct contact with the Masters as inner spiritual teachers.

Thus readers will see two trends in Besant's teachings on psychic and spiritual development. The first consists of her definition of psychism and her cautions against its dangers. The second consists of her outline of a path of psychic and spiritual unfolding that avoids these dangers. This path involves the development of the bodies on their respective planes up to the point of establishing communication with a trustworthy and reliable inner spiritual teacher—a Master.

How far had Besant gone in achieving such a goal? In a self-published pamphlet entitled *H.P.B. and the Present Crisis in the Theosophical Society*, Countess Constance Wachtmeister (1838–1910), the constant companion of HPB's last years, a member of HPB's inner group, and herself gifted with clairvoyance, wrote the following:

> H.P.B. always told me that her successor would be a woman, long before Annie Besant had become a member of the T.S. She made various attempts with different people, hoping to find one, but was quite unsuccessful, so that she became terribly depressed and downhearted, saying "There is nobody left to take my place when I am gone." It was only when Annie Besant joined the movement that her hopes revived, for she seemed to feel that in her she would find a successor. H.P.B. told me this, but I had been so discouraged by the previous failures, that I was determined to be on my guard and not accept Annie Besant unless entirely convinced of her disinterestedness of purpose and of her integrity. I thought it just possible that she might be an ambitious woman entering the Theosophical Society with the thought of governing and getting all into her own hands, so I watched her narrowly, criticizing her every action according to that point of view. But as I noticed her life of daily self-sacrifice and continued endeavor to overcome her failings and shortcomings, how she took herself with an iron hand to task, and how with indomitable willpower

she overcame one obstacle after another, I was obliged to confess to myself that my surmises had been both unjust and wrong.

One day I saw Annie Besant enveloped in a cloud of light—Master's color. He was standing by her side with his hand over her head. I left the room, went quickly to H.P.B., and finding her alone, told her what I had witnessed, and asked her if that was a sign that Master had chosen Annie Besant as her successor. H.P.B. replied. "Yes," and that she was glad I had seen it.

Again, one evening I accompanied Annie Besant to a small hall in London, where she lectured to workmen, when suddenly the Master was by her side, and she spoke with an eloquence which I had never heard from her lips before; it came flowing from her like a torrent of spiritual force. I may add that I have since then here in India had repeated proof of her being in direct communication with Master.

During the last year of H.P.B.'s life, when living in Avenue Road, Annie Besant used to spend some time every evening with H.P.B. to receive occult teachings. One day she was told by H.P.B. to go to America, and on the evening of her departure H.P.B. called me to her room. After a few words of salutary advice to myself, she informed me that Annie Besant had gone to America, to bear a message from H.P.B. to the American Section, and also to become better acquainted with W. Q. Judge, as on account of his power of organization, he would be most useful in the exoteric work of the Society, and therefore it would be well for them to work together. H.P.B. then, turning to me, said: "Master really communicates directly with Annie Besant, her development in this life is a very rapid one, it is the sudden bursting through the shell of all the development and knowledge gained in her previous lives of occultism." H.P.B. continued: "Annie is soon coming very near to Master, and you may rely on her." H.P.B. then went on to speak of her other pupils, but there my lips are sealed.

In confirmation of what I have here stated, I will quote from a letter, written by H.P.B. to W. Q. Judge, dated March 27th, 1891, of which I have a copy in my own possession. In this letter H.P.B. speaks of Annie Besant as *"the soul of honor and uncompromisingly truthful,"* and describes her heart as "one single unbroken diamond . . . transparent so that anyone can see how filled to the brim it is *with pure, unadulterated Theosophy and enthusiasm.*" "UNSELFISHNESS AND ALTRUISM," continues H.P.B., "is Annie Besant's name, but with me and for me she is Heliodore, a name given to her by a Master, and that I use with her, it has a *deep meaning*. It is only a few months she studies

> occultism with me in the *innermost* group of the E.S., and yet she has passed far beyond all others. She is not psychic nor spiritual in the least—all intellect (H.P.B. told me that it was through the intellectual plane that Annie Besant would pass on to the spiritual plane), and yet she hears Master's voice when alone, sees His Light, and recognizes his voice from that of D____. Judge, *she is a most wonderful woman*, my right hand, my successor, when I will be forced to leave you, my sole hope in England, as you are my soul hope in America." The italics in the above quotation are all H.P.B.'s, and not mine.[6]

Such testimony is suggestive, though it was brought forward fifteen years after the conversations with HPB supposedly took place and deals with unverifiable clairvoyant perceptions. A curious explanation of the "deep meaning" of HPB's name for Besant, *Heliodore*, occurs in a tribute published after Besant's death by her lifelong friend Bhagavan Das (1869–1958), a TS member and Sanskrit scholar living and teaching in Benares (now Varanasi). His words are especially startling when we consider that his forty-year-long friendship with Besant was often strained for extended periods by his outspoken opposition to her policies in guiding the TS:

> In earlier days she often wrote over the penname of *Heliodore*. The word means "Given by the Sun," *Surya-datta*. Appropriately she named herself so, by subconscious memory. The old books say: "The messengers, the orderly officers, the envoys and ambassadors, of the high gods who have their abode in the solar sphere, are always flashing along the pathways constituted by the sunbeams, to all parts of the solar system, adjusting the affairs of the *jivas*, the living beings, that make up the kingdoms of animate nature everywhere; and human souls also which, by their virtuous deeds, have won the right, are led, after they leave the earth, with sweet songs of invitation and of welcome, by those same deeds of sacrifice in visible shape, along these rays, to their appointed places of reward and rest in the solar heavens."
>
> To those of us who have been nurtured in such traditions it is easy to believe that her soul of fire and light was such a servant of those who brood over humanity as parents over their children, and came to and dwelt on the earth for a few decades for the awakening of men to higher things, and has now gone back for a while, to rest and then to come again, as she has promised.[7]

Whether such statements are to be considered as hagiography or as an intuition of what could be called Besant's "superphysical" career depends on people's attitude toward her. She is still revered as a spiritual teacher by some Theosophists and viewed as a controversial and possibly untrustworthy figure by others. During her many decades of involvement with the TS, she championed various unpopular persons and causes and opposed others that many contemporary TS members held dear. A book of its own would be required to examine these controversies with fairness to all parties.

Aside from such considerations, I believe there is much of value in Besant's teachings on psychic and spiritual development. My guiding light in selecting the texts included in this book comes from HPB herself, when speaking to her specially chosen students, the members of the Esoteric Section of the TS (later called the Eastern School of Theosophy), established in 1888:

> The attitude of mind in which the teachings given are to be received is that which shall tend to develop the faculty of intuition. The duty of members in this respect is to refrain from arguing that the statements made are not in accordance with what other people have said or written, or with their own ideas upon the subject, or that, again, they are apparently contrary to any accepted system of thought or philosophy. Practical esoteric science is altogether *sui generis.* It requires all the mental and psychic powers of the student to be used in examining what is given, to the end that the real meaning of the Teacher may be discovered, as far as the student can understand it. He must endeavor as much as possible to free his mind, while studying or trying to carry out that which is given him, from all the ideas which he may have derived by heredity, from education, from surroundings, or from other teachers. His mind should be made perfectly free from all other thoughts, so that the inner meaning of the instructions may be impressed upon him apart from the words in which they are clothed. Otherwise, there is constant risk of his ideas becoming as coloured with preconceived notions as those of the writers of certain otherwise excellent works upon esoteric subjects who have made the occult tenets more subservient to modern Science [or some political or spiritual cause] than to occult truth. (*CW* 12:492–93)

These are wise words that pertain to the manner in which we might assess *any* spiritual teaching we consider worthy of exploration—if only we are willing to take on the challenge of reviewing it in such a light.

Selections

I have divided the texts in this anthology into four sections, arranged (with one exception) chronologically by date of publication. Part 1, "Occultism: Light and Dark," includes two undated pamphlets from the 1890s that have been unavailable for a century or more: *What Theosophy Is* and *Introduction to Theosophy*. Since most of Besant's writings on psychic and spiritual development require a basic grounding in the Theosophical worldview, and since she was such an eloquent expositor of this worldview, I chose to include these texts instead of providing my own introduction to Theosophy. The first covers the territory in brief for an audience that knows little or nothing about Theosophy except perhaps the name. The second goes into detail about the founding and purpose of the TS and the esoteric doctrines taught by Madame Blavatsky and the Eastern spiritual Masters who were her teachers.

Besant introduces in the first text, and in the second elaborates on, a set of concepts crucial to Theosophy and to her explorations of the third object of the TS, to explore the "powers latent in humanity." These concepts include the seven principles of the cosmos and of human consciousness, the seven planes of existence, and the subtle bodies by means of which we may explore such planes.

These selections are followed by a lecture given in 1895 to the Blavatsky Lodge in London, of which Besant was longtime president (1890–1904): "The Light and Dark Sides of Nature." Many of Besant's most interesting and least known lectures were given under the auspices of the Blavatsky Lodge. The present lecture further develops the scheme of bodies and planes and provides a theoretical framework for laying to rest some inevitable questions about the safety of exploring psychic and spiritual development.

Next comes "Occultism, Semi-Occultism, and Pseudo-Occultism," another lecture given to the Blavatsky Lodge. Though it remains in print as a pamphlet, this lecture benefits from annotation and from being placed in context with other writings by Besant on psychic and spiritual development. The questions of safety raised in the previous selection are dealt with here in an eminently practical way.

Part 2, "Higher Life Training," begins with a lecture originally delivered in 1902 but not published until 1930. "The Higher Life" represents a transition from Besant's teachings on the subject in the 1890s to her more in-depth, comprehensive, and practical treatments in the first years of the twentieth century.

"Methods of Unfoldment," from 1904, considerably expands upon the topics outlined in "The Higher Life." Its keynote is the need to develop the bodies along two lines: that of consciousness (how the bodies are used to act, feel, and think while we are in the waking state) and that of the vehicles (how the bodies are used to explore higher planes while we are in other states).

"The Reality of the Invisible and the Actuality of the Unseen Worlds" considers the intriguing notion that experiential rather than merely theoretical knowledge of superphysical worlds might beneficially change our beliefs about ourselves and the universe and our conduct toward ourselves and others. For Besant, this is one of the strongest rationales for the pursuit of psychic and spiritual development—a point she makes more trenchantly in a later selection, "Investigations into the Superphysical."

"Occultism and Occult Training" is perhaps Besant's most important lecture on psychic and spiritual development. Here, she lays out a comprehensive plan for developing the astral and mental bodies in order to explore higher planes and states of consciousness. Her later writings on the subject, both here and elsewhere, frequently draw upon these ideas. This text was first published in the transactions of a 1904 Theosophical convention and subsequently disappeared from view until Nancy Lehwalder, the librarian at the Theosophical Library in Seattle, accidentally made me aware of it in 2009.[8]

"The Conditions of Occult Research" was delivered in 1905 at another convention and was similarly buried until the late 1940s.

Perhaps in response to critics of her advocacy of the third object of the TS, Besant provides a rationale for pursuing the line of development laid out in "Occultism and Occult Training." Why should an organization based on the principle of human brotherhood and on administering to the physical, emotional, intellectual, and spiritual sufferings of the world involve itself in the development of psychic and spiritual abilities? Besant's answer is that such abilities are developing anyway as part of the natural course of human evolution. Further understanding is needed about the nonphysical bodies and planes so that we can be of better service to humanity along psychic and spiritual lines.

Part 3, "Investigating Different Worlds," begins with a new phase in Besant's Theosophical career, her election to the presidency of the TS. "Psychism and Spirituality" was delivered in the summer of 1907, in London, just after her election. It demonstrates how the intentional development of psychic abilities—disparaged by some members of the TS—relates to our process of spiritual unfolding.

Originally published in 1909 as a two-part article, "Communication between Different Worlds" poses the greatest challenge for contemporary readers. The first half deals with the familiar subject of planes and bodies. The second half applies this information to various types of communication with the Masters. Besant is writing for a knowledgeable audience and makes many references to historical and then-current issues in the TS. Much annotation is required to provide context.

Toward the end, a political subtext for the piece emerges, along with controversial views of the events under discussion. Besant attempts to justify what she calls the "Adyar manifestations"—alleged appearances of the Masters at the International Headquarters of the TS in Adyar, Madras (now Chennai), India, at the time of the death of its cofounder and longtime president, Henry Steel Olcott (1832–1907). A crisis of leadership was in the air. Several persons, including HSO, claimed to see visions of the Masters, who allegedly expressed their support of Besant as the next president of the TS. Besant was present at Adyar during some part of this anxious period. Whether naively or self-servingly, she announced these visitations to the membership and ignited a firestorm of protest that continued to plague her well after she was elected.

Eighty years after Besant's death, the details of this controversy may seem important only to historians. Yet a larger issue relevant to the membership and governance of any spiritual organization was playing itself out—and Besant's attempts to resolve it bear consideration in this light. What is to be done when an organization is split along the lines of experiencers and nonexperiencers of psychic and spiritual development, clairvoyance, occult phenomena, and mystical states of knowing?

The experiencers, usually a minority, may include individuals at all levels of natural ability, training, and accuracy, as well as intentional and unintentional deceivers. The nonexperiencers, usually the majority, may include believers, agnostics, skeptics, and naysayers. Ideally, the basis of the TS in the notion of universal brotherhood (considered by HPB to be the most important of its objects) should allow for the peaceful coexistence of experiencers and nonexperiencers. But what if the former are in leadership positions and the latter do not understand or trust their decisions or the occult authority they claim—even when this authority is attributed to high spiritual beings such as the Masters?

Besant grapples with such problems in this article. Her solutions may seem hollow to some readers. Yet she returns to these problems in later selections, confronting them in somewhat more satisfying ways. Sadly, the ideal of brotherhood she develops in these responses to her critics may never be realized during our current contentious evolutionary stage. The sixth subrace, with its more evolved sense of unity consciousness, is still far off in our future, despite Besant's hopes that its forerunners were to be found in the TS of her day.

The next selections, "The Larger Consciousness and Its Value" and "Revelation, Inspiration, Observation," come from Besant's lectures in London during the summer of 1909. The first tells us how to know when the astral and mental bodies are developing as they should. The second deals with how students of Theosophy should assess the vast body of Theosophical literature available at the time, including several volumes of clairvoyant investigations by Besant and her colleague Charles W. Leadbeater (1847/54–1934).[9] Though Besant considered these volumes to be nothing more than catalogs of observations subject to refinement and correction by subsequent generations of clairvoyant investigators, some members of the TS tended to see them as quasi-scriptural revelations. Besant notes the dangers of such an attitude. Her insightful remarks have kept this lecture in print as a pamphlet for many years.

Part 4, "Science of the Superphysical," contains four selections. The first, "Theosophy as Science," appeared as a chapter in *Theosophy*, part of a popular series entitled the People's Books, published by a non-Theosophical publisher in 1912. This book contains a diagram that brilliantly synthesizes Besant's and Leadbeater's teachings on the bodies and the planes of existence with HPB's teachings on the principles. However, it has disappeared from the awareness of most students of Theosophy, with unfortunate results.

In Leadbeater's *A Textbook of Theosophy* (1912), a note appeared to the effect that "the President [Besant] has now decided upon a set of names for the planes, so for the future these will be used instead of those previously employed." There follows a list of the old and new names.[10] Readers were apt to wonder about the authority of a president who could make such an official—and apparently arbitrary—proclamation. To some, it seemed as if Besant had abrogated HPB's authority in the matter of naming the planes. Perhaps to pacify those who objected to such abrogation, later editions of the book changed this note to read, "Dr. Annie Besant has *proposed* a set of names for the planes . . . "[11] The restoration to the Theosophical canon of the diagram that prompted Leadbeater's note may lay such concerns to rest.

The 1912 article "Investigations into the Superphysical" was composed to explain the methods and the rationale of producing a collaborative book of clairvoyant investigations with CWL, published that year: *Man: Whence, How and Whither*. Written on the eve of the secession of the German Section of the TS under the leadership of Rudolf Steiner (1861–1925), and its reformation as the Anthroposophical Society, this article advocated for tolerance in assessing clairvoyant information, especially when a variety of sources apparently contradict each other.

The final selection, a brief article of 1914 entitled "Occultism," continues the discussion, begun in part 3, on the distinction between psychism and spirituality. It stipulates two paths of spiritual development: That of the occultist embraces psychism—the mastery of the bodies and the exploration of the planes to which they give access. That of the mystic embraces true spirituality—the seeking of union with the divine, without regard to the bodies and planes. Each path is equally valid and leads to a different goal—in the first case, becoming a Master who remains to work within the world as a liberated being, retaining a physical body; in the second, becoming an Adept who leaves the bodies behind (especially the physical body) and works for the benefit of humanity in superphysical states of being. Touching on many of the themes treated in earlier selections, this brief essay forms a fitting close to the book.

Toward the end of 1913, Besant turned her attention to Indian politics, campaigning for home rule for much of the next two decades. About this time, she renounced further clairvoyant investigation.[12] Though she subsequently published two books treating the bodies and planes, *Man's Life in This and Other Worlds* (1913) and *Man's Life in Three Worlds: A Booklet for Beginners* (1919), neither broke new ground. The former focused primarily on our experience in the afterlife. The latter was a reorganized, updated, and nontechnical presentation of the material Besant brought out nearly twenty-five years earlier in *Man and His Bodies* (1896).

Except for sporadic mention in lectures on other topics during the 1920s, Besant virtually dropped the subject of psychic and spiritual development until one of her last lectures, "Occultism in Daily Life," delivered at an international conference in Geneva in 1930, when she was eighty-two years old. Comparison of the published transcript of this lecture with "The Higher Life" of 1902, included here, reveals the same basic outline and a similar treatment of the bodies and planes—so I chose not to reprint it.[13] Nevertheless, this late lecture demonstrates that Besant's ideas on the subject of psychic and spiritual development remained remarkably consistent throughout her more than forty years of involvement with the TS. The best of these ideas are presented in this collection.

Sources

Many of Besant's major writings have been continuously in print for a century or more in a variety of editions—some supervised by her, when her thinking on a subject changed, others altered after her death, often without acknowledgment of the rationale for such changes. The texts included here are mostly drawn from books and pamphlets that have long been out of print and were generally not subjected to such treatment. In the case of *Occultism, Semi-Occultism, and Pseudo-Occultism* and *Revelation, Inspiration, Observation*, both of which are still in print from the Theosophical Publishing House, I have used the earliest appearance I could find.

Since Besant's works entered the public domain in 2003, there has been a proliferation of reprint and online versions of many of her books and pamphlets, with no scholarly oversight as to the reliability of the editions used. In some cases, typographical errors and unacknowledged changes in format (such as the loss of original italics or the rearrangement of diagrams) have been introduced into the texts because of the peculiarities of digitizing scanned books (e.g., misprision by optical character readers) or of creating HTML documents for display on the Internet. When I have drawn from such versions rather than scanning texts myself, I have carefully checked them against original published versions to correct such problems.

More complete information on the sources of individual texts may be found in the listing on pages 369–72.

Editing

I have corrected typographical errors, modernized spelling and punctuation, broken up long paragraphs, and shortened sentences. Many of Besant's essays and addresses are transcriptions from the spoken word. The transcribers tended to place all the material on a particular aspect of her subject into a single paragraph and to string sentences together with semicolons, posing serious challenges for the reader's attention. In a few cases, when Besant was quickly summarizing a subject, I have rearranged the original presentation in outline form—so much information crammed into a single sentence was virtually unreadable.

I have regularized Besant's idiosyncratic capitalization, maintaining it only when she refers to entities and concepts she held in reverence, such as the word *Adepts* (spiritual masters) and its cognates. I have not altered her use of *man* and *his* in reference to humanity—e.g., in the title of the book *Man and His Bodies*. Though some might argue that her message was to the world and therefore updating it to be less paternalistic and more inclusive of women is justified, I contend that with such changes her speaking voice in the lecture form is lost. This voice is natural, intense, intelligent, passionate, intimate, and often inspired. I would not want to deprive readers of the chance to sense Besant's charismatic personality through her language by updating it for the sake of political correctness.

During her lifetime, Besant was considered the greatest female orator in English. The sound of words was important to her. Thus, though I have Americanized her spelling, I have left such Briticisms as *towards*, *upwards*, and *downwards* because they are part of the sound world of her speech (though she seems to follow her own rules when using *upward* and *downward*, which may or may not carry a final *s*). I have also retained some unusually placed commas when they indicate rhetorical pauses in the delivery of Besant's lectures, whether for breath or for emphasis. On rare occasions, I have silently made slight modifications of tense, syntax, or usage if the sense was otherwise unclear—but always ensuring that Besant's voice would not be lost. As the son of one of her closest Indian colleagues said, "She was a great artist in words, which in her mouth were like music, and her voice rose and fell as the waves of the sea in perfect rhythm when she spoke."[14]

When Besant is discussing the seven principles using her own English terms instead of HPB's Sanskrit originals, I have added the Sanskrit equivalent in brackets. For example, Besant sometimes refers to *atman*, the seventh principle in HPB's system, as the spirit. The word *spirit* has so many connotations for us that Besant's use of it as a technical term is weak. When we read *atman* in brackets after *spirit*, a moment of deeper recognition and insight occurs that might otherwise have been lost.

Diacritical marks have been removed from Besant's texts and from all citations as problematical for those who use e-readers, which may not be able to generate the required characters. Emphasis in citations, such as words or passages in italics or upper case, is original unless otherwise specified.

In Besant's texts, the anglicized Sanskrit word *akasha* has been used in preference to various spellings (such as *akasa*) found in original sources and later editions of such sources, including HPB's *Collected Writings*. Similarly, *kosha* is used instead of *kosa*. Following the lead of Boris de Zirkoff, editor of the *Collected Writing*, I use the more familiar *atman* instead of *atma* and *Dhyani-Chohans* instead of *Dhyan-Chohans* as more grammatically correct.

Annotation

When Besant herself supplied the source of a scriptural quote, whether from the Bible, the Upanishads, or the Bhagavad Gita, I have surrounded it with parentheses. Those I have supplied myself are in brackets. All biblical citations refer to the Authorized King James Version. Translations from Indian scripture vary so widely that a reader who looks up Besant's references may wonder whether the citations are correct. I have consulted numerous sources to ensure accurate identification. But it has been impossible to ascertain Besant's own sources. Some translations from the Upanishads resemble those by Edward Roer (1805–66), published in the 1850s by the Royal Asiatic Society of Bengal in a series entitled Bibliotheca Indica. (These may be found by using the search words *upanishads roer* at www.hathitrust.org). Besant was a Sanskrit scholar, so the wording sometimes may have been her own. Most references to the Bhagavad Gita can be easily correlated with her published translation, which is still in print.[15]

I have moved footnotes in the originals back to the endnotes and indicated that they were Besant's.

Some selections use terms familiar to students of Theosophy but not to a general audience. When Besant does not explain these terms, or when her explanation would be insufficient for a reader new to Theosophy, I provide definitions and context in the notes.

Besant often conjures up the intellectual or spiritual atmosphere of the past or of her present with the names of philosophers, mystics, and scientists. A contemporary reader would be justified in skimming such passages without loss of the sense of a text. Though Besant regarded the teachings of Theosophy as timeless, the evidences she presented in favor of them were a product of her time. For those interested in the intellectual climate of the late nineteenth and early twentieth centuries, I have tried to identify the many persons and publications she cited. Except where indicated, birth and death dates and capsule biographies are based on information from http://en.wikipedia.org. Because of the large number of such references, I have not cited them individually, unless the source article title is different from the person's name as listed in boldface at the head of each note.

Besant's writings are dense with allusions to the works of HPB. I have attempted to track these down and present them verbatim in the endnotes. Linking Besant's allusions with the passages in HPB's works to which she was referring results in a double illumination: Besant's points take on added depth and dimensionality and HPB's points are clarified by the context into which Besant places them. Besant's allusions thus become an invitation for the reader to discover HPB's teachings for the first time or to go back to and reconsider them in a new light.

I have edited citations from older editions of Besant's works to match the style used in the rest of the book. Citations from HPB's works and those of others may include idiosyncratic spelling and capitalization.

Any Besant text mentioned in this introduction or in the endnotes is fully documented in the bibliography. Other authors are included in the bibliography only when quoted directly or mentioned significantly by her or by me.

Annie Besant Chronology[1]

1847 October 1, Annie Wood born in Clapham, London, to William Burton Persse Wood (1816–52) and Emily Roche Morris Wood (d. 1874).

1867 Marries Frank Besant (1841–1917), an Anglican clergyman, younger brother of writer Walter Besant (1836–1901).

1869 Son, Arthur Digby, born (d. 1960).

1870 Daughter, Mabel Emily, born (d. 1952).

1873 After several years of religious doubts, refuses communion, separates from husband, pronounces herself an atheist.

1874 Delivers her first public lecture, "The Political Status of Women." Joins the National Secular Society, befriends the political reformer Charles Bradlaugh (1833–91).

1877 Becomes subeditor of Bradlaugh's *National Reformer* and with him forms the Freethought Publishing Company, which brings out many pamphlets on their radical political and atheistic views. Arrested with Bradlaugh for reprinting a pamphlet by Charles Knowlton (1800–1850) on birth control, resulting in a famous obscenity versus free speech trial in which she represents herself.

1880 Supports Bradlaugh in his successful election to Parliament.

1881 Becomes coeditor of the *National Reformer* (until 1887).

1883 Begins publishing her own journal, *Our Corner* (until 1888), as her political views shift toward socialism.

1885 Under the influence of playwright George Bernard Shaw (1856–1950), joins the Fabian Society, a recently founded organization for the nonrevolutionary promulgation of socialism.

1887 Elected to the London School Board, campaigns for free education and meals for needy children, regardless of sex (until 1891).

1888 Organizes the Matchgirls' Strike, leading to the formation of the first Matchmakers' Union. Begins studying spiritualism. Joins the Marxist Social Democratic Federation. Participates in Bloody Sunday in Trafalgar Square, when police brutally break up a free speech demonstration.

1889 Reviews *The Secret Doctrine*, meets its author, a founder of the Theosophical Society, Helena Petrovna Blavatsky (1831–91), and joins the TS. Visits HPB in Fontainebleau when the latter is writing *The Voice of the Silence* and experiences her first encounter with one of the Theosophical Masters. Meets Henry Steel Olcott (1832–1907), another founding member of the TS and its president for life. Begins editing the Theosophical journal *Lucifer* with HPB.

1890 Meets Charles Webster Leadbeater (1847/52–1934), a former Anglican clergyman who had gone to India with HPB in 1884. Elected president of the Blavatsky Lodge in London. Establishes the headquarters of the European Section of the TS in her home at 19 Avenue Road, building a lecture hall for public presentations and an occult room for secret meetings of the Esoteric Section (ES) recently established by HPB. Resigns from the National Secular Society and the Fabian Society, dissolves the Freethought Publishing Company with Bradlaugh.

1891 First lecture tours in the United States. HPB dies on May 8, and AWB becomes head of the Esoteric Section in Europe, takes over editorship of *Lucifer*.

1892 Four-month coast-to-coast lecture tour of America, beginning in November.

1893 Attends the Theosophical Congress at the World Parliament of Religions in conjunction with the World's Fair in Chicago. Publishes her *Autobiography*. First visit to India. First series of lectures at the International TS Convention in December in Adyar, Madras (now Chennai), India—the international headquarters of the TS—which becomes a quasi-yearly tradition for the rest of her life.

1894 Four-month lecture tour of India, delivering 121 lectures to audiences of 600 to 6,000. Tours Europe, Australia, and New Zealand.

1895 First clairvoyant investigations with CWL, involving Atlantis, Devachan (the heaven world), the early history of our planetary chain, Lemuria, the occult chemistry of the atom, and thought forms. American Section of the TS secedes under the leadership of William Quan Judge (1851–96), one of the original founders of the TS, after several years of controversy over the leadership of the TS and the ES.

1897 Six-month coast-to-coast lecture tour of America, involving magic lantern slides of clairvoyantly perceived thought forms, causing a sensation. Publication of *Occultism*, the so-called third volume of HPB's *The Secret Doctrine*, including various "esoteric instructions" and "oral teachings" from the final months of her life. *Lucifer* renamed the *Theosophical Review*.

1898 Establishes Central Hindu College in Benares (now Varanasi) for the advanced education of young Hindu men within the context of their own religion, rather than that of English

colonialism. Quasi-yearly lecture tours of England and Europe during the hot season in India.

1899 Lecture tour in Burma. Last meetings of the Blavatsky Lodge on Avenue Road and transfer of the TS European Section Headquarters to another location. Takes up residence at Shanti Kunja (Grove of Peace), a bungalow built for her on the property of Central Hindu College at Benares. Splits time between Benares and Adyar when not touring India or traveling around the world. India is now home base.

1902 Joins Co-Masonic Lodge (a society based on the principles of Freemasonry that admitted women).

1905 CWL relocates to Adyar after years of residence in England and extensive touring in America and Australia.

1906 CWL resigns from the TS over allegations (never conclusively proved) of sexual impropriety with young boys.

1907 HSO dies. AWB elected president of the TS for a seven-year term. Takes over editorship of the *Theosophist*, resigns editorship of the *Theosophical Review*. Lecture tours in Europe and America. Further clairvoyant investigations with CWL on occult chemistry at Weisser Hirsch, Germany.

1908 Lecture tour in Australia and New Zealand. Begins publishing the *Adyar Bulletin*. First edition of *Occult Chemistry* (with CWL).

1909 Lecture tours in Europe and America. The *Theosophical Review* discontinued (merged into the *Theosophist*). CWL reinstated in TS, returns to Adyar, and discovers J. Krishnamurti (1895–1986; nicknamed Alcyone, after a star in the Pleiades; also Krishnaji), the fourteen-year old son of an Indian Theosophical worker. AWB and CWL begin training Krishnaji as a possible spiritual teacher of world importance. Further clairvoyant investigations with CWL.

1910 AWB takes over guardianship and education of Krishnaji and his younger brother from their father. Clairvoyant investigations with CWL for *The Lives of Alcyone* and *Man: Whence, How and Whither?*

1911 Tours Burma. Inaugurates the Order of the Star in the East (OSE) to promote Krishnaji as the vehicle of a future manifestation of the World Teacher, identified with the Second Coming of Christ.

1912 Retires to Taormina, Sicily, with CWL, Krishnaji, and others to pursue further clairvoyant investigations and complete *Man: Whence, How and Whither?* Lawsuit filed by Krishnaji's father over custodianship of his two sons.

1913 German Section of the TS secedes, under the leadership of Rudolf Steiner (1861–1925), in protest over AWB's teachings regarding the World Teacher. Represents herself in court case against Krishnaji's father (prevailing, after several losses in court, upon appeal to Privy Council in England in 1914). First lectures in Madras on Indian politics.

1914 Renounces clairvoyant work, begins active political work for Indian home rule, publishing a daily journal, *New India* (until 1932), and a weekly, the *Commonweal* (until 1920). Reelected for second term as president of the TS. After touring in Europe and returning to India during the first half of the year, is unable to leave India for the duration of World War I (1914–18).

1917 Interned by the government of the Madras presidency for three months under suspicion of sedition. Afterwards elected to presidency of the Indian National Congress.

1919 First lecture tours in England and Europe following the war.

1920 Political tide in India turns against AWB as a result of her opposition to the program of noncooperation advocated by Mohandas K. Gandhi (1869–1948). Controversy in TS over

AWB's promotion of the Liberal Catholic Church (LCC), a remodeling of Christian doctrine and ritual along Theosophical lines whose proponents (including CWL) claimed apostolic succession.

1921 Lecture tour in Australia. Reelected for third term as president of the TS. Agitation against AWB over the LCC and further unproven allegations of CWL's sexual impropriety with young boys.

1922 TS agitation against AWB spreads to United States and Canada, including a "Back to Blavatsky" movement.

1923 Drafts a Commonwealth of India Bill and actively campaigns for it, first in India and later in England. TS agitation against AWB in America, Australia, and France.

1924 Celebrations in London, Bombay, and Madras of fifty years of AWB's service in social and political causes. TS agitation against her spreads to England.

1925 Lectures in England on the Commonwealth of India Bill and on the coming of the World Teacher. Celebrates the golden jubilee of the founding of the TS. Commonwealth of India Bill read in British Parliament (never advanced).

1926 Lectures in America on the coming of the World Teacher. Winters in Ojai, CA, with Krishnaji.

1927 Returns to Europe for more lecturing, then home to India.

1928 Reelected for fourth term as president of the TS. Worldwide membership peaks at 45,000.

1929 Last tour in America. Krishnaji renounces his role as World Teacher and disbands the OSE.

1930 Last tour in Europe.

1931 Withdraws from political work. Celebrates the centenary of HPB's birth at Adyar. Last public addresses in India.

1932 Celebrates twenty-five years as president of the TS and the centenary of HSO's birth at Adyar.

1933 September 20, passes away at Adyar, just before her 85th birthday, and is cremated with honors. Half of her ashes are deposited in the Ganges, near the site where a portion of HPB's ashes were cast, and half at a Garden of Remembrance at Adyar.

Part One

OCCULTISM LIGHT AND DARK

Chapter One

What Theosophy Is

(ca. 1896)

No religion, no philosophy, no science, worthy the name, can be understood in all its bearings on life, can be explored to its obscurest recesses, without careful and prolonged study from the person who desires to understand. The metaphysics and the philosophy of Christianity have given birth to a literature totally incomprehensible to the "man in the street," but it does not therefore follow that Christianity is to be set aside as an obscure and difficult study, with nothing in it intelligible to the average man and woman. Christianity has its popular as well as its philosophical side—and so with Theosophy. Its subtle metaphysics may task the keenest intellect, but its main outline is intelligible to anyone of average mental capacity, while its ethical teachings may be rendered attractive to a child.

It is with its main outline that I am here concerned—its outline as a philosophy and a science. Its ethical teachings have been familiar to the world for millenniums and found exquisite expression in many of the sayings ascribed to Zoroaster in Persia, to Lao Tzu in China, to Krishna and Buddha in Hindustan, and to Jesus in Palestine. The moral teachings of all these great sages are identical, and Theosophy can only reiterate on this head the unanimous declarations of these teachers, endorsed as they are by the conscience, though not by the practice, of mankind.

"To him that causelessly injures me," says Buddha, "I will return the protection of my ungrudging love. The more harm goes from him, the more good shall flow from me."[1] "Hatred ceases not by hatred at any time; hatred ceases by love." [Dhammapada 1.5]

"The good I will meet with goodness; the not good I will meet with goodness also; the faithful I will meet with faith; the unfaithful I will meet with faith also" [Tao Te Ching 49]. "Overcome the greedy by liberality, the liar by truth" [Dhammapada 17.223]. So Lao Tzu taught his disciples.[2]

"Love your enemies, do good to those that hate you" [Luke 6:27]. "Be not overcome of evil, but overcome with good" [Rom. 12:21]. Such was the doctrine of Jesus.

To maxims of conduct such as these, Theosophy can add nothing more noble. But it *does* claim to add a compelling motive, rooted in a rational philosophy—a motive which will have an effect on conduct which the simple enunciation of these maxims has failed to produce.

The justification of the Theosophical propaganda lies in the present condition of Christendom, to say nothing of the condition of Eastern lands. The wars, the labor strifes, the heartbreaking poverty, the unbrotherly competition, the brutality, the prostitution, the drunkenness—all these evils are rife in a civilization that calls itself Christian. And those who love man, who seek for the progress of the race, cannot but welcome into the field as allies in their warfare against sin and sorrow those who bring in their hands the priceless weapon of a knowledge which explains man's nature and the nature of the universe, and so opens up the road to his final triumph.

"The first object of the society," wrote one of those Great Souls who sent their messenger to found it for the helping of the East and the West alike, "is philanthropy. The true Theosophist is a philanthropist. Not for himself, but for the world he lives." And this true philanthropy is not only the helping of the suffering in material ways, but also the feeding of the starving mind with knowledge. For "this and philosophy, the right comprehension of life and its mysteries, will give the necessary basis and show the right path to pursue"[3] [*LMW* 1:101].

The first principle to grasp in the esoteric philosophy—spoken of as Theosophy in modern times—is that beneath all phenomena is an Eternal Existence manifesting itself, unfolding itself, in the universe. This Existence manifests as a trinity—the *Logos*, or *Word*, being the name by which the manifested God is described in Theosophy, and the Logos having three aspects: the First, Second, and Third.[4] From Him proceeds the universe, He, as it were, breathing it out; a universe which is subtlest spirit at its core, physical matter at its outermost manifestation.

Spirit and matter are the two poles of the evolving universe, and at every point in that universe both are found—spirit the parent of energies or forces, matter the parent of forms. This is the duality so marked in nature, the "pairs of opposites": positive/negative, light/darkness, male/female, and so on. The Logos in His evolving work uses as His agents and ministers the perfected men of past universes, the archangels and angels of the Christian scriptures.

Next, this universe evolves in seven stages—each successive stage being marked by an increasing latency of the spiritual side, by an increasing manifestation of the material side. It is the One robed in garments becoming denser, until at last the garments hide the life within. As Goethe sang,

> At the roaring loom of Time I ply,
> And weave for God the garments thou seest Him by.[5]

Thus the universe at last takes its physical shape, and is but the materialization of the divine thought. Having reached the point of densest materiality, it begins a slow return, evolving the spiritual forces which had been involved during the densifying process, and rendering the material form which the thought had taken instinct with energy, radiant with life.

The question may here arise: "Why seven stages? Why not ten, seventeen, fifty?" Nature is ever repeating this number seven, which lies at the basis of our cycle of evolution. Why seven is the number which underlies our present evolution I do not know. But that it is so may be found by observation.

The moon, that so largely influences our life periods, marks them in multiples of seven, for it completes its cycle in twenty-eight days (the lunar month). The fourth of this, the quarter of the moon, gives our week, consisting of seven risings and settings of the sun. Periods of gestation last for multiples of the lunar months. The seventh year of postnatal life marks a stage of development in the growing child, as does the fourteenth. Fevers reach their critical stages on the seventh, fourteenth, and twenty-first days.[6]

Illustrations might be indefinitely multiplied. All this repetition of seven in nature shows that this number is not a fanciful and arbitrary choice of the mystic, but that he merely recognizes a fact and accepts it.

The next important principle is that the universe and man mirror each other—all the forces that exist in great in the universe existing in small in man. Man is correlated to the universe, and this correlation enables him to investigate all regions of the universe, gaining in each, by the exercise of the corresponding faculties in his own nature, direct knowledge which he can register in his own consciousness. Thus he possesses

1. *A physical body*, divided into dense and etheric parts. By the first part, he comes into contact with the dense universe—the cells of his body receiving impressions from outside, and conveying those impressions inward. The eye, the ear, the touch, the taste, the smell, all are avenues of knowledge from the external universe. The second, or *etheric double*, is the vehicle of the life forces, of electric and magnetic energies, and is correlated to the ethereal world. In this plays the vitality which keeps in orderly activity all the cells and molecules of the physical body.

2. *A body of desire*; a graphic epithet, which expresses the collective whole of appetites, cravings, desires, and passions which are found in connection with the body. It is the bridge between the physical body and the mind. Pleasure and pain have in this their seat. Heat and cold, hunger and thirst, sexual desire, love and hatred, in their simplest forms, are contacted by the soul through this body of desire. This body is made of astral matter and is correlated to the astral world.

3. *A mental body*; this is made of mental matter and is correlated to the lower levels of the mental world. It is the immediate garment of the soul, and is often called the *lower mind*—the organ for all concrete thinking.

These three bodies, with the vitality that throbs through them, are the three garments of the soul, in which he is clad for his experience of life in the corresponding regions of the universe. In these he dwells in our physical world, and may range the astral and mental planes of existence, gathering knowledge of each.

While man possesses these three garments and (4.) *vitality*, he is

5. *A soul*, that is, a living intelligence, capable of learning by experience and evolving into a nobly intellectual and spiritual entity by the discipline of life on earth. This is the real man, or thinker, our word *man* being derived from the Sanskrit root *man* ("think").

6 and 7. *Spirit in its vehicle*, for which the English language has no distinctive name. By this, the realms of spirit may be directly known, instead of being taken on faith.[7]

This analysis of man gives us a key to his complicated nature, enabling us to trace and to understand the workings of consciousness alike in the saint, the criminal, the average man and woman—and by understanding these, we learn how best to help the good towards expression, how best to help the higher to dominate the lower, to aid the *man* in his struggle to control, educate, and evolve the lower constituents of his nature.

At death, he shakes off the physical and astral bodies, the time occupied in the disrobing process varying according to conditions which I have not here space to discuss. The freed soul, clad in the mental body and brooded over by the spirit and its vehicle, then passes onward into a serene and happy state, in which he assimilates the experience gathered in the life passed through. Then the mental body also disintegrates, the soul weaving into his own nature all that in that life is worthy of immortality. For the average person, this rest of the soul lasts for about fifteen hundred years, but the period varies with the stage of evolution at which the soul has arrived.

Then comes the time for the return of the soul to earth to learn another lesson in life's school. The place of his incarnation, the nation, the family, are determined by the affinities he has formed in past lives. The soul that yielded to the cravings of his passional nature will be drawn to parents showing similar characteristics. The dominating ideas of one life govern the conditions of the next—hence the enormous importance of ideals and of the tendencies of our thoughts. The thoughts of one life make the character of the succeeding lives, and this can be escaped by none.

In each life the soul seeks experience—for by experience the soul gains knowledge, and by knowledge the power to increasingly guide the man of flesh in whom he dwells. A life which is sorrowful to outward vision may be a life in which the soul rejoices, for every obstacle conquered and every pain endured are transmuted, by this spiritual alchemy, into new forces and new qualities. Measure the difference in power and usefulness of the soul in some low type of savage and that in some hero or saint, and you will understand why the soul seeks experience and how his growth proceeds.

Thus the soul journeys on his way from life to life until all that earth can give him of experience has been reaped. He reaches the greatest altitude compatible with life in this world—and then a choice is before him. He can pass onward triumphant into realms of loftier nature and there expand and grow. Or, this glorious prize within his grasp, he may turn back to earth patiently again to bear the burden of the flesh until the lowliest child of man has reached his own level and he enters into peace with all his race.

The Great Souls that choose this lot are the saviors of the world, and they wait, watching to help whenever help can be given—the Elder Brothers of our race, the perfected Sons of Man. Blessed beyond all blessings are they who in any fashion can aid them in lifting the heavy burden of our world, and can cooperate, even if it be in humblest way, in hastening the evolution of the glorious destiny of man. For the service of man is the noblest of privileges, and to work for the world the richest of prizes. Our philosophy, our science, our religion have worth only as they make us more useful members of the brotherhood of man.

Chapter Two

An Introduction to Theosophy (1896)

The Theosophical Society

The Theosophical Society was founded in New York City in the year 1875, the day recognized as its official birthday being November 17. Regarded as a spiritual movement inaugurated in the first year of the closing quarter of the nineteenth century for the helping of men, it has for its true founders certain great spiritual teachers, who devised this means of reawakening the East and awakening the West to the knowledge of the springs of spiritual truth that lay hidden in Eastern philosophy.

The spread of materialism in the West, with its consequent spread in the East, was threatening the very existence of spiritual life among men.[1] The triumphs of Western science—so dazzling in their effects on material comfort and luxury, as well as in their intellectual promise—were alluring the most promising of the youth of every land towards a philosophy becoming more and more materialistic, while the minds whose bent was more religious than intellectual were slipping further and further into superstition. Already, the cry was being raised that between Rome and atheism there was no sure and defensible standing-ground, and that the battle of the near future was between a religion devoid of all science and a science devoid of all religion.[2]

It was at this crisis that the great guardians of spiritual truth stepped forward, and sent into the arena a new combatant, the esoteric philosophy. As a center for those who held this philosophy, round whom might gather others who—agreed or not on philosophy—were willing to cooperate for the spreading of love and true brotherhood among men, they instigated the founding of the Theosophical

Society. Regarded as an organized society existing in the world with definite objects, rules, and organization, it had for its founders Helena Petrovna Blavatsky, a *chela* (disciple) of the spiritual teachers above spoken of, and Colonel Henry Steel Olcott, whom she brought into contact with these same teachers.

Helena P. Blavatsky was a Russian of noble birth, descended on the father's side from the branch of the von Hahns settled in Russia, and on the mother's from the Fadeyevs and the Dolgorukis, she being the granddaughter of the Princess Helene Dolgorukova of the elder branch, and daughter of Helene Fadeyev. These facts have been certified by her uncle, Major-General Fadeyev, of the Tzar's staff, and Joint Secretary of State in the Russian Ministry of the Interior.[3] She was the widow of a Councilor of State, General Nikifor Blavatsky, late Vice-Governor of the Province of Erivan, Caucasus. Renouncing rank and wealth, she had traveled in all lands, searching for occult knowledge, and had finally passed under the tuition of a great Eastern Adept, to the carrying out of whose directions in the service of man the whole of her later life was devoted. She passed from this life on May 8th, 1891, at 19 Avenue Road, Regent's Park, London.[4]

During the period from 1875 to 1891, she was the heart and soul of the Society, the chief link between it and the teachers of the esoteric philosophy. She held but a nominal office, her work being that of a teacher, not of an organizer, and her books—*Isis Unveiled, The Secret Doctrine, The Key to Theosophy, The Voice of the Silence, The Theosophical Glossary*—and her numerous articles in the *Theosophist*, in *Lucifer*, in the *Path*, as well as in other magazines, are a mine of information for the student.[5] As an exponent of the esoteric philosophy, she stands unrivalled in the present generation—but she claimed for herself no infallibility. She frankly stated that there were many mistakes in her writings, and she strenuously asserted the right and the duty of each to use his own intellect and judgment and not to accept blindly the authority of any writer.[6]

Colonel H. S. Olcott was a man who had played a highly honorable part in the war between North and South, and had held a responsible appointment under the USA Government.[7] He was also a journalist of repute, and was engaged in investigating and reporting on the famous spiritualistic phenomena at the Eddys' farm when he met Madame Blavatsky there among the visitors.[8] Attracted by her evident knowledge of occultism, he became her friend, and he was selected as president for life of the new Society. To it, he devoted himself with splendid courage and loyalty, battling against ridicule, slander, and opposition of every kind, side by side with his heroic woman colleague. He is still living, the "President-Founder" of the Society, and has his home at Adyar, near Madras [now Chennai], India, at the Headquarters of the whole Society.

The Society has now six sections, each with its general secretary and autonomous organization, and all working under the general constitution of the TS and acknowledging Colonel Olcott as president for life. The Sections are those of India, Europe, Sweden, America, Australia, and New Zealand.[9]

The Society has three objects:

1. To form a nucleus of the universal brotherhood of humanity, without distinction of race, creed, sex, caste, or color

2. To encourage the study of comparative religion, philosophy, and science

3. To investigate unexplained laws of nature and the powers latent in man

Of these three objects, the first is the only one which is binding on all members—the two others being meant to subserve the first. The carrying out of the second, revealing the East and West to each other, tends to break down the barriers of race and creed. There is no brotherly service the East can do to the West comparable to the unveiling of her hidden treasures of spiritual knowledge, the pouring out of her jealously guarded spiritual truths. Ever has the East been the mother of religions—and she comes now again to the aid of the West, sorely pressed by the advancing hosts of materialism.[10]

The third object also tends to brotherhood, in that it leads man to understand himself and his environment, and finally demonstrates to him the underlying spiritual unity of all beings. But both these objects require for their prosecution special capacities and special opportunities. They are not, therefore, binding on members, but are voluntarily taken up by those who are attracted by them and who are able to pursue them. Leaving such aside, probably most members have a sympathetic feeling towards them, and many even pursue them in a dilettante sort of fashion. But a person may be entirely indifferent to them—and yet if he believes in human brotherhood and is willing to work for it, he has full welcome and standing in the Theosophical Society.

For this promotion of human brotherhood is nearest the heart of the Sages who work for the welfare of man. On this point, they have left no possibility of doubt. Thus Master KH wrote to Mr. Sinnett:

> The chief object of the T.S. is not so much to gratify individual aspirations as to serve our fellow men. . . . You have ever discussed but to put down the idea of a Universal Brotherhood, questioned its usefulness, and advised to remodel the T.S. on the principle of a college for the special study of Occultism.[11] [*ML* 8 (Barker); 8 (Chin)]

This the Brotherhood refused to do. If an Anglo-Indian Theosophical Society was to be formed it must be only as

> a Branch of the Parent body, as is the British Theosophical Society at London, and contribute to its vitality and usefulness by promoting its leading idea of a Universal Brotherhood, and in other practicable ways.[12] [*ML* 9 (Barker); 9 (Chin)]

A yet higher authority wrote very plainly on the subject:

> Shall we devote our selves to teaching a few Europeans fed on the fat of the land, many of them loaded with the gifts of blind fortune, the *rationale* of bell ringing, cup growing, of the spiritual telephone and astral body formation, and leave the teeming millions of the ignorant, of the poor and despised, the lowly and the oppressed, to take care of themselves and of their hereafter the best they know how? Never. Perish rather the Theosophical Society with both its hapless Founders than that we should permit it to become no better than an academy of magic and a hall of occultism.[13] [*LMW* 1:7–8; *ML* 479 (Chin)]

> And is it we, the humble disciples of these perfect lamas, who are expected to allow the T.S. to drop its noblest title, that of the Brotherhood of Humanity to become a simple school of psychology? . . . He who does not feel competent enough to grasp the noble idea sufficiently to work for it, need not undertake a task too heavy for him. But there is hardly a theosophist in the whole Society unable to effectually help it by correcting the erroneous impressions of outsiders, if not by actually propagating himself the idea.[14] [*LMW* 1:9; *ML* 480 (Chin)]

With equal clearness, and by the same two great Easterns, were laid down the lines on which work should be carried on and the objects which, in their minds, the Theosophical Society might accomplish by spreading abroad the Aryan teachings.[15] Said Master KH,

> The same causes that are materialising the Hindu mind are equally affecting all Western thought. Education enthrones skepticism but imprisons spirituality. You can do immense good by helping to give the Western nations a secure basis upon which to reconstruct their crumbling faith. What they need is the evidence that Asiatic psychology alone supplies. Give this, and you will confer happiness of mind on thousands [third object of TS]. The era of blind faith is gone; that of enquiry is here. Enquiry that only unmasks error, without discovering anything upon which the soul can build, will but make iconoclasts. Iconoclasm from its very destructiveness can give nothing, it can only raze. But man can not rest satisfied with bare negation. Agnosticism is but a temporary halt.
>
> This is the moment to guide the recurrent impulse which must soon come, and which will push the age toward extreme atheism, or drag it back to extreme sacerdotalism, if it is not led to the primitive soul-satisfying philosophy of the Aryans [second object of the TS]. . . . You and your colleagues may help furnish the materials for a needed universal religious philosophy; one impregnable to scientific assault because itself the finality of absolute science; and, a religion, that is indeed worthy of the name, since it includes the relations of man physical to man psychical, and of the two to all that is above and below them. Is not this worth a slight sacrifice? And if after reflection you should decide to enter this new career, let it be known that your Society is no miracle-mongering or banqueting club, nor specially given to the study of phenomenalism. Its chief aim is to extirpate current superstitions and skepticism, and, from long sealed ancient

> fountains to draw the proof that man may shape his own future destiny, and know for a certainty that he can live hereafter, if he only wills; and that all "phenomena" are but manifestations of natural law, to try to comprehend which is the duty of every intelligent being.[16] [*ML* 475–76 (Chin)]

With equal plainness did the other Sage, previously quoted from, write as to the dangers menacing our present civilization and the functions of the Theosophical Society:

> The intellectual portions of mankind seem to be fast dividing into two classes, the one unconsciously preparing for itself long periods of temporary annihilation or states of non-consciousness owing to the deliberate surrender of their intellect, its imprisonment in the narrow grooves of bigotry and superstition, a process which cannot fail to lead to the utter deformation of the intellectual principle; the other unrestrainedly indulging its animal propensities with the deliberate intention of *submitting* to annihilation pure and simple in cases of failure, to millenniums of degradation after physical dissolution. Those "intellectual classes," reacting upon the ignorant masses which they attract and which look up to them as noble and fit examples to follow, degrade and morally ruin those they ought to protect and guide. Between degrading superstition and still more degrading brutal materialism the white dove of truth has hardly room where to rest her weary unwelcome foot. . . . [original ellipsis]
>
> It's time that Theosophy should enter the arena. . . . The Theosophical Society was chosen as the corner stone, the foundation of the future religions of humanity. To achieve the proposed object a greater, wiser, and especially a more benevolent intermingling of the high and low, of the alpha and omega of society, was determined upon.[17] [*ML* 477–78 (Chin)]

Such, then, are the aims of the Theosophical Society, such the scope of its work. Anyone who enters its brotherhood should consider himself pledged to serve men as brothers, and it is this service that is reckoned as the essence of Theosophy. No acceptance of the esoteric philosophy, no search after knowledge, no desire for occultism, suffice to make a man a Theosophist, if his life be not one of helpfulness to man:

> He who does not practice altruism, he who is not prepared to share his last morsel with a weaker or poorer than himself; he who neglects to help his brother man, of whatever race, nation or creed, whenever and wherever he meets suffering, and who turns a deaf ear to the cry of human misery; he who hears an innocent person slandered, whether a brother Theosophist or not, and does not undertake his defense as he would undertake his own—is no Theosophist. [*CW* 8:171; HPB quoting a Master]

The members of the Theosophical Society are thus connected by an ethical rather than by an intellectual bond, and their unity rests on a sublime ideal, not on a formulated creed. The Society has no dogmas, insists on no beliefs, endorses no church, supports no party, takes no sides in the endless quarrels that rend society, and embitter national, social, and personal life. Everywhere it cries to men, "Peace! Ye are brothers" [Acts 7:26]; everywhere it proclaims, "There is no religion higher than Truth."[18] It seeks to draw no man away from his own religion, but rather impels him to seek in the depths of his own religion for the spiritual nourishment he needs.

The teachings it presents, as the results of its second object, those of the esoteric philosophy which underlies all religions, it presents as subjects for study, not as dogmas to be blindly accepted. Those who find them to be intellectually, ethically, and emotionally satisfying, accept them. Those who do not, reject them. Others accept some and reject others. That each should show to the religion of others the respect that he claims for his own is understood as an honorable obligation in the Society, and perfect mutual courtesy on these matters is expected from members. More and more this leads to cooperation in the search for Truth, to softening of prejudices, to liberalizing of minds, and to the growth of a gracious friendliness and willingness to learn. Thus the Society not only strikes at the twin foes of man, superstition and materialism, but it spreads wherever it goes a gentle and refining influence of peace and goodwill, forming one of the forces that make for good amid the conflicts of modern civilization.

From its early days, there has been within the Society an inner circle of members who have undertaken heavier obligations than the light one of ordinary fellowship. All these members definitely accept the esoteric philosophy, believe in the Masters, regard H. P. Blavatsky as their messenger, and are willing to make sacrifices for the advancement of the Society and to work for all its objects perseveringly and unselfishly. They enter this inner circle in order that they may become more useful servants of humanity, seeking spiritual knowledge with the one object of helping man—and so cooperating, however feebly, with the great Brotherhood that is ever working for the spiritual progress of mankind.

At first, this inner circle was called the second degree, or second section, of the Society. In 1888 it was more fully organized as the Esoteric Section, and in 1890 its name was changed by H. P. Blavatsky, its head, to that of the Eastern School of Theosophy, and its official connection with the Society was severed by her, so that the perfect neutrality of the Society might not be imperiled. Only members of the TS, however, are eligible for admission, as the main object of the School is to form devoted workers for Theosophy, and the TS is the agency chosen by the Masters for the spreading of Theosophical teachings through the world. The School forms a doorway for those who seek the Masters for the sake of serving man more wisely and effectively, but the finding of them depends on the love and devotion brought by the candidate to the search. Those who desire to enter it must write to Mrs. Annie Besant, its present head.[19]

The esoteric philosophy

The esoteric philosophy is a body of knowledge embracing all truths that can be known during the present cycle of human evolution. These truths have been discovered, verified, and reverified by men in whom the spiritual nature has been so fully evolved that, for them, nature has "no veil in all her kingdoms" [*VS* 14]. These men have in all ages formed a brotherhood, in whose charge this body of knowledge remains, and they give it out gradually as the races of men become capable of assimilating it.

Truths relating to man's spiritual nature have been imparted from it and have formed the basis of the various great religions of the world. Truths of an intellectual kind have been given out as the lines on which the great philosophies have been built. Truths touching physical nature have been taught to give fresh impulse and direction to science. These benefits have been brought to men by members of the brotherhood who have been worshiped or persecuted, adored or slain, according to the temper of the times in which their mission lay. Such have been the founders of great religions, as Zarathustra, Lao Tzu, Krishna, Osiris, Buddha, Jesus. The identity of the origin of religions may be proved by the identity of their fundamental teachings, both as to the spiritual nature and as to ethical obligations:

1. The universe has its source in One Life.
2. Man's spirit is the offspring of that life.
3. Man may therefore rise to his source and re-become one with it.
4. Human life on earth is a means to an end, and that end the perfecting of the soul.
5. Man is an immortal spirit linked with a lower nature.
6. The purification of the lower nature and its union with the spirit are the means whereby the lower may share the immortality of the higher.
7. All men are brethren.
8. The law of love is the law of progress.

Such are some of the truths that will be found in every religion, however great may be the differences in the intellectual presentment of them as dogmas, or in the rites and ceremonies used in different communities. As the same water may be held in vessels differing in size, in shape, in decoration, but drawn from any of them quenches the thirst of men, so may the water of spiritual life be found in all religious vessels, and may be drawn from them for the refreshment of the soul athirst.

Thus also with philosophies. The Great Sages who gave to India the Upanishads belonged to the same brotherhood as did those—of whom Plato was one—who gave to Greece, and to the Western world through her, the immortal teachings that have molded the systems of the modern world. The thought of Pythagoras, faded from the West, was revived in the sixteenth century by Giordano Bruno, and he, "the second Pythagoras," renewed the intellectual impulse on the old lines of Greek and of Indian thought.[20]

And in our own days, not by the coming of one of these Great Ones, but by lesser men inspired by the study of their writings (as in old India were the rishis who founded the Indian schools of thought), we have from every side—from Germany in Fichte, Kant, and Schopenhauer, from America in Emerson, from England in Berkeley, not to mention the noble succession of mystics, Eckhart and Boehme, Fludd, Vaughan, St. Martin, Swedenborg—echoes of the early teachings, repetitions even of the early conceptions, mixed indeed with much alloy, but none—and this is significant—none scaling loftier heights, none plumbing more abysmal depths, than were measured by those gigantic teachers of the past, round whose feet cluster the teachers of today. Those who would test these statements need only study the world's philosophies, and they will find the same identity of fundamental conceptions running through all the nonmaterialistic [ones] as may be found in the religions of the world.[21]

And thus, also, with the sciences. We find in India the beginnings of astronomy, geometry, medicine, with psychology carried to a point unapproached in modern times. In China, Egypt, Chaldea, Greece, science flourished. And in all these lands, applied science left triumphs of engineering skill at which our punier world still looks with amaze. In mediaeval Europe, Paracelsus gave the impulse which guided chemistry, medicine, and magnetism to the lines on which modern triumphs have been won.[22] Van Helmont, Greatorex, and Mesmer made possible Charcot and Liebeault—and the French experimenters had done sounder work had they followed more closely the lines of their greater predecessors.[23] Today, Crookes, Lodge, and a whole group of young and progressive thinkers are pressing on into regions of psychology and physics already mapped out by the esoteric philosophy and familiar to its devoted students.[24] For in science, as in religion and in philosophy, the esoteric philosophy, the *atma-vidya* or spiritual wisdom,[25] is the complete body of truth, and by the study of it we may learn what men shall know in the future as well as that which they are learning with toil and pains—and with much loss of time in devious byways—today.

Thus we postulate a great brotherhood of spiritually illuminated men, guardians of a body of teachings, existing from an immemorial past down to the present day, and we point in proof to the succession of great world teachers, giving out identical doctrines in garbs fitted for the times of such unveilings. They have been called Initiates, Adepts, Mages, Hierophants, Mahatmas, Elder Brothers, Masters. Little matters the name; that humanity should have such helpers, that is the sublime truth and consolation. Always, and in many ways, they work for man—and the Theosophical Society is one of the agencies started for man's helping on their impulse. Their blessing rests on it just so far as it is faithful to its mission, but they do not directly guide, save where guidance is strenuously sought and eagerly obeyed.[26]

The main teachings of the esoteric philosophy are

1. The One, from which all proceeds, in which all exists, and to which all must return. As to *that*, all words are idle, all thought impossible, all speculation useless. By us, the manifested and conditioned, the unmanifest, the unconditioned, cannot be known

2. Universes coming into manifestation by the outgoing of the Great Breath from the One[27]

3. The Logos, or Word, coming out of the Silence, the beginning of manifestation, emanating as the primeval Trinity, the threefold aspect:

   a. the First, substance beyond our imagining

   b. the Second, dual—spirit/matter, energy/form, life/condition—the subtlest roots from which spring all manifested things, essence of spirit, essence of matter, incognizable by human faculties

c. the Third, the Great Mind, universal consciousness, or Being as conditioned, moving within the limitations inseparable from manifested existence

From these, in endless gradations, endless combinations of subtle and gross, endless varieties of consciousness, all things come forth. Hence every part of the universe, from loftiest spiritual entity to tiniest molecule in grain of sand, has life, has consciousness, has form. For each is from the Logoi, reflects in its own measure the Logoi, has its own dual aspect of spirit/matter. No spirit without form, no form without spirit—such is the law in all manifested worlds.

As rays from a sun, all spirits flame forth from the Great Mind. Here is the source of their being, here the central fire whereof all are sparks. Hence the underlying unity of all beings, and as they approach nearer and nearer to their fount, they come nearer and nearer to each other. The realization of this unity of origin makes them see the supreme soul in all things, all things in it, and thus the sense of separateness is destroyed and the One is recognized as All.

From the Logoi proceed first the higher spiritual entities that are concerned in the great cosmical processes, they who build up the universe and direct the cosmic forces. These are the gods of the Hindu religion, as of the Egyptian, Chaldean, et cetera; they are the archangels of the Christians. In the esoteric philosophy, they are spoken of as the builders, the *Lipikas*, the *Dhyani-Chohans*, or lords, and the planetary Spirits.[28] To them succeed the entities concerned with natural forces of a more restricted character: the lower gods of Hinduism, the angels of Christendom, the high elementals of the esoteric philosophy. Then the hosts of inferior entities less developed in consciousness than is man, known by an almost endless variety of names, and classed as the lower elementals in the esoteric philosophy.[29]

The point to be grasped in this department of the esoteric philosophy is that nature is not to be regarded as a soulless unconscious machine, but as a congeries of living entities; that every force, every energy, is the expression of consciousness, of will, ensouled by these entities; that each grade works in obedience to more highly evolved consciousnesses; and that therefore all kinds of material activity in nature can be controlled by the soul, by the action of the will consciously directed to command these inferior entities, as higher kinds can be controlled by the use of spiritual energies. This is the rationale of what has been called "practical magic," and its possibility is an inevitable corollary from the constitution of nature as taught by the esoteric philosophy, and as known to the occultist—i.e., to the man who studies the workings of the universal mind in nature.

Every atom in the universe mirrors the whole in its constitution, but man is a miniature image offering special advantage for study, partly because he is the most available, partly because the various regions of consciousness are more developed in him than in the other living things that surround him. Faculties latent in them are functioning in him, and so may be studied in activity. Each region, or "plane," as it is called, of consciousness which he develops in himself puts him into rapport with the corresponding plane in the universe—and as he becomes self-conscious on each, he may gain direct knowledge of that plane.

These planes are seven in number, according to the esoteric philosophy, and they are generally numbered from below upwards. Five of them are concerned with our cycle of evolution. They may be regarded as stages in consciousness, in each of which consciousness works in a different way because working under different conditions. Thus spirit working in dense matter organizes the mineral, vegetable, and animal kingdoms, or physical nature—the matter becoming more and more ductile, and making higher combinations as this evolution, guided by spirit, proceeds.

All this makes the physical plane. And man's physical body—consisting of the dense body and its etheric double—belongs to this, and is built up of tiny living particles. By means of this body, man comes into contact with physical nature, and the particles of this body, set in motion by impulses from without, are the instruments whereby he is able to gain knowledge of the physical plane, and to affect it in turn. He is always taking in and giving off minute molecules, the materials out of which the cells of his body are builded. He stamps on all parts of his body his own characteristics, and, scattering them abroad, thus physically affects his surroundings directly, and affects them indirectly—mentally, morally, and emotionally.

Through his etheric double the forces of vitality play, called *prana* or breath. The Great Breath, or *jiva*, is called prana when it is appropriated in man, and it is the coordinating life force that keeps the physical body as an organized whole.[30] At death, its vehicle, the etheric double, withdraws from the body, carrying with it this coordinating force—and then the tiny lives that make up the body run riot, disintegrating the whole.

Dr. Richardson's "nervous ether" is one aspect of this etheric matter, and the existence of electrical currents in the body proves the presence of this ethereal medium, without which no such currents could pass.[31] A great part of the etheric matter may be withdrawn from the body during earth life, but such withdrawal leaves the physical body but half-vitalized and is not unattended with danger. Such a withdrawal occurs in trance, sometimes in illness or during sleep.

The second plane is the astral, and a body of astral matter, interpenetrating every part of the physical body, is the vehicle of the desires, passions, and emotions of the animal nature, and is called that of desire, or *kama*. The phenomena of clairvoyance and clairaudience, and many of those of mesmerism and hypnotism, belong to this plane, and are connected with the conscious or unconscious use of the astral body and of the inner senses working in astral matter.

This astral body completes the lower man, sometimes called the animal man, and these four "principles," as they are often termed—physical body, etheric double, vitality, astral or desire body—make up the instruments whereby man feels, suffers, enjoys, experiences, in the world of these two planes. And that which works in and through them is the real man, the thinker, technically *manas*, or spirit working on the third plane of matter (counting upwards) manifesting as intellect, ideation, self-conscious will—that which corresponds in the human being to the Third Logos in the universe.

This manas, the fifth principle, is the human soul, immortal, imperishable as regards its essence, embodied in animal man for the sake of gaining experience and so evolving further towards union with the spirit, and also for the sake of individualizing spirit and making it active and self-conscious on all planes of existence. To the achievement of this double purpose its nature is adapted. It has its higher aspect, the higher manas, reaching up towards spirit and storing experience. It has its lower aspect, the lower manas, uniting itself to kama, the fourth principle, and through it reaching the three lower principles.

This is what we know as "mind": the lower manas and kama, called *kama-manas*. It works in the brain, is the user of the inner senses which are correlated to the outer ones (those of the body), and may either be submerged in the animal man, held captive by desire, or may purify and raise the animal man and lift him towards that third plane of consciousness to which it belongs rightfully itself.

Manas is the "god fallen into matter," or the "germinal god," and the lower manas is that part of the god that is submerged.[32] The whole process of distinctively human evolution is the struggle of this god to develop individual consciousness on his own plane, unifying with himself the lower nature he has redeemed. That lower nature informed by him is the personality, and the success or failure of each earth life depends on the extent to which the essence of the personality is assimilated with the immortal soul. For a personality may wreck itself and perish, wrenching away in its downward plunge the lower manas from its source. Or it may be so purified that the lower manas, withdrawn into its source after death, may carry back with it the essence of that personality and so give it immortality.

Thus manas becomes dual when it incarnates, and re-becomes one when disembodied. lower manas is breathed out into a body and breathed in again after death, as the Great Breath causes a universe and draws it in again when manifestation is suspended. The whole period of its pilgrimage is thus divided into alternate stages of embodiment and disembodiment. The stages of embodiment are called reincarnations, because it takes on a body over and over again. And in each earth life, it learns some lesson of experience and garners into itself the result thus obtained.

Manas is the storehouse of all these accumulated experiences of many lives, and the character manifested in any particular incarnation is the result of these experiences—or, more exactly, of such part of these experiences as can be manifested through the embodiment then in use. The whole of manas is colored, as it were, by these experiences, and the ray (the lower manas) has the color of its source. By these repeated incarnations the soul evolves, becomes strong and wise, and gains an ever-increasing mastery over physical, astral, and kamic conditions. As this mastery increases, the successive bodies take more strongly and swiftly the impress of the soul, and become more and more ductile instruments.

Thoughts mold successive astral bodies, and as the physical bodies are built for these, their form also ultimately depends on thought—which, in man, as in the universe, is the great molding and arranging energy. Further, as evolution proceeds, the illusions of matter have less power over the lower manas, and the ray being less clouded more closely resembles its source and shares its higher consciousness. Gradually, the accumulated knowledge and experience of manas pass freely down its ray into the brain of the personality, and the higher and lower consciousness become unified: "God manifest in the flesh" [1 Tim. 3:16]. This is one of the lower grades of adeptship, the commencing triumph of soul over matter.[33]

The stages of disembodiment, after the soul has shaken off the perishable part of the personality, are spent in a state of consciousness which has been named Devachan—a blissful and specially guarded state on the mental plane, in which the soul assimilates the experiences of the earth life just closed, and works out all the unfinished trains of thought started in that life.[34] A life that is poor in thought and in love will be succeeded by a poor and barren Devachan, while one rich in these respects will be followed by a rich and varied Devachan. Unselfish love, pure aspiration, noble thought—these products of the soul fill the devachanic state with bliss. And hopes and desires for human good and human progress which have failed of realization may be so worked out during the devachanic life that on return to earth the soul may be able to carry them out into action, having learned wisdom by failure and the way of successful effort by meditation.

As souls are separated from each other by the illusions of matter, and as the veil of illusion in Devachan is (though still present) thinner than during earth life, the union between souls that love each other is closer there than here. In fact, Devachan is the normal life of the soul, and the successive incarnations are brief interludes that break into it. For average persons, it is said to last for some fifteen centuries, but it has no exact period that can be set down, as it varies within very wide limits.

The period between the time at which the soul leaves the body and that at which it enters Devachan also varies widely, depending on the nature of the earth life just closed. The withdrawal of the etheric double, which carries with it the other principles, is "death," and for a very brief space these principles remain with the etheric double. They then shake it off, leaving it to disintegrate as the dense body also decays.

The four remaining principles (prana escaping immediately), pass on into the astral plane, where is the region of Kamaloka—the land of kama or of desire.[35] And here, the lower manas has to disentangle itself from kama, and so break the link which holds the soul in bondage. The process is long or short according to the relative strengths of kama and manas. If the mind has been fixed on earthly things—on material luxuries, pleasures, appetites—so that kama has been fed and manas starved, a long and painful struggle ensues between the soul that strives to free itself and the brute that holds it down. But if the life has been temperate and pure, and filled with noble thoughts, then it is the animal that has been starved, and the soul sleeps peacefully for a brief space while the earth links fall off it, and it wakes into its devachanic life.

As the soul thus passes successively through earth lives, lives in Kamaloka, lives in Devachan, while it takes up body after body, each differing from its predecessor, it will readily be seen why the soul is regarded as the real man, the individual, the eternal pilgrim treading constantly the path of evolution. The transient personalities, each of which contributes its quota of experience to this individual, cannot be regarded as the man, as the real "I." They are but the garments that the soul puts on, and that it casts away when they are worn out.

It will also be seen that in all these stages, these lives in different regions, the man reaps ever as he has sown. Unbroken causation everywhere, the harvest according to the seed. This truth is expressed by the word *karma,* a Sanskrit word meaning literally "action," but used to express the unbroken sequence of cause and effect.

As a Master has pointed out, a man generates thoughts, and these thoughts take form. These thought forms coalesce in the astral world with elementals, and so take on a life of their own as entities, beneficent or maleficent according as the thought was good or bad [*ML* 472 (Chin)]. These, peopling the astral atmosphere of the soul that gave birth to them, form his karma—and life after life, he works out his destiny amid the surroundings which he has thus made for himself. He cannot escape his karma, but the way in which he meets it generates fresh good or fresh evil for the future. He must work today amid the surroundings he has made, but his work is making changed surroundings for tomorrow. As surely as the present is the outcome of the past, so is the future the outcome of the present—so that man is not the slave of destiny but its master, in that he is its creator.[36]

But no one soul can separate itself and its destiny from that of other souls, since it is constantly affecting them and being affected by them on all planes. On the physical plane, the continual interchange of the tiny lives of which all bodies are composed brings about a physical brotherhood that we cannot escape, and lays on each a duty to purify all lives to which he is host, and to send them out improved, not worsened, by their stay with him. On the astral plane, we affect each other by the subtle vibrations of astral matter that carry varied influences—vital/magnetic, emotional, intellectual—and so establish a bond of brotherhood that is a source of blessing or of curse according to the nature of the influences sent forth by each.

We must influence others, but we can choose what kind of influence we will use. We cannot escape brotherhood, but we may either help or harm our brothers. And the vast ethical value of the esoteric philosophy is not only that it establishes the fact of human brotherhood, but that it also gives the knowledge which enables us to make that fact fertile of good for man. Now it may be seen why the true founders of the Theosophical Society, as the guardians of the esoteric philosophy, made the establishment of a nucleus of universal brotherhood the one essential and obligatory object of the Society.

There are two principles remaining, not yet touched on, to complete the evolution of man—latent today in all save Initiates, but nonetheless present in all. The sixth principle, working on the fourth plane, is *buddhi,* and no description of it at this stage is possible. We can see its effects in the great Initiates who have founded religions, in their clear vision of spiritual truths, in the authority of direct knowledge which marks their utterances. It has been called the spiritual soul, the faculty of spiritual discernment. Manas united to buddhi becomes the spiritual ego, and that union is the achievement of the *arhat*.[37]

One step more lifts man above the power of material nature, makes him master of life and of death, and opens to him nirvana, the third plane, the state of perfect knowledge, of perfect bliss.[38] There, shining on all beings, source of their existence, sun whereby they live, is *atman,* the One Self, the self of all. "He who sees me in all things, all things in me," says Sri Krishna, "of him I will never let go, and he shall never let go of me" [Bhagavad Gita 6.30]. On this let us meditate in silence—we cannot know until we become.

Such is a brief, bare outline of some of the leading teachings of the esoteric philosophy.[39] Men of all religions will recognize among them doctrines familiar to them under other terms in their own faiths, and they will see that the esoteric philosophy comes to the world as a friend of religion, and makes possible a strong intellectual defense for much that has rested merely on faith and on the intuitions of the human heart. Not only so, but by showing the rock whence the varying faiths have been hewn, it enables men of goodwill everywhere to work for religious peace and for mutual respect among those of different creeds. Its aspect towards all religions is, therefore, that of helper, friend, and peacemaker. It deepens and instructs religious faith and stands as breakwater against the waves of materialism.

Towards Western science, its aspect is that of opponent when science becomes materialistic, denies occultism, dogmatizes on spiritual things, scoffs at the soul, undermines religion. But when science investigates nature, records its discoveries, patiently works by way of experiment, accumulates facts, systematizes knowledge, it has nothing for it but good words and readiness to encourage. If help is asked for, then, to gain it, science must ally itself with love of man and seek to employ its knowledge for human help only, and not for human destruction. It must become moral in its aims, and seek knowledge not for the sake of knowledge only, but in order that knowledge may subserve human good. Thus has a Master spoken, and on such a matter the word of a guardian of the esoteric philosophy is decisive.[40]

Chapter Three

The Light and Dark Sides of Nature (1896)

Everything in this universe of differentiated matter has its two aspects, the light and the dark side, and these two attributes applied practically, lead the one to use, the other to abuse. Every man may become a botanist without apparent danger to his fellow creatures; and many a chemist who has mastered the science of essences knows that every one of them can both heal and kill. Not an ingredient, not a poison, but can be used for both purposes—aye, from harmless wax to deadly prussic acid, from the saliva of an infant to that of the cobra di capella [sic]. [1]

—H. P. Blavatsky [*CW* 12:602]

In one of the scriptures of our race, it is pointed out that at the very beginning of the universe the pairs of opposites appeared.[2] "The pairs of opposites" may be taken as a general name for the light and dark sides of nature—and a word on this general meaning of the pairs of opposites and on what they imply in nature may fitly be said in opening.

First, it is impossible to think at all without pairs of opposites. We can think, that is, only by and through duality. If there were but a single thing undifferentiated, always the same, always everywhere, no thinking could arise in that thing. There must be at least two—the thinker and the thing thought of, distinguishable from himself, before what we call "thought" can exist at all.

Not only so, but in thinking, we find ourselves continually distinguishing one thing from another, we perceive the presence of these opposites: light and not-light, dark and not-dark—put in the most general form, A and not-A. To recognize identity (A=A), and to perceive difference (A is not not-A), is the condition of thinking, the law of the mind. Without this, no mind, no thought can be.

It is because this fact is recognized that in philosophic religious books the phrase which strikes many Western thinkers as not only strange but nihilistic is used: Brahman is "without mind."[3] So long as only the One exists, nothing that the incarnate intellect can call "thought" or "mind" can be present. There is something deeper than "thought," something which is the form of "thought." But thought as known by the brain must always imply duality, for without this we are unable to perceive—perception depending on distinctions.

While this formal statement may be unfamiliar, it must at once be seen to be accurate when it is understood. For the very moment anyone thinks of anything, he distinguishes it from other things by its differences, and assigns it relations by its identities. He distinguishes it from everything which is not itself, and he recognizes in it identities with things previously perceived, things to which it is akin. We know things only as we separate them by differences from the things they are not, and classify them with the things they resemble.

The pair of opposites that we are now taking for our consideration is the fundamental pair of opposites—one therefore of vast importance. This pair has long been called "the light and dark sides of nature." It is the primary pair of opposites arising from the One, the fundamental duality, known to all students as being the nature of the second or manifested Logos.

The Second Logos in Christian phrase is the "Word made flesh," and in philosophic phrase (apart from any special religion) is spirit/matter, male/female, life/form, positive/negative—the two aspects of the One between which the whole universe revolves. "Father-mother spin a web," the web of the universe [*SD* 1:83].

In this Logos, the manifested Word, the manifested God, the two poles of existence appear, and between these poles the universe is builded. They exist always together. They are coeternal—one cannot be without the other. They are never known separated in nature. Without the one, the other could not be—could not even be thought. Fundamentally the same in their essence, they differ only in their manifestation.

The whole of evolution is the progress of these two, side by side, and evolution consists in the differences of proportion between the two. One is more manifest and the other less manifest; one is predominant and the other subservient—always, however, together in whatever part of the universe we may be.

In the highest spiritual region, life is not alone—but there, form is so subtle that it lends itself to the slightest change of the informing life. In the densest region of the universe, life is present—but there, form is predominant, is rigid, unplastic, and the life is concealed beneath the rigidity of the form.

Life implies consciousness, and form is that in which consciousness becomes manifest—and necessarily implies limitation. The two best words for this fundamental duality are really *life* and *form*, sometimes called in Eastern books *name* and *form*. For name has in it the molding potency and shapes the form it inhabits—therefore has name always been secret and sacred, and all potency lies in the "word."[4] If name/form has become restricted to the lower plane, it is because occult knowledge has been lost. Truly is it written that "Life is concealed beneath name/form" [Brihadaranyaka Upanishad 1.6.3]—and these are the manifested universe.

Now the light side—the side of spirit, life, or the positive—is the constructive and motive side. The dark side is the side of matter, form, or the negative, and is always subject to destructive transmutation—for only by destruction of forms can a fuller manifestation of life be made.[5] Light and dark in nature, then, are the constructive and the destructive forces, both of which are necessary for the evolution of the universe—equally necessary, strange perhaps as that at first may sound.

The light and the dark are equally manifestations of the One. The light and the dark are equally necessary for the manifestation of the One. For without the light, there would be no construction, and therefore no universe, no manifestation. Without the dark, there would be no destruction, and therefore no evolution. For as each form is constructed, it becomes a mold in which the life is held—and there could be no evolution, no progress in the universe, unless that form can be destroyed and give place to a form which is higher and nobler.

Within that form, the life has been accumulating experience which has caused internal growth and differentiation. The form which expressed the life ere that experience was gathered now cramps its further growth and hinders its further expansion. If the life is to evolve, the form that imprisons it must be broken, and a new form must be constructed which will express the new powers of the life. Life is continuous, while forms are transitory and are shaped to successive stages of the life. The form that prisons is broken to set the life free to enter the form that expresses it. That also will become a prison in its turn to be broken—and so on, stage after stage.

Thus all evolution depends on the presence of this destructive side of the one divine existence, breaking down every form—not for the mere purpose of destruction, but because death is only the dark side of birth, and there is no death in one region of the universe which, looked at from another region, is not birth. Death and birth, in fact, are only two correlative names, and they are used in relation to the standpoint of the speaker. The passing of a life out of the region in which it is, is death to its form in that region. But as it passes out of that region by death, it appears in the next region by birth. Therefore, birth and death are rightly called the wheel of existence—both equally necessary, both equally fundamental; construction and destruction continually succeeding each other, both stages in evolution, and stages which are equally necessary.

The manifested Logos, call Him by what name men will, is spoken of in all religions as creator, the unmanifested as destroyer. Sometimes He is styled the regenerator, a name which includes both—creation and destruction being thus seen as the two poles of the one life. And in all manifestation these two are present.

The next stage in our study is an understanding of the three great regions to which the general evolution of ordinary humanity is at present confined. And it is necessary that it should be clearly understood that the question of good and evil does not come into play with regard to these regions *in themselves*. I want to get rid of the idea which is lurking in many minds that "spiritual" means "good" and "material" means "evil." Spirit and matter, life and form, are never separated, and in themselves are neither good nor evil.

But *spiritual* is a name often used to define a particular region in nature where form is dominated by life, just as much as material is used to indicate another region in nature where life is dominated by form. Neither life nor form, spirit nor matter, is good or bad in itself. Both these poles are present in every plane, in every entity—and the entity is good or bad according to the end to which its activity is directed. There is good and evil spirituality just as there is good and evil materiality.

The words *good* and *evil* have nothing to do with the fundamental constituents and forces of nature, and people are constantly getting into a confused condition of mind because they take "spiritual" as meaning good—and then try to deal with the "dark spiritual side" of nature, finding themselves face to face with what they recognize as evil and yet find existing in the "spiritual" region. The forces of any region are nonmoral, though both constructive and destructive entities are good or evil as they use these forces for or against the divine will. We shall avoid confusion if we consider the planes of nature as they really exist, and then define each clearly, so far as it concerns us.

The word *spiritual* being used so loosely is apt to be misleading. The third and fourth planes (counting from above downwards) form a region beyond the reach of moral evil, and if these alone were termed spiritual, evil would be excluded from the conception of spirituality. But the word is often applied to the manasic, or intellectual, plane by Theosophical writers—and as the Brothers of the Shadow function thereon, its forces can be turned to evil purposes and are often thus turned.

The two highest planes of the septenary [sevenfold system of planes] do not concern us, as human evolution in this *manvantara* does not touch them.[6] We have thus left five: the atmic or nirvanic; the buddhic or turiyic;[7] the manasic or mental; the kamic or astral; and the physical. The atmic and buddhic planes will be touched by ordinary humanity only in future rounds, so that for practical purposes we are confined to the three lower planes—the mental, astral and physical. In these, man spends each of his life periods, repeating the cycle over and over again.

Diagram 1

	Atmic or nirvanic	Spiritual
	Buddhic or turiyic	
Ordinary	Manasic or heavenly	Sometimes called Spiritual
human evolution	Kamic or astral	Psychic[8]
in 4th round	Physical or earthly	Physical

Thus, for ordinary humanity, we might name the three lower planes spiritual, psychic, and physical. And in this way they are often distinguished, for they are the regions of heavenly, astral, and earthly life—and heavenly or devachanic life is that which satisfies all the part of man's nature usually regarded as spiritual. This use of the word *spiritual* brings us into line with the use of it by the different great religions, as with St. Paul's "spiritual wickedness in high places" [Eph. 6:12], the Hindu *asuras*, the Buddhist Mara and his hosts, the occultist's Black Magicians or "Brothers of the Shadow."[9]

Further, the word *spiritual* is not inappropriate, as in that region of the universe the spirit or life side is predominant, while the matter or form side is completely subordinate.[10] Matter is very rare, very subtle, very ductile, very plastic, and it changes its form with almost inconceivable rapidity. Sometimes the higher region of this plane is even spoken of as formless.[11] It is formless to everything which is below it, because the senses of the lower cannot appreciate the forms of the higher. But, to those who are upon it, form exists. For without form—which is fundamentally extension, that is, matter—manifested existence cannot be. The lower part of this plane is the region of the lower mind, but matter still remains quite subordinate to spirit, form to life.

In the next, or psychic, plane, form is denser, though still plastic, and life is more veiled. Both are active, but they are more balanced. Above, life is predominant. In the middle, life and form are balanced. In the lowest plane, or the physical, form is predominant and life is hidden. That is perhaps one of the simplest and clearest ways in which we may recognize the characteristics of these planes. In the first, life or spirit predominates. In the second, life and form are balanced—it is the battleground of nature. In the third, form triumphs.

In the lowest stages, very many Western people do not recognize life at all. They regard it as one of the Theosophical follies to say that there is life in the lowest forms of material existence. But amongst some of our more advanced and younger chemists, the phrase *evolution of metals* is being used, and "the life history of metals" was lately spoken of in a lecture given at the Royal Institution.[12] So that it looks as though science would soon no longer oppose the reasonable view—would begin to understand that life is everywhere in a universe which proceeds from life.

To pass now to good and evil. Everything which is in accord with the divine will—and in a moment I will define what I mean by that phrase—and which therefore works for progress and for happiness, is good. Everything which works against progress and happiness is evil, no matter whether it be on the highest, on the middle, or on the lowest plane. It is not the forces which are good or evil in themselves, but the use that is made of them; not whether they are spiritual, psychical, or physical, but whether spiritually they are used for good or evil, whether psychically they are used for good or evil, whether physically they are used for good or evil. The good or the evil depends on whether they work for progress or against it, whether they work towards the happiness and the perfecting of the universe or against it. On each plane, there are forces which can be thus used. The forces in themselves are not good or evil, they are merely spiritual, psychical, or physical. They become good or evil according to the purpose for which they are used, and the end which they bring about.

Electricity, for instance, is neither moral nor immoral in itself. It is used immorally if it be employed to kill. It is used morally if it be turned to help and to comfort. And so in other regions of the universe.

A spiritual force is evil if it be used against progress, for the causing of misery and of destruction. It is good if it be used for progress, for the bringing about of the happiness and the perfection of the universe. On each plane, you may find good and evil—the distinction being in the use of the forces and not in the nature of the plane.

Let us now examine the meaning of the phrase *divine will*. The one existence emanating a universe may be described as causing a great circle of existence, a vast cycle. It is said that "spirit descends into matter." That is a phrase consecrated by long usage and one to which there is no objection if its meaning be understood. But it is apt to be exceedingly misleading if people think of spirit as being somewhere up aloft, and matter separated from it somewhere down below, and spirit falling from above into matter.

That is the conception which a good many people really have, though they might not put it quite so plainly. And as they think spirit climbs up again out of matter to where it was before, they not unnaturally ask: What is the use of the whole proceeding, why should it start if it is only going to return? Sometimes the Theosophist who is not quite instructed is apt to be a little irritated with his questioner, but the enquirer is really quite justified in his challenge—for where we Theosophists have expressed ourselves badly, it is quite right that a question put to us should point out the clumsy way in which we are saying what is yet fundamentally true.

There is a vast cycle of manifestation which may be regarded for convenience's sake as a circle. At every point of the descent, spirit and matter are side by side—but there is the change of proportion before mentioned: the spirit becoming more hidden and the matter more evident. The change in the ascending line is that the matter becomes more subtle and the spirit becomes more predominant.

The divine will is the law of progress. This existence, manifesting itself, wills to bring a universe into existence, and to conduct that universe by evolution to perfection. It may of course be asked, why should it will to emanate? That is a question which we cannot answer fully. But we find in existence at the end of a universe a number of self-conscious individuals who were not in existence at its beginning, and who are capable of perfect life, perfect knowledge, perfect bliss.

Even from our limited standpoint, it must be admitted that this is a reasonable and sufficient purpose for the existence of the universe. It brings into conscious being these blissful all-knowing intelligences, who share with the divine life that gave them birth its own existence, its own knowledge, its own joy.

What a universe is to the manifesting life no words of limited mind may tell. What it gives to those who gain self-consciousness, bliss, and knowledge by the process is sufficiently evident to anyone who thinks at all. It is the difference between knowing nothing and knowing everything—a difference far more than between a stone and the highest archangel. For there is evolution behind the stone as well as in front of it—an evolution that prepares its existence as well as an evolution that carries it on into the highest ranges of self-conscious being.

Now this process, at first and all through, must be regarded as double—the light and the dark sides. One of the streams of divine energy is constructive, the other destructive. One of them is life, building forms. The other is death, breaking them up. Both are equally necessary, for destructive energy is going to destroy every form when it has served its purpose, in order that the materials used in the form whose purpose is over may be taken up by the constructive energy and built into a higher form. This process is what we call evolution.

At every stage of the downward curve in which form becomes more prominent and life more veiled, forms will be brought into existence by this descending energy. Against it, there will be working a destructive energy, which breaks up these forms as soon as their purpose is served, and they become outworn.

There are thus two opposing streams of energy, by one of which forms come into existence, and by the other of which they are constantly broken up, in order that higher forms may be built from their materials. There is no increase of matter, it must be remembered—constant change, constant transmutation, but no increase and no diminution. Evolution consists, on the form side, of this process of destroying the lower forms that the higher forms may come into existence.

The next point is at first a little difficult to conceive, even a little startling. Growth is at first from the one to the many, from one existence to a universe of countless forms. "It willed, 'I will multiply'"

[Chandogya Upanishad 6.2.3]. Then this descending line must be a process of separation, of making differences in order that an ever-increasing multiplicity of forms may be brought into existence. The keynote of evolution will be separation.

As far down as the lowest or most outward point of evolution, the keynote of progress is separation. The perfection of a universe is in the multiplicity of its forms, in the variety of the existences that are found in it. The universe exists in order to bring all these separated forms into manifestation, and all through this early process, evolution will work for separation. Using the phrase *the divine will*—that will which is "I will multiply"—the divine will will work for separation, will work to make forms which are more and more separated and diverse from each other, in which the fundamental unity of life is more and more hidden.

The whole of this growth will be a process of increasing separation. It is said to be a coming down into matter, and we may venture to use the phrase now that we have guarded ourselves against mistake. As things become more and more material, they obviously become more and more separated. We may see that in the very density of matter as we know it.

A piece of sulphur, for instance, is more separated from a piece of iodine than if both are sublimed to gas. The analogy is clumsy, for the gases remain separate molecularly, though mingling in mass, so that there is no real union. But as we pass from the subtle to the dense, this separateness of form is the thing that strikes us; whereas when we are dealing with very subtle things, their unity is more prominently characteristic.

If we understand this "descent into matter," we shall see that under the circumstances of the descending arc the opposition to progress would be the desire to remain one, would be the refusal to take form, would be the unit setting itself to maintain unity instead of accepting separateness. Hence setting itself against the divine will—wrong because it is against evolution, against progress, against the perfecting of the universe at this stage—would be, strange as it may sound, the refusal to take form in more and more material shapes.

Theosophists who have really studied may here see a gleam of light on what otherwise may have seemed to them strange. In the wonderful Stanzas of Dzyan, it is said that the sin of the mindless is preceded by the refusal of the "Sons of Mind" to incarnate. That is, that the refusal of spirit, as we will call it for the moment, to take to itself separate form goes before the great sin which was wrought by the mindless men, and has left its traces in some of the higher animal forms [*SD* 2:18–20; 161–98].[13]

Intelligences awaiting incarnation set themselves against the law of progress. They looked on it as degradation to clothe themselves in the available bodies, as lowering their position to take forms in this lower world, and they refused to come down. Thence came the great primary transgression, known to students as "the sin of the mindless." To remain out of gross matter was against the law of progress, against evolution and the perfecting of the universe.

What at first seems so strange is that everything that now is right—the seeking of unity, the getting rid of separateness, the dominating of the material—at that stage of progress was wrong. The duty of these intelligences was to descend from the psychical to the physical, in order that a universe might come into existence in multiplicity of forms, in order that this building process might go on in which they were necessary helpers, coworkers with the divine will. Opposition to that will, as ever, brought evil. But the nature of the opposition in this case was the refusal of spirit to enter physical forms, to veil its light in dense matter.

As the evolutionary process went on, the spiritual was veiled in the psychical, and then the psychical was veiled in the material, and the most material race of men appeared. Yet it was really a rising—descent though it seemed—for it was part of evolution. It was the way to the swifter bringing into existence of self-conscious individuals of our humanity. Without this, the perfected manifestation would have been long delayed. Without it, self-conscious spiritual intelligences could not have developed so rapidly as the harvest of the universe, as the justification of this emanation of the divine.

Thus, in this downward sweep of evolution, what we now rightly call evil was then really good. To become separate, to become material was good in those far-off eons. For separation was necessary in order that a more perfect unity might finally be gained. Intellect could not evolve without spirit working through the lower forms of matter. The coming thus into the closest connection with matter of the physical plane brought into existence the human brain, the physical basis of all the faculties of the lower mind, and made possible the acquiring of the knowledge without which the individual could not expand into the divine.

In the process of evolution, this lowest point was thus reached—and then there was a change. The utmost separation having been achieved, the utmost multiplicity of forms having been achieved, the utmost multiplicity of forms having been brought into being, then what we call the upward curve began. Life, having made this infinite variety of forms for its own manifestation, began to work upon the forms to render them plastic. First, the process of differentiation to get the forms, then the working in the forms to make them ductile as the expression of the life. These are the two great stages.

The form must be brought into existence, and that means separation. Then there must be work from within to make the form the plastic expression of the life. The whole of the upward curve is used for that second half of the work. Life constantly toiling within these separated forms to make them more plastic, more transparent, working towards unity. Unity must be regained, or immortality could not be achieved, for that which is composite cannot last forever. But it is a unity into which has been absorbed the very essence of all the differences that have been passed through during the circle of evolution.

The subtle life form clothes itself in varied garments, subdividing and becoming more and more separate as it comes downwards—then a life form separated from all other life forms by this clothing of denser matter beginning the upward path, in which it will work on its material garments, making them more transparent, more subtle, more a mere delicate film—and yet that film containing in itself the essence of every separated form through which it has passed.

When at length it arrives on high, having passed into the intellectual sphere, it has in high and spiritualized forms the faculties which were latent in it at the beginning, and has become self-conscious and not only conscious. Then it becomes one with others, but has the memory of its separateness behind it, reaching a stage which words must fail to describe, but which—borrowing a phrase from Madame Blavatsky—I may perhaps call "a conscious entity becoming consciousness."[14] It keeps the memory which has made it an individual, and yet shakes off from itself everything which separates it from other individuals. It shares their experience and knows their knowledge, and yet is itself. It reaches the state which is spoken as of nirvana, which is the very antithesis of annihilation—which extinguishes separateness, but keeps everything which by separateness has been gained. It is the All, and yet in it is preserved the subtle essence of memory which was gained when each knew itself as one of many.

In this upward sweep, therefore, it is separateness which is to be gotten rid of—and therefore separateness is called "the great heresy," therefore it is called "the great sin,"[15] therefore it is the fundamental evil, therefore it has become the mark of what is called the Black Magician, the brother of the dark side. To keep the self separated from other selves, to seek everything for the separated self, and not for the common self of all, is now the worst sin. The Black Magician seeks for strength in order that he may be strong, whereas the White Magician seeks it in order that all may be strong. The Black seeks knowledge that he may be learned; the White that all may be wise.

When the White Brother reaches the spiritual plane, everything that he has gained in upward climbing becomes part of the general store, everything that he has gathered in his passing through the world becomes a common light which radiates in every direction. It is his own, truly. But he has shaken off everything that separated him from others. He is able to shed all he has over the whole world of living things. Everything that he has gained as a separated self radiates out from him as an unseparate self to the universe of unmanifested existence. For where he stands, there is no separation. There is love, and love knows no separation. There is perfect wisdom, and perfect wisdom knows no separation. It is by ignorance that separation exists, and perfect wisdom clears away the veils that divide, and makes man realize that he has only become separate in order that he may gather, and has re-become one in order that he may give. In that region, everything is common property. There is no longer "mine" and "thine," for all selves are one.

In the upward path then, the dark side will evolve by the desire to be separate—thus working for disintegration, and against progress. The Black Magician evolves by clinging to the separate form, by the desire to possess for the separate self. If that determination to be separate continues, if the desire to be apart from everything instead of being a part of everything persists as man rises upwards, then this one possibility remains: for a time, by the tremendous strength that he has gathered, by the mighty knowledge that he has won, by the almost omniscience that he has gained in the long striving upwards, he can for a time, even in the spiritual region, hold his own against all others; for a time, even in that world of unity, can preserve a separated self. Not forever, only for a while. He has won such tremendous force and energy and knowledge that he can hold his own for a time even against the divine will. He can keep himself apart even against everything which tends towards unity.

Even in the *arupa* region of the mental plane,[16] there may be for a while separated existences which work for themselves, which are selfish, which refuse to hold for the common good and for the common enrichment—who are learned as separated selves, strong as separated selves, who use their strength to rule and to hold instead of to serve the world and lift it higher. Those are the great Black Magicians that are spoken of, the "Lords of the Dark Face," mighty in their power, mighty in their knowledge, mighty in the spiritual height that they have gained—very gods in the manifested universe, but selfish gods, anti-gods, and therefore incapable of immortality. For only that can live which is one with the All—and they must break in time.

The separated form built apart from its fellows and keeping itself separate whilst the universe is gradually becoming one—being against this upward trend, against the law of progress, against general evolution—is always striking itself against the law. It is deliberately dooming itself to disintegration. For the divine energy breaks up every form, and if it keeps separate form, it also must be broken up. Though the dark spiritual powers—the god of the dark side of nature, as they may have been called, the *deus inversus*[17]—may last for many an age, for many and many a millennium, yet as they have chosen form, and all form is perishable, they must at length perish. The forms that they have chosen must be disintegrated, and if they have identified themselves with the separated forms, then as forms they cease to exist.

Having chosen the forms that perish, when those forms break, their consciousness goes back into the vast ocean of consciousness. They have failed to extract the essence, to transmute it into consciousness per se. They have chosen a self-conscious individuality which is separate, and when the separateness breaks, the consciousness goes back into the ocean and self-consciousness is lost.

Any, if he will, may choose that side. We all of us are choosing it from time to time. For every force that works for disintegration works for its own destruction. Every force that at this period of the world's progress works for its separate self is throwing itself against that mighty stream of destructive energy which breaks and grinds everything to powder in order that it may be rebuilt anew of higher mold. Every agency which works against the whole, everyone who separates himself and works for himself against his brothers—every such force is a force that is working for self-destruction, destruction which is self-chosen and which nature cannot refuse to give.

Now we can realize what evil means. Evil is everything which works against the divine will in evolution. It is everything which works against truth which is God, against unity which is God, against love which is God. Every such force is working against the whole. And if it comes into conflict with the general force which is working upwards, and with those who are the embodiments of that upward tending force, it must inevitably be broken into pieces.

The Great White Lodge wars against none, but it goes its way, and that which wars against it is broken into pieces. It does not war with hatred; it passes upward. It does not use the weapon of wrath and of anger, but it passes upward. Everything which flings itself against it is, by its own act—and not by the act of the White Brotherhood—broken into shivers. It breaks into fragments, while the great force goes on.

Some imagine that the force of the White Lodge is used for destruction, but it is not so. That Lodge is on the upward arc, and the

White Brothers are ever on the side of unity. Where there is conflict, it is the disunity flinging itself against the unity. And as that is unchanging and ever going towards its end, those which fall against it are broken into pieces. Here is the occult meaning of a phrase which is familiar in the Christian scriptures: that those who fall upon the stone which is the head of the corner are broken [Luke 20:17–18]; not by the action of that mighty cornerstone, but by their own action; not by its disruptive energy—for of disruptive energy it has none—but by virtue that it is changeless and cannot be broken, and that everything that works against it must shiver from the energy with which it flings itself against the law.

The whole mighty sweep is the law which passes downwards and then upwards once again. Everything which is against it is broken, everything which separates itself from it must fall to pieces. Every separated existence must break. Only in unity can life proceed. Therefore, when we study the light and dark sides of nature in their bearing on our practical life, we find that every force of hatred, of disruption that makes against unity, that works for separated fragments and not for one mighty whole—everything that works on that side is under the Black Lodge, is an agency of the Black Brotherhood. When we speak of the dark side of nature and of those who incarnate the disruptive forces, as the White Brotherhood incarnates the law, the good law of the universe, we know that every one of us must be on the one side or the other—working for brotherhood or working against it, working for construction or destruction, for building or for breaking, for unity or disuniting.

That is the practical outcome of this study. Each of us, in striving to lead a life which we would fain should lead us on the upward course and bring us at length into that unity wherefore the universe exists, will do well to scrutinize our own hearts and our own lives to see whether the forces in us are tending to truth, to love, to unity. Everything that is of these is white. Everything that is against these is black. We *must* cooperate with the one side or with the other—and according to our final cooperation will be the final end of the individual soul.

Chapter Four

Occultism, Semi-Occultism, and Pseudo-Occultism (1898)

Speaking to the lodge for the first time after returning from India,[1] it will not seem to you, I think, either strange or inappropriate that I should take for my subject one which is largely drawn from Indian history—not the history of the outside nation, but the history of that inner line of thought which is of the deepest interest to us as students and as Theosophists. And inasmuch as history continually repeats itself, such a study may offer points of instruction to us in our own time. For I am going to ask you to consider with me what I may perhaps define—although definition is a little difficult—as, first, occultism, then what may be called semi-occultism, and, thirdly, the outgrowths which follow and surround these, and which are specially marked and active at any time when true occultism is working in the world.

It is a very common blunder, made by many people, to suppose that spiritual forces have in them something which they are pleased to call unpractical. And we continually notice an assumption, which is taken for granted without argument, that if a nation, for instance, should turn itself towards a spiritual ideal, or if individuals should devote themselves to the spiritual life, that then such a nation is likely to be undistinguished along other more evident and visible walks in life, and such an individual is likely to lose much of what is called his practical value in the world. Such a view of life is a blunder—and a blunder of the most complete kind.

The liberation of spiritual forces, the setting free of energies on the spiritual plane, has a far greater effect, both on the individual and on the nation in the other regions of its activity, than can be produced by any of the forces that are started on the lower planes of life.[2] When a spiritual energy is set free, it works down through the other planes of being, giving rise on each plane to a liberation of energy, and bringing about results great in proportion to the nature of the spiritual force. So that it is true in history (as you may find by study) that when spiritual forces are liberated, the intellectual life of the nation will also leap forward with tremendous energy, the emotional life of the nation will show fresh development, and even on the lowest plane of all—the physical—results will be brought about entirely beyond anything that could have been achieved by the energies of the physical plane which are set to work and which apparently cause these results.

That is a principle, a law, which I will ask you to bear in mind through all that I have to say to you—that every force initiated on the higher planes, as it passes down to the lower, brings about results proportionate to itself. So that it is the shortest-sighted view of human life and of human activity which imagines that devotion to the spiritual life, the evolution of the individual in the spiritual world, is anything but an immense addition to all the forces of progress that work on the earth, anything but a lifting up of the world on the great ladder up which it is climbing.

But there is another principle that we must also bear in mind in our study, and it is this: that as forces are liberated on any plane, the results brought about by those forces will vary in their character according to those who utilize the energies after their liberation. As we have often pointed out to you here, energies on the different planes of nature are not what we call good or bad in themselves. Force is a force; energy is an energy. When we bring in the idea of good and evil, of right and wrong, of morality and immorality, these ideas are connected with the results brought about by individuals in the utilization of the forces.

A time, then, of great spiritual energy, of great liberation of forces from the spiritual plane, will be marked to a great extent by activities of opposed characters on the lower planes of being, and those energies which are liberated on each plane may be taken up and used by individuals for what we should call either good or evil. The great mark of good or evil, looking at it from this standpoint, is the use that the individual is making of these forces, or such part of them as he is able to control—whether he is using them for the uplifting of humanity, whether he is regarding them as the divine energy which he may use to forward the divine purposes, or whether he is simply trying to grasp them for his own separate ends, striving to apply them to that which he desires to grasp and to hold, serving his own purposes without regard to the divine economy.

This, then, as I said, we will bear in mind in following out, first, as a lesson, something of the past in India, and then in applying the lesson that thus we learn to the movement which we know amongst ourselves at the present day—that great spiritual movement which is manifesting itself in the world and of which the Theosophical Society is one of the potent expressions.

To begin with, what is occultism? The word is used and misused in the most extraordinary ways. H. P. Blavatsky once defined it as the study of mind in nature,[3] meaning by the word *mind*, in that connection, the study of the universal mind, the divine mind, the study of the workings of God in the universe—the study, therefore, of all the energies which, coming forth from the spiritual center, work themselves out in the worlds around us. It is the study of the life side of the universe: the side from which everything proceeds and from which everything is molded, the looking through the illusory form to the reality which animates it. It is the study which underlies all phenomena. It is the ceasing to be wholly blinded by these appearances in which we so continually move, and by which we are so continually deluded. It is the piercing through the veil of maya and perceiving the reality, the One Self, the One Life, the One Force—that which is in everything and all things in it.[4] So that, really, occultism, in the true sense of the word, may be said to be identical with that vision which, as you know, is spoken of in the Bhagavad Gita, where Sri Krishna declares that "He who sees Me," that is, who sees the One Self, "in everything and everything in Me, verily he seeth" [Bhagavad Gita 13.28].

Such a study, if you understand at all what is implied in it, must necessarily mean the development, in the one who sees, of the highest spiritual faculties. For only by the spirit can the spirit be known. We speak continually of proving this, that, or the other spiritual thing. There is no real proof possible of spirit, save through spirit. There is no proof of the intellect, no proof of the emotion, no proof of the senses, which is proof when you come to deal with the reality of the spirit. Nothing of the nature of proof along those lines, whether sensuous, emotional, or intellectual, can be anything more than a suggestion, a reflection of the truth, an analogy which may lead us on the right path—but proof in the true sense of the word it never can be. And it has been written truly in one of the great Indian scriptures, and repeated over and over again in the other scriptures of the world, that there is in the full sense of the word no proof of God save the belief in the spirit, for only the spirit that is akin to Him, and that is Himself, is able to know, is able to touch [Mandukya Upanishad 7].

Now looking at real occultism as thus defined, realizing that no one can be in the full sense of the word an occultist save one in whom the spiritual nature is developed and active, we should, in our next step, be able to separate off from this true occultism very much that goes by its name, both in the past and the present, amongst those who went before us and amongst ourselves today. But we should need, in separating off all these forms of so-called occultism, to distinguish between those which may be said, in a sense, to be stepping-stones to the real—which were intended as stepping-stones by those who gave them to the world, and which may be used as stepping-stones and utilized for progress—and other forms which are not really included under the name of *occultism* in any true sense of the term, those things which H. P. Blavatsky once spoke of as occult arts, and which for many people seem to include everything they regard as occultism—arts in which certain forces of nature are utilized and in which faculties are developed on various planes in nature below the spiritual. For there are worlds above what we call the physical, but still below the spiritual regions, with which the development of certain faculties brings man into touch, enabling him to control and utilize their forces.

There are almost myriad arts and lines of study of this kind which ought never by any real student, by anyone who is seeking the higher truth, to be included in his thought when that thought is turned towards occultism. And some of you might clear up much confused thinking on this subject if you would refer to the writing of H. P. Blavatsky on "Occultism versus the Occult Arts," where she draws the dividing line extremely clearly and shows the position that these occult arts hold, and should be recognized as holding, when we are dealing with human evolution [*CW* 9:249–61].

True occultism, then, is that to which at first I would ask you to turn your thoughts—and its pursuit implies, as I have said, the development of the spiritual nature. Now the moment we speak of the development of the spiritual nature, we must at once recognize that for the larger number of us that development must necessarily lie in the future, but that we may begin to work towards it today; that it is of enormous import to our true progress that we should recognize it and work towards it, and not, by misunderstanding the nature of that development, waste our time—waste possibly many lives—by following blind alleys and mistaken roads.

The development of the spiritual nature must succeed—and this is one of the most important points that we can realize—must succeed the purification of the lower parts of our nature. We must be pure emotionally and intellectually, we must have reached a certain stage, at least, of the elimination of the personality before anything that can rightly be called spiritual progress is within our reach. No amount of mere intellectual development—and I will come back to that point, for I do not wish in any way to depreciate that most necessary line of human growth—but no amount of mere intellectual development will of itself bring about the growth of the spiritual nature. With the fundamental reason for that I shall deal more fully in a future lecture.[5] But I must say in passing that the development of the spiritual nature and of the intellectual nature are on one vital point in direct opposition.

The principle that we call the intellect is the analyzing, the dividing, the separative principle. The very purpose of its evolution is the building up of the individual. Its root lies in the *ahamkara*, or the "I-making" faculty.[6] It is that which limits, which defines, which separates, which marks off the man from every other man—which makes what we may call that coating of selfishness which is absolutely necessary as one stage in evolution, which is one part of our growth in this world. It is a stage through which all humanity must pass, but which, regarded by itself, makes all those illusions which the spirit transcends, and gives the touch of apparent reality to the separated self—the antagonistic self, the self that covets and grasps and holds and sets itself against all others. So that what we might call the very principle of illusion is represented by this intellectual faculty.

Necessary as its evolution is, nonetheless it is, on this point, in antagonism to spiritual evolution. For spiritual evolution means the recognition and the growth of the One Self into manifested activity: first, within that sheath which has been formed by the intellect,[7] and then by transcending it and bringing about that realized unity which is the object of our human evolution. It is for this that we place the unity of mankind in the spiritual regions. It is for this that we proclaim the brotherhood of man as a spiritual reality. For the spirit is One, and it is only as that unity is recognized, consciously known—not simply intellectually seen, but consciously realized—it is only as that is done that the spiritual nature is in course of evolution.

Inasmuch as the intellect is separative and the spirit unifying, inasmuch as the one gives rise to illusion while the other transcends it, as the one is the source both of individuality and of personality, whereas the other is the source of that Oneship which we seek and shall realize—you will readily see how in the course of evolution these two parts of the nature cannot be regarded as causally related in the strict sense of the term, and we cannot say that by the evolution of the intellectual nature the spiritual nature will inevitably develop. On the contrary, we have to learn that we are not the intellect, but are to use the intellect as an instrument; that we are not the separated self, but the One Self living in all. That is the object of our evolution, that the goal of our pilgrimage.

And therefore occultism, which means the study and the development of the spiritual nature, must transcend completely the intellectual evolution. It may even in many of its earlier stages find—

and does find—its bitterest antagonist, its most dangerous enemy, in that very maker of illusions that you may remember we are warned against in *The Voice of the Silence*, that most spiritual book which so many of us have found as opening up the path to us to the spiritual life.[8] Recognizing this, we shall naturally look forward to the spiritual evolution as a thing to be worked for, rather than to be accomplished, from the stage at which we are at present. We should also be prepared to realize the immense difficulty of such an achievement, to understand how much will have to be done with the character and with the nature, how tremendous are the demands that we shall have to meet, before anything which in the strict sense of the term can be called occultism will be at all within our reach.

In the history of the past, when true occultism was the life of the world, when that great fount of spiritual life flowed from the Beings in whom the spiritual nature was wholly developed, when the world was drawing its light and its life from such Beings, it was obviously not possible that their knowledge, their powers, their work could be largely shared by undeveloped humanity—or even by the comparatively advanced humanity that surrounded them.[9] Still less was it possible that any great part of their teaching, or any true comprehension of their work and their methods, could be known to the people at large. And yet it was necessary that links should be made, that steps, as it were, should be created. The result of this necessity was that men who were advanced—although in them the spiritual nature was not yet wholly evolved—men of great powers, who stand out in history as giants of humanity, strove to make possible for the advancing ranks of mankind some understanding of the upward path that should be trodden, some realization of the methods that might be adopted whereby approach might be made to the spiritual regions.

These men, great as they were, were not, as I have said, men in whom the spiritual nature was wholly developed, supreme, complete. Their evolution in many cases—and I speak with all reverence of those so much greater than ourselves—may even be said to have gone along one line in excess of other lines of their growth. So that one man might have enormously developed intellectual power, but less perfection perhaps of moral character. Another might have made great advance in devotion, and might not have developed so much of intellectual force. Another might be keenly alive to the religious necessities of man, and not so much interested in his philosophical evolution. Another, again, might have turned his attention towards the development of certain sides of man's nature which would touch the physical regions of existence—and even to the forcing of faculties in man, which, when built up from below, would bring him into touch with parts of the astral or the lower mental world, and might force those faculties and the part of his nature to which they belong in advance, alike, of mental and moral evolution.[10]

Along these various lines you will readily see that individuals might have progressed, and that each man would be characterized, in his thinking and in his endeavor to serve mankind, by his own qualities, the attributes which he had specially evolved. So that, looking back into the ancient history of India, we find great teachers—*rishis* as they were called—of many different types, each giving to the nation some great gift from his thought or from his knowledge, intended to help the more advanced souls of that nation toward progress which should end in spiritual evolution.

Hence, to take one line of growth, the great philosophical systems which we find in Indian thought—such a system, for instance, as the Vedanta.[11] Regarded as an intellectual system of pure philosophy, it puts in a magnificent intellectual form a view of the universe—of the One Self, of the One Life, and of its manifestations—as illusory in the deepest philosophical sense. That serves as an intellectual training, as a step which men must take in learning something of the mysteries of the universe. This system, when studied apart from the yoga that alone can make it practical, may be classed under the head of semi-occultism. It is a system—true within its own realm, a system intended to help forward the progress of mankind—capable of being grasped, of being followed, of being studied, only by souls already advanced in mentality. But nonetheless it is not the spiritual truth. It is only an intellectual presentment of one aspect of it, an intellectual showing forth of one side of it.

It is a thing that must always be remembered, that the spirit can never be expressed in terms of the intellect—that the One can never be grasped in the terms of the many, and that any intellectual presentment of spiritual truths must necessarily be partial, must necessarily be imperfect, must be, as has often been said, a colored glass through which the white light is seen. A ray is passed through the prism of the intellect which breaks up the white light of the spirit, showing it in varied colors as these scattered beams, each one of which is imperfect in itself.[12]

One, then, of the great gifts to ancient India—coming in this way, as the result of true occultism, as the result of the mighty spiritual life—was the philosophy of the Vedanta and all those intellectual systems intended for the training of man, and giving, so far as the intellect could give it, a view of the spiritual reality. But remember the saving clause "as far as the intellect could give it." The intellectual view is only a partial view. And such a view, however much it may help man to see intellectually something of the possibilities of the higher life, can never make him realize it in consciousness, or give the true knowledge which comes, alone, through the evolution of the spiritual nature itself.

Along another line of activity would come the many schools of yoga. These schools, as you well know, were exceedingly various in their nature. Some of them were designed to develop the higher intellectual consciousness in man by means of concentration, by means of meditation, and thus to bring him into touch with the higher regions of his being. They were intended to lead him, stage by stage, to get free from the body, to pass consciously into higher worlds, so that his consciousness might function in those more extended realms of being. And we find many of the teachings of yoga—you may read many of these systems at your leisure, those which come under the great classification raja yoga—carefully adapted to aid the growth of the mind, the evolution of the loftier mental faculties, the rising on to the higher intellectual planes, the passing into states of consciousness far beyond the reach of ordinary humanity. They are, again, a stepping-stone offered—but still coming under this heading that I have called semi-occultism.[13]

Other schools were founded which dealt with man in different fashion, which strove to force his faculties from below, to force the evolution and the training of the astral faculties, to bring him first into touch with the astral world, to make him familiar with a part of the phenomenal universe closely allied to the material. These have generally been classed as the schools of hatha yoga. And in them, various methods were employed dealing with the lower vehicles of man. By these methods the body was trained, was to a great extent purified and rendered an obedient instrument. The power of the will was also enormously developed. The man was taught to be master of his lower nature, and so to take what in very many cases was a real step upwards—although we cannot include it in any sense of the term under the heading of true occultism.[14]

It must be remembered when dealing with all these schools, when looking at them and striving to learn alike their use and their abuse, that it is a great thing for a man to become master of his passions. It is a great thing to subject the animal nature, to be able to stand unshaken, no matter what temptations may assail the lower man. And very, very many of these schools, which it is often the fashion in the West to scoff at and despise, have yet in them this element—that they at least recognize that man's intellectual nature should be master of his sensuous nature and that he should learn complete control over the body, complete control over the passions.

And even along many of the darker lines of evolution, even in the schools that tread the path which all those who would reach the highest should most carefully avoid, it is nonetheless true that the subjugation of the lower nature is most rigorously insisted upon. It is only the ignorant who suppose that those darker schools are all given over to sensuous practices. Many of the followers of those schools lead lives which, so far as that side of the nature is concerned, might be taken as examples by an enormous majority of the men of the Western world.

Now the whole of these different schools rose and flourished in ancient India as the result of the great downpouring from the spiritual regions onto the lower planes, and naturally they were used both for selfish and for unselfish purposes. But in dealing with all those schools of yoga which train the intellect and develop the higher forms of intellectual consciousness, it is well to remember that they are real stepping-stones to the higher—and that it is a necessary stage of our progress that we should practice concentration, that we should use meditation, that we should be accustomed to contemplate intellectually and emotionally the ideals which appeal to us by their grandeur and their nobility. Those are stages in our upward path, and stages that very many of us might well be utilizing now, with a view to the higher growth, the deeper wisdom of the future.

Men took up these varying lines of evolution, stirred fundamentally by the prompting of the divine life within them, ever seeking to raise them and to help their upward growth—stirred, so far as they themselves were conscious, by the natural and rightful desire for higher evolution, for further progress, for growth in life. For, as we have often seen when we have been studying progress, we cannot leap at a bound to the heights of the spiritual life. We have to climb step by step. We have to utilize the higher thoughts in us for the subjugation of the lower, and then in turn to outgrow that higher when a greater height comes within our sight and within our reach.

We have learnt, as we know well, in our studies, that we may constantly eliminate lower ambitions by nourishing a higher ambition, and that, though that higher ambition be still attached to the personality—or even transcending the personality, be attached still to the individual—it is nonetheless a stepping-stone; it is one of the ways by which we climb. It is well continually to kill out our lower by our higher desires, though even those higher, in their turn, seem lower as we are rising above them and greater perfection comes slowly within our gaze. So that this longing for a higher life, this desire to develop, this yearning for progress, had—and have—their rightful place in evolution. And it is out of the ranks of those who feel these, out of the ranks of those who use the methods which make progress possible, that are taken those who are capable of further evolution.

They learn gradually to transcend the hope for individual progress—and learn that that also, in the fullest sense of the term, is illusory, inasmuch as the separated life is an illusion and cannot exist as separate in the higher regions. The true life is the life which is spent as part of the divine life, pouring itself out for others. And no life is true, no life real, no life spiritual, save when the very idea of the separated life is entirely transcended, and all the thought of the being, all the energies of the life, are poured forth as part of the One Self, and no distinction is recognized. Service is then the natural expression of the life, helping is that in which the true existence is felt. But ere it is possible that this ideal can be even intellectually realized, some progress, at least, must have been made in transcending what we recognize as the personality. And it was in order to make that possible to every man immersed in illusion—as all men have been, and are—that the various methods were suggested by those who would fain help their fellows forward, as steps on the upward path.

Others, seeing in the religious instinct in man—in that side of his nature allied to the emotions, in which devotion finds its root and the possibilities of its growth—seeing in that his easiest upward path, gave to the world the various forms of religion, in all their variety of adaptation to human needs, thus making the path upwards suitable for those whose constitution attracted them chiefly in the direction of love and of service. Seeing, then, that all these methods of growth were most active at the time when the real life was working at the heart of things, it will not be difficult to understand how—as that life found fewer channels for its expression in the world, fewer who were ready to transcend their own limitations and to give themselves wholly as channels of the divine life—all these methods lost their vitality and a great part of their usefulness.

And so we find, in looking around the India of today, that many of those things that were living are now dead, that many of the systems that were vital are now mere shells, forming subjects for intellectual controversy or for individual pride—but no longer stepping-stones to the higher life. Here and there, still, some gleam of the true life survives, some real use is being made of these stepping-stones upward. But, so far as the great masses of the people are concerned, mere shells and forms remain—evidences of what existed in the past, evidences, may we dare to hope, of what may be in the future.

It is hardly worthwhile to remind you that while semi-occultism may serve as a stepping-stone to real occultism, pseudo-occultism is generally a distinct obstacle and hindrance. Under this heading may be classed all the "occult arts," in the study of which many promising beginners have lost their way and wasted their lives. Geomancy, palmistry, the use of the tarot, et cetera—all these things are well enough for those who want to tread the byways of nature and to gather knowledge of her obscurer workings. They may be harmless, interesting, even useful in a small way, *but they are not occultism and their professors are not occultists*. A little success in their pursuit—and success does not demand high qualities of either head or heart—is apt to breed the most absurd vanity and pretentiousness, as though this dalliance with the *apsaras* of the kingdom of occultism converted a commonplace man into one of its rulers, a mage.[15]

A man may be past master of all these arts, and yet be further away from occultism than is a pure and selfless woman seeking only to love and to serve, or a generous, clean-souled man, devoted to the helping of his fellows. And if these arts be turned to selfish purposes, or if they nourish vanity, their professor may find himself approaching perilously near to the gateway of the left-hand path.

Looking for the application of this to our present movement, the lesson springs easily enough to our gaze. Again, in our own days, a great outpouring of real life has occurred. Again, an effort has been made by those who are the guardians, the reservoirs, of that life for our humanity, to pour out the true spiritual energies for the helping and the uplifting of man in every region of his being, the manifesting again of the possibility of the real life. This has been marked by certain definite statements made from time to time, by hints thrown out here and there by her who was the special messenger in our own day of this possibility opening up for our own race.[16] And there is one passage in that paper to which I referred at the beginning, which gives us in a phrase the reality of life: we are told that when a man becomes a real occultist he becomes only a force for good in the world.[17]

Here is a sentence that people read without realizing at all its meaning, a sentence that comes in the middle of many other statements, and does not strike with its full force on the unprepared mind and heart. For many things may be said which are missed for want of receptivity, and many truths are proclaimed which remain dark and silent, save to those whose eyes are beginning to be opened to see, and whose ears are beginning to be opened to hear. And that statement, which really puts the occult life in a few words, is one that most readers pass by without realizing its significance.

There is no true spiritual life, there is no real occultism, until the man at least recognizes that the goal of his living is to become a force for good, and that only, in the world. He is no longer to seek his own progress, no longer to seek his own life, no longer to seek his own development—no longer to ask aught that heaven or earth or any of the other worlds can give him for himself. There is only one thing left within him, the longing to be of service; only one thing the motive of his being, to be a channel for the great life of God, to enable that life to be scattered more effectively over the world of man, and over all worlds where that life exists.

When that is recognized, even afar off, when that ideal first dimly dawns upon the human heart—come it by way of intellectual apprehension of its sublimity, or by way of devotional recognition of its truth—then, for the first time, the spiritual life stirs within the man, the first germ of the spiritual nature begins to quicken into life. And so we begin to realize that if true occultism would be reached and understood by any of us, we should have to begin the preparation for it by working at character in the way that every religion has taught.

How often do we hear it said amongst ourselves, "We know all these moral truths; there is nothing new in Theosophy when it simply reiterates the old morality. When we are told to be unselfish, to seek to help others forward, to eliminate the personality, to kill out our faults, it is all an old story that we have heard to weariness. We want something new, we want some fresh knowledge, some facts of the astral world, some strange things of the mental region—that is what we demand from Theosophy, that is what we are seeking, and we do not desire to have pressed upon us these ethical maxims, these continual repetitions, these old-world stories which every religion has made familiar, and which we can hear from any pulpit."

And yet the truth of the matter is that along that path, only the spiritual life has been and is possible for man; that the divine teachers who gave the religions to the world, with their perpetual insistence on morality, gave them knowing the spiritual life, and knowing that only along that line the real progress of man into unity with God was possible. And when it was again declared by the lips of the Christ that only he might gain his life who lost it [Luke 17:33], that those who would be perfect must sacrifice all that they had—when he again reiterated the ancient teaching that narrow was the path and straight was the gateway [Matt. 7:14]—he was only repeating what all true occultists have taught as to the necessity of the training for the spiritual life.

As progress is made, all those methods of yoga which tend to help forward the individual, which are followed in order to gain progress, practiced in order to evolve faculties, and used in order that the individual may faster forward himself—all these are dropped, and yoga is regarded, not as the means of self-evolution (as we are accustomed to regard it here), but as the using of great forces for the lifting and the helping of humanity, with utter disregard for the going forward of him who is using them, with no thought of progress on the part of him who is wielding them for the helping of man. For in truth, all control of higher forces, all utilization of these vast energies, ought to come only within the grasp of man when he has transcended the personality and has learnt to use them only for the helping of all.

We readily admit this in the common things of life, and recognize the difference between learning the use of an instrument and the mere holding an instrument without knowing how to use it. A pen, for example is one of the most useful of instruments, but its utility depends upon the brain and the heart behind it, upon the knowledge and the skill that wield it. And a pen in the hands of a child is of no more use than any fragment of wood that the same child might pick up to use as a toy in its play.

Very much the same is the grasping of the forces of the superphysical world by those who have not yet conquered the lower nature, eliminated personal desires, and consecrated themselves wholly to the divine service. They are, truly, picking up an instrument which may be used for the highest and noblest ends. They are, truly, placing their hands upon a tool which, in hands that know how to use it, may serve for the salvation of the race. But unless the spiritual nature be developed, that tool fails in its highest purposes, that instrument fails in all its noblest possibilities. And it has this peculiarity—that, whereas the pen that I used as a symbol might be comparatively harmless in the hands of the child, the grasping of those forces by one in whom the personality is not eliminated may become a source of danger alike to himself and others, and may tend to retard the progress of the race instead of lifting it upwards.

That is why some of us who have learnt but the mere alphabet of these great truths lay so much stress—stress to weariness, as I know some of you think when I am speaking to you—on the moral training which must precede all attempt at occult study. H. P. Blavatsky gave us the same lesson when she herself said that she had blundered, in teaching part of the alphabet of occult knowledge without insisting upon that old precept that the moral growth must come before the occult training, and that the character must be purified, raised, and spiritualized before anyone should dare to lay his hand upon the latch of the occult gateway.[18] Hence it is that those qualifications that we have so often studied are made qualifications for initiation. Hence it is that there has even been the demand that only the pure should enter, that only the selfless should come in.

If I have spoken of the past to you tonight, if I have reminded you that amongst us today the very outburst of the new spiritual life will cause activity on all the lower planes, it is because I would bring the experience of the past to reinforce a lesson so often given from this platform. It is because I would warn you of the dangers that surround us on every side—dangers that some of us are beginning keenly to recognize, and to recognize just because they have to some extent struck us, and have therefore made progress the more difficult.[19] So that it is our duty as Theosophists, as would-be students of the science of the soul, to be careful that in all things character precedes any attempt at the gaining of power, that purity, selflessness, devotion, utter self-surrender, be found in us ere we touch the ark of occultism—for without these any success is a defeat, without these any attempt is doomed to failure.[20]

And surely it is better for us to learn from the experience of the past than by the bitter suffering that grows out of the personal experience of today; better to learn by the authority of the great teachers, who have proclaimed the lesson over and over again, than to have to learn it by the suffering that follows from grasping powers ere we are ready to use them, from plucking the fruit of knowledge ere it is ripe for our consumption, from striving to rule ere yet we have learnt to obey, and from endeavoring to snatch at the mighty forces of the spiritual realm until we have learnt that great lesson of the spirit—that only by giving is the spirit shown, that only by utter abnegation is the true life realized.

As the very life of God in manifestation is a life that gives everything and asks nothing back, so those who would reach unity with Him, and realize what the spiritual life means, must learn to give and not to take, to help and not to hold, to pour out without seeking or looking for return. Only as we learn that do we become fit candidates for the higher knowledge. Only as the heart is thus rendered absolutely pure may we dare to face the presence of the Master, hoping that when "he looks at the heart, he may find no stain therein."[21]

Part Two

HIGHER LIFE TRAINING

Chapter Five

The Higher Life

(1902)

This is a subject for thoughtful, serious people who realize something of the object of life. The first thing that is necessary to consider is whether one really desires to lead the higher life, for it is only a strong will that will enable us to win footing on the spiritual plane.

Desire Ardently

It is useless to think of treading the higher path unless in one's heart is the *ardent aspiration* to achieve. Therefore, with the force and energy which is likely to give needful strength, we must desire. Compare for a moment the very feeble way in which we desire spiritual progress with the way in which worldly people desire wealth, fame, power, success. If even one-half the energy we spend in worldly matters were put into spiritual aspiration, it would carry us far into spiritual achievement. The prayer of an ancient devotee might profitably be used by us: "May I love and seek Thee as men in the world love and seek wealth."[1]

Swami Vivekananda, speaking in America, told a somewhat graphic story in order to impress upon his hearers how very little, as a rule, people really long for God. He told of a young man who came to a religious teacher and said he wanted to find God. The sage smiled and said nothing. The young man returned time after time, ever repeating the intensity of his desire, his longing to find God. After many days, the sage told him to accompany him as he went to the river to take his morning bath, and when both were in the river the sage took hold of the young man and plunged him under the surface of the water and held him there. The young man struggled and struggled to shake off his hold. Finally, he raised him out of the water and said to him, "My son, what did you long for most when under the water?" "Air!" gasped the youth. "Thus must the would-be disciple long after God if he would find him. If you have this breathless longing after God, verily he shall be found of you."[2]

When that longing after God has been awakened, a longing as intense as the drowning man had for air, it will not be satisfied until the higher life is found.

The first qualification, then, is *desire*. There is no compulsion in the matter, there is no harm in following the ordinary evolution of humanity, there is no disgrace in not striving to quicken your evolution and step out of the beaten track. The whole world is an expression of the divine will and the divine beauty.

Lead, then, if you prefer it, a life happy and harmonious and useful to those around you. There is no reason why any person should make up his mind to enter the probationary path[3] unless there is no other way possible for him, unless no other way satisfies. As long as the outer world holds your interest, try to lead an ordinary good life, for the time for the inner has not yet come.

The Good Law

In *Light on the Path* we read,

> Remember, O disciple, that great though the gulf may be between the good man and the sinner, it is greater between the good man and the man who has attained knowledge; it is immeasurable between the good man and the one on the threshold of Divinity. [*LP* 21]

Most religions simply try to make people good, to turn the sinner into the saint. But leading the higher life has to do with that part of our evolution between the good man and the man divine. It is not merely a question of becoming a saint, but a sage as well. That is the crown of human evolution to which human life leads.

A man must have a firmer conviction of, and faith in, the good law. Those of you who believe in that law should never be anxious about your work. You know that so much effort put forth means so much progress, for such is the law. It is not a question of thinking at one time that you are making progress and at another time fearing you are not—the law that progress follows effort is as certain as that fire burns. This conviction leads a man to be neither anxious nor hurried over his work. Success or failure comes not into his consideration. He does his work. He "fears no failure, courts no success" [*VS* 31].

We cannot judge our progress by our feelings. There is nothing more deceptive. In reality, we often make more progress in what seem to be times of deadness, coldness, and indifference, than in times when we feel the most joyous.[4] We are dealing not with the things which are seen, or felt, which are temporal, but with the things which are not seen or felt, which are eternal—for growth in the higher life is a matter of eternity, not of time.

The natural laws of the spiritual world are as certain as the natural laws of the physical world, for a law of nature is only a statement of conditions, not a command. And so also with the laws of the higher life—the candidate for it is shown what is needed to produce such and such results.

Environment and Opportunity

It is surely necessary, then, first to study the conditions. Study yourself, then your environment. See what are your capacities. Recognize definitely your nature and your powers, that you may understand how to work with that nature. Then study the things around you, your environment. This environment has nothing whatever to do with your progress. You must get rid of that idea. It is very common for people to say, "If I were in different circumstances, amid different surroundings, I would do much better." All that idea grows out of ignorance. If you cannot make progress where you are, you cannot make it anywhere. Any artificial change would only lead to disappointment.

The difficulties which lie in our way in the spiritual life are not in our environment, but in ourselves. We have in the past made certain relations—pleasant or unpleasant—with people. Karma brings us together again to work out these relations. They form part of our environment. If our lot is cast among people who are uncongenial to us, we only make things worse and bind them to ourselves indefinitely by discontent and trying to get rid of them artificially. Our relationship with them must be worked out. Thus, and thus only, shall we rid ourselves of our uncongenial surroundings. The relations must either be made permanent, by struggling and artificial methods, or concluded, by working them out.

And so with disadvantages of position and lack of opportunity for work. The lack of opportunity means that the desire for work needs strengthening. It is a result of choice in the past. It is idle to fret against opportunity. The desire must be strong to create the opportunity—and in the meantime we must wait with the patience of knowledge.

What can we do as regards our environment? Our attitude towards our surroundings is the only thing which marks our capacity for attempting to live the higher life. You must change your attitude towards your surroundings. Cease quarreling with them. Change yourself, not your surroundings.

A Christ would be the same in whatever conditions he were placed, and would quietly change those surroundings by the benediction of his presence.

Similarly with the social problems with which we are brought face to face. It is useless to attempt to alter the surroundings first. It is beginning at the wrong end. Improve the people, and the surroundings will inevitably improve. Improve the inner nature, and the outer will inevitably follow suit.

Consciousness and Its Vehicle

Study yourself and your constitution, your consciousness and the forms in which the consciousness expresses itself. First must come the evolution of consciousness, then the improvement and evolution of the vehicles. Consciousness is there in the germ in each, not yet in flower. It is self-unfolding, but you can aid it to unfold more rapidly than if it were left to nature alone. The vehicles of consciousness must then be purified and controlled. The question then lies before us: how to unfold the consciousness—how to purify and control the vehicles.

You must study the nature of consciousness in order that you may understand. You cannot unfold the self [atman] until you have knowledge of what constitutes "myself." This must be mastered intellectually. The self in man reveals itself in three aspects: will, intelligence, activity.[5] All three must be unfolded, and each of the three is unfolded differently.

Will and Desire

It is necessary to understand something of the nature of *will* in its various aspects. Desire is the working of will on the lower planes.[6] There is no fundamental difference between the two. They are the force, the energy of the consciousness going outwards. We live because we will to live.

We are accustomed to look upon the desire nature as an enemy to progress, an obstacle to be done away with.[7] On the contrary, it is a good thing to have strong desires, provided they are under control. It is perfectly true that uncontrolled desires lead a person into endless trouble, but a person with no desires at all is apt to be very weak and wishy-washy. We might compare a man with a strong desire nature to a spirited horse. With a rider who can control him, he is a magnificent instrument. While a man with a very weak desire nature (very little will force or energy) is like a weak, broken horse, practically good for nothing. So long as the spirited horse is unbroken, plunging about with no control over him, he is dangerous. But a horse with no energy in him—what can be done with him?

You must have force. Without that, you can do nothing. Strong desires are troublesome, yes. But they are to be brought under control. There is a great deal of truth in the old saying, "The greater the sinner, the greater the saint." You cannot change one into the other in a moment—purification is needed. But the force, the energy that makes a man great in sin, when turned in another direction, carries him to sainthood.

Terrible as the struggle may be with the personality, the force within gives promise of future achievement, for the material is there which, when awakened, insures rapid progress. The desires which ruin when uncontrolled, elevate when controlled.

Use intelligence and discretion in curbing the desire nature. If you use exaggerated efforts, a recoil may set in. It is far wiser to try to conquer a desire which is low in its tendency by another which is nobler. For instance, a young man who has strong animal desires may fight strenuously against them. A wiser plan is to conquer them with, say, artistic emotions—to put something higher in their place. You should study your whole desire nature, and use those desires which have an upward tendency to curb and conquer the lower ones. Bring all your intelligence to bear upon it.

When you have thus brought out the force of your desire nature into the side of the *good*, you have begun the evolution of the will—which is the energy of the self [atman] directed from within, not from without, guided by reason, not by external objects.

Connected with this is the whole question of emotions. Understanding them, you will learn to control them. Strive earnestly to understand how you may control evil emotions and stimulate good. Study also the relation of emotions to each other, and of those in you to those in others. It is not an easy task—it is troublesome and arduous. Therefore is determination needed, therefore the will to tread the Higher Path must be strong.

Intelligence and Activity

The evolution of faculty is of far more importance than the mere gaining of information. In the one case, you are creating an organism; in the other, filling up a receptacle. It is not developing the mind to be merely filling it with other people's thoughts. As the physical body cannot live without food, still less without time for digestion and assimilation, so neither can the mental body grow without intellectual food and assimilation. Carry into practical life those rules of mental growth with which we are all familiar. Those who succeed are those who practice the art of independent thinking.

The activity of the self [atman] is the way in which consciousness affects all that is not itself. Study the rationale of action. Cease to plunge blindly along into one line of action or another simply because others recommend it, or because it promises immediate good. Think it out—and then follow, or not, as your consciousness dictates. Never forget that invariable sequence: desire, thought, activity. Bearing this in mind, you will find one of your strongest helps in the conduct of life. Everything begins by *desire,* is carried into *thought,* and expresses itself in *action.*

Purification of the Bodies[8]

Let us turn our thoughts towards the purification and control of the vehicles of consciousness. In each case, again, this is a threefold process. There are three vehicles to be purified and controlled: the physical, the astral, and the mental—each having its own laws. The denser portion of the physical body depends on food, health, and cleanliness. According to the kind of body you want, according to the kind of work you wish it to do, you must choose the food with which to build it up. Pure food will help to build up a pure body. Even the selection of the kind of food you wish to use can be made a means for the strengthening of the will.

Think out carefully your rule of life, and having thought it out and determined that you will build only pure materials into your body, then stick to it. Thus will your willpower develop. Do not be thrown back by the temporary rebellion of the body and its desires against these reforms. Realize that you are the master, not your body. If you are full of doubts instead of full of will, your body will break down under any diet. Be fully convinced of the life you mean to follow—and the body will, sooner or later, be your obedient servant.

The purification of the etheric part of your physical body is carried out by the magnetic quality of food.[9] Find out what things have good magnetism and what bad. Magnetism is largely affected by the cleanliness, or otherwise, of the external surroundings. Impure air affects the magnetism of the food we take. This, of course, makes it more difficult for those who have to live in our large manufacturing towns—for the magnetic conditions there are bad. But there is no need for discouragement, as these conditions can be somewhat modified by keeping one's own vehicle pure and positive.

One's personal magnetism is also greatly affected by the company we keep. If you are much influenced by your companions, then refrain from going into bad or doubtful company unless your duty compels you so to do. Only very strong souls can afford to mix in the magnetism of bad company.

Purification of the Astral Body

To get rid of an evil desire is a hard task because the ingrained habit of the past resists the change. Suppose an evil desire comes to you. Refuse to consider it. Turn resolutely away from it, and think of something pure. Refuse to attend to an evil thought and turn your attention to one of a pure and noble nature. By simply turning your attention thus away from impure to pure desires, allowing only pure ones to effect a lodgment, you finally purify your astral body.

Desires still leave traces on the astral body after you have conquered them—the reason being that the astral vehicle does not change so rapidly as the consciousness. The consciousness may have evolved beyond evil desires, yet the astral body, having once responded to them, has matter within it still capable of responding to vibrations of the old desires.[10]

There are many earnest, eager students who are greatly distressed by evil desires. Do not be discouraged—they do not belong to you now. But so long as there is matter left in your astral body which used to respond to these things, it is liable to be vivified by any desire form passing by, or by evil thoughts of those you happen to be among. Continue earnestly and determinedly to desire the opposite kind, and this coarser matter will be gradually shaken out. The same applies to the thought body.[11]

Control of the Bodies

While purifying your vehicles, you must also bring them under control. This control again is threefold: 1) control of thought, 2) control of tongue, 3) control of action.

First, you must act as you think. Suppose you are in the habit of thinking carelessly, superficially. Then, inevitably, your action will follow suit. Here, in thought, lies the secret of control. If you try to control each action by itself, it is a never-ending task. It is as if a gardener cut off the tops of the weeds instead of rooting them out. Checking one objectionable action alone is comparatively of no use, for it will arise again and again.

The root of an action is *thought*, and this must first be purified and controlled. To work with this law in mind would be to determine definitely, deliberately, to *think* before acting. Give a certain time every morning to such meditation. You want your actions to be deliberate, considerate, compassionate. Think thus, while meditating, and your actions will express them. Give the time for thinking, and thus make the conditions possible.

Next follows the control of tongue. This is a difficult thing to do. It is said in the Laws of Manu, "One who controls the tongue has conquered everything" [Shrimad Bhagavatam 11.8.21].[12] Learn to control your words—*think* before you speak. Half the mischief in the world is done by unconsidered speech. Want of thought is the root of much evil. You do not stop to think, and there the fault lies. Consider before speaking, "Is it worth saying? Is it true? Is it useful?" Otherwise be silent.[13]

The habit of frivolous chattering makes a person superficial. Be willing to wait for a few moments before speaking. It will make you slow in speech—but that will be no great loss to the world! Thus you will never be a party to mischief-making, to gossip, to idle repetition of unkind stories. Never speak what is untrue. Never speak what is not courteous. Never speak what is not kind. When thought and tongue are controlled, action inevitably follows suit. This is a triple subconscious cord which every candidate for spiritual progress must wear.[14] Unless this is attempted and accomplished, the higher life is impossible.

Finally, control all your actions. Be in the world as a divine instrument. Try to realize what it is which the Logos is striving to bring about, and help in the shaping and guiding of the world's *purpose* to its *goal*.

Our Spiritual Attitude

We desire to be instruments with which the Logos can work—tools in His hands to shape the material, rather than stones on which the tool is exercised. Recognize the divine beauty of the work to which we are called. What should be the attitude of the spiritual man to the world at large? The spiritual man does every action because it *ought* to be done, not because he wants to do it for personal reasons. He does not seek activity, neither does he shrink from it. He holds himself in his own place, where the Logos has put him, that the divine life may flow through him, accomplishing the divine purpose.

We are agents of His life, the instruments He has in His hands. We lose the sense of being workers, and realize that He is the only worker, and we are the organs through which He expresses Himself in His universe. Then the result must always be that which is best for the whole. Actions fail in being best only when we try to guide them for the fulfillment of our personal wishes. When the divine idea and the divine wish take the place of our personal ideas and wishes, then we shall have become a channel of the divine will.

Unless we can be kept at full stretch of activity by that motive, it is better to be moved by desire for personal success—as otherwise inactivity ensues. It is far better that a man should be moved by ordinary worldly things, such as the gaining of wealth and the acquiring of power, than for him to be inactive. It is better that the lower motive should hold until the higher motive is realized.

The whole desire of the spiritual man is to do the will of the Logos, to be a channel through which the divine life may flow—and to realize that for him, the one supreme law is the divine will.

Chapter Six

Methods of Unfoldment (1904)

I propose tonight to say something about the methods of unfoldment, meaning by that the way in which people may develop themselves as to the inner man, and so gradually acquire certainty and knowledge where at present they are puzzled and bewildered. For this new psychology that we have been dealing with will never be thoroughly understood until people can "see"—and trace out that which gives rise to those many phenomena which are put together under the title of coming from "the unconscious"—without any kind of explanation.[1]

In the course of these lectures, I have tried to show the different sources whence these phenomena arise, so that theoretically, as it were, you may be able for yourselves to classify them—to say, as you read about this or that phenomenon, "That belongs to such-and-such a part of the nature of things; this to another part," and so on. But it is much more satisfactory if, instead of simply taking the theory to work upon and applying it, you are able, by your own perceptive ability, to decide, when any new case arises, what is its real source. Therefore, it seems to me useful to put before you certain lines of possible development—and the more useful, perhaps, because some of these lines are undesirable and dangerous, whereas others have been, if not perfectly successful, at least useful to those who practice them in quickening their development, even if in the present incarnation they have not time to complete the work.

We must first consider what it is which is to be developed, because the method will depend on the part of the nature in which development is sought. And we see that along two main lines human evolution will inevitably go: one, the side of consciousness; the other, that of the vehicles. The consciousness itself will be greatly unfolded, and show out a deeper, clearer insight, a fuller and firmer grasp. So that we shall have to deal with methods of development as applied to the consciousness. And that is, in the most literal sense of the term, a question of unfoldment—because the consciousness has all these possibilities existing within it, and it is only a question of bringing them to the surface, just as a bud may unfold into the perfect flower.

But it is not only a question of the development of consciousness in which we are interested—because, as the consciousness unfolds on one plane after another, it does not thereby follow that the consciousness will be able, from the higher planes, to directly affect the physical brain, so as to bring about effects in what we call the waking consciousness. For it is quite possible for a person to be so developed that, both as regards the consciousness and the higher bodies, they may be active on their own planes—and yet the knowledge acquired there may not be brought down into the physical mind and "remembered."

But when the consciousness is developed so as to be able to work, then comes in the question of the vehicles in which it is to work: the various bodies which it uses. And we are concerned with only three of those—for if three of them are in active working order, the possessor does not need further physical instruction to learn anything of the value or practice of unfoldment. If a man has control of his physical, astral, and mental bodies, he can gain for himself the knowledge that comes out of what the psychologists call the unconscious—and from the higher and valuable side of it, the superconscious.[2]

But it is rarely that there will come down, at the present stage of evolution, information from the consciousness above the mental body. Of course, it does happen in the case of the genius, for there are many cases of genius in which the illumination comes from the causal body—the lasting treasure house in which all memories are stored. It may also occur in the case of those who, by gradual evolution and definite practice, have perfected their outer vehicles so that they are able to work in the causal body.

Mostly, however—and for our purpose, entirely—these three lower bodies are those with which we are concerned. And we want to know how to unfold our consciousness, how to improve our physical body, how to bring the astral body into working order, and how to do the same for the mental body. So that, on the side of consciousness, the powers may be unfolded, and on the side of the forms, the organs whereby these powers express themselves.

Now, along some methods of evolution, all the force is directed to the vehicles, while the unfolding of consciousness is left unattended to. And where that is the case, the results are peculiarly unsatisfactory, because the person may be developed as to the psychic senses, which may yet remain practically useless—because, although they are developed as organs, the consciousness is not ready to work through them. It is an artificial forcing. Instead of the consciousness bringing about the evolution and presiding over the building, it is possible to some extent to force the evolution of the organs, and take them, as it were, ahead of the evolution of consciousness—so that people may see and hear many things which they do not in the least understand. And that is most often the case when people are born "psychics"—people who have developed these qualities in previous lives.

Generally, when people are not very highly evolved, and yet are born with these psychic powers, they have in previous lives devoted themselves to the methods which work upon the bodies, leaving the consciousness unattended to. The result is considerable psychic development. But, the unevolved consciousness being unable to use these powers intelligently, they are of comparatively little value, and more an annoyance than a treasure to their possessor. Such people are by no means to be envied. And if they find themselves possessed of powers that they do not know how to use, and which tend to disturb and distress them—bringing into their life a number of phenomena which they do not understand and cannot control—the only thing such people can wisely do is to set themselves to the deliberate unfolding on the side of consciousness, and so make up in this life what they have failed to do in a previous one.

I think we shall most readily follow the methods of unfoldment if I put briefly, first, the theory as it is held, especially in India, where these things have been studied for thousands of years; and secondly, the methods we find recommended amongst ourselves today.[3] We may then see to which of these two great divisions of unfoldment the methods amongst ourselves belong. It is always advisable to have a complete theory—because then, when a new thing comes along, you have a niche in which to put it. And as no such theory exists in the West just now, we must go to the East for one, and see how it bears upon things happening among ourselves.

In the ordinary psychological science of India—a psychology many thousands of years old—there are two great forms of yoga: the hatha yoga, and the raja yoga. And under these two divisions all development naturally and inevitably falls. The theory of hatha yoga is this:

- that, on the whole, it is easiest to begin with the physical body, because then you are dealing with a thing of which you at least know something;
- that, starting with your physical body, you can bring it under control to a well-nigh incredible extent;
- that, as the physical body corresponds in its various parts to the organs of the higher bodies, it is possible to reach those organs of the higher bodies by stimulating the organs in the lower;
- so that, starting with the physical eye, you would gradually develop, going upwards, the corresponding organs in the astral body, thus developing clairvoyance; that, starting with the physical ear, you can, by stimulating that, bring about a corresponding growth in the astral body, and so hear things on the astral plane.

That theory of correspondence is perfectly true. Our senses are not really in the physical body, but in the astral, and the centers of those senses are in the astral body. All sight on the physical plane—before it conveys any knowledge to the inner man, the perceiver—passes from the retina back to the optic centers in the brain, and from those in the astral body to the corresponding centers which are really the centers of the senses. The brain is merely like a telegraph wire along which the message goes. You see by the stimulation of these astral centers. That is the first thing to remember.[4]

But hatha yoga includes much more than the stimulation of the senses. It includes a complete control over every part of the physical body, so that all the muscles, voluntary and involuntary, are all brought under the control of the will. The hatha yogi goes through a number of processes, many of them extremely troublesome and even painful, in order to bring under the control of the will every portion of his physical body. And, being taught also the correspondence in the astral body, he works up from one to the other in the way I described with respect to sight and hearing.

There are in India a considerable number of these hatha yogis who are willing to show off their powers. They can do some very extraordinary things. They can stop the beating of the heart or the working of the lungs, and many other things of that sort. And it is rather surprising until you know how it is done. Only when you have done all this, the question arises: "Of what use?" Is it worthwhile to go through this long training in order to do things that, after all, you do not really want to do?

The only thing in which you may say there is some use is with regard to the seeing, hearing, and feeling on the astral plane. And that they attain only to a very limited extent—and after the novelty of the thing is over, inevitably the man wants to go further and ask what it means. In many cases, they are not able to connect together the centers in the astral body and the organ of the physical senses; so that they do not in many cases succeed in [astral] seeing or hearing, as far as their brain knowledge is concerned. They go into trance, and when they come out of it, they are as wise as when they went into it.

Nearly all hatha yogis can go into trance. But when they have done it, what happens? Simply this: that the physical and astral bodies are separated. In some cases, the astral body is at work; so that, as far as that is concerned, the man is having experiences, although they cannot be conveyed to the brain consciousness. Still, the fact that it is able to work is an advantage, because much may be learned on the astral plane which will filter down to the physical plane—not as memory, but as knowledge which gradually makes its way through. But, in many cases, when the physical and astral bodies are separated, the astral stays quite close to the physical, practically useless and asleep.

So far as I can find, along that line no very great increase of knowledge is attainable. But one thing they *do* attain, and that is magnificent physical health. They develop a muscular strength and power of endurance which enable them to carry the body through fatigue which would crush an ordinary man. They also develop, through the difficult nature of the practices they do, and the perseverance necessary to obtain any results, a great power of will.

Now, what theory lies behind that, as well as the correspondence between the physical and astral? When we look at it, we notice this: that in the course of evolution consciousness has gone a little ahead of organs, and the working of the consciousness has brought about the building of the organ. That is a point of enormous and practical importance. The function of life always precedes the shaping of the organ—the organ being built by the exercise of the function.

Tracing on the evolution, the next thing that strikes one is that, as the consciousness develops, as the thinker evolves more and more power of thought, he puts aside one thing after another that he has done by the exercise of his will, handing it on to the automatism of the body, and turning his attention to higher and more useful things. So that when we see the hatha yogi bringing again within his conscious control the things that in the course of evolution he has let go, we find he is going backwards instead of forwards, burdening himself again with a number of things which are really done very much better by the automatic mechanism of the body—and on which, if he interferes, he must spend a great deal of trouble in order to reach the same perfection as the mechanism has done by his previous work upon it.

We find we are going backwards also when we come to deal with stimulation of the astral senses in this way. The astral center was first developed, and through that the physical organ of sense, so that to use the physical organ to stimulate the astral center into independent working is to retrace the path of evolution. And it does not bring out the true sight or hearing in the astral body, but brings into abnormal and undesirable activity those sense centers which have built for their own expression the sense organ in the physical body—the astral having a set of senses of its own which do not necessarily communicate directly with the organs in the physical body.

The astral senses are directly related to the astral plane, whereas the sense centers are bridges for communication between the thinker and his physical vehicle. You do not want to make those active independently, for they will never serve your purpose thoroughly and completely. You are taking an instrument made for one purpose and clumsily adapting it to another.

What you want to do is to evolve in the astral body its own sense organs—the chakras or "wheels," which belong to that body as a body, and not to that body as a means of communication between the thinker and his physical vehicle. To stimulate those centers which are bridges, instead of evolving the living "wheels" which are the right organs of the astral body, is a complete blunder. You are falling into an abnormal evolution, and one which is utterly undesirable and likely to be mischievous.

Let us now see what Western methods of unfoldment partake of this hatha yoga principle—that you are to stimulate the physical body and thus arouse certain powers in the astral. All methods which begin by turning any of the senses to the careful close observation of a physical object are part of this hatha yoga method. For instance, the favorite Eastern method, which is now being advised for practice over here, is to make a black spot on a white ground and stare at it for hours together. Crystal gazing is another method which is recommended.

I have received a large amount of American literature suggesting all sorts of things on these lines. All these belong to the hatha yoga system, and are fundamentally mischievous—not only because they are going backwards in evolution, but because of their exceedingly injurious effect on the physical organs.[5]

One result of gazing at a black spot for hours is that it spoils the sight. The axes of the eyes are often put out of order, producing strabismus, more commonly called squinting. Another thing you find is a gradual dulling of the physical sight, due to the overstrain of the nerves of the retina, which overstraining gradually passes back through the optic nerve to the optic center—so that, after many years of practice, atrophy of the optic nerve may arise, causing dimness and even blindness.

There is a difference here between the Indian and the Westerner. The Indian does not care about the physical result. The European or American does. When the Indian gets a well-established squint, he is as happy with it as without it. He does not want to look at the things round about him. He has set his mind on something different, and he is not disturbed by the squint. He does not mind even blindness. But the Western man minds it very much.[6]

Over in India, these things are known—but that is not so over here. And it is rather a cruel thing, it seems to me, that systems of that sort should be scattered broadcast all over the West without any explanation of the dangers that every Indian knows are connected with them. Some few people may get safely through, but many are injured. And even supposing a man does escape these things, and throws himself into a trance—when he comes out of the trance, he is as wise as before. He has simply performed self-hypnotization, and doing that is of no value to the man who does it.

So also with hearing. It is quite possible to hear sounds by breathing in a certain way. But it is only through pressure on the nerves connected with the ear, in the throat. People seem to think that doing this opens up the astral senses.

There are many things like that which you can read if you like. But do not practice them. It is better to give them a wide berth. The fact that the people who circulate these things among an ignorant public do not tell of the effects likely to be brought about by these practices may be because they are ignorant. I do not suppose they do it maliciously.

Crystal gazing, also, leads to nothing but the very lowest order of clairvoyance. I was once very much puzzled by a fact with regard to crystal gazing. I happen to know one of our members who has developed astral sight to a remarkable extent, and I asked him one day, for my information and amusement, to look into a crystal and tell me what he saw. He gazed at it, and turned it in all sorts of ways—but not a solitary thing could he see, although he worked at it for some time.

The reason for this is quite clear when you come to think about it. The vision of the physically developed man is a vision which comes not through a stimulation of the sense centers in the astral body, but from the chakras. And the man who is using the one would be the last man in the world to be using the other—which is only wanted, so to speak, on the downward path of the bridge, in order that physical impacts may reach the thinker and give him information.

I have never known a case of crystal gazing which went beyond the possibilities of the lower astral plane. It is true that you can, by practice, see—but you do it at a serious risk. I strongly advise you not to go largely into crystal gazing, popular as it is; for, although you may gain some small results from it, you will be shutting yourselves out from the higher possibilities.

Turn from that line of evolution to the raja yoga system. That starts quite differently. It starts with thought, with a process of meditation. And before that process of meditation, which is the beginning of the raja yoga, there is a preliminary course to be followed by the man desiring to practice. He must to a certain extent have purified his physical body—not because he is going to use that body to stimulate the astral, but because, as the powers of consciousness grow, they will work down into the physical body. And unless it be prepared to receive their workings, it is likely to be injured, and hysteria, diseases of all kinds, breakdown of the physical health, sometimes even lunacy may result. All these things have been observed and studied in India. And it has been found by practical experience that if a man starts these methods with an unprepared body, while he may get some very remarkable results by the play of the consciousness downwards, he will very soon break up as regards his health and he will become a nervous wreck.

The purification of the body is effected by an elaborate system of food, drink, sleep, and so on, of which the center note is moderation—not starvation, not lying awake so that the nerves are overstrained, but moderation in everything. The kind of food the raja yogi takes is to be *sattvic*, a term generally translated "pure," but which I think is better translated as "rhythmic"—that is to say, food in which the vibrations are regular, harmonious, balanced. This is based on their theory of matter having three attributes—one, inertia, which, predominating in the human body, would mean sloth and heaviness, so that foods tending to produce this quality are barred. So also, all foods that tend to produce ill-regulated activity, restlessness, in which predominates the second of the attributes of matter, mobility, are barred. That leaves the foods in which the quality of rhythm predominates. A whole system relating to the foodstuffs is built up to help in the preparation of the body to vibrate in answer to the higher consciousness when it is wanted.[7]

The next step is the complete mastery of the emotions, so that a man may never be carried away by them. A man must have made some advance along this line before it is thought safe to teach him the methods of yoga itself.

When he has thus partly purified his body, and learned to control his emotions, there comes in the training of the mind—the "great enemy," as they call it [Bhagavad Gita 6.6]—because all the ordinary use of the mind is to run out to the outer world, and that mind is usually regarded as the best which moves most rapidly from one thing to another, which is able to grasp one thing and then turn to another, and so on. Now, those qualities are exceedingly hindering when you come to the evolution of the higher consciousness. And the raja yogi turns all his efforts to the evolution of this higher consciousness, which demands the quieting of the mind, in order that it may shine forth. So his practice consists partly in the steadying of the mind, which is done by the use of the imagination, to a large extent—a mental picture being formed and the attention fixed on it; then withdrawn from all the picture but one point, and fixed upon that; that point finally being dropped, so that the mind remains absolutely still. The difficulties here in the West with regard to this method are these: that the mind is more restless than it is in the East, by the line of evolution—and, again, that people expect results too rapidly.

The first result of trying to fix the mind is to discover that it is much more restless than you thought it was. A mind which thought itself fairly steady is found to be restless and all over the place when it is ordered to fix itself on a thing which does not attract it. Then, again, you must practice this for years before you get a really satisfactory result—and that is a thing which seems rather long to the hurrying and busy life we find here in the West. If you have done it some lives before, you will do it soon now. But if this is the first life, it will be a weary task—but it is inevitably necessary if you desire to grow along the path that means wisdom, power, and service.

When the mind has grown fairly steady, so that it can be reduced to quietude and kept there without thinking, then comes the time when the higher consciousness asserts itself—and with that one enters on the real practice of yoga. In addition to the fixing and gradual emptying of the mind in this way, there will be considerable practice simply in concentration, keeping the mind on a single thought—not so much now on a mental picture as on an idea, and, as it were, sucking out of that idea everything it has in it, by a curious process in which the idea takes possession of the man.

What really happens is that the mental body molds itself into the form of the idea, so that the idea becomes part of the mental body of the thinker. And when he can do that, those fixed thoughts mold and shape and create the organs in the mental body necessary for the work which he has to do. When those organs are partially developed, then the thought power comes down through them onto the astral, and builds there again the organs that it requires.[8]

You see, you are coming down, along the true line of evolution—the higher builds the lower—and this more highly developed consciousness, having shaped the mental body, proceeds to the shaping of the astral. And as the man proceeds with his meditation and concentration day by day, the thought comes down onto the physical plane, and shapes the brain, also for the expression of the higher powers. And when the thought currents at last pour down, they find an instrument which is able to vibrate without injury. And in addition to that, the whole of the man's previous thinking has improved the cells of the brain, has enlarged them and made them very much more complex, creating a better instrument—both in the organization of the cells by the whole course of thinking, and by the power of vibrating to the subtler currents when they come down from the higher planes.

Now that is the practice of raja yoga, put in a general way. Laborious, difficult, demanding a great sacrifice of time and labor, it must become the first thing in life ere one can expect success. But, after all, that is only what is true of every other science. The man who is going to be a really great mathematician must give his life to it. The man who is going to be a great scientist of any kind makes the science in which he chooses to be an expert the one object of his life, bending all his efforts that way. And can you expect [that] the science of the soul—hardest, most complex, and most subtle of all sciences—shall be mastered with less of effort than is given to the ordinary science, which works in the physical plane and by the physical brain?

If you think of it, you will see that this, only, can be the rule of evolution, here as elsewhere: that the man who would really be a raja yogi must make it the object of his life. And as he proceeds in this way, notice the sequence: consciousness unfolding first, and then the organs of the body shaped for its expression. That means that whenever the organ is able to work, the consciousness will be able to understand and master. It means that the man has evolved within, and so will be able to deal with all that meets him on the different planes of existence—and as he enters into one plane after another, he will find that the powers that he requires on that plane are evolved in his consciousness, and that none of the mechanism that has been created by their use goes beyond, in its power of response, the powers of the consciousness to understand.

I grant that it is much more difficult than the other plan—but then it takes you somewhere. It really quickens our evolution and makes our lives nobler and grander than otherwise they can possibly be. It is the road of evolution traced by the divine will for the whole of humanity. And all that the raja yoga does is to quicken evolution. It does not turn aside from it, nor go against it.

Along this line of meditation and of practice it is that the great teachers of the past have gone. It is the road that they have proved to be safe for human feet to tread. And the prize that lies at the end of the efforts is great beyond all speaking.

I have been talking here, all the time, of this new psychology. But the understanding of that is as nothing—is but, as it were, child's play to those who are working for the evolution of these higher and nobler faculties. For there is only one motive that makes the strength, the courage, and perseverance to follow this toilsome road to its end, and that is the will to serve, and to become a channel of the divine will in evolution.

You may tread part of that way with the desire to serve your separated self. You may find something of courage, endurance, and patience by the prizes of power held out to you along this path. But this also will fail as the difficulties grow greater. For the man who fixes his thoughts on power for the separated self is working against the divine will, which works for unity—and although he may become splendidly intellectual, although he may develop to a great extent that body which for age after age is not born nor dies, he cannot touch the innermost life of the spirit, which knows no separation, but lives by unity alone.

Along these paths of unfoldment I have mentioned, you are truly unfolding consciousness and form. But the highest path of all, on which the eyes of those who tread these paths are set, is that spiritual evolution which means the recognition that all lives are one and not separate; that all beings live but in the self [atman], and the self in them—that knowledge, which is of the highest, in which all are seen as one and not as "others." So that the man who reaches the threshold of the spiritual world [i.e., the buddhic consciousness and plane] sees in that world himself indeed, but himself as part of a common, universal life; realizes that all the forms that lie on the lower planes are his, so far as his life and his powers are concerned, and that the one particular form that he has been evolving by his struggles and his labors is in very truth no more his, as a separated thing, than any of the other objects which he sees around him in the universe, whose life is one. So that it is not for him, as his eyes open to the greatness of the spiritual world, to see differences in those around him anymore, nor to think of himself as other than they. The criminal, in his lowest degradation, to him is part of himself, and the form of the criminal is his form, as much as his own highly evolved one.

It is the glory of such a life that it can share any form—however low, however base or vile—and, pouring part of itself into that form, can raise it a little higher than by its own unaided efforts it could climb. That it is to be a savior of the world: to know no difference, to look on the saint and criminal with equal eyes, as both manifestations of the Divine, as much identified with the one as with the other—perhaps even more with the lower than with the higher, because the lower needs aid and effort more than does the higher and the more intelligent.

That it is to be a savior of the world: to be wise, but only that the wisdom may go out among all the ignorant and make every ignorant man a little wiser because one has known. To go out among the foul and the impure, having gained purity, and make them a little cleaner because one has risen to the heights of purity. To learn, but only to share. To gain, but only to give. To rise to the highest in order to be able to touch most effectively the lowest. For this is true: that the higher you climb, the more easily you can touch the lowest—not by stooping down to them, but by feeling your own unity and identity with them.

It is the part of the truly spiritual man to feel himself one with the sinner, and to share his own purity with him. That is what is meant by the spiritual life—beyond all intellect and beyond all enveloping form. That is the true glory of divine manhood; that the reality of the spiritual life. Worthless is all unfoldment, worthless all swift evolution, worthless all development, unless it subserves this one supreme end—to put an end to separateness. To think no more of others as different from oneself, but to know that the whole universe, inasmuch as it is in its Creator, is also in every life that is one with him. To know that, as we share the divine life, we come nearest to every form in the universe. For true is it only of that which is of spirit: "Closer is he than breathing, nearer than hands and feet."[9]

Chapter Seven

The Reality of the Invisible and the Actuality of the Unseen Worlds (1905)

The majority of civilized people today, in every country, profess a belief in the existence of worlds other than the physical globes scattered through space, the suns and planets of our own and other systems. However vague may be their ideas of the nature of such worlds, invisible, superphysical, supersensuous; however much the ideas vary, according to the religion professed by the believer, they yet cling to a belief that "not all of me shall die" [Horace, Odes 3.30], that death does not put an end to individual existence, that there is "something" beyond the tomb.

But if we estimate the value of the belief by the criterion suggested by Professor Bain—that the strength of a belief may be tested by the influence it exerts over conduct—then we find that, despite the nominal profession, the belief itself is of the flimsiest character.[1] The conduct of people is ruled by their belief in the visible world rather than in those invisible. Their thoughts, interests, affections, all center here. And so markedly is this the case that the behavior of anyone who is really influenced by the thought of the superphysical worlds is deemed eccentric and morbid.

A patient's body may be worn out by extreme old age, or tortured by a disease that must shortly end in death. Doctors, nurses, relatives, will strain every nerve to scourge the will to hold on to the useless body, will pour into it drugs and stimulants to put off for a few days or weeks its dissolution, as though the life beyond this world were a mirage, or a thing to be avoided as long as possible by every means.

This lack of the sense of the actuality of the superphysical worlds is more common in modern than in ancient times, in the West than in the East. Its wide prevalence is due to the conception of man as a being who possesses no present relation with those worlds, and no powers which would enable him to cognize them. Man is regarded as living in one world—the world of waking consciousness, the world of the triumphs of the senses and the intellect—instead of in several worlds, in all of which his consciousness is functioning, more or less definitely. He is no longer supposed to possess the powers which all religions have ascribed to him—powers which transcend the limitations of the body. And the active agnosticism of the scientist, of the leaders of thought, is reflected in the passive agnosticism of the intellectual masses, whose lip belief in the superphysical is mocked by the conduct belief of ordinary life.

It is not enough that we should think of the superphysical worlds as worlds that we may, or even shall, pass into after death. The realization of these worlds, if they are to influence conduct, must be a constant fact in consciousness—and man must live consciously in "the three worlds," the physical, the astral, the heavenly. For that only is actual to man to which his consciousness responds. If his consciousness does not answer to a thing, for him that thing has no existence. The boundary of his power to respond is the boundary of his recognition of the existent.

A man might be surrounded by the play of colors, but were it not for the eye, they would not, for him, exist. Waves of melody might sweep around him, but without the ear, there would, for him, be silence. And so the worlds invisible may play on a man, but while he is unconscious of their presence, for him they do not exist. So long as that irresponsiveness continues, no amount of description can make them living, actual. To him they must remain as the dream of the poet, the vision of the painter, the hope of the optimist—beautiful exceedingly, perchance, but without proof, without substance, without reality.

But can the invisible worlds be made present in consciousness; can we respond to them, and share their life? Are there in man powers not yet unfolded, but to be unfolded in evolution, so that he may be likened to a flower not yet opened—powers that lie hidden like the stamens, the petals, in the bud? Are the prophets, the saints, the mystics, the seers, the men in whom these possibilities have flowered, and are their methods of prayer or of meditation the scientific means of culture which hasten the unfolding of the bud?

In seeking to answer this question, we may look back into the past or analyze the present, we may study the religions of ancient times, or we may scrutinize our own constitution and seek to understand its constituents and the relations of these to our environment. Along these lines, it may be, some results may be obtained.

Looking back over the religions of the past, we find one idea dominating them all—that the visible universe is the reflection of the invisible. Egypt sees the world of phenomena as the image of the real world. To India, the universe is but the passing expression of a divine idea—there is but one Reality, and the universe is its shadow.[2]

The Hebrews in their philosophic books assert that God made the universe of ideas before the universe of forms. The celestial man, Adam Kadmon, is the original, whereof the terrestrial man is the copy. And Philo says that God, intending to make the visible universe, first created the invisible. In the Talmud, it is regarded as axiomatic that if a man would know the invisible he should study the visible. And the Hebrew Paul declares that the invisible things are plainly seen by those that are made [Rom. 1:20].[3]

Pythagoras tells of the world of ideas, and has "real forms" existing in the intelligible world—the world of ideas in the universal mind—ere the ideas were manifested as the physical universe. So again Plato and his followers.[4]

Everywhere is this dominating thought: that there is an invisible which is real, and a visible which is unreal, a copy, a reflection. Only the Real is eternal, and only the Eternal can satisfy, since "Thou art That."[5] The Real manifests as the unreal, the Eternal masks itself as the transitory. How strange the paradox, how complete the subversion, when the unreal is considered to be the only reality, and the transitory the only existence.

During the immense period of time covered by these and by other religions, man was regarded as an immortal consciousness veiled in matter, the consciousness becoming more and more limited as the veils of matter grew thicker and thicker. His deepest relations were with the world of ideas, and each world grew more unreal, more illusory, as the matter which composed it grew more and more dense and gross. The phenomenal worlds were, as their name denotes, worlds of appearances, not of realities—and man must pierce through these appearances to reach the core of reality.[6]

This spirit endued the garment of mind, and over the mind the garb of the senses, in order to come into relation with the intellectual and sensuous worlds. And man, the resulting composite, must rise above the senses, must transcend the mind, in order to be self-consciously spirit. As in himself, as spirit, he knows the spiritual, so in his mind garment he knows the intellectual, in his sense garment the sensuous.[7]

The sense garment is threefold, and each layer relates him to a material world—the heavenly, the astral, the physical. All these are truly visible, each cognizable through sense organs composed of its own state of matter. But only the grossest is visible to the normal man, because in him only the grossest layer of the sense garment is in thorough working order. As the finer layers of the sense garment are gradually evolved into similar working order, the finer phenomenal worlds will become sensuous to him, tangible to his senses.

Thus was it taught in elder days. Thus is it now taught in Theosophy. The pseudo-invisible—that which is capable of being seen although invisible to the eyes of the flesh—will become visible as evolution proceeds, bringing into functioning activity the finer layers of our sense garment, and then "the three worlds" will become "the visible universe." Such functioning activity may even be brought about, at the present stage of evolution, by special methods, and man may live consciously in "the three worlds" at once. For such men, the actuality of the lower invisible worlds is established on that so-called indubitable evidence, the evidence of the senses. And it is of this sensuous evolution that many, perhaps most, people think when they speak of obtaining proof of the persistence of individual consciousness on the other side of death. Such evidence, however, must remain, for a considerable time to come, out of the reach of the majority of people, although the minority able to obtain it is ever-increasing and is certain to increase more rapidly in the coming years.

The available evidence for the existence of the finer layers of the sense garment, and for man's relations through it with superphysical worlds, is abundant and is continuously receiving additions. Clairvoyance, clairaudience, premonitions, warning and prophetic dreams, apparition of doubles, thought forms, and astral bodies, et cetera, are beginning to play a part in ordinary life and to find unjeering reportal [*sic*] in the daily press. Signs of evolving sense organs are thus around us, and the unimportance of death will be more and more recognized as these multiply.

It is no longer possible for a person, instructed in the well-ascertained facts of mesmeric and hypnotic trances, to regard mental faculties as the products of nervous cells. It is known that the working of those cells may be paralyzed while perception, memory, reason, imagination manifest themselves more potently, with wider range and fuller powers.

Those who have patiently and steadily observed the phenomena occurring at spiritualistic seances know that when every doubtful happening is thrown aside, there remains a residuum of undoubted facts which prove the presence of forces unknown to science, and of intelligence that is not from the sitters or the medium. Automatic writing has been carried to a point where the agent concerned cannot be the brain consciousness of the writer. Thought transference—telepathy—has passed beyond the range of controversy and has established itself as a fact by reiterated and exact proofs.

The worlds unseen are becoming the seen, and their forces are asserting themselves in the physical world by the production of effects not generated by physical causes. The boundaries of the known are being pushed back until they begin to overlap those of the astral world. The evidence increases so rapidly that the materialist of forty years ago threatens to become as extinct as the dodo, and the whole attitude of the intellectual classes to life is changing.

And yet, amidst all this, it may be well for us to realize that these extensions of knowledge, valuable as they are, can only, at the best, give us proofs of a prolongation of life, not of our immortality—for the three worlds are all phenomenal, all changing, and therefore all transitory. They add to our physical life an astral life and a heavenly life. They give us three visible worlds instead of one. They enlarge our horizons, and add to our material inheritance. They do not, and they cannot, give us the certitude of immortality.

To say this is not to undervalue the further improvement of our sense garment, but to put the senses in their right place as regards our knowledge of the superphysical worlds, even as we have learned to put them in their right place in our knowledge of the physical. If we analyze carefully the knowledge which we gain through observation every day and at once utilize for our conduct, we find that very little of it is directly obtained through the senses.

At our present stage of physical evolution, the experiment to prove this is not quite easy, but it is not impossible. If we would make the experiment, we must proceed as follows. We shut out all that the mind has deduced from previous observations, and narrow ourselves down to pure sensuous perception of an object, such as a face, a landscape. We mark only what the eye reports, and as far as possible add nothing to that sensation from the mind that has perceived, noted, registered, compared, so many previous similar sensations. We see, as an infant sees, outline and color, with no distance, no depth, no relations between adjoining parts, no *meaning*. When we now look over a landscape, we see into it countless observations, movements, and experiences made from our babyhood upwards.

The infant's eye is as perfect as our own, but does not measure the near and the far, the relation of parts that makes a whole. When the eye sees under quite new conditions, it is easy to deceive it. The senses are continually corrected and supplemented by the mind.

Now, when first the finer sense organs of our sense garment begin to work, they are as the eyes of the infant on the physical plane. But behind them is an actively functioning mature mind, full of ideas built up out of physical plane sensations. This content it throws into the outline supplied by the astral sense organ, and the man "sees" an astral object. As on the physical plane, by far the greater part of the perception is mind supplied. But while the mind on the physical plane supplies details collected by countless physical plane observations of similar objects, and thus adds to the sense report its own store of congruous memories, the mind on the astral plane projects into the sense perception the same store of memories—now incongruous, for it lacks the astral observations which should form its contribution to the total perception. There is a fertile source of error, continually overlooked. And hence early observations are most misleading, and the observations of the untrained continue to be earth filled.

In order that we may be sure of our immortality, something quite other than this refining of the sense garment is necessary—something that is related to life and not to life vehicles.[8] We may climb rung after rung of the world's ladder, and yet remain unsatisfied. For infinities stretch ever above us, as below us infinities stretch—and stunned, dwarfed by the immensities above and below, it seems to matter little whether we occupy one rung or another of the ladder. This is ever going outwards, adding one mass of phenomena to another mass, a true weaving of endless ropes out of illimitable sand. And if the word of the mystics be true, we must turn inwards, not outwards, when we would seek wisdom instead of learning.

It is indeed obvious that no extension, no refinement of the senses can introduce us into worlds really invisible—into that which is not phenomenal, into the world of thought, not the world of thought forms. For this, the consciousness must unfold the powers ever within it, and make manifest the divinity which is its hidden nature. Consciousness is the Real, conditioned by matter, and we must "plunge into the depths of our own being" if we would find the certitude of immortality in conscious union with the One.[9] All other proofs are supplementary—this is primary and final, the alpha and omega of life. Consciousness is the Ever Invisible: "Not in the sight abides his form; none may by the eye behold him" [Shvetashvatara Upanishad 4.20]. Yet herein resides the full certainty of the reality of the Ever Invisible, of that which escapes alike the senses and the mind.

As the eye responds to light, the ear to sound, the material to the material, so must consciousness learn to respond to consciousness, the spiritual to the spiritual. When this is learned, the question of death can never more distress us, nor doubt of the necessary existence of worlds for the continued life of the imperfect discarnate assail us. For when consciousness realizes its own inherent immortality, it knows itself essentially independent of the three worlds, a spiritual entity belonging to a spiritual world.[10]

The answer to the question, Can we know this, not only hope it? comes alike from religion and from philosophy. The greatest of our humanity declare that this knowledge is within the reach of man. It is the *brahma-vidya*, the gnosis, Theosophy.[11] And the ancient narrow path along which men have trodden from times immemorial, along which have gone the teachers of every religion and the disciples that have followed in their footsteps—that ancient narrow path is as open for the treading of men today as it was open to the men of the past. The human self is as divine in the twentieth century as in the first, or as in thousands of years before. The life of God is as near to the human spirit. For the spirit is the offspring, the emanation of Deity, and it can know because it is like its parent.

It is said in an ancient writing that the proof of God is the conviction in the human self.[12] That is the one priceless evidence, that testimony to the divine reality which comes from the Real in us. Hence man may know the reality of the Ever Invisible, as well as the actuality of the—at present—invisible worlds.

In search of this testimony, religion bids the believer tread the road of prayer. By intense concentrated prayer, when the life is pure, a man may so rend the sense garment that spirit may commingle with spirit, the human with the divine. The rapt ecstasy of prayer may lift the devotee to the object of devotion, and he may feel the bliss of union, the ineffable joy of the Lord. Never again may he doubt the reality of that high communion. And, far short of this, the man of prayer may have experience of the inner worlds, may feel their peace, their joy, may bask in their light.

These experiences are facts in consciousness, and lift the man beyond all possibility of doubt as to the reality of the invisible. To call them "subjective," to talk of the "reflex action" of prayer, does not explain nor destroy their value.[13] That the consciousness may be widened, uplifted, illuminated, is the all-important *fact*. The man feels himself in touch with a fuller consciousness, an upwelling life. His hunger is appeased, and the food reaches him from realms that are not physical. Along this road of prayer, he may reach sureness of the existence of the Invisible. For the simple, the devotional, this path is the easier to tread.

There is another road to which philosophy points, in which man turns inwards, not outwards, and finds certitude of reality within himself. The one certainty for each of us—needing no proof, beyond all argument, incapable of being strengthened by any act of the reason—is the sure truth: "I am." This is the ultimate fact of consciousness, the foundation on which everything else is built. All save that is inference.

We argue the existence of matter from changes produced in our consciousness by other than ourselves. We argue the existence of people around us from the sensations we receive from them. All is inference save the one central fact of consciousness. All else changes—but that, never. In that stability, that changelessness, is the mark of the Real. The Real is the changeless, the eternal, and this one changeless thing is the Real ingarbed in form.

If, studying man in his present stage of evolution, we seek to know the seat of this self-consciousness, we find that in most of us its throne is the lower mind [kama-manas]. In truth, the place in evolution of each conscious being may be judged by the recognition of the seat of consciousness. If that seat be in the physical body [sthula sharira], we find consciousness, but not self-consciousness. There is not there the power of distinguishing the "I" from the impact of impressions causing sensations.

Higher in the ladder of being, consciousness is seated in the second layer of the sense garment [kama-prana], and this is the case with animals and with large classes of men.[14] The life with which these identify themselves is the life of sensations, and of the thoughts which serve sensations. From this, they gradually rise to a consciousness which identifies itself with the mind, which has risen from the life of sensations to the life of thought. From this life of the lower mind [kama-manas], in which sensations still play so large a part, man rises to the life of the intellect [buddhi-manas], and the lower mind becomes his instrument, ceasing to be himself. From the life of the intellect, he must rise to the life of the spirit [atma-buddhi], and know himself as the One.

The seat of self-consciousness is moved from the lower mind to the higher by strenuous thinking, by the intellectual travail of the student, the philosopher, the man of science—if the latter turn his thoughts from objects to principles, from phenomena to laws. And as strenuous thinking can alone lift the seat of self-consciousness from the mind to the intellect, so can deep concentration and meditation alone raise that seat from the intellect to the spirit.

The man who would deliberately quicken his own evolution must, having transcended the life of the senses, strive to make his life the life of the intelligence, rather than the life of mere outer activity. As he succeeds, he will become more, not less, effective in the outer world—for he will fulfill all his duties there with less of effort, with less dispersal of energy. A strength, a calmness, a serenity, a power of endurance, will be marked in him which will make him a more effective helper of others, and a more efficient worker in his daily tasks. While he discharges these faithfully, his true life will be within, and he will practice daily the higher powers of the intellect as they unfold.

As these become familiar, he will gaze into the darkness beyond the intellect, seeking by concentrated meditation to find the light that is beyond the darkness—the light of the Real, of the self [atman]. In that silence will arise within him the spiritual consciousness, responding to subtle thrillings from an unknown world. First feebly, and then more strongly, with a courage ever-increasing, that loftier consciousness answers to the without and realizes the within. He knows himself as spirit. He knows himself divine.

To such a one, all worlds are open; nature has "no veil in all her kingdoms" [*VS* 14]. The heavens spread around him, and living selves, discarnate and incarnate, people the various worlds. He knows that death is nothing, that life is ever-evolving—not because he has seen with the finer organs of the sense garment the astral and mental bodies which clothe the departed, and can thus view the unbroken continuity of life here and there, but because he knows consciousness as eternal, not subject to death.

To him, the universe is rooted in life, and the changing forms are unimportant, since the Real *is,* however forms may change. This sure conviction needs no phenomenal proofs to make it more sure. It is based on the nature of things. The actuality of the unseen worlds is, indeed, known to him—but his rock is the reality of the Ever Invisible. All worlds are actual, because they are the masks of the reality, but they might all fade away as shadows, and yet would the Real remain.

Chapter Eight

Occultism and Occult Training (1906)

Occultism has been defined by H. P. Blavatsky as the study of the divine mind in nature. And, taking it in its broadest and deepest sense, I do not think that we can better that definition—the study of the universal mind as shown forth in the universe. Now, those who have made such study, and have given some of the results of their study to the world, tell us that the universe exists first in the universal mind—that it exists there as idea before it comes into manifestation in the grosser forms of matter. And, as you know, that view of the universe is found in all the great philosophies and religions of the world.

We find the Greek philosophers speaking of an intelligible world, then of an intellectual, and later of the worlds of grosser matter. We find the Hebrews speaking also of a world of mind, of which the physical world is but a gross and rough reproduction. We find it stated in the teachings of the Hindus and Buddhists that the universe is but the thought of the Supreme. And Theosophy, dealing with this a little more closely and more precisely, as its fashion is, draws for us a picture of the beginnings of a universe in which these ideas in the universal mind are drawn out by the great architects. And then the builders take them from the architects and shape them into grosser kinds of matter, mental, astral, and physical.[1]

The occultist, in trying to carry on his studies, finds himself face to face with two kinds of evolution, along both of which he must go. He is bound by the very name of his study to devote himself to the understanding of the divine mind in nature. And inasmuch as that mind manifests itself through form in subtle matter, on which the grosser forms are modeled, he finds it also necessary, in his study of the thoughts of the Supreme Thinker, to prepare himself for the observation of the subtle forms in which those thoughts are clothed. His evolution, then, must be twofold.

On the one side, he must evolve his own consciousness, so that that consciousness, working on higher planes, may be able directly to contact, to see, to study, to vibrate with, the thoughts in those subtler worlds. And, while he is evolving his consciousness to be able to intuit those thoughts, he must also evolve his subtler vehicles in which that consciousness may function upon the higher planes, and so be able by the development of his subtler senses to observe the various forms on those planes and see their relations with the physical plane. For when we say—as we say truly—that mind underlies the universe, and when we say that nature has a life side, we are dealing with rather different kinds of ideas, although ideas that are closely allied. For, in studying the mind that underlies the universe, we are clearly on the side where form is not. We are in a realm of ideas in the subtlest sense of the term, where formlessness (as is often said) is to be found.

When we come to deal with the manifestation of these ideas in the worlds we call invisible, and also in the visible, then in those worlds invisible we have to do with what is called the life side of nature. For by that phrase we intend to say

1. that nature is no dead mechanism, no soulless apparatus;

2. that all that science knows as forces or as energies are really expressions of subtle lives;

3. that all those forms and energies in nature that form one great part of the study of scientific men are really, on the higher planes, living beings; and

4. that these living beings express themselves on the physical plane as the forces or the energies of the physical universe.

So that we may trace down a line along which the occultist would study the evolution of the form side in nature: He would begin with the Logos of a system. He would pass from him to his viceroys, those we call the Planetary Logoi, each ruling over a department of his own. And then he would see round each Planetary Logos the great rulers of the elements which are to be the fundamental forms of matter in that department of nature. He would see there those who are called in Hindu parlance the Kings of the Shining Ones, those who have for their bodies the great elements in nature—meaning by that word *elements*, not the chemical elements of the physical plane, but elements as spoken of in ancient philosophies describing the types of material used in the shaping of a universe. So that we should find one of these elements, earth; and one that we call water (not water on the physical plane, but on the plane above the physical, the astral); and then above that the plane of fire; and above that the plane of air; and above that still higher the plane of *akasha*, the ether—the five planes with which here we have to do, and two higher yet, at present unmanifested and to us unknown.[2]

Now, each of these elements, from the occult standpoint, forms in its entirety the body of one of these great Kings of the Shining Ones—those who in Christian parlance would be called the seven archangels, rulers of the angels, having each beneath him and under his control a vast angelic host. And the conception of the occultist with regard to such an immense life is that you have a great spiritual intelligence who has evolved in past universes and comes into this world to be one of the great builders of a universe, having as his body all the matter which is of one kind.

Thus one of these Beings would be clothed in ether as a totality, and every force that played in the ether would be the working of his intelligence, the expression of his thoughts. Another would be clothed in the supernal fire, and all forms of fiery matter would be his body, or made of the material of his body. And all the energies that play in those forms would be his thoughts—the life, the fire, the energy, that play in that fiery matter. And so on all the way down.

So that you have this conception of nature—that it consists, on the side of life, in great spiritual intelligences, each of them ruling over a vast department of nature, and each of them clothed in a particular kind of matter—matter which is one of the elements, in the ancient sense of the term. And when we come down to our physical plane, we find that each of these elements and each of these great Beings has his own representative in the physical universe also. For that which is a subplane of matter in the higher world is a plane of matter in the physical universe, and each subplane in the physical corresponds with, or represents, a plane in the higher—and each element is reproduced in the physical as a subplane of the physical, and gives its name to that subplane.

Thus down here on the physical plane, while the whole is all the great element earth, the solid earth would be taken as the corresponding subplane; while the watery matter belongs to the great plane of the astral, and liquids on the physical plane would be the corresponding subplane or subelement. So again with fire, which here is represented by the gaseous bodies in nature. And above that, in the occult sense of the word, air, by the lowest of the ethers is represented. And above that, the next higher great plane, the divine flame, is represented down here by the second of the ethers. The subatomic and atomic subplanes are the representatives of the two highest, the unknown elements.[3]

In this way, finding in the physical universe subplanes corresponding to each great kosmic plane, and thus subplanes corresponding to each of the primary elements in the kosmos—in this way, the occultist, in studying even the physical, would not look on it quite from the standpoint of the ordinary scientific man. For he would see what he would call the subelements here—the solid, the liquid, the gaseous, the etheric, et cetera—as directly connected with the great lord of the element in the kosmos or solar system.[4]

And so, if he is studying the life side—that which is behind the phenomenal appearance of the subelement—he would then study the workings of the intelligence of that Being as shown out in the countless hosts of lower intelligences who reproduce his thoughts in miniature and manifest his powers in miniature. Thus the whole of his study would be conditioned by this greater thought, and he would see in the manifestations of the physical plane the lowest expressions of the thought of a higher plane. And that would have a very practical bearing upon his dealing with nature in a fashion I will return to in a moment.

The occultist who is trying to develop himself would deal first (in far more detail than I have outlined) with this great theory of worlds or systems of worlds and would become quite familiar with it in detail. That would be his first step, and a necessary step—for until he has mastered it as a theory, it would be hopeless to attempt to practice it as an occult science. He must learn this theory, as laid down by those who have verified it and studied it at firsthand, in order that when he starts on his first practical and firsthand study, he may bring to it a trained intelligence, a cultured mind, and a consciousness which knows at least in theory what it is going to study.[5]

Our would-be occultist, then, having mastered this theory in its details, will next concern himself with the evolution of his own consciousness. He will endeavor, by hard and strenuous thinking, by prolonged and careful meditation, to train the mental instrument with which he is to work upon the higher planes. And now will come his first great difficulty: he cannot begin to be an occultist until his mind is thoroughly under his control. As you know, men are for the most part under the control of their minds, where they are not under the control of their senses. But even the more developed are under the control of their minds, and do not control them.

Until the mind is under control, it is useless as an instrument of occult research. For if it is to run about here, there, and everywhere, as it pleases, dragging its owner with it, it is clear that it will tend downwards towards the lines along which it has come in its evolution, impelled by desires, moved by attractions and repulsions—whereas the occultist who desires to know cannot afford to have attractions and repulsions. He is to study everything in the clear dry light of reason, and is not to shrink from one study nor to be attracted to another. The whole universe is before him. The divine mind is manifested in every part of it, and all that the divine mind has thought is worthy of study. There is nothing in that mind, rightly understood, that can possibly repel. So that he must master his mind completely, and that is the first step the would-be occultist must take.[6]

I say the first step, because I take it for granted that no one is thinking of becoming an occultist until he has purified his life and laid a firm foundation of virtue, of noble thinking, and of noble living. It does not do to leave that out of regard, though I am taking it for granted as being well known to you, for it is of vital importance to him in his later studies.[7] No man whose life is not pure, whose thoughts are not noble, whose character is not unselfish, should venture to touch occultism at all. For every fault he has will assail him, every failing will dig pits for his feet. And until he has laid his foundation of virtue, he must not try to build on it the temple of occultism. Nor must he try to build that temple until his emotions and senses are thoroughly under his control.

Let me put to you very briefly why this complete control of the senses, of the emotions, of the thoughts, is necessary for the occultist. Presently, we shall find that he is going to move on subtler planes and use subtler vehicles. Now, these vehicles he is going to practice in, made up as they are of very fine and delicate matter, will move and vibrate under far less force than will move and vibrate the physical body.

It is a very simple fact, known to every one of you, that the same amount of force put to the moving of a light body will drive it farther than if applied to a heavy body. A push that would not move a railway wagon would send a ball skimming many yards away. Now, apply that well-known law to the vehicles in which the occultist is to work. So long as he is in the physical body, he thinks and feels—but before the thought expresses itself, it has used up almost the whole of its power in making the brain work at all. Before an emotion shows itself as an emotion, the greater part of it is exhausted in moving the heavy physical matter by which that emotion is expressed—so that you get only a very small residuum of thought and emotion showing themselves in the physical world.

But now let the emotion go on to the astral plane. What happens? The same amount of thought, of emotion, moving in the astral body, will throw it into the most violent and fearful passion. If the man is not careful at first, he will run the risk of tearing his own astral body, and of doing great damage to those who are around him on the astral plane by the tremendous vibrations he sends out. He might knock another senseless, or even shatter his astral body, by the thought which down here would only show itself by a strong emotion. Hence the need to control the thoughts and emotions. That is one of the reasons why, until the control of thought and emotion is achieved, no one will help another to go to work upon the astral plane in the definite wide-awake fashion.[8] Uncontrolled people are like so many [fire]crackers or rockets flying all over the place—a danger to others, useless to themselves. So it is necessary that our would-be occultist should get the mastery of his mind and emotions, in addition to that purity of nature of which I have spoken.

Then comes the time when he is to work for the development of what are called the subtler senses. I am supposing he has gone along the line of evolution by which his consciousness has been unfolded—so that his consciousness is ready to understand, ready to receive impressions, ready to answer. When the consciousness is ready, the vehicles must be brought up to a fine point of response, and the subtler senses must be evolved. Now, these must be evolved in very definite ways—still all along the line of meditation—of a somewhat different type from that which evolves the consciousness: a meditation that deals directly with the astral and the mental senses, sets them to work, makes them active, and brings them under his control. When he has made progress along these two lines of evolving the consciousness and the subtler senses, the occultist will be ready to work upon the next two higher planes.

Then, as he begins to work, he will find a difficulty facing him—the difficulty of distinguishing between what he contributes to those two planes and the things which exist there independently of himself. And here he will make many a blunder for a very considerable time. Every feeling he has there takes to itself astral matter and presents itself as a living being. Every thought clothes itself in mental matter and presents itself as an independent existence. And the first blunder that he will make, when he is able to see and to understand, is that he will always be getting back his own thoughts, he will always be finding his own ideas confirming themselves, apparently by external agency. Hence many of the mistakes made by those whom we call untrained seers.[9]

If any such has a strong desire in his mind, he is sure to find it on the astral plane, presenting itself as a most magnificent picture—and he will be convinced that it is his duty to follow out that image he has seen. And if it be one that can be reproduced on the physical plane, he will be wild to reproduce it here. So also with doctrines, beliefs, convictions, of all kinds—the nearest thing to him will be the crowd of his own thoughts, emotions, and wishes. They will crowd all round him when he wakens on the higher planes, and it will be some time before he learns to quietly put all that crowd aside and to study the plane itself, and not only his own creations upon it.

Here comes in the value of his moral and unselfish training: for the more his thoughts are pure, the more they are under control, the more easily he will be able to manage them on the higher plane and give them their proper place. And the more they are free from all the promptings of desire, the safer he will be against the danger of hearing the echo of his own voice as his Master's voice, and regarding the figments of his own brain as commands put upon him by his Master.

As he goes on, he will learn to distinguish. And there is one kind of touchstone which is very useful in the earlier days. If the thing he brings back is only the reflection of his own thought, a wish he desires to carry out upon the physical plane, then you may be sure there will be a great deal of feeling mixed up with it: grievous impatience, hurry, excitement, and anger, if the carrying out is opposed. Whereas, if it be really a teaching of his Master, then he will show down here on the physical plane a calm, a peacefulness, an utter absence of excitement and passion of any kind. Now, inasmuch as it is his Master's will, he will know that his will must work itself out, if only he does not oppose it; and that what is wanted on his side, that the Master's will may be done on the physical plane, is simply devotion, calm, and patience—putting no obstacle in the way, but waiting until the impulse comes from the higher plane, which has in it the certainty of self-realization.

And the man who is trying to be an occultist will test himself in this way. If he finds himself very excited, he will refrain from action, knowing that excitement is alien from the spiritual impulse. But if he finds a steady conviction which is able to wait for its realization, with no hurry, no excitement—which knows that every necessary circumstance will be brought into being by the Master—he may be sure his inspiration is from above, and that he is not being led away by the echoes of his own desires. Hence, again, the enormous importance of that purifying process I alluded to, before real advance is made in occult knowledge and power.[10]

Now, a great change takes place in the higher vehicles of the occultist—a change which is slow but steady, and which must be completed before he is really available as an instrument on higher planes than this. You have read in some of our Theosophical books (mostly in some books or papers by Mr. Leadbeater) that the astral and the mental, as well as the physical, matter of which our bodies are composed, is elemental essence with a tendency downwards. That is to say, the ordinary mental body is made up of elemental essence—that of the higher kingdom—coming downwards towards the astral plane. So, on the astral, the essence of which our astral body is composed is striving to come downwards to the physical. Hence a continual downwards movement in the very matter of our bodies.[11]

Now, as the occultist evolves, a change takes place in the material of which his astral and mental bodies are composed. The change consists in the rearrangement of the matter—and that rearrangement of the matter gives vehicles respectively for different kinds of life. The former arrangement of the matter gives vehicles for the downward-coming wave of the life of the Logos. The new arrangement of the matter of the astral and the mental bodies gives vehicles for the upward-climbing life of the monad, the spirit of the man himself. So that, as this change goes on, the downward wave of the life of the second Logos leaves his astral and mental bodies—and his own life, the life of his own spirit, takes the place of that downward-sweeping wave.

The result is an entire change in the direction and tendencies of these bodies. Before, they tended to go down. Now, they tend to go up. Before, the life pushed them downward. Now, it is drawing them upward. So that, in the perfected body of the occultist, his own spiritual life is the ruler of the molecular arrangement, and it is that life which forms its vehicles of the subtler matter and shapes the matter into the bodies that thereafter he uses on the higher planes. This vast and wondrous revolution makes his body useful to him in the future, instead of a hindrance, taking away that downward pulling, of which he has ever been conscious, and giving him, as it were, wings in his body—wings that lift him instead of clogs that drag him down.

Here, again, comes in the need of that moral growth in self-consciousness of which I spoke. The only safety in this process is in the moral character, in the inner power of the man himself.

When he has thus builded his bodies, when he has thus evolved his consciousness, when he has thus developed his psychic senses, then is he an occultist indeed. Then he will be able to study without fear of error. Then he will be able to investigate without fear of failure. For, at that point, he will be at the threshold of liberation—he will be ready for the initiation that makes a man a Master.[12]

All through his discipleship, he has been going through these stages, working along these different lines, and improving himself year by year. In his earliest studies, he will make many blunders. And there is no mistake greater, on the part of those who have not yet developed any of these faculties, or opened up their consciousness, than to suppose that when a person unfolds some of the astral, or even of the mental, subtler senses, that he becomes an infallible prophet, an infallible seer. Quite the contrary: he is liable to endless blunders, continual mistakes. And his only safety lies in the honest statement of what he believes to be the truth, and in a readiness to correct and amend it when clearer vision shows him to be mistaken. For there are many possibilities of mistake that open before the growing occultist.

I have told you of those that face him on the very threshold. Putting these aside, his next difficulty will be that there exist on the plane nearest to the earth many who will deliberately try to deceive him, to lead him wrong, to delay his growth, and to impede his gathering of knowledge. He can only gradually eliminate those—feeling them, sensing them, rather than seeing them, recognizing that subtle touch of magnetism which puts him on his guard, the signal of danger.[13]

And even when seeing straight and clear, the limitations of his vision are a fruitful source of error, for a thing does not look the same when you see it out of proportion. Seeing a fragment of a picture, you will have very little idea of that portion of the picture hidden from you, and you will not even see correctly the color of the bit you are able to sense. For colors are very much modified by surrounding colors, and are not really the same to your vision when you see them surrounded by many other colors that influence the whole—as when you see one fragment shown with, perhaps, a white surrounding surface. Not only is this true of color, but it is also true of form, and shapes seen out of proportion look quite different from the same seen in proportion. And seeing a fragment of the higher planes is often misleading because out of proportion to the whole. So this lack, this limitation, bringing about a disproportion, is also one of the dangers against which the growing occultist must guard himself.

And then there is the subtle temptation of pride and power, of thinking himself different from others and not realizing that he can only be an occultist in the higher sense when the forms are as nothing to him and the one life represents all being. Therefore is separateness called the great heresy, for to the occultist there is no more dangerous noose in which his feet may be trapped. If he thinks of himself as separate, at once he drops downward.[14] If he thinks of others as separate from him, at once he is enmeshed in the web of delusion. He must keep clear the vision which depends on unity, nor allow the pride of superior knowledge to make him hold himself as distinct from the ignorant and the unevolved.

Such are some of the difficulties that surround him. And yet none of these difficulties can daunt the soul who has set his heart on knowledge, on the greater service of the world. True, they are difficulties. But difficulties exist only to be overcome. True, they are dangers. But dangers make brave the heart, make strong the muscles of the spirit. So that one who is ready for the occult pathway will not be affrighted by the dangers, nor depressed by the difficulties. But, taking patience in both hands, and with the perseverance that marks the true student, he will address himself to his difficult task—secure in his faith in his Master, secure in his faith in the God that is himself, profound in his love for humanity, whom he is resolute to serve. And thus armed with patience, perseverance, faith, and love, he will tread his difficult path and become an occultist indeed.

Chapter Nine

The Conditions of Occult Research

(1907)

The subject we are to study this evening is one, I think, of practical and immediate interest to all members of the Theosophical Society. It is one on which a great amount of misunderstanding appears to exist, and I thought it might perchance be useful to try to lay before you some of the difficulties and conditions which surround occult research, and something, perhaps, about the attitude with which those who carry it on should be regarded.

The conditions surrounding the work of occult research at the present time are entirely new in the history of the world. In the past, a man who was gradually unfolding the faculties necessary for this research was practically shut away from the crowd and bustle of cities or large communities. The moment a pupil of a great teacher began to develop the faculties of the astral or mental sheaths, he was called into retirement. He was shut into an atmosphere kept calm and serene by the thoughts of his teacher—that mighty aura serving for him as a protection from the throng of outer influences. Everything that could be done to purify the bodies and to strengthen and concentrate the consciousness was done for him.

He was necessarily somewhat ascetic in his life, but it was a careful asceticism—neither exaggerated in the hardships imposed upon the body, nor in any sense lopsided in its conditions. With all physical things, a medium path was followed. He must neither so strain the body that there would be a danger of hysteria, nor pamper it so that it would not readily respond to the vibrations from the upper worlds.

The whole arrangement was based on an experience that had lasted for tens of thousands of years, until it had reached perfection—an arrangement of all surrounding circumstances so that the least possible difficulty from outside might come in the student's way.

For those who have to carry on occult research in the West, or the ordinary East, under the conditions of normal human life today, it is obvious that none of these precautions exist. And in the West, especially, there is a certain impatience of any restrictions in relation to these matters, a vague confusion of psychic and spiritual development, and irrelevant questions asked, such as: "Can it make any difference to the spirit whether I eat peas or mutton?" Well, it does not. The spirit, as such, is not concerned with the question—but the vehicles in which the spirit is to work are very much concerned with these matters. And I am bound to say to you that a fairly strict regimen along these lines is necessary if research is to be carried on with safety to the body.

Among the various people whom I know who do follow lines of psychic evolution and occult research, I do not know one single case where restrictions of diet have been disregarded which has not been followed by a breakdown of the health of the physical body. And the only ones I know who carry it on without injury to the body are those who yield to the old rules with regard to these restrictions.[1]

Then, in addition to that physical training, it is necessary that the emotions shall be well under control, and that the mind shall be trained to concentration—for the simple reason that in the earlier stages of this research much difficulty arises on the astral and mental planes with regard to the nature of the objects observed, as to whether they are inhabitants or objects of the planes or projections from the investigator himself. This is one of the most fertile sources of error, and one which is far subtler and far more difficult to escape than many in their earlier investigations are inclined to admit. Obviously, if the emotions and the mind are uncontrolled, the chaos on the astral and mental planes will be unspeakably increased, so that the old habit is not only to train and prepare the body, but also the consciousness as regards the emotions and thoughts.

But it is not only a question of what is called purification. It is also a question of the higher and finer development of each of the bodies—the physical no less than the astral and mental. Certain changes in the atomic structure must take place with the bringing down of the consciousness of the higher planes into the physical brain. It is not only a question of being conscious on the higher planes, but of translating that consciousness by means of the physical brain. And in order to do this effectively, certain parts of the atom have to change and evolve, and the higher orders of *spirillae*—which, at our present stage of evolution, are lying with their sides against each other like limp India-rubber tubes—have to be forced open by the currents from the higher planes, so that they may become physical instruments of consciousness.[2]

As physical matter yields but slowly to all forces, it is necessary to give time when those changes have to be brought about. They are brought about by the action of strenuous, definite thinking. And as that is carried on, one after the other of these more delicate spirillae begin to open. This shows itself by a heaviness of feeling in the brain—and if it be disregarded, then by pain growing more and more acute.

Suppose, for instance, a person in whose brain some spirillae are ready, so far as the manasic consciousness is concerned, desires to pass on to the buddhic plane. He will at first lose physical consciousness and pass into a trance. In that condition, he will be able to find the required knowledge, and by impressing it on the manasic sheath, utilize the manasic spirillae in the physical brain. When he first tries to keep his physical consciousness at the same time that he is using his buddhic consciousness, he will find a great physical pressure, and he dare not persist for more than the briefest space of time. Fraction of second by fraction of second, he must lengthen the period of pressure, never carrying it on one iota beyond pressure to pain—for pain means absolute danger, whereas pressure is only the danger signal. It is not only the physical brain he has to prepare for the work. He must reorganize his astral, and later his mental body, in the same way.

That reorganization can be simply described. I am taking it for granted that you are familiar with the ordinary facts as you find them in our books. You know that what we call the sense centers of the astral body are in full working order with every one of us; that it is these that build up the physical sense organs; and that these sense centers in the astral body have nothing to do with astral sight or hearing. They are merely the mechanism whereby the consciousness builds for itself the sense organs on the physical plane.[3]

A great deal of indefinite astral information, however, reaches the physical brain by way of these sense centers, in the case of undeveloped persons (the savage, and types at about the same level)—the second sight of the Highlander; the vague premonitions of approaching disaster, of sorrow or trouble; intimations of events on the threshold of the physical plane; and so on. All these things come from the astral plane by a general vibration caused in the astral body by vibrations coming out from the coming events. The whole astral body vibrates in answer. And when the vibrations pass down to the sense organs, they often produce sights or sounds of various kinds—because any pressure on the nervous mechanism of the body produces, when you are dealing with a sense organ, the kind of result to which that sense organ normally gives rise. So that anything that comes from the astral center of sight and touches the mechanism of the physical eye will start a vision.

I came, in India, across one very interesting series of experiences of that kind, which the people thought to be astral experiences, but which, as a matter of fact, were physical. By a certain process of strain placed upon the sense organs—by external pressures, and so on—they were dulled for a time to external impact, and under those conditions a considerable number of people heard musical sounds. On looking into it, I found there were two factors at work: one, the impressions on the astral body, which, touching the astral center of hearing, passed down to the delicate harp-like mechanism within the ear and set it vibrating; and, two, the pressure on the auditory nerves, which produced a vibration in those ultimate cells, and caused the sounds heard. I have even known them to be caused by purely physical means—by the pressure of blood, alterations of the pressure giving rise to vibratory action within the nerves, which again translated itself as musical sounds. Now, I do not think there are so many observations on what may be called in psychological language "auditory hallucinations" as there are on "visual," but no doubt they may be carried to an extreme extent.

The occult researcher has nothing to do, in his researches, with these centers. He is concerned with those astral centers which serve him on the astral plane as the sense organs serve him on the physical—the chakras and the organs connected with them in the astral body itself. Whatever comes to them comes clearly, so far as the immediate sense impression is concerned. And I want now to make one general observation before going more into detail.

When you are dealing with observations on the astral or mental plane, you are dealing with observations that are made under the same laws as observations on the physical plane. You are dealing with consciousness using a vehicle in order to contact a particular plane—and there is no difference in principle between observations made by your eyes and ears on the physical plane and the observations made by your astral eyes and ears on the astral plane. Both are observations, not revelations. There is no sudden illumination which reveals to the seer the objects of another world.

Illumination belongs to the inner consciousness, not to the outer observations, whether physical, astral, or mental. That which is gained by illumination is quite a different thing from occult research. It is not research at all. It is simply the higher mind [buddhi-manas] illuminating the lower [kama-manas], sending a beam of light, and enabling the consciousness to understand—but not to observe.

Observations belong to the vehicles, not to the consciousness. Much error arises from students imagining that when a person begins to develop astral sight, for instance, everything becomes known by some miraculous process of illumination. It does not. That depends on the evolution of consciousness—a very different thing—and has to be evolved in very different ways. It is the path of the prophet; it is not the path of the occult researcher.

Let us, then, apply to the first observations on the astral plane some of the laws which we know work when we are dealing with observations on the physical plane. I am speaking now of early observations, because I want you to see how these are surrounded with difficulties. As the best seer has gone through these early stages, it is well that those who, perhaps, are beginning to see shall understand some of the difficulties surrounding these earlier visions.

One of the most misleading, because the most subtle, difficulties is the question of how much the astral eye sees and how much the consciousness, trained in physical experience, adds to the observations of the astral eye. Every student knows that when he says, "I see so-and-so" (on the physical plane), that sight carries with it a mass of previous experiences of similar observations. If you go into the country of a race differing very much from your own—say India—all the faces appear the same. Thirty people are introduced to you. You do not know one from the other. You constantly blunder. But the Indian will say the same thing when he comes for the first time over here. To us, it seems absurd. I look at the faces in this audience. No two are alike—but an Indian who had never seen English people before would say, "How can you tell one from the other?"

That means that you do not see very much. You supply by the mind much more than you see—and there is the first great difficulty of the astral seer. He sees the astral object, but he sees it as the baby sees a physical object—as a sort of blob, outline, color perhaps; no knowledge of astral distances, no power of realizing different dimensions. But into that, he reads all the memories of the physical past, and he sees an astral outline with a physical content. He does not know that, and only finds it out after long experience. It is quite inevitable until his astral experience has gradually made up for him a content of astral consciousness, which he will gradually begin to read into the astral sight, and then he will begin to see more accurately the astral world.

Hence you continually find in the records of seers that they are only giving you, when they tell you about heaven, copies of the earth—golden thrones, and streets of gold, and gates of pearl, et cetera. They have read into the heavenly colors that which, down here, they connect with the colors which they see. It is true that when the student is being taught, he passes through this stage more rapidly than if he is quite alone. But nevertheless, for many a month—or many a year—more or less of that difficulty will surround his astral seeings.

Pass from this to another difficulty—the difficulty of the confusion of one's own aura with the astral colors. That comes out very curiously if you talk to a number of different clairvoyants. You will find people read an aura in the same way. But if you ask them what colors they see, they will tell you quite different colors. One clairvoyant, for instance, may say: "Oh, there's a great deal of green, yellow, and pink in that aura—it means so-and-so." The next clairvoyant may say: "There is a great deal of violet, red, and blue in that aura," and will read it the same—because the consciousness working in the astral body receives a distinct impression as to the temperament and the consciousness of the person who is being looked at, but the astral vision, confused by the aura of the observer, mixes that aura with the observed object, and you get a mixture of the two.

I will mention a similar case on the physical plane, because it will probably strike you as even stranger. When palmists read the hand, they have certain name for the lines, and by that tell the character of the person. I have had my hand read by both English and Indian palmists. Now, the Indian names all the lines quite differently—the English "line of life" is the "line of head," and so on. Yet out of his different lines, he reads the same character. The same thing happens as on the astral plane, and the reason is the same. He does not only go by the lines. He goes also by the impression made by the consciousness of the person at whose hand he is looking—and that is really stronger than the lines.

Not only does this take place in the looking at auras, but another difficulty arises from the crowd of thought forms which surround the person when first he makes his astral observations. How often have we said, "If you find an astral person praising you, telling you [that] you are a very wonderful person, mistrust that astral appearance. It is more than likely your own good opinion of yourself, appearing there as a thought form, and translating your own idea of your merits into an outside testimony to the greatness of your evolution." And the other day, when I met a harmless gentleman who told me he had been hearing voices which told him that he was in his last incarnation and could not commit any more sin, I knew very well the voice he heard was the voice of his own self-opinion, and not of some astral person on the level of a Master, as he imagined.

These difficulties, of course, are obvious. What I want to point out to you is that they persist much longer than most of us are inclined to think—that the trained seer, unless his training has carried him to the threshold of mastership, may still be liable to these blunders in his observations. Quite honestly, his temperament will influence his observations. Quite honestly, something of himself will mingle in what he sees. And though he may have outgrown the coarser blundering of mistaking thought forms and desire forms for heavenly and astral inhabitants, nonetheless there will be a residue of that clinging round him for many a year.

And even when that is over, there is one other difficulty you must remember—you who read the books written by some of us in whom these faculties are partially developed. You may often find differences of observations, and such discrepancies are inevitable. Every man observes most the things which attract him most. If three or four people send you an account, say, of a foreign city, those accounts will differ greatly if the people have been working independently—one will have observed the architecture, another the type of people, another the contents of the shops, another will have gone to the libraries or the picture galleries. Such discrepancies are a good test of observation. If you find with a general identity a large amount of detail discrepancy, you may take it that something has been observed.

I look on those discrepancies as of value—partly, as showing that the people are really trying to see for themselves, and not repeating the great thought forms made by ages of thought in particular directions; and also, because they may do something towards checking that tendency in the Theosophical student to repeat blindly on authority that which others have tried to see by careful investigation. Nothing is more fatal to the growth of faculty than the constant acceptance of unverified observations. The more discrepancies, the better for the careful observing of the other world. We are not in a realm of miracle, but in the realm of observation—and human observation is subject to error on whatever plane it may be carried on.

Let us pass from that to one other difficulty before I take up the latter part of my subject. According to the development of the vehicles of the student will be the amount of observation he can carry on at the same time that he is working in his physical consciousness. There are two ways of observing. In one, you observe while your physical observation is also alive. In the other, you try to shut out the outer world—and the more quiet your surroundings the easier will it be to let the astral sight play unchecked while the physical eyes are open.[4] This double observation makes considerable strain upon the nervous system, which shows itself constantly in an increase of nervous irritability on the part of the person who is using the consciousness along two or three lines at the same time. Very often, such a person may be blamed for his irritability. Certainly, it would be better if he were not irritable. But it is almost inevitable until great progress has been made.

It is for this reason that, in the earlier days, people were secluded in the carrying on of the work. For when a person has developed the astral faculties, and the physical body is becoming more sensitive at the same time, loud noises, as in the London streets, come like thunder on the nervous system. The mere rolling along of a dray shakes the physical system as though it were a great electric shock—and in this way, you often get nervous irritability which the unfortunate person is fighting against, but cannot entirely control.

Let us pass from that to the question of how the researcher can find out the facts which he is asked for—the method he must use and the limits of his power. Suppose, for instance, a question is asked, such as the question which led up to the observations made by Mr. Leadbeater and myself on the atoms some ten years ago. The process was first of all to get quiet. We went to Box Hill for a week, so that we could have pure air and surroundings which were not full of thoughts and vibrations of every kind.[5] We lay down on the grass and shut our eyes.

The next step was simply to intensify the sight—which meant a projection of the will on the astral center which corresponds to vision on the physical plane, and through that to stimulate the physical senses, so that the etheric sense would be active, as well as that normally used in vision. The result was a very great increase of rapidity of vibration in the ether connected with the physical eye—and side by side with that, a rapid magnetic action in the astral chakra and the corresponding physical center between the eyebrows, so that there was a sense of great pressure and of rapid whirling between the eyes.[6]

Then comes the direction of the will to find an atom floating in the atmosphere around. One is selected. You may not know what it is, but you have before your intensified vision the form of an atom. You then intensify more and more, just as you would screw a microscope into focus, until there comes out clearly before the intensified vision the subdivisions of the chemical atom.

The first thing you get after seeing the atom as a whole (by intensification, like magnifying it more and more) is the first subdivision of the atom on the next etheric plane, and by a further intensification, the subdivisions within those—and so on, until you come to the ultimate atom. If you try to press it further, you suddenly find a mass of astral matter.[7]

It is through those stages the observation goes: the will steadily kept at work, and a slow, careful seeing of the parts, just as you would look at them through a microscope. And when you have done, you are very tired. Your brain, your nerves, your attention, are tired.

It is absolutely necessary in a task of that sort for the attention to be fixed on the one thing without wavering. You have to hold your attention for half hours at a time without wavering. That process you must repeat over and over again, to be sure you have not blundered. You leave out all kinds of things you do not see, and, going back later, find these things out. It is the same as a physical observation carried on with a microscope—and you have to do it as carefully and as repeatedly. No answer on these matters is worth having which is not worked out in that way.

Research work on the astral plane is as laborious as research work on the physical. I want students to realize that, because they ask one the most extraordinary questions, to find a really honest answer to which would mean weeks of research given to that one thing. And you know how much time the people who do this have left from the other pressing claims on their strength and their time. You cannot have much of this occult research unless a certain amount of time is set aside for it, and that has to be taken from other work—and it is all a balance as to which work is the most useful, not to a few people, but to the world.

I want to ask you to be a little patient with those who have heavy burdens of work upon them, and who cannot, with the best goodwill, answer the innumerable questions poured upon them. The moment one fact is stated, twenty new questions start up, and the moment one of these is answered another crop immediately comes.

There is one very great difficulty in occult research which very much limits its value for the outer world: you have absolutely no proof. We could not prove what we saw about the atoms. We could only say we saw them. When you look at a thing, you see it. You cannot prove anything about it. We have not the mathematical, chemical, electrical knowledge necessary to explain the whole of that in the scientific way—and the occult researcher must always lie under the imputation of dogmatism. He can only say, "I do not ask you to receive the results of my sight as though I could prove them." And he has no right to be offended if anyone says, "I do not accept your observation." If their minds or prejudices reject it, he can only repeat, "I see it." And that is not proof.

What, then, is the value of occult research, if we cannot prove it? I think this: that it may give hints which may possibly, if scientific men would take them as working hypotheses, facilitate investigation and quicken the discoveries which otherwise might be long delayed. I do not claim anything more than that. I do not think any scientific man ought to accept our visions and think them true. But I think he might utilize them if he sees anything in them to give a hint of a line of possible discovery.

Therefore, I think we ought to continue to make such observations as far as we can, and publish them without caring for what people say. Only, on the other side, let those who make the observations say, "That is the thing as I see it, but I may be reading into it conclusions that are not there. I may be drawing entirely erroneous deductions. I give you my best, but your best attitude towards it is that of careful analysis and rigorous scrutiny."

That is the service that I think the occult researcher has the right to demand at your hands. For if you blindly swallow everything he says, if he is an honest man, you make him hesitate to say. While, if he is a dishonest man, he is likely to mislead you. The honest man leaves it to time to justify his observations.

Those observations on the atoms, by the way, I find *are* being justified. They have been verified because, along other lines, scientific men have gradually built up scientific proof, which we can never give. We are simply people who see, and record the facts seen.[8]

And another thing to remember is that we are not omniscient. Our observations are often very imperfect. We see a little bit of a thing, and give it out as the whole. Or we see it out of relation, and that gives a wrong impression. There are so many difficulties in the way, and so few ways of getting help. For there are few people who have come to the point where they can look quietly on the astral world and record what they see there. Those who can have often difficulty in comparing observations, because separated far from each other, and have difficulty in meeting and joining forces so that the observations may be confirmed.

I think, then, that in observations made by only one person, they ought to be issued as seen only by the one person, leaving them open for later confirmation, if that should come. So that we may gradually get a body of literature, however small, founded on occult research—which no one is asked to accept, no one blamed for rejecting, which shall be gradually verified by repeated observations of different people. If that is done, occult research will play a great and useful part in our movement. If it is not done, it is more a danger than a help—a double danger, for the seer may be misled by not having other observations to correct his own, and a danger that the readers may be misled by taking as some infallible revelation the single observation of a fallible man.

It is under these conditions that I desire that occult research should go forward—a willingness to correct wherever wider knowledge shows error to have been made; a willingness to repeat and verify, and to accept no observations without investigation and careful thought. If that be done, there will be no danger in it. But there is a danger, today, where only a few people observe; where those people say they see and are continually warning people there may be errors—but where others who do not see, but perhaps love and respect those who do, take criticism of them as though it were an insult, instead of being the best help that can possibly be given to the researcher. And, on the other hand, I would say that ungenerous criticism, unkind remark, imputation of motives—which we find from those who are not in favor, perhaps, of these lines of research—are as mischievous as the over-receptivity on the other side.

Cannot we be sane and rational, and keep our equilibrium in these matters? Give fair play to the researcher, but not blind acceptance. Do not accuse him of being conceited, opinionated, dogmatic, because he speaks out the things he sees honestly and frankly. But do not hamper him by giving blind faith where intelligent thought is demanded.

Part Three

INVESTIGATION OF DIFFERENT WORLDS

Chapter Ten

Psychism and Spirituality (1907)

Our subject tonight consists of two words: *psychism; spirituality*. I am going to speak to you on the subjects denoted by these two words, because there is so much confusion about them in ordinary conversation, in ordinary literature—and out of that confusion much of harm arises. People think of one thing and use the name of the other, and so continually fall into blunders and mislead others with whom they talk.

I want tonight to draw a sharp and intelligible division between psychism and spirituality; if possible, to explain very clearly what each of them means. So that, thoroughly understanding the meaning of these things, people may choose for themselves which of the two they desire to evolve, or unfold, within themselves. For if a person, desiring to unfold the spiritual nature, uses the means which are adapted only for developing the psychic nature, disappointment, possibly danger, will result. While, on the other hand, if a person desires to develop the psychic nature, and thinks that he will reach that development quickly by unfolding his spiritual powers, he also is equally doomed to disappointment—but in the second case, only to disappointment for a time. For, while it is not true that the great psychic is necessarily a spiritual person, it is true that the great spiritual person is inevitably a psychic.

All the powers of nature are subject to the spirit, and hence, when a man has truly unfolded his spiritual nature, there is nothing in the lower world which is not open to him and obedient to his will. In that sense, then, the man who follows the spiritual path will not ultimately be disappointed if he is seeking psychic development. But the very seeking for it will, on the spiritual path, act as a certain barrier. I shall return to the point again presently, and show you in what sense—and why—it is true that the development of the psychic powers may hinder the unfolding of the spiritual.

Now, to distinguish clearly between the two, I will begin with two brief definitions. They will be expanded, naturally, in the course of the lecture—but I will define each of these two words in a single sentence so as to make the definition clear and brief. Spirituality is the self-realization of the One; psychism is the manifestation of the powers of consciousness through organized matter. Each word of that definition has its own value.

We are far too apt, in our ordinary thought and talking, to limit the words *psychical*, *psychic*, or *psychism* in a quite illegitimate way—and the popular use of the term is illegitimate. It is generally used amongst us to mean unusual manifestations of the powers of consciousness. Whereas, properly speaking, the word ought to cover every outer manifestation of consciousness, whether on the physical, on the astral, on the mental, or on the buddhic plane. It does not matter in what world you are moving, in what matter your consciousness is acting. So long as it is utilizing organized matter for its own expression, so long are those manifestations psychic—and are properly included under the term *psychism*.

You may perhaps wonder why I lay stress on this. You will see it at once if I remind you that, unless we keep this definition in mind—accurate, legitimate as it is—we shall be making a division between the manifestation of the consciousness on the physical and on the astral and mental planes, between its manifestation in the physical and those in the astral and mental bodies. And if we do that, the whole of our thought will be on mistaken lines.

You need practically to be pressed back to what you know of consciousness on the physical plane before you can thoroughly follow its manifestations on the astral and on the mental. If you try to separate off manifestations which are the same in kind, though differing in degree, according to the fineness of the matter which is employed, if you try to separate them off, you will always regard what you call psychism—that is, astral and mental manifestations in the subtler bodies—in an artificial and unwise manner. If, on the other hand, you realize that consciousness is one, that its manifestation on any plane is conditioned by the matter of the plane—that it is one in essence, only varying in degree, according to the lessening or the increase of the resistance of the matter of the planes—then you will not be inclined to take up exaggerated views with regard to what people are so fond of calling psychism. You will not denounce it in the foolish way of many people, because, in denouncing it, you will know that you denounce all intellectual manifestations—an absurdity of which very few people are likely to be guilty.

If you take your intellectual manifestations in the physical world as admirable things, to be always encouraged, strengthened, developed, then you will be compelled, by parity of reasoning, to understand that the manifestations of the same consciousness in finer matter, astral or mental, are equally worthy—and no *more* worthy—of development, of consideration. You will not find yourself in the absurdly illogical position of declaring it a good thing to train the physical plane consciousness, while it is dangerous to cultivate the astral and mental plane consciousness. You will understand that all psychism is of the same kind, that on each plane the development of psychism has its own laws—but that it is absurd to admire the working of consciousness on the lower plane and shrink from it as something dangerous, almost diabolical, when it appears on a plane higher than the physical.

It is this rational and common-sense view which I want to impress upon you tonight, to get you out of the region of mystery, marvel, wonder, and fear, which to so many people surround what is called psychism; to make you understand that you are unfolding consciousness, showing out your powers on one plane after another according to the organization and the fineness of the bodies in which your consciousness is working; and that if you will only keep your common sense and reason, if you will only not allow yourself to be terrified by what at present is unusual, you may then walk along the psychic pathway in the astral or mental world, as resolutely, and with as great an absence of hysteria, as you walk along the psychic pathway in the physical world.

That is the general idea. And, of course, this is the meaning in which, after all, the word is often used down here. When you say "psychology," you do not mean only the workings of consciousness in astral and mental bodies. You mean the whole consciousness of the man, the workings of the mind, wherever the mind is active—the whole of that you include under *psychology*. Why, then, when you change its form, should you narrow it down, as though that which is mind on one plane is not also mind on all planes on which the mind is able to function?

Now, let us consider for a moment the workings of the mind on the physical plane: they are familiar. There is, however, one important point about them. In the materialistic science of the last century, you had very widely spread, amongst scientific men, the view that thought was only the result of certain kinds of vibration in certain kinds of matter. I need not dwell on that. But you are aware that both in England, and more especially in France and Germany, most elaborate disquisitions were written to prove that thought was only the product of nervous matter. You rarely—I think never—now find a well-trained scientist prepared to commit himself to that position. Those who survive as representatives of that same school may do so, but they are literally survivals.

The mass of psychologists of today admit that the manifestations of mind cannot any longer be regarded as the results of vibrations in the physical brain—that at least we must go beyond these limitations when dealing with the results of the study of consciousness, as it is now studied amongst scientific men. They will no longer, then, regard thought as the product of matter. They certainly will not be prepared to go as far as I now propose to go, and say that the thinking organism is the production of thought—the very antithesis, you will agree, of the other position, but which is vital to the understanding of the unfolding of the powers of consciousness through matter.

It is recognized in ordinary biology that the function appears before the organ. There, I am on safe scientific ground. It is recognized that the exercise of the function gradually builds up the organ. All the researches into the simpler forms of organisms go to prove that. It is also recognized that when the exercise of the function has built the organ in a very simple form, the exercise of the function continually improves the organ which originally it built.[1]

So far we are hand in hand with ordinary science. I think I shall not go too far in saying that a large number of the more scientific psychologists of today will at least agree that the brain, as you find it in the adult man, is very largely the result of the exercise of thinking through the earlier years of life. I do not think they would go so far as to say that thinking has literally produced it. They would, however, judging by very many things that have been said, be willing to admit that by hard thinking we can improve our apparatus of thought. That is one reason for thinking hard—in order to think better. And the harder you think, the more will your thinking instrument improve.

In my next step, however, I cannot by any stretching of ordinary science persuade it to accompany me, or give me a foundation. For the point is that your consciousness, working on the next plane above the one on which the organ of consciousness is being built, is the shaper of that mechanism. To put it concretely: your physical brain is built up from the astral plane—and it is your consciousness working in matter finer than the physical which builds up the brain in the forming child within the limits laid down by karma. Now, that is a general law for healthy evolution. You will see the importance of this law a little further on.

Every body which we possess—physical, astral, mental, buddhic—is always built up by consciousness working in the plane next above it. The next plane, or world, is a world very much more "next" than you are next each other sitting here—not far away beyond the stars, removed by great spaces. It is interpenetrating you in every portion of your being. It is only "next" in the sense that the solids, liquids, and gases of your bodies are next each other in the body—not far away, but here. So that the working is of the closest and most intimate kind.

Some of you who are students of Theosophical literature will remember that HPB has spoken of all of us as working in the astral consciousness. You will see that you are not working with a physical consciousness in the literal sense of the term, if you think for a moment. How much do you know of the consciousness working in the various cells and tissues of your physical body? Practically nothing, except when you are ill. Only when the body is disorganized do you become conscious of that working. Normally, the motion of your blood, the building up by assimilation of your muscles and nerves, the life of your cells, the protective action of some of the living cells in your body—the "devourers," as they are called—go on without your knowledge, without your thought, without your giving one moment's conscious attention to them.[2]

In the perfect man, the consciousness of all this is ever present. But in us, imperfect, it is not. We are not yet sufficiently vitalized and unfolded to carry on the whole of our consciousness, with full awareness of all its activities. We are able to manage only a very small part of it, and so have let go the consciousness that keeps at work the physical body, to concentrate ourselves in a higher world, and utilize the nervous mechanism as the apparatus of our thinking. That law obtains, then, all through.

If you want to organize and build up your astral body, you can do it only from the mental plane. You must raise your thought to a higher power by concentration, by regular meditation, by deliberately working on the consciousness, before you can raise it to that power from which it shall be able to organize your astral body, as it has already organized your physical body. That is the reason why meditation is necessary in all these things—because, without the creative power of thought, we cannot organize the body in the world which is nearest to the physical.

Now, supposing that we recognize that our consciousness working in the physical brain—the instrument over which we have complete control—is continually at work contacting the outer world, using the brain as an instrument on which it can play, and continually bringing down from higher worlds impressions which it transmits more or less perfectly to the physical plane. We need not dwell upon our ordinary thinking. Let us take thinking a little more unusual, where the finer part of the brain, its etheric matter, is being more largely vitalized, more definitely used. The powers of the imagination: the creative power, the artistic powers, all creative in their nature—these utilize most the ethers of the brain, and, by working in those, bring into activity the lower and coarser matter of the dense brain.[3]

Now, the thought passes from the consciousness through vehicle after vehicle to find its clear expression here. But do you not have many mental impressions that are not clear, not well defined, and yet which impress you deeply, and of which you feel sure? They are of many kinds, and reach you in many ways. What is important to you is simply this for the moment: that being surrounded by the astral and mental worlds, contacts from these are continually touching you, continually causing changes in your consciousness. If your astral body were thoroughly organized, like your physical, the impressions made would be clear and sharp, like the physical. If your mental body were well organized, the impressions of that plane, the heavenly plane, would be clear and sharp, like the physical.

But as the astral and mental bodies at this stage of evolution are not well organized, the impressions received by them, causing changes in the consciousness, are vague and indeterminate—and it is these which are generally called "psychic." And when you have a Psychical Research Society, it is not dealing with the ordinary processes of thought, but with those which are not ordinary.[4] And all those things to which it gives many strange names are all workings of the consciousness in sheaths or bodies of which it has not yet gained the mastery, which it has not yet definitely organized for its purposes. Slowly and gradually, they become organized—and strenuous thinking is the method for the astral body, and the working of the pure reason is the method for the mental body.[5]

Let us consider, with regard to this, whether there is any other way of bringing the astral body and mental body into activity. For you may have noticed that I use the words *normal evolution*—orderly evolution on the lines of natural evolution, always from above. But you may stimulate it from below. It is possible to stimulate the astral body, at least, from the physical plane. But you do it at the cost of higher evolution a little later on. And the reason you can do it is simple enough. In the astral body are all the centers of your senses.

You know how after death a man's desires are the same as they were during his physical life. You know how in dreams your desires resemble desires that you may have in your waking consciousness. The center of all your psychic powers—of your conscious powers—the centers of these are in the astral. And if (especially with your senses, each of which has its own center in the astral body) you overstrain the physical senses down here, you will get an action on the astral plane, but an unhealthy, because disorderly, one—one not going along the line of evolution, but trying to create from below instead of from above.

Nonetheless, you may have some results. And in the two famous Indian systems for developing the powers of the consciousness, and for unfolding the consciousness itself, you have this recognized—and you read of raja yoga and of hatha yoga, of the "kingly yoga" and of the "yoga of effort." The yoga of effort is hatha yoga, and is practiced by physical means and followed by physical effects. The eye is stimulated in certain ways, and the effect of straining the physical eye is to bring about a certain limited kind of clairvoyance. You can gain it in that way by gazing into crystals, and so on. They do stimulate the center of physical sight, but not the astral—and that is why they cannot go very far. You can get a certain amount of clairvoyance by these means, but you are only expanding your physical sight, and working on centers of the astral body connected with the physical organ of vision, the eye.

The true astral sight is an entirely different thing. That comes from a center of its own in the astral body. It has to be created from the mental body, as the organ of the physical was from the astral. The center of that sight will be in the mental body, and not in the astral—and only the organ of it in the astral body.

The method of the kingly, the raja yoga, is always by thought—concentrate, meditate, contemplate, think. By that means, in a healthy, normal, natural way, you will inevitably develop the powers of sight on the astral, as in the course of nature the powers of sight were developed on the physical plane. And if you realize that your consciousness is one, building its bodies for its fuller and more complete expression—that you are here in order to become masters of matter instead of its slaves, to become lords of matter, using every organ of matter for knowledge of the world to which that matter belongs, and not to be blinded by it, as we are for so long a time in our climb upwards—then you will see that this natural development of astral powers is inevitable in the course of evolution, and all that you can do is to quicken it, following the line which nature has traced. As nature slowly will evolve in every human being the power of using the astral body as freely as you use the physical body now, so can you quicken the coming of that day for yourselves by understanding the powers of thought and turning them to the object you desire to obtain.

There are many ways in which this may be done, and many rules you may learn for your guidance. Those rules may be summed up under two heads: (1) clear and strenuous thinking; (2) discipline for the bodies that you are trying to evolve—and also, I should add, for the body below them in evolution. Those are the two great laws for the safe evolution of these so-called psychic powers—what I call the powers of the consciousness on the astral and mental planes.

There must be a discipline for the bodies, for you have to choose the material which will serve you best in the work you are doing out of the innumerable combinations of matter with which nature presents you. You must choose the combinations that will serve your purpose, which you can utilize in the building of the organs of sense on plane after plane. Just as really as the man who is a drunkard will injure his nervous system by his excesses, and by supplying coarse and overactive compounds will injure the physical body, so making it a less useful instrument for the man—as any excess, not only drunkenness, but gluttony, profligacy, and so on—[just] as these injure the physical body as an instrument of consciousness (and to have full and perfect consciousness here, we must train, discipline, build up our body with knowledge and with self-control), so also is that true on the higher planes.

A regimen is necessary when you are dealing with the organization of the subtler matter of the astral and mental worlds, for you cannot build up your physical body out of the coarser combinations of matter on the physical, and have finer combinations on the astral and mental. The bodies have to match each other. They have to correspond with each other. And as you find all sorts of combinations related the one to the other on every plane, you must choose your combinations on the physical if you desire to choose them also on the astral and mental.

You cannot make your physical body coarse, and organize the astral and mental bodies for the finer purposes of the man—and you must settle that in your minds, if you wish to try to develop these higher powers of consciousness. Not only because, if you gather together the coarser materials of the astral world, you will find yourself hampered by them in the higher expression of consciousness, but also because the presence of these combinations in you exposes you to a number of dangers on the astral plane.

The purer the elements of your astral body, the safer you are in your earlier wanderings on that plane. It is important to mention this, because in some of the schools of thought which are trying only to develop astral powers, you will find that they deliberately use other methods in order to make their astral body active. Many schools of the "left-hand path" in India will use spirits, wines, meats of all sorts, in order to bring about a certain astral condition. And they succeed, because by these means they attract to themselves, and for a time govern, the elemental powers of those lower planes—the elementals of the lower astral worlds. So that you may find that an Indian, who knows a little of this and wants to use it for his own purposes, will deliberately use these things which are attractive to the elementals of those lower worlds, and gather them around him and use them. But he does it knowing what he does, and aiming at that which he desires to conquer.

But amongst those who practice black magic of the higher kinds—of the mental kinds—you have an asceticism as stern and rigid as has ever been used by those who are trying to develop their higher bodies for nobler ends. It is a mistake to think that the brothers of the dark side are, as a rule, licentious and indifferent to what you call morality. On the contrary, they are exceedingly strict. Their faults are the faults of the mind, not the faults of the lower desires, of the organs of the different bodies which may gratify them. Their faults are the more dangerous faults of mental powers misused for personal ends. But they realize very well that if they want the mental powers and the higher ranges of those powers, they must be as rigid in the discipline of the lower bodies as any pupil of the White Lodge could be.

Take it, then, that to develop in this way, a regimen for the bodies, as well as the strict working and training of the mind, is absolutely necessary. But, with these, the result is sure. You cannot set a time for the result, for it depends where the worker is beginning in his present life. In all these matters, nature's laws will not permit of what is called miraculous growth—and if you find persons developing psychic powers very rapidly, when perhaps they have been meditating only a few months, it is because in a previous life they have cultivated these powers and are taking up their lessons again in a more advanced class of evolution, and not in the infant class, as many do in the present life. So that there are differences.

Some now beginning are not likely to succeed in their present incarnation. But if that discourages them, one can only say: "If you do not do it now, you will have to begin again next life, and so on and on and on. For nature's laws cannot be violated, and nature knows no favoritism and no partiality. Sometime or other you have to begin, and the sooner you begin, the sooner will you succeed."

Now the whole of this, you will remark, is the training, the organizing of *bodies*. And psychism implies that. You must train, purify, organize, in order that the powers of the consciousness may show forth. You will see very fully now why, at the beginning, I urged you to realize that the whole of these manifestations are similar in kind, so that when you find someone saying to you: "Oh! So-and-so is a psychic," as though that were to condemn the person—"Such-and-such a person is a mere clairvoyant," and so on, as though the fact of possessing clairvoyance were a disadvantage rather than an advantage—then the proper answer is, "Are you prepared to go the whole way with that?"

Many Indians do so (it is the point to which I said I would return). They say that the *siddhis*, the powers of consciousness manifested on the lower planes, are hindrances to the spiritual life.[6] And so they are in a sense. The spiritual life goes inwards: all psychic powers go outwards. It is the same self [atman] in either case—the self turning inwards on itself, or the self going outwards to the world of objects. But it does not make one scrap of difference whether it goes out to physical, astral, or mental objects: it is all the objective consciousness, and therefore the very reverse of the spiritual.

But the Indian does not shrink from that as, ordinarily, the man in the West does. He is perfectly honest. He says, "Yes, the powers of the intellect applied to the objects of the world are a hindrance in the spiritual life. We do not want them, do not care to think about it. We give up all the objects of the physical plane when seeking the self." And if you are prepared to say that, then by all means turn aside from psychism. But do not at one and the same time encourage intellectuality on the physical plane and denounce what you call psychism on the others, because that is mere folly.

If it is better to be blind here than to see—and the Indian will tell you it often is, because it shuts out all the distracting objects of the physical plane—if you are prepared to say that, and say, "Yes, I would rather be blind than see," then you may go on to denounce seeing on the astral plane. But if you value your physical sight, why not value the astral sight—it is a stage higher—as well? And the mental sight—which is a stage higher yet—as well?

Why denounce astral and mental, and praise up the physical? Why admire the power of sight of the painter, who sees more shades than you can see, and denounce the sight of the clairvoyant, who sees very much more than the cleverest painter? They all belong to the object world. They all lead the self away from the realization of himself, and they are all exactly on the same level. It seems strange when one sees the same person exalting the psychic on the physical plane and denouncing it on the astral and mental.

But now let us turn to *spirituality* and see what that means. "The self-realization of the One"—not the declaring that all men are one, that all men are brothers. We can all do that. Anyone who has reached a certain stage of intellectual knowledge will recognize the unity of mankind; will say, with the writer in the Christian book, that God has made all men of one blood [Acts 17:26]—quoted again from what is called a pagan book.[7] That intellectual recognition of the unity is practically universal among educated people. But very few are prepared to carry out the intellectual recognition into practical life and practical training.

Now, for the development of what are called psychic faculties, some amount of retirement from the world is very useful. For the development of the spiritual consciousness, no such retirement is necessary. In fact, for the most part, except in the earlier stages perhaps, seclusion is a mistake. For the world is the best place for the unfolding of the sense of unity, and best amongst men and women and children can we call out the powers of the spiritual life—and that for a simple reason. In the lower world, the spirit shows itself out by love, by sympathy. And the more we can love, the more we can sympathize, the greater will be the unfolding of the consciousness of the self within.

It was a true word of the early Christian Initiate, that if a man loves not his brother whom he hath seen, how shall he love God whom he hath not seen? [1 John 4:20]. And if the perfection of the spiritual consciousness be that vision of the Supreme—the consciousness which knows itself to be one with God—then the way to the realization will be by the partial realization of loving sympathy, for which the world is the most fitting field, and our brethren around us the natural stimulus.

Love, sacrifice—these are the manifestations of the spirit on the physical plane, as is right knowledge also. For the spirit is not a one-sided thing, but a trinity, and knowledge is as necessary as love. The special value of love lies in its unifying power, and in the fact that it makes what the world calls sacrifice natural and delightful. You know it in your own experience. Just in proportion as you love another is it a joy and not a sorrow to give up things in order that the happiness of the other may be increased.

It is no sacrifice for a mother to give up personal enjoyment for the sake of giving it to her children. A deeper joy is felt in the happiness of the child than could possibly have been felt in the enjoyment of the thing by herself. A sweeter, finer, profounder happiness is the enjoyment of the happiness of the beloved. And that a little widens out the consciousness—and hence family life is one of the best schools for spiritual unfolding. For in the continual sacrifices of the family life, springing from love and rendered joyful by affection, the self feels itself a larger self, and reaches the sense of unity with those immediately around. And after the family, the public life, the life of the community, the life of the nation: these also are schools for the unfolding of the spiritual consciousness.

For the man who is a good citizen of the community feels the life of the community as his own life, and so becomes conscious of a larger self than the narrow self of the family. And the man who loves his nation, his self widens out to the boundaries of the nation, and he is conscious of a larger self than the self of the family, or the community within the State. And just in proportion as the love widening does not grow superficial and shallow (for if you have only a certain amount of water and you make your dish wider and wider, the water will become shallower and shallower) does it approach spiritual love.

Too often, love becomes unreal with those who try to love the far off when they do not love the near. But if you avoid the temptation, and remembering that the spirit has no limitations, and that you can draw and draw and draw on the love within you and never find the bottom of the source of love—if you are strong enough to do that, then the love of the family, of the community, of the State, will widen out into the love of humanity, and you shall know yourself as one with all, and not only with your family, or your community, or your nation.

All these local loves are schoolmasters to bring us to the wider love of man. But do not blunder in the idea that you can have the wider unless you have gone through the narrower. For the bad husband, the bad citizen, the bad patriot, will never make a real lover of humanity. He must learn his alphabet before he can read in this book of love, and must spell out the letters before he may pronounce the word.

Nonetheless, these successive stages are all stages towards the spiritual life, and prepare the man for the consciously spiritual realization. And if you would really train yourself for the unfolding of this life within you, practice it on those who are nearest to you by meeting them with love and sympathy in the daily paths of life. Not only those whom you like, but those you care not for as well; not with those who love you only, but with those who dislike you also.

Remember that you have to break down barriers—barriers of the bodies that bar you out from your fellow selves in the worlds around you. And that breaking down of the barriers is part of the training in the spiritual life. Only as barrier after barrier is broken down, only as wall after wall is leveled to the ground, will the freedom of the spirit become possible in manifestation on every plane and in every world.

The spirit is ever free in his own nature and his own life. But, confined within the barriers of the body, he has to learn to transcend them before, on these planes of matter, he can realize the divine freedom which is his eternal birthright. So long as you feel yourself separate from others, so long are you shut out from the realization of the unity. So long as you say "my" and "mine," so long the realization of the spirit is not yet possible for you.

Love of individual possessions, not only physical, but moral and mental—not the vulgar pride of physical wealth only, but moral pride, intellectual pride, everything that says "I" as against "you" and does not realize that I and you are one—all this is against the spiritual life. Hardest of all lessons when brought down to practical life, most difficult of all attainments when effort is made to realize it and not only to talk about it and imagine it. It is best practiced by continual renunciation of the individual possessions on every plane and the constant thought of unity.

When you are trying to live the life of the spirit, you will try to be pure. You do well, but why? In order that you may be pure, and leave your impure brethren in their impurity? Oh no! You must try to be pure in order that there may be more purity in the world to share amongst all men, because you are pure. You are not wanting to be purer than others, but only gathering purity that you may spread it in every direction—and most joyous when your own purity lifts someone from the mire, who is trampled into it under the feet of the world.

You want to be wise. You do well, for wisdom is a splendid possession. But why? In order that you may look down on the ignorant and say, "I am wiser than thou," as the pure man might say, "I am holier than thou"? Oh, no! But in order that the wisdom that you gather may enlighten the ignorant, and become theirs and not only yours. Otherwise, it is no spiritual thing. For spirituality does not know "myself" and "others." It knows only the One Self, of whom all forms are manifestations.

We dare not call ourselves spiritual until we have reached that point which none of us as yet has reached, for to reach it means to become a Christ. When, looking at the lowest and basest and most ignorant and vilest, we can say, "That is myself, in such-and-such a garb," and say it feeling it, rejoicing in it—because if there are two of you, and one is pure and the other impure, and the two are one, then neither is perfect, but both are raised above the level of the lowest—that is the true atonement, the real work of the Christ. And the birth of Christ within you means the willingness to throw down all walls of separation, and the stature of Christ within you means that you have accomplished it.[8]

For the most part, we claim our unity above; we do not take pride in claiming our unity below. We are glad to say, "Yes, I also am divine. I am a Christ in the making. I am one with him." Harder to say, "I am one with the lowest of my brethren, sharing with them the same divine life." Yet our divinity is realized only as we recognize that same divinity in others.

You may remember that exquisite story of Olive Schreiner, breathing the very essence, first, of the unspiritual, and then of the spiritual life. In the first case, a woman, pure and spotless, her garments shining with whiteness, and her feet shod as with snow, went up to the gates of heaven and trod the golden streets. And as she trod them in her shining robes, the angels shuddered back, and said: "See, her garments are blood-spotted, and her sandals are stained with mire and blood." From the throne, the Christ asked, "Daughter, how is it that your garments are blood-spotted and your sandals stained?" And she answered, "Lord, I was walking in miry ways, and I saw a woman there, down in the mire, and I stepped upon her that I might keep my sandals clean." The Christ and the angels vanished, and the woman fell from heaven, and wandered again in the miry ways of earth.

Once again, she came to the heavenly portal and trod the golden streets, and this time she was not alone. Another woman was with her, and the garments of both were blood-flecked, and the sandals of both were stained with the mire and blood of earth. But the angels, seeing them pass by, cried out, "See how whitely their garments shine! And see how white are their feet!" And the Christ, when they came before the throne, said, "How come ye here in garments that are soiled?" And the answer came: "I saw this my sister trampled upon, and I bent down to lift her up, and in the picking of her up my garments were soiled, but I have brought her with me to Thy presence." And the Christ smiled and lifted them up beside him, and the angels sang for joy. For it is not the sin and the shame that are shared that soil the garments of the spirit, and leave upon it the mire of earth. [9]

If, then, you would lead the spiritual life, go downwards as well as upwards. Feel your unity with the sinner as well as with the saint. For the only thing that makes you divine is the spirit that lives in every human heart alike, in all equally dwelling—and there is no difference in the divinity of the spirit, but only in the stage of its manifestation. And just as you and I climb upwards and show more of the spiritual life in the lower worlds, [so] should we raise our brethren with us, and know the joy of the redeemer, and the power of the life that saves. For those whom we call Masters, those who are the Christs of the world, those are reverenced and beloved, because to them there is no difference, but the sinner is as beloved as the saint—nay, sometimes more, because compassion flows out to the weaker more than to the strong.

Such is the spiritual life, such the goal that every man who would become spiritual must place before his eyes. Very different from the psychic, and not to be confused with it—the unfolding of the divinity in man, and not the purification and the organization of the vehicles. Both are good, both necessary—and I finish with the words with which I began, that while to be psychic is no proof of spirituality, to be spiritual is to possess every power in heaven and on earth.

Choose ye each your road. Tread whichever you will—but beware that by the growth of your powers here, in separation, you do not delay the growth of the spirituality which is the realization of the unity of the self. For everything which divides becomes evil, by the very fact of its dividing. Every power which is shared is a wing to carry us upwards, but every power that is kept for the lower self is a clog that holds us down to earth.

Chapter Eleven

COMMUNICATION BETWEEN DIFFERENT WORLDS (1909)

The Theosophical Society is differentiated from most of the religious movements of the day by asserting the continuance in our own time of communication between the different worlds in which humanity is living. All religions assert that such communication took place in the past. They all claim for their founders, and generally for their associates and immediate followers, that such communication was enjoyed and enabled them to "speak with authority." Some, as the Hindu and the Roman Catholic, allege that in sporadic cases scattered through their respective histories such communication was established—though rarely, if ever, found today.

But the Theosophical Society definitely asserts the existence of powers which lie latent in all men, and of the forces in nature that are as yet hidden from common knowledge, and makes it one of its objects to study these. Some of its members have so successfully followed these studies as to evoke these powers and control these forces, using methods taught by the Masters of the Wisdom, whereby such communication may be normally established and carried on, without provoking the difficulties and disadvantages embarrassing the methods known as spiritualistic. The latter remain, however, as the only methods within the immediate use of the untrained, and hence are of the greatest value in destroying the prejudices of the scientist and the materialist, and in giving physical and tangible proofs, available to everyone, of the continuity of consciousness through death. They are a sign of the changing age through which the world is passing, a herald of the approaching era in which the barrier of death will be broken down, the invisible become the visible, and the physical and astral worlds will intermingle.[1]

In order thoroughly to understand the subject before us, it is necessary to grasp certain fundamental laws of nature. When these are clearly seen, it is comparatively easy to apply them to special cases that may come under our notice. And it must be remembered, in order that this study may be useful, that all fear of the unusual must be put aside. The student must realize that there are many things around him which he does not see, and that they become less dangerous, though sometimes more alarming, when they pass from invisibility into visibility. It is the unknown which may be dangerous. It is ignorance which is full of fears. The child unused to strangers screams and hides its face in its mother's dress at the terrifying sight of a harmless man or woman. Accustomed to such meetings, the child has no fear. The sight of a "ghost" startles on the first occasion. After a while, it is no more alarming than the sight of a passing stranger in the street. Our ignorance is our real danger, and that can be gotten rid of only by experience.

A reasonable and thoughtful person, pure of life and bright of intelligence, may train himself for normal communication with other worlds without any danger worthy of consideration, provided that he is habitually self-controlled, deliberate, and energetic. Such a one may evolve himself rationally and quietly, and not only convince himself of the reality of other worlds, but may become a source of help and comfort to others—lessening and even removing their fear of death, and softening the anguish of separation from their beloved.

Such a person normally guards himself in the physical world, where danger is far more potent than in subtler worlds, because dense physical matter is far more resistant to control by thought than is the subtle matter of higher worlds. Human power of self-defense against danger is smallest in the physical world. In other worlds, fear is the worst enemy, because it paralyzes thought and will. I do not say there are no dangers in the subtler worlds. Dangers there are. But the more we know, the more are we safe—and there are dangers for the ignorant everywhere.

The first fundamental fact is that each individual is a single consciousness, a unit of consciousness, and that varieties in the form of communication arise from difference of bodies, not from difference of consciousness. A consciousness may, of course, be more or less unfolded, may have brought into manifestation more or less of his powers. One unit of consciousness may differ widely from another unit. But the same unit—i.e., the same individual—remains the same in all communications, however restricted or unrestricted by the particular body, gross or fine, through which the communication is made. If we compare two units of consciousness, one advanced and one backward, the difference in evolution will be marked in each world in which they function. But the manifestation of each will be determined by the material conditions of manifestation [in each world], and these will introduce a variety in the form of communication, but will not affect the unity of the manifesting intelligence.

It is well also to bear in mind that all consciousness are fragments, parts, of the one all-pervading consciousness, and hence their characteristics are fundamentally the same, however differing in degree. All will possess the three essential attributes of will, wisdom, and activity—though will may have reached only the point of unfoldment at which we call it desire, though wisdom may be seen only in its embryonic form of cognition, and though activity may be manifested only in the shape of restlessness. There are no essential differences in the units of consciousness trying to manifest themselves in various worlds. But there are innumerable differences in degree, from the mighty and luminous consciousness of the highest seraph to the dim, and scarcely even groping, consciousness in the mineral. There is but one consciousness in the universe and all so-called separated consciousness are phases thereof.

The second fundamental fact is that these units of consciousness are embodied—i.e., are closely related to portions of matter which they have temporarily appropriated. For the purposes of our study, we need not concern ourselves with the highest of these appropriations. We may content ourselves with recognizing the fact that there are finer grades of matter than those to which here we confine ourselves, and may indicate these by the general term of the *spiritual body* without further particularizing them. Those who can freely use the spiritual body are certainly not in need of any explanations such as those given in this article.[2]

We are concerned, then, only with three well-defined grades of matter, those which answer to, and are the instruments of, thought, desire, and action—mental, astral, and physical. From the mental matter is organized the mental body; from the astral matter, the astral body; from the physical matter, the physical body, which is functionally divisible into its etheric and gross parts. These are the vehicles, the instruments of the unit of consciousness, his means of affecting, and being affected by, the outer worlds in which he lives. These may be highly or poorly organized, may be composed of fine or coarse materials. Such as they are, they are his only means of contact with the worlds surrounding him, and his only means of self-expression.

These three bodies—mental, astral, and physical—are separable from each other, and under abnormal conditions the two parts of the physical body may to some extent be dissociated during physical life, and are completely dissociated at physical death. While a man is awake and in his ordinary everyday state of consciousness, he is using these three bodies all the time. When he goes to sleep, he leaves the physical body and uses only two—the astral and mental. At death, the grosser part of the physical drops away, the finer part clinging to him for a short period (normally), and then dropping away from him as did the grosser part, and he uses only the astral and mental bodies in the postmortem condition for a period varying in length. Later, the astral body also drops away from him, and he remains clothed in the mental body during the long mental—or heavenly—life, intervening between the intermediate state and rebirth into the physical world. When this also drops away from him, he finds himself on the threshold of reincarnation, of the building of new bodies for his next period of physical life.

The third fundamental fact is that man is living, functioning, in three worlds during the waking periods of his life on earth. These three worlds are the worlds composed severally of physical, astral, and mental matter—the worlds from which are severally drawn the materials for his physical, astral, and mental bodies. These worlds are not separate from each other, but interpenetrate and intermingle, while remaining distinct.

Just as gas may pass into water but remains distinct from it, so does astral matter interpenetrate physical matter while remaining distinct from it—and so does mental matter, being still finer, interpenetrate the astral. Physical ether interpenetrates the gases, liquids, and solids of the physical body, moving through every part of it unhindered. So does superphysical matter interpenetrate physical, moving unhindered through every part of it by reason of its greater subtlety. Nature everywhere repeats herself, and we may understand much of the superphysical by studying the physical and reasoning by analogy. But we must ever remember that the superphysical is the original and the physical the copy, and not vice versa.

The astral world, while intermingling with the physical, is not conterminous with it. It forms a sphere round the sphere of the earth, and a radius of this astral sphere would extend from the center of our earth to the moon.[3] The mental, or heavenly world, again, is a similar concentric sphere, stretching far beyond the limits of the astral, although interpenetrating both it and the physical.

According to the development of the respective bodies will be a man's consciousness of each world. As a man physically blind cannot see the physical world which stretches around him, so a man astrally blind cannot see the astral world, though it ever environs him. Similarly may a man whose astral sight is open be mentally blind and fail to see the mental world encompassing him. The matter in each body must be organized in order that consciousness may use it as an instrument of perception. The physically blind, at the present stage of evolution, are a small minority. The astrally blind are a huge majority. But blindness of organisms does not change the worlds in which they live—except to themselves. Thus men are living in three worlds at every moment of their waking consciousness, though normally conscious only of the densest.

In sleep and after death, they are living in two, but are normally conscious only of the intermediate world—and not always of that. At a later period of their postmortem condition, they are living in only one, and conscious but of their immediate surroundings in that. As evolution proceeds, the astral world will become visible to those who occupy the crest of the wave of normally advancing humanity—and at a far future time, the mental will also become visible, so that men on earth will live consciously in the three worlds, the three bodies having become organized as vehicles of consciousness, available for ordinary use.[4]

The fourth (and, for our purposes, the last) fundamental fact is that each body is affected by the embodied consciousness and affects it long before it is sufficiently organized to convey to that consciousness definite information as to the world from which its materials were drawn. We may notice this to a very considerable extent if we watch the workings of the waking consciousness in a new infantile body. The consciousness answers to the discomfort of the body—from want of food, pain, et cetera—before it is able to obtain through that body any definite idea as to its surroundings or any grasp of its own relations to them. And the astral and mental bodies answer to changes in consciousness by changed vibrations [in those bodies] for ages before they hand on to the consciousness definite news of the events that are taking place around them in their respective worlds. Hence communications constantly take place between the worlds in which the man is normally living without the man knowing anything of their passage. He becomes conscious of a thought only when it affects his physical brain, and knows nothing of its origin or of the course it has followed ere its arrival in his physical body.

Let us begin our study of communications between different worlds with the everyday constantly arriving communications, and thus establish ourselves thoroughly on the normal before we enquire into the abnormal. Just as the (to us) inappreciable interval between the touching of a hotplate with the tip of a finger and the withdrawal of the finger is occupied with the passage of a wave in the sensory nerves from the periphery to the brain and the passage of a return wave from the brain through the motor nerves to the periphery, so is there the passage of a vibratory wave from the physical matter to the astral and from the astral to the mental, and a corresponding change in consciousness.

It is the consciousness which feels the pain of the burning, and memorizes the fact for future guidance. The communication has run inwards from the physical body through the astral to the mental—a communication from world to world. Similarly is the change in consciousness (the will to move the finger from the hot substance) the cause of a vibration in the matter of the mental body, and this causes a vibration in the astral body, and this in turn in the physical brain—a communication from world to world.

In all processes of thinking, there is a series of changes of consciousness in the mental world. These are answered by a corresponding series of vibrations in the mental body. These cause a series of corresponding vibratory changes in the astral body, strengthened by the consciousness—the *same* consciousness, remember, in all the bodies—and these set up similar vibratory changes in the etheric part of the physical. These etheric vibrations are largely electrical in character, and affect the cells of the dense physical brain, setting up vibratory changes therein.

Here you have the normal communication between the worlds, going on repeatedly, continually, varied by the reverse process, where the initiative is from outside. Something occurs in the outer world which starts such a series of changes—one of the senses receives a stimulus and a nervous wave is set up. It passes from the dense to etheric matter, or begins in the etheric, is answered by a change of consciousness, runs up through astral to mental, intensifying the change, and the consciousness receives and registers the communication.

It is not a waste of time to place clearly before our minds that communications are constantly running up and down the ladder of our bodies—each body a step in the ladder, and each step in a different world. The maintenance of our mental balance and of our powers of reasoning and of judgment in the face of the abnormal is rendered very much more easy when we understand that the abnormal is only an extension of the normal. If a person feels that he is facing something strange and unknown, something that he is inclined to regard as supernatural, he loses too often both judgment and reasoning faculty. But if he understands that the phenomenon before him is only a subtler repetition of a familiar happening, he is then able to observe accurately and to reason sensibly and acutely.

As M. Jourdain was astonished to find that in his ordinary conversations he was talking prose, so may the student be astonished to find that he is continually communicating from world to world.[5] Your consciousness may turn its attention outwards in any world in which it possesses a body to serve as window. You may look out through your physical, astral, or mental window, but it is always the same *you* that looks out, that receives impressions.

Let us consider the next class of communications. A person becomes conscious of a thought, or rather an impression, arising in his waking consciousness, rather vaguely and somewhat indeterminate, which he cannot relate to anything in his physical surroundings, and which does not seem to be originated in his own consciousness. It seems to him to come from outside, but it lacks the sharpness of definition to which he is accustomed in the presence of real objects. Such impressions as premonitions, warnings of danger, apparently causeless depression or elation, feelings as to the mental, moral, or physical condition of friends, as to illness, death, misfortune, good fortune, et cetera—intimations which do not come with the clearness of the spoken word or written message, but nonetheless cause a change in consciousness. What are these? They are due to impacts made upon the astral body in the astral world, impacts which set up vibrations in its matter and thus give rise to changes of consciousness. The absence of precision of definition is due to the lack of organization of the astral body, and its consequent incapacity to receive clear impressions.

The physical body has been in process of organization for millions of years, and can receive sharply defined series of vibrations, and the consciousness through this immense period of time has been learning to relate impacts to objects, to analyze and coordinate impressions made on its body, and thus to understand their meaning. Experience has evolved it into an admirable vehicle and instrument of consciousness. But the astral body is a very different case. In every fairly civilized and educated person, it is partially organized, sufficiently organized to receive and reproduce sequences of vibrations thrown upon it from the astral plane. But its special sense organs—the whirling wheels, or chakras—are not as yet generally evolved in such persons, and hence sharply defined impressions cannot be received.

With closed eyes, you can distinguish between the light and the dark. If, when the sun was shining on your eyelids, a hand were interposed and threw a shade over them, you would be conscious of the difference—but you would not discern the hand. Or if shadows were thrown on a sheet, your open eyes would see the shadow dance, but it would only imperfectly convey a story which you could easily gather from a drama acted by persons visible to sight. So is it with the astral body of the average educated man. If, at some distance from you, an event takes place of great interest to yourself, bringing to you joy or grief, or if some persons think strongly of you, the vibrations thereby set up in astral matter will be propagated through space, like a Marconi message, and will impinge on your astral body, setting up similar vibrations therein.[6] But unless the astral sense organs are developed, a sharply defined picture cannot be produced, and hence only a vague impression will be made on the consciousness.

The astral body and the astral sense organs differ as do the physical body and the physical sense organs, although much more substitution is possible in the one than in the other. The astral bodies of the educated are fairly well developed in form and general constitution, but are poorly organized as regards the sense organs. There are, however, in the astral body very well developed centers connected with the physical organs of the senses—a center connected with the eye, one with the ear, and so on. These are sometimes stimulated into action by violent vibrations in the astral body, and then we have the phenomenon of second sight, the vision of phantoms, wraiths, phantasms of living or dead persons.

It is also possible to stimulate the physical senses, but in a rather unhealthy way, by stimulating these centers through their appropriate physical organs—as by crystal gazing, the use of magic mirrors, and other similar means. In this way, an extension of sight on the physical plane may be gained, or even of vision in the lower regions of the astral world. But this is not a gaining of astral senses, but an unhealthy stimulation of physical senses, causing an abnormal increase of sensitiveness in the astral centers to which they are attached.

It is the law of nature that development comes from above, and the forces of evolution work from above and organize that which is below. Life organizes matter, matter does not produce life. The consciousness working in the astral world organizes the physical sense organs. The consciousness working in the mental world organizes the astral sense organs, and so on. There is a continual working of consciousness for the improvement and the refining of its lower vehicles.

As your evolution proceeds from the stage it has now reached with the most thoughtful and cultured persons, it is possible to quicken the unfolding of the astral senses by strenuous and clear thinking and by purity of desire and action. As these become active, the communications received through the astral body will become clear and definite, like those received through the physical body. These are blurred now because the instrument is imperfect.

As the consciousness unfolds on plane after plane, in world after world, and organizes its vehicles in the world below that on which its own center is established, the lower bodies for all practical purposes unite into one body. If a person has the center of consciousness established on the mental plane, the astral and physical bodies function as a single body, and he lives consciously in two worlds.

In the high consciousness of those whom we call Masters, all the worlds are to them as one world in which their waking consciousness is ever functioning—and they focus their attention at any point without leaving the physical body. The worlds on which attention is not fixed are "out of focus," but are not invisible.

When we are using physical sight only, things we are looking at are clear and distinct. The surrounding things are visible, but not clearly defined. So if a man be living in two worlds, physical and astral things intermingle in his normal field of vision—but if he looks at the physical, the astral is out of focus; if he looks at the astral, the physical is out of focus. But a communication from any world can reach a Master, and by focusing his attention on it, he sees the world from which it comes—and can, if he so will, answer it by sending the reply through the appropriate body. All his bodies function as one body for his consciousness. But each is, there, a perfect instrument for action in any world.[7]

We, who have not reached that high perfection, may have to move from world to world, or leave one body to function in another. Or, if we have passed that elementary stage of the higher evolution, we may have partly unified our lower bodies, and may be able to function on some planes as the Master does on all those which are manifested. Then, by paying attention to any message, we can know from what world it comes. It is all a question of the development of our bodies, the one consciousness receiving impressions from any world in which it is using a well-organized body. The whole question, therefore, is one of evolution—the unfolding of consciousness, the organization of bodies.

But there are many forms of communication that do not depend wholly on ourselves: forms used by other persons who desire to communicate with us, and which demand no growth on our own part—communications which present themselves to our normal consciousness in the physical body, and are surrounded with more or less of difficulty and danger because of the letting loose of forces not usually employed on the physical plane by the person making the communication. It is to these that we will next turn, remarking only that it is our own want of development that makes necessary the employment of these means, that forces more highly evolved Beings to come down to our level because we are not able to rise to theirs.

It may be taken for granted as a general rule that no Being who is functioning on higher planes will go to a great expenditure of energy to manifest himself physically at a point far removed from that at which his physical body is living, if he can do the work he needs to accomplish without such manifestation. He will always use the smallest amount of power necessary to achieve the aim he sets before himself. He will take the easiest way, employ the easiest method.[8] If the person with whom he wishes to communicate has so organized his higher bodies as to be able to receive communications on the subtler planes, then most certainly he will not go to the expenditure of energy necessary for appearance on the physical. Still, it is sometimes necessary (and in olden times it was usual) for a Master to teach on the physical plane when his physical body is far away from the place at which the teaching is to be given. In such case, the question arose, and arises: "What is the best method of communication?"

The ancients answered this question in a simple and definite way. They said—and truly said—that the best method of communication was to use a pure, carefully trained, and carefully guarded body, highly organized as to the nervous system, from which the legitimate owner could easily step out, or be sent out, leaving this body an empty tabernacle into which the teacher—whose own physical body was far away—could step, and use as his own. Such a body is like a well-made garment out of which the owner can slip, leaving it to be put on and worn by another.

If a body is to be thus used, it is necessary that it should be guarded with scrupulous care. The surroundings should be beautiful and peaceful. No rough or jarring vibrations should be allowed to ruffle the atmosphere. Coarse and impure persons should not be allowed to approach it. Its diet should be nonstimulating, nutritive, and free from all products of ferment and decay.[9] Careful physical culture should preserve it in health.

In the ancient temples, ruled by those who were themselves initiates of the lower or higher mysteries, such bodies were to be found—those of the vestal virgins, or sibyls. These virgins were originally young girls brought up with extreme care within the temple precincts, and allowed to come into touch only with those who were pure and noble—and such a virgin would be chosen as the means of communication. Seated on a stool or chair isolated from the earth's magnetism, the girl would leave her body—if trained to do so at will—or she would be thrown into a trance. Then a Master, or a high initiate, would take possession of the body, and through it teach the disciples gathered for instruction.

That was the favorite way of teaching among the ancients. And it was a good way, for it caused little disturbance of normal, physical forces. It merely afforded to a higher Being a vehicle which he could use, while the vestal was no more disturbed than by an ordinary going to sleep. This was the way in which Pythagoras was wont to give instruction to his disciples in more lives than one.[10]

In modern days, such an organism is spoken of as that of a medium, and the lack of knowledge has brought about a degradation of the office. A person who is born a sensitive is taught to be passive, allows himself to be thrown into a trance and his body to be taken possession of, without knowledge of the entity who is going to use it, without discrimination or power of self-defense. Such persons usually pollute their bodies with flesh and alcohol, meet all people indiscriminately, allow anyone to sit with them, live amid sordid surroundings. The results are naturally trivial or repulsive. For this, one cannot blame the mediums. It is ignorance which leads to such conditions.

If Mr. Stead be able to carry out the plan that he and his astral world friend Miss Ames—"Julia"—have formed, he will raise the medium to a far higher position, will guard sensitives from evil surroundings, and will fence his seance room against undesirable intruders belonging both to the physical and astral worlds. Julia's Bureau is the first attempt in modern days to open systematic and carefully guarded channels of communication between the living and superliving along this particular line. Nor are the absent living excluded from using it, if they are able to go thither in their astral bodies.[11]

In our own days, H. P. Blavatsky was largely used by her Master and other teachers as such a means of communication. She was a most extraordinary and rare compound. Her body and nervous system were of the most sensitive type. She was born a medium, and was surrounded during her childhood and youth by a wealth of mediumistic phenomena.[12] But she had also an intelligence of extraordinary vividness and a will of steel. Rarely, indeed, is such a combination found—but it was ideal for an occultist. In fact, a Master said that no such body had been available for two hundred years.[13]

Her character was positive and imperious, and her occult training made even stronger her already strong will. Throughout her life as one of the founders of the Theosophical Society, she was constantly stepping out of the physical body, in order to place it at the service of her own Master or at that of one of the teachers—the face and voice sometimes so much changing as to bewilder unaccustomed spectators. Colonel Olcott has told us in his *Old Diary Leaves* that most of his own occult instruction reached him in this ancient way. She would step out of her body, a Master would step in, and through her lips would teach the eager, devoted disciple.[14]

Of all ways of communicating, as I said above, this is the best, because it causes least disturbance. But there are few people who are fit to serve as such a channel. Not understanding the conditions necessary to make the body fit for the use of a Being on the level of a Master, people do not train and keep their bodies sufficiently well to be used in this way. And, for the most part, what is done nowadays along these lines is not of the nature of possession, but rather of inspiration, when the mind is raised above its normal level by contact with the mind of the Master, and some of his thought flows through it.

The very opposite of this means of communication, as dangerous as the other is safe, is where a materialization of a physical body is brought about. Our Masters have used also this method, and in the early days of the Theosophical Society it was not infrequently employed. The Master comes in his *mayavi rupa*—phantasmal body—and densifies it on the spot where he chooses to appear by drawing out of the atmosphere, or out of the body of someone present, the particles which, built into the subtle body, make it visible and sometimes tangible.[15]

Colonel Olcott saw his Master first in this way in New York. So also I saw him for the first time in Fontainebleau in 1889.[16] In this way, several of the Masters and of their initiated disciples have appeared to members of the Theosophical Society. Mr. Leadbeater, Damodar, Pandit Bhavani Shankar, and Mr. Subbiah Chetty are some of the various witnesses of such appearances at Adyar and elsewhere.[17]

The question will naturally be asked: Why should so impressive and satisfactory a means of communication be dangerous? Because of the universality of the well-known law that "action and reaction are equal and opposite." Whenever the forces of the higher planes are caused to affect the lower directly, there is a reaction equal to the action caused—and the direct action down here of a Brother of the White Lodge is followed by a similar direct action here of a Brother of the Dark Lodge. One of the Masters in an early letter [*ML* 1 (Barker); 1–2 (Chin)] explained this dangerous reaction from the phenomena worked by H. P. Blavatsky, and the destructive results on those around her, and many of us have seen plenty of confirmation of the law.[18]

Wherever these manifestations of force occur, there is storm and trouble—and those who seem, at the moment, to be most highly favored are those on whom falls the weight of the inevitable recoil. They suffer physically or mentally: there is loss of [mental] equilibrium or [there is] nervous disturbance. The nervous strain to which H. P. Blavatsky was subjected by the wealth of phenomena produced by her broke down her physical health and aged her before her time. And it is noteworthy that because of the strain involved by this play of forces in the life of discipleship, physical health has ever been in the East a condition of discipleship.[19]

Biographies of seers, of saints, are full of evidence of the working of this law—and without definite training, no physical body can stand the strain of psychic experiences. So constantly have hysteria and seership been found together that some regard all exhibitions of seership as resulting from disturbance of mental equilibrium. And it is true in very many cases that psychic sensitiveness and overstrained nerves go together. Magnetic, electrical, and other forms of etheric vibrations are set up on the physical plane with the exhibition of the subtler forces—and unless people within their reach know how to protect themselves, they pay for their presence in disordered nerves and strained brains.

Another means of communication is the sending of a message by the Master through a disciple. Such a message would often be given by the disciple in his Master's form. For astral and mental bodies follow the thought of their wearers, and if the disciple bearing the message is thinking intently on his Master, his body might assume his appearance, and the sender of the message would appear as its deliverer. The mental or astral body assuming that form, the denser material built into it would also follow it, and thus an appearance of the Master might take place—although he himself was not present.

Similarly, again, a thought form of the Master might bring the communication, and that happens more frequently than the actual coming of the Master to any particular place. It has been observed, quite apart from any question of a Master, that one person will see the form of another when only a thought form has been sent, and no visit has been paid in the astral body. A person whose mind has been fairly well-trained may send such a thought form, and it will assume the form of the sender. I have myself very often been told that I had appeared in particular places and had done certain actions, and those who had seen the phantasm were not easily to be convinced that I had not paid them any visit, but had only thought of them. If the percipient had been trained to close observation, he would have been able to distinguish between a thought form and a person. But in the absence of such training, a person may say quite honestly, "I saw my friend," when he had seen only his friend's thought form.[20]

Moreover, it is possible for a person to project a thought form and then to perceive it as an external object. A Master may send a thought to a student, and thus bring about a change of consciousness in that student on the higher levels of the mental plane. That change of consciousness caused by the Master will bring about corresponding vibrations in the student's causal body, and these will be reproduced in the normal way in the mental and astral bodies, and thus carried to the etheric. A person most readily affected through the auditory nerves might, under such circumstances, hear the Master's voice—and hear it either inside or outside his brain. One most readily affected through the optic nerves might equally see the Master's form. Each might believe that he had heard or seen the Master himself, when he had unconsciously manufactured in his etheric brain the voice or the form. In such cases, the communication would be a real one, but the shape it would take on the physical plane would be illusory.

It is stated in the Acts of the Apostles that when the Holy Spirit came down upon the twelve, everyone in the assembled crowd heard them speak in his own tongue [Acts 2:1–6]. To the person who does not understand matters such as those with which this article deals, the story seems incredible. Yet it is not so. For the thought of the apostles caused in each hearer a mental change, reproducing itself in the mind of each. That change became each man's thought, and reached each man's brain in the ordinary way. There, it clothed itself in words—the words into which each man was accustomed daily, unconsciously, to translate his own thoughts. The man thought that he heard the apostles speaking words in his own language, whereas they spoke in thoughts, and he translated them into his own tongue.

Similarly, if a worker on the astral plane finds that he cannot communicate with someone whom he desires to help through the medium of a common language, he will—if he has learned to use his mental body—transmit the thought to the mind of his companion, leaving him to translate the mental image into his own language. He does the translation, but he will consider that his friend has spoken to him, whereas he has only received from him a mental impression which he has himself translated after his accustomed fashion.

That wonted interaction of mind and brain—the normal translation of mental image into words—is used by those working on higher planes as offering a convenient means of communication with those on lower planes who use a language unknown to themselves. Thus an Eastern Master, not knowing English, will "speak in English" to a Western pupil. He may even write it by taking from the pupil's brain the words he needs.[21]

There is one other possibility that should not be omitted: the personification of a Brother of the Light by a Brother of the Shadow, or of a disciple of the one by a disciple of the other. It may happen that for the deceiving of a person possessing wide influence, and the consequent harm that may be wrought by such a one when deceived, a Brother of the Shadow may personate a White Brother, and give a mischievous order or direction. In such a case, everything depends at first on the intuition of the one whom it is sought to mislead, and then the matter passes on to the intuition and judgment of others. Should such a possibility be before the Society, each member must form his own opinion on the veracity and reliability of the communication, after considering all the circumstances of the case—the knowledge and the character of the supposed victim, the bearing of the communication on the welfare of the Society, and all collateral happenings.[22]

Sometimes the question can be finally decided only after the expiry of a considerable period of time. Thus, in the case of the Judge secession, time has spoken by the continuance and growth of the original Society, its output of literature, its increasing vitality and power, compared with the breaking up of the secession into various smaller bodies, the decrease in adherents, the paucity of literature, the small influence on the public.[23]

Time proves all things, and its verdict is without appeal. So will it be with the controversy aroused by the Adyar manifestations. "In patience possess ye your souls" [Luke 21:19], and after using your best judgment await that verdict.[24]

The fire of time proves all things. It burns up dross and leaves the gold purified and resplendent. The Lord of the Burning Ground throws all things earthly into his fires. Let us await the results without fear, willing that our dross shall be consumed and hoping that some pure gold may, in the end, remain.[25]

It will be evident to those who consider these various means of communication that it is well-nigh impossible for persons at a distance from the place where a communication has been made to decide on the form it may have taken, unless they have at their command occult methods of investigation. The nature of the manifestations which took place at Adyar in the winter of 1906–7 could not be decided by the ordinary member of the Society, unversed in occult phenomena. He was forced either to rely on the good faith and accuracy of those present during their occurrence or able to study them occultly, or to suspend his judgment. The data were insufficient for an independent decision in the matter. And such is the case with regard to most of the phenomena which have occurred in the history of the Society. Unless we can accept the good faith and the competence of the witnesses, or have the power to investigate the past for ourselves, we must perforce suspend our judgment.

Irrational credulity and irrational incredulity are both signs of an unbalanced mind. And, where evidence sufficient to satisfy us is lacking, our right course is to abstain alike from affirmation and denial. It is clear that in such matters each must decide for himself, and that none has the right to dictate how any other member shall think. A person who has definite knowledge may affirm that such and such a thing happened, but he cannot claim authority to impose his knowledge on others as sufficient proof of the happening. Nor should he blame them if they deny his competence as a witness. The entire freedom of each member to exercise his own reason on these matters is necessary to the security and progress of the Society.

The paucity of communications permitted to be made public during many years was a proof of the want of balance, judgment, common sense, and calmness in the general Society. People had come to regard communications from the Masters with doubt, suspicion, and fear. And consequently, as they caused much turmoil, they were withheld, save when absolutely necessary. In the earlier days, they were common, because the fact of the open door was very generally recognized. Now they are rare, because of the turmoil they cause.[26]

But if we believed what theoretically most of us accept, that we are living in three worlds all the time and are related to those worlds by the inclusion of their matter in our body, we should regard it as natural, not unnatural, that we should receive by way of our appropriated matter impacts from each of the three worlds. On our receptiveness, not on these outer worlds, depends our knowledge of them and our communication with them.

It is all-important for the progress of the Society that, however true the fact of communication between these worlds, neither the fact itself, nor any particular instance of it, should be imposed upon the members of the Society by authority—either open or tacit. Each member must be left free to accept or reject on his own responsibility that which is affirmed by any other. If, in the exercise of this discretion, a member rejects what is true, that is his own loss—and it is far better that he should lose than that the Society should be deprived of the liberty which keeps open the path of progress.

If a majority of the Society rejected a true and important communication—a communication from a Master—then the Society would perish as an organization, and the minority would be left to carry on the work. That was the peril in which the Theosophical Society stood after the manifestations at Adyar and the expression to Colonel Olcott of the Master's wish as to the nomination of his successor. But the great majority of the Society obeyed the Master's wish, and the danger was averted.[27]

Such a peril might again confront us, but we must not buy security from it by restricting the freedom of members to think for themselves.

Every member must be left free to believe or not to believe. None has the right to say, "I believe it, therefore you must accept it." None has the right to say, "I do not believe it, therefore you must reject it." There is no coercion in saying: "I know this to be true," any more than there is coercion in saying, "I know that putting those substances together will form an explosive compound." If anyone chooses to put them together, then he will find out by his own experience that such a compound is formed.[28]

As a Master once said when he was accused of uttering a threat because he stated what would follow a certain line of action, "A warning is not a threat."[29] Elder students may see a danger that younger students do not see, and they are sometimes bound to put their knowledge at the service of the younger. But the younger must be left free to accept or to reject the warning—and in the latter case to buy their own experience at the cost of suffering that would have been avoided by utilizing the experience of their elders.

Progress is made along both lines and is, for the most part, gained by a blending of the two methods. The laws of nature do not change because we are ignorant of them, and if we make a mistake, however conscientiously, we shall suffer as we strike against the law. The conscientious decision will improve our character, and our knowledge will be increased by our experience. Those who have already gained that knowledge may rightly offer it to their fellows, though they may not impose it on them—otherwise would they lay themselves open to the reproach: "You knew we were ignorantly running into danger; why did you not warn us?"

The Theosophical Society, as the nucleus of the coming race, must encourage variety of opinion within its borders, in order that it may gather up within itself all seeds of truth, even though they be enclosed within husks of error. The husk will drop away and the seed will remain and grow.[30] The Society will never be destroyed by varieties of thought—if only we practice perfect tolerance, and put no barrier in the way of freedom of expression. But do not let us encourage negations while discouraging affirmations, lest we should grow towards the darkness rather than towards the light.

While we guard liberty of thought and expression and encourage the fullest discussion of differences, let us not forget courtesy and gentleness, lest difference of thought should glide into vituperation of those who think differently from ourselves. Personal attack and imputation of evil motives are the weapons of attack used by the uncultured and the vulgar, and should find no place in Theosophical discussion. Love is as vital as knowledge for the growth of the future—and the knowledge which is without love is useless to the master builders of the coming race.[31]

Chapter Twelve

The Larger Consciousness and Its Value (1909)

Friends: During the whole of the lectures, of which the discourse of tonight is the last, I have taken for granted the existence of a larger consciousness in man than that which we know at the present time as our physical or waking consciousness.[1] Over and over again, I have had occasion to allude to it. Once or twice, I dwelt for a few moments upon it. But I could not interrupt the course of what I had been putting to you by any detailed description of the larger consciousness, or of the instruments of that consciousness—the body or bodies of man.

It seemed to me that the work I had been trying to do would remain somewhat imperfect unless I tried to place before you, ere quitting the subjects I had been dealing with, something with regard to this larger consciousness in man: a consciousness which exists in every one of us, which functions intermittently in all of us, which is in [the] course of unfolding in humanity at the present time. And side by side with the unfolding of the consciousness there goes a continual evolution of the bodies in which that consciousness expresses itself—and it is that subject that I want to deal with tonight, trying to put before you clearly and definitely the theory which is studied by Theosophists with regard to this matter, a theory which some of us have proved to be true by our own investigations, and (which is a far more important thing) confirmed by the great scriptures of the world's religions, the testimony which has been given to man by seers, by prophets of the highest, the most inspired, order.

Sometimes we are inclined to lay more stress on contemporary evidence than on the evidence that comes from the great scriptures of the world. It seems to me as though that were a little along the line of hiding the sun by holding a plate quite close to the eyes. For it is quite clear, when you come to think of it, that testimony which may be given nowadays by half-developed students cannot in the nature of things be nearly as valuable as that of the great prophets and seers of humanity, embodied, however mystically and allegorically, in the great bibles of humanity. In fact, the testimony of the modern-day investigator should be checked and governed by those mightier and wider revelations. And it is always a point of satisfaction, a point of confirmation to the modern and partially developed seer, when he finds that his own investigations throw light on some of the statements of these scriptures, and that the bibles of the race become more illuminating in some of their obscurer passages by the light that he may have been able to gain by his own investigations.

I am not, then, pretending for one moment that anything I put to you now is comparable in value with what you might find out for yourselves, if spiritually illuminated, in these great bibles of religions. But I do think that the investigations of today help us to understand those great revelations, though much that is there said is necessarily obscure to us because of the immense difference in knowledge between the speaker and the student. Therefore, though we may call our knowledge today a farthing light, it may be of value in the deciphering of these great manuscripts of the past, so that even a little knowledge of our own may enable us to go more deeply into those great wells of truth which have come down to us from antiquity, which have been given to us by the saviors of the world.

In order to make what I have to say clear to you, I shall have to ask you to pardon me if I go in the beginning a little into definition and detail. If you want to study your own body, comparatively simple as that is, you must be willing to learn the difference between a bone and a nerve, between an artery and a vein—and so on, through the whole of the more or less familiar terms which the physiologist uses in explaining the anatomy and the physiology of the body. No person can have clear and definite ideas if he is not willing to study the mere nomenclature of that which he wishes to understand. And while it is quite possible to avoid using words of other languages, it is not possible to avoid some demand on the consecutive "thought power" of the student if he desires to be anything more than a mere superficial hearer, without any definite understanding of the subjects which he supposes himself to be studying.[2]

There is a very good and simple description of man's constitution in one of the Pauline epistles, where a triple division is given [1 Thess. 5:23]—and a perfectly accurate division, although subdivisions again are possible and practicable. But for my purposes now, that division into three, and then certain subdivisions of each, will be sufficient to give you a very clear and definite idea of consciousness in man. And then, by your own experience, you can decide how much of the larger consciousness comes into your waking consciousness, or how much of you is still without vehicle of expression, still without the power of manifesting in worlds related to our own.

That division, as all of you will at once know, is spirit, soul, body. It is curious how indefinite the mass of Christian people are with regard to the meaning of the first two terms, *spirit* and *soul*. I am not quarreling with the fact that different definitions may sometimes be given. I am quarrelling with the fact that most Christians have no definition at all; that they use the words interchangeably; that they constantly talk of man as a duality, always using the word *body*; sometimes using the word *spirit*, and sometimes *soul*, for all that which they exclude from the body. Thus you hear people talking about spirits manifesting in various ways. Sometimes you hear about the human soul and its immortality, and so on. But a clear, distinct definition of what is spirit, what is soul—that, for the most part, is wanting among even the students of theology.

Let us see if it be not possible to define them in a way which may at least be clear. You may, of course, differ with the division, for the reason that you may think some other dividing line is better. I am concerned chiefly, for the moment, with giving you a clear definition, and then you may correct or amend it according to your own thought, or your own knowledge. The definition will, of course, govern me in all that I say tonight.

First of all, then: What is spirit [atman]? Spirit is a germ of divinity unfolding itself gradually in human evolution, appropriating certain kinds of matter which it gradually organizes into an instrument for self-expression—we may shorten that by saying a germ of divinity encased in matter. That germ of divinity, as you might naturally expect, shows out in itself the triple division of its divine parent. Just as you find God, manifesting in a universe, ever manifesting three supreme attributes—sometimes personified into what is called a Trinity—so you would naturally expect to find in the germ that which you find in the parent: that the triple nature of divinity should show itself out in the triple nature of the spirit which is man. And that is so.[3]

You find spirit showing itself forth in full divinity, taking for a moment the Christian names as most familiar, in the form of power in the Father [First Logos], in the form of wisdom in the Son [Second Logos], in the form of creative activity in the Holy Spirit [Third Logos]. If you will take those names for the time as being most familiar to your own thought, and therefore introducing nothing of difficulty to you—if you will remember those accepted ideas for the time, and translate them into terms of consciousness (limited, because these are not all fully unfolded in man)—you will be able readily to distinguish in man's spiritual nature (and even more distinctly, for the moment, in the lower reflection of that with which I will deal presently); you will be able to distinguish the threefold division, and so to obtain, as it were, a clear picture of your own spiritual nature.

That which in Divinity we call power, the will by which the worlds exist, shows itself out in our own spiritual nature as will [atman]. The wisdom which upholds the worlds shows itself out in the human spirit, also, as the pure and compassionate reason, which is the wisdom, the Christ, in man [buddhi]. The third, creative activity, shows itself in intellect, the highest, the noblest form of creative activity—the intellect, the pure intellect in man [manas] is the third reflection in man of the creative activity of God. And if you link what may be less familiar with the familiar, it will be very easy for you to keep the thread of that which I desire to put before you. Think first of all, then, that the spirit, the germ of divinity in man, has to show out in the gradual unfolding of its hidden powers these three supreme attributes with which you are familiar in the thought of Divinity itself.

Then, passing from that highest part of our nature to what St. Paul calls the soul, what is the soul in relation to the spirit? It is the temporary reflection in grosser matter of the eternal spirit; the image of that which is the eternal object; the reflection in the mirror of a world of that eternal life which passes from world to world, unfolding, but is never subject to the transitoriness which marks the ever-changing worlds.

The soul in man is the spirit [monad] working in grosser matter. And hence in our own natures, so familiar to us—for now we come into a region that psychological science deals with and tries to define and understand—we have, when we look at our own consciousness, the soul, the reflection of the spirit in grosser matter. We have the mind [kama-manas] reflecting the pure intellect [buddhi-manas] with all its activities—imagination, judgment, reason—all these powers of the mind. Then we find a part of our nature that we call the emotional [kama]. There we have the reflection of that pure and compassionate wisdom [buddhi] that I spoke of which shows itself in the lower worlds by love, the highest and loftiest of the emotions, the root whence all virtues spring. For the same principle of unity which expresses itself as wisdom in the spiritual world expresses itself as love, which draws the separated lives together in the world where matter has overcome spirit, where spirit is blinded by matter.

The unity that the spirit knows, the soul seeks by love, which is the attribute that draws towards unity—and that which in the spiritual world is known, in the lower world is sought by this exquisite attribute of the soul. And that which in the higher world we call will becomes desire in the lower. For the difference between will and desire is that will is self-determined, whereas desire is determined by the attractiveness of objects outside the consciousness.

You are moved by desire when some pleasure attracts you, some pain repels you—when your activity goes along the road that is determined by an outer attraction, an outer repulsion. You are moved by will, the spiritual attribute, when the whole of your inner nature, drawn up to a single point, self-determined, sends that nature along the road that within yourself you have chosen, whether it leads to pleasure or pain, whether it leads to gain or loss in the lower world. Will is determined from the spiritual self [atman]. Desire is guided and stimulated by objects in the lower world. Hence that which is will in the spirit is desire in the soul. And so you find the soul represented by these three well-known attributes: *mind*, with all its powers; *emotion*, the root emotion being love; *desire*, the reflection of the determining power in this lower world.[4]

When you come down into everyday life, you find the whole of these make up your waking consciousness, showing itself out in the denser matter of the brain. In your waking consciousness, you know the working of the mind. In your waking consciousness, you know the working of the emotions. In your waking consciousness, you know the working of desire. So that the waking consciousness—the limited, the conditioned, the smaller consciousness—is that which is within the limitations of your brain or physical body, but is none other than the larger consciousness which shows itself in the subtler worlds as soul, in the spiritual world as spirit.

If you realize clearly that outlining, with its subdivisions, you will find that consciousness is a unit, and the differences are differences of the material in which it is working rather than in itself. The triple division is the only one, whether you look at it in the brain, in the subtle body, in the matter of the world where the spirit rules. Everywhere, consciousness is one, expressing itself in three modes, by three qualities—but everywhere a unit, yourself, the reality within you.

What is body? For there is a third factor in St. Paul's definition of man. Naturally, the body also has in it the same triple differentiation as the consciousness. And so we find a spiritual body [buddhi-manas], the clothing of the spirit [atman] in the highest worlds of consciousness. We find also what St. Paul, again, calls a natural body.[5]

There is a natural body, he says, and there is a spiritual body [1 Cor. 15:44]. But that natural body divides itself into two—the subtle body in which the soul is working; the dense body in which the waking consciousness is working, the reflection of the highest. Those two naturally go together, and might well be classed roughly as the single natural body, for it is transitory, impermanent, belongs to the three worlds of change—the physical world, the intermediate, and the heavenly; has a certain life through which it passes in the three worlds, and then gives back its elements to the worlds to which they respectively belong. Whereas the spiritual body [buddhi-manas, or casual body] is a relatively permanent thing, lasts through the whole of the long life of the individual, passes through birth after birth, death after death, knows neither birth nor death in its own nature, passes through them, but is not affected by them—the spiritual individuality, the real man, is eternal in his own nature, and has a permanent clothing of the matter of the spiritual world, unfolding his powers, organizing his matter, but remaining ever the same in essence, the consciousness ever living in those worlds, the matter the same, only becoming more and more definitely organized.

In that spiritual body remains the memory of all the experiences through which you have passed. In that spiritual body resides your true individuality, that knows neither birth nor death. In that spiritual body which is ever yours, all the experiences of the past are gathered up, and part of those experiences is put forth, birth after birth, in order that the soul may clothe itself in new bodies for new experiences and new developments. So that the part of you that lasts is the spirit [atman] in the spiritual body [causal body or individuality]; the part of you that changes, the soul [personality] in the temporary body, whether you take the subtler [mental and astral bodies] or the denser [etheric double and physical body] parts.

Supposing you accept that definition of man in his triple division, it will be easy enough then to follow out step by step what the higher consciousness is as apart from the lower, the larger as apart from the smaller. You will start with the great conception of a living spirit [atman] coming down into denser and denser matter, with the object of acquiring that matter and subduing it to his own purpose—appropriating it, wrapping himself up in it, and temporarily blinded by the veil, but a veil that he is going to turn into an instrument, so that by it he may know all the worlds, and come into contact with every portion of the universe. For that, he appropriates the matter of every world. For that, he wraps himself round in these material garments.

And working upon these, he turns them to his own purposes, shapes them by his own will, molds them in order that he may use them for that which he desires to effect—contact with matter, the condition of his becoming master of the worlds. And by making matter his servant and his instrument, all the worlds become open before him, and he can function in any one of them.

That, the pure spiritual being cannot do. He can function only in worlds of the spirit, those lofty eternal regions where Divinity itself resides and manifests without the blinding effect of the denser matter that we wear. But just as Divinity emanates these coarser forms of matter in order that the spiritual germs may be sown therein, and therein gain the experience by which their powers will be unfolded from within—just as Deity is manifest in matter—so must the germs of Deity grow therein, until matter is subject to them as it is to the Father of light, whence they come.

So, in looking at this consciousness unfolding and these bodies becoming organized, we can trace throughout the purpose of that long unfolding—to make the spirit master of matter, to enable him to act in every world. And when we catch a glimpse of that great purpose, we realize how perfect is the plan, how complete our triumph will be.

First we notice, when we are looking at the lower forms of consciousness in ourselves, that we can understand a certain relation between matter and spirit which we are told exists all the way up to the highest spiritual world. And so far as investigation has been carried by the students of today, they find that relation in each successive world that they enter and finally subdue. It is a relation, then, that runs right through between consciousness and form, between spirit and matter. It is this: that every change in consciousness has a corresponding vibration in matter, and that every vibration in matter has a corresponding change in consciousness.

We are told that that relation is imposed by the Logos Himself in His first shaping of the matter side of His universe; that all the vibrations of which He makes the atoms capable answer one by one to changes in His own consciousness; and that throughout the whole of His universe, in all the mighty realm of spirit/matter that He rules, this correspondence is universally, unchangeably found—for every change in consciousness a corresponding change in vibration, for every change in vibration a corresponding change in consciousness.[6]

Let us see how that would work if anyone whose eyes are a little opened looks at the aura of a person—the lowest part of that aura, if you will, in etheric or astral matter: let us say, astral. You will notice a large number of colors continually flashing through it and changing. And if you examine those colors, every one, as you know from your ordinary study, representing a certain definite vibration in matter—every color is nothing more than a certain vibration in matter, a vibration with a definite wavelength. If you watch those changing colors in the aura, you will find that they either are generated by a state of consciousness or give rise to it.

Suppose, for instance, you find a person in a mood of devotion, engaged perhaps in prayer. You can see them by the score in any Christian church. Watch the astral aura of that person, and you will find that the whole of it is vibrating in a way that gives you the color of blue—blue everywhere predominating, the whole of the aura suffused with that color. But you will also find, if there is in that congregation a quiet person who was not feeling devotional when he came into that congregation, that gradually his astral body will be affected by the vibrations in the astral bodies near him, and that those vibrations imposed upon him from without will produce a devotional mood within him. You can start it, then, at either end: either the mood producing the appearance, the vibration, or the vibration producing the mood.

Take it in another form. Have you never felt when you yourself were perfectly good-tempered and some very irritable person came up to you, have you never felt that you yourself were becoming irritable? Not that you had anything to be irritable about, but merely because the other man was—and you need considerable control over the astral body to prevent the irritation of the person who comes near you from affecting your own previously placid mood. If you have not observed this, keep watch over yourself during the coming week, and you will find how continually you reproduce the emotions of the people with whom you come into contact.

What is the mechanism of it? Very simple. That person's astral body is vibrating in consonance with the emotion he is feeling. Those vibrations of his astral body set up vibrations in your astral body, a perfectly mechanical thing. But because it is your astral body, the matter you have appropriated, those vibrations in it produce in you the corresponding mood of irritation. Hence the common ethical precept given by every great teacher, to return good for evil. That is, by a deliberate effort of the consciousness, to throw yourself into the mood which is opposite to the evil mood of the person with whom you come into contact.

If you do that, then your own mood will overbear in your astral body the vibrations imposed upon it from without, and your astral body will begin to vibrate in correspondence with your own good emotion instead of with the evil emotion imposed from outside. The further result of that, if you be strong enough, will be to correct the bad vibration in the astral body of the man who is near you—and so, by correcting that vibration into harmony with your own, to produce in him your own good emotion, instead of having your emotion controlled by his.

That is the ordinary science of the emotions that every aspirant for the higher life is set to practice in his daily life. He is first told the theory, so that he may understand what he is doing. And then he is set to the practice, so that by the practice he may realize the truth of the law that his teacher has explained.

Sometimes the ethical teacher only says: "Love your enemies, do good to them that hate you" [Luke 6:27]. With the unspiritual hearer, the question will very readily arise, "Why should I give love when hatred is given to me?" Only knowledge will enable you to understand the wisdom that underlies this precept of all the great teachers of the past. Speaking in an age when authority was valid, and when people were willing to accept the precept from one whom they recognized as greater than themselves, they only proclaimed the law, and the docile hearer tried to obey. In our own more critical and combative age, it is necessary to justify wisdom to a more critical and carping generation, and so the full explanation is given which shows you the scientific truth which underlies the ethical precept.

That runs through the whole of the working of our bodies, the whole of the changes in our consciousness. You can work it out step by step, or you can read the working out which has been made by a thoughtful student, and so you will have a veritable science of the emotions.[7] And you will go out into the world a source of peace, a source of blessing, a source of all good emotions, helping the weaker by your own knowledge and your own strength, and so enabling them to climb more quickly by giving this helping hand out of the knowledge that you have learned.

By that fact, then, we have power over matter, we can throw it into the vibrations we desire. We can do more than that: we can shape it into organs of expression for the consciousness that is unfolded within us. Understanding these laws, we begin to realize that by these bodies we may come into touch with the various worlds around us. Let us see, again, the method.

When first the spiritual germ descends into matter, gathering round itself the matter that it needs, that matter is like a mere cloud. It is still so in the highest regions for most. It is becoming organized into definite instruments of consciousness in the three lower worlds in all the more advanced members of our present race—to a very large extent in all of you.

If you pause for a moment on the physical body, you will see exactly what is meant by the phrase *the organizing of the body*. You have here now in your physical body a valuable instrument, first for acquiring knowledge of the outer world, and then for acting on that world, carrying out the knowledge you have gained.

You have, as you know, in your body two sets of nerves, called sensory and motor. By the sensory, you gather knowledge from without. By the motor, you act upon the outer world, utilizing the knowledge you have gathered to bring about the results that you desire. And your physical body is well organized for its work. By the evolution of the senses, by the gradual growth of the whole nervous system, by the development of your brain, you have largely become master of this densest world, the physical world, to which your body is related. All that is needed further is a comparatively small evolution—the development of the other two senses, the conquest of the realm of ether, that which science is now investigating.[8]

So far, then, you have one instrument, the instrument of your waking consciousness. Through that, spirit and soul alike are working, the powers of the soul showing out as far as the density of the matter will permit.

Coming into denser matter is very much the same as if you brought a light through thicker and thicker glass. The light would remain the light, but that which would show out through the glass would be less and less according to the opacity of that glass. So with the light of the spirit shining through the soul and the body.

Your next work is the organization of the next finer body of matter, that which I called the subtle. In that, your emotions are working. In that, your thoughts are working. And, to a very large extent, your mental and emotional bodies—we call the emotional the astral—are organized at the present time. But here more variety comes in. Some of you will have your astral body so well developed that it is fit for separate working in the intermediate world. Some of you will have it well developed so far as consciousness is concerned, but not so far as the reception of impressions from the outer intermediate world. That is, your consciousness will be working there in that finer matter that has not yet sufficiently organized the astral body to receive impressions from without.

Gradually, as evolution goes on, the organization of the astral body will go on in everybody. But it is possible, as I suggested to you a few Sundays ago, very largely to quicken that evolution, and gradually to make the astral body what it ought to be, as perfect an instrument for contact with the astral world as the physical body is for contact with the physical world.[9] That is, of course, what a very considerable number of people have done, and they are able to act either in or out of the physical body. We will take both cases in a moment.

Take the finer part first of the subtle body—the mental body. In most of you that also is fairly organized. But, again, it is organized for working within yourself, but not receiving from the outer mental world all that hereafter it will be able to receive and utilize. And only a few of you, comparatively, would be able to leave the denser and the astral body behind, and live in the heavenly world, in full consciousness, working there as thoroughly as you can work in the physical world.

What signs are there by which you can judge how far the organization of the astral and the mental bodies is going on, so that if you work to quicken their organization you will be able partly to judge how far your work is effective? Let us take the working in the body—the physical body—first. As these other higher forms of consciousness begin to become coordinated with the physical, and to hand on to it the impressions that they receive, the mental body is becoming highly organized. When the person possessing it is strong in science (physical science), above all in the grasping of principles, in the power of observation, in the ability to draw conclusions from the observations that have been made, organization is improving—among the scientific men of our own time that mental body will be very highly developed, chiefly for use in the waking consciousness, very imperfectly as yet for direct reception on the higher planes.

The higher development of the astral body will show itself in forms of art and of high emotion, and just in proportion as those are transmissible to the waking consciousness may you realize that the astral body is becoming more definitely organized. When the body of the intellect [buddhi-manas]—the lasting body [causal], part of the spiritual body [buddhic]—is becoming organized, then it is that you find fine metaphysical ability, great philosophical profundity of thought, the highest conceptions of idealistic art, the highest achievements in idealistic literature. Those are the faculties that belong to the beginning of the spiritual body in man, transcending the transitory, beginning to shape the permanent instrument of the spirit [atman].

Where you have great talent, where the mental body is highly organized, where you have the highest genius, there the spiritual body is beginning its organization. For that highest genius is the flashing down, from the organized spiritual body into the lower nature, of knowledge which in those regions alone can be gained. And when art and literature become illuminated by the spirit, then you have the mighty geniuses of history that outlast the passing generations and shine out in the world of thought.

What signs may we find other than those of the organization of these bodies through which the larger consciousness will work? Genius is the highest of all, save that which I spoke of as the manifestation of the Christ, the wisdom spirit [buddhi] in man. But if we leave those loftiest manifestations of the larger consciousness alone, what signs may we find amongst ourselves of the growing organization of those higher bodies and the unfolding of the larger consciousness? There are very many signs today of the organizing of the astral body, and it is in the lack of discriminating these from genius that we find a great absence in power in the new psychology.

You find the organization of the astral body showing itself forth in the power to receive impressions directly from the astral plane, and the power to translate them into the waking consciousness. In the body, those first signs are seen in telepathy, where it is well developed, where people are able to communicate with one another without the ordinary physical means of communication—and that is not so very infrequent a thing among the more thoughtful of our own time. That is a power you can develop, if you like, by definite and regular practice. Only remember that all development of power means regular practice and patient and reiterated experiment.

One finds, for the most part, that after a few weeks or months of practice people are apt to drop the whole thing if they have not in that time gained startling results. That is not the way that powers grow. The law is sure, that if you choose to concentrate your mind so as to make a clear image, that will be reproduced in astral matter. Then, by an effort of the self-determined will, you can send that astral thought form to whomsoever you choose. And if you practice that day after day, week after week—nay, even month after month, and year after year—you will find that you will ultimately develop the power of sending thought clearly and definitely, so that you will be able to communicate with the absent as surely, as certainly, as any physical plane communication can be sure and certain.

Practice along these lines can do you nothing but good. It increases the power of the will; it increases the concentration of thought. But remember that, without concentrated thought and fairly strong will, you are bound to have a very long practice before you will have results tangible in the outer world. The person who cannot keep his mind steady for a couple of minutes at a time, the person who cannot concentrate definitely on one thought—such a person certainly cannot transfer that which he is unable to create. And for a very considerable time, people will have to practice by creating the thought image before they will have anything to be definitely sent to another. But that is one of the means of organizing the astral and the mental body as an instrument of the larger consciousness.

Some people, of course, have it by nature, as you say. But what does that mean? Only that they have practiced it in previous life. No one gets anything for nothing from nature. On the other hand, nature is a good paymaster, and pays the exact wages that we have earned, never withholding anything. If you can do it easily, it is because you have done it before. If you find it difficult, it is because you are beginning that definite kind of work. But no one obtains it without labor, no one can develop it without long and continued practice.

But there is one form in which the astral body shows its organization when you are out of the dense body and not in it: in the form of dream. Whenever you go to sleep, you leave your dense body behind.

Some dreams belong only to the brain. It is because people do not distinguish dream from dream that so much foolish ridicule is sometimes cast on the dream state altogether. It is perfectly true that there are dreams which grow out of conditions of the physical body, where a little change in the circulation, a momentary block in some vessel of the brain, will cause a dream, incoherent, senseless, without meaning or illumination. That is the physical dream. It may be caused by any disturbance of the body—indigestion, a hundred other things.

The dream that shows that the astral body is becoming organized is a dream in which some definite knowledge is conveyed, in which some definite warning is given, in which something is added to you that you had not before, or in which you come into contact with someone who has passed out of the physical conditions through the gateway of death, and whom you may meet in the astral world when you yourself have temporarily dropped the dense body. Those dreams are coherent, rational, sometimes illuminative.

Remember how many dreams have now been put on record in which a man has gained in the dream state knowledge that he had not in the waking state. How often that knowledge gained in the dream state has enabled him in the waking state to cover over some gap that he was before unable to bridge. You will find in Myers's book on *Human Personality* some of these dreams given, although not very definitely explained.[10] And if you find in your experience that those are becoming more frequent, then you may be sure that your astral body is becoming a vehicle of consciousness, an instrument by which consciousness can work in the other world.

It is true that in some dreams, especially of warning, the thought may be thrown into your mind from without when you have not found it out for yourself, but have been informed of it by another. Such a warning may come through, given you by some friend, some helper, someone whom you love, who may have passed onwards, and so has the advantage of the astral vision.

But in all those cases, there comes into the waking consciousness something from the larger—and as you perfect the astral body, all those come more and more within your control. As it becomes organized, there is less and less need to leave it in order to exercise its powers. You will find yourself seeing, hearing [astrally], while the physical senses are active, while the consciousness is working normally—the waking consciousness in the brain. So that, slowly and gradually, you will unify the physical and the astral bodies and live in the two worlds continuously at one and the same time, finding those worlds intermingling and interworking. And so you will gain that much of the larger consciousness which belongs to the expression of the soul through the subtle astral body.

Exactly on the same lines with the heavenly worlds, the mental world, your evolution will go on. And for this there is one condition regarding the consciousness, there is one condition regarding the instrument for the unfolding of consciousness—regular and steady meditation. There is no other way. If you find anybody telling you that by any physical means you can really unfold your consciousness, tell them that they do not realize what they are talking about. You can start a little astral consciousness on the lowest parts of the astral world by causing vibrations in matter in the physical that affect the astral, and so bring about a change in consciousness in that lowest part of the astral world—but you can go no further.

I have seen in India men who, by the use of difficult physical means that none of you would care to use—for they bring about the gradual spoiling of the physical body—I have known them able to leave the physical body and live for the time being in the astral. But in that astral body they were unconscious, not conscious. They were not coming into touch with the astral world, nor using the larger consciousness at all. They had only forced themselves into that world in the astral body where it was not organized enough for the reception of impressions, nor the consciousness unfolded to understand them—and they had injured the physical brain and rendered that practically useless for physical utility. So that they had lost both worlds instead of gaining the higher that they sought.

When one has seen that happen in India, one realizes that those methods are not methods that it is desirable to spread in the West. And it is along that line that so many of those pseudo-occult books are going which come to us from America, promising that if we follow those practices, we shall be able to get the better of other people in business transactions, and hypnotize them for our own advantage and our own gain.[11] Wherever you find that the method of working and that the object aimed at, be sure that you are dealing with a form of unfolding and of evolution that can only injure. It cannot really serve. The worst of it is that those forms tend to atrophy the parts of the brain that you want to bring things through, after a higher consciousness is active and the higher body is organized. By this means, you injure the brain, and, with the brain, the connecting link between this world and the next—so that you injure yourself along that line, as well as along the other, and make yourself incapable, until you have a new body, of that higher unfolding at which you aim.

There you have the danger of people picking up fragments of an ancient science of the East, without realizing all the protection with which in the East that science is surrounded. And if, even there, one finds occasionally such cases as I have mentioned—of the ruined physical frame and the undeveloped astral body—then how much more dangerous it is when given to people of different physical heredity, without the conditions which in the East are ever imposed!

Meditation, then, is the one safe way of unfolding the consciousness, and thus organizing the vehicle. And the other condition is purity of thought, purity of desire, purity of physical life. That is the matter side of the training. Your thoughts must be pure, otherwise your mental body will be unfit for higher development. Your desires must be pure, or your astral body will not be fit for that unfolding at which you aim. Your physical body must be pure—otherwise, when the developed mental and astral pour down their power on the physical, the physical will be unable to answer, and you will have hysteria instead of the wider consciousness you seek.

Those, roughly, then, are the conditions: meditation for the consciousness, purity for the evolution of the instrument. If you are willing to accept those conditions, then the path of the higher evolution opens before you, and according to your courage, your perseverance, and your ability will be the rapidity with which you can tread that path.

The object before you should be the helping of others, the gaining of these powers in order that you may be more useful—not in order that you may be greater than your fellow men. Of the purity of your motive, there is only one test: are you using the powers you have now for the helping of your race? If you are not, then no profession that you will use the higher powers for good will be effective in bringing you help in their unfolding.

I have met many a man, many a woman, who is anxious to be an invisible helper—that is, a worker on the astral plane. But I do not always find that those people are visible helpers as far as their present powers go. And I do not understand why people should want to go about in astral slums when they keep carefully away from the physical slums which are already within their reach. So far as you can go by your own power you have the right to go, but if you ask for help from those more highly developed—from the great teachers of the race—then you have to bring in your hands the proof. And that proof is life, and not words—that, as you are using well the talent you have, you deserve to be helped in the gaining of others.

There is the underlying meaning of those strange words ascribed to the Christ, that he who has much, to him shall be given [Matt. 13:12]. Those who have used well that which they have, those alone have claim to be helped in gaining more. For by their life they have shown that they do the best with what they possess, and that is the guarantee that with more they will utilize that also for the race.

And so in the old rules of discipleship, it was said that when the disciple came to the teacher, he must bring with him in his hands the fuel for the fire. It was the fire of sacrifice, and the fuel was everything that the pupil possessed in mind, body, and estate. And he brought that in his hands as offering to the teacher, and then alone was he accepted by the one who knew. And so in these days, also, that higher evolution, quickened by the power of the Great Ones, can be opened up only to those who bring in their hands the fuel for the fire of sacrifice.[12]

You must be willing to give up everything you have, and own nothing, material or immaterial. You must hold everything you have and everything you are at the service of the Great One from whom you ask the gift of knowledge. When that is brought, the gift is never refused; when that door is thus knocked at, it never remains closed.

True it is that the gateway is narrow. True it is, now as of old, "Strait is the gate, narrow is the way, and few there be that find it" [Matt. 7:14]. But the fewness does not depend on the grudging of the teacher—it depends on the want of self-surrender by the disciple.

Bring all you have and all you are, lay it at the feet of the Master of the Wisdom. He will open the gateway. He will guide you along the path. But dream not that words are heard in that high atmosphere where the Master lives and breathes: only high thoughts can reach him, only noble acts can speak the thoughts you have conceived. For voice, there, is the life that is lived; and only the life that speaks of sacrifice can claim the teaching at his hands.

Chapter Thirteen

Revelation, Inspiration, and Observation (1909)

Friends: Those who seriously take up the study of Theosophy should not be satisfied with the mere reading of the voluminous Theosophical literature poured out into the world through the centuries of the past, and continuing to flow into it in our own days. They should, in addition, if they have any innate faculty for such investigation, prepare to develop the faculties by which they may verify for themselves that which they are told by others. But in all cases, much theoretical study is desirable before passing on into the practical. And in most cases, it may not be possible to develop the subtler senses within the limits of the present incarnation, although a good foundation may be laid for such development in the next. Hence theoretical study must form a large part of the training of every Theosophical student—and his attitude towards such study is a matter of serious importance. He needs to discriminate between the books he reads, and to suit his attitude to the type of the book. He must seek to understand what is meant by Revelation, what by Inspiration, and to distinguish revealed from inspired literature, and both from the records of observations.

Some scriptures which are regarded as authoritative lie at the back of all the great religions. Thus Hinduism has the Veda. The word means "knowledge," and this knowledge is of that which is eternally true. It is the knowledge of the Logos, the knowledge of the Lord of a universe; the knowledge of what *is*, not of what *seems*; the knowledge of realities, not of phenomena. This abides ever in the Logos. It is part of Himself. In its manifested form, as revealed for the helping of man, it becomes the Vedas, and in this form goes through many stages—until finally, little of the original remains.

All Hindu schools of philosophy acknowledge the supreme authority of the Vedas. But after this formal acknowledgement is made, the intellect is allowed to range freely at its will—to inquire, to judge, to speculate. Rigid as Hinduism is in its social polity, it has ever left the human intellect free. In philosophy, in metaphysics, it has ever realized that truth should be sought, and no penalty inflicted on error—error being sufficiently penalized by the fact that it *is* error, and breeds misfortunes under natural laws. Even today, that ancient liberty is maintained, and a man may think and write as he will, provided that he follows in practice the social customs of his caste.

The Hindu divides all knowledge into two types—the supreme and the lower. In the lower, he places all his sacred books—following in this the dictum of an Upanishad—together with all other literature, all science, all instruction. In the category of the supreme, he places only "the knowledge of Him by whom all else is known" [Mundaka Upanishad 1.1.4–5].

There you have Hinduism in a nutshell. When once supreme knowledge has been attained and illumination has been experienced, all scriptures become useless. This is asserted plainly and boldly in a well-known passage in the Bhagavad Gita: "All the Vedas are as useful to an enlightened Brahmana as is a tank in a place covered over with water" [Bhagavad Gita 2.46]. What need of a tank when water is everywhere? What need of scriptures when the man is enlightened? Revelation is useless to the man to whom the self [atman] is revealed.

In the early days of Buddhism, the Vedas held high place—for the Lord Buddha, as Dr. Rhys Davids says, "was born and brought up, and lived and died a Hindu."[1] But the character of intellectual freedom for Buddhists is contained in the wise advice of their teacher:

> Do not believe in a thing said merely because it is said; nor in traditions because they have been handed down from antiquity; nor in rumors, as such; nor in writings by sages, merely because sages wrote them. . . nor on the mere authority of your own teachers or masters. But we are to believe when the writing, doctrine, or saying is corroborated

> by our own reason and consciousness. For this I have taught you: not to believe merely because you have heard; but when you believed of your own consciousness, then to act accordingly and abundantly.[2]

Even revelation, for the Buddhist, must be brought to the touchstone of reason and consciousness. There must be a response to it from within, the interior witness of the self, ere it can be accepted as authoritative.

In the Christian and Muslim faiths—both largely influenced by Judaism—the authoritative nature of revelation is carried further than in any earlier faith. In modern days, the yoke of a revealed scripture has been much lightened for Christianity by the growth of the critical spirit and by the researches of scholars. The modern Christian student is little more hampered by his revelation than is the Hindu by his. A conventional reverence is yielded, a lifting of the hat, and then the student goes freely on his way.

What is revelation? It is communication from a Being superior to humanity of facts known to himself, but unknown to those to whom he makes the revelation—facts which they cannot reach by the exercise of the powers that they have so far evolved. These facts can be verified at any time by one who has climbed to the level of the revealer, who may be an *avatara*, a rishi, a founder of a religion.[3] They "speak with authority," the authority of knowledge, the one authority to which all sane men bow.

We do not find that these great Beings wrote down their teachings themselves. They taught, but they did not record. Some follower, some disciple, it may be after the lapse of many years, even of centuries, wrote down what he or his forefathers had heard. Hence the revelation—and to this rule there is probably no exception—is inevitably to some extent colored, narrowed, distorted by the transcriber. That which was heard originally by those round the divine teacher exists indeed in the akashic records, and may ever be recovered thence by those who have developed the inner sense by which those records may be read.[4]

In many cases, true records will have been made at the time by highly qualified persons. But such precious books are kept securely in the custody of their chosen guardians in secret temples, in rock libraries, available for the study of high occultists, but of none other.

The Muslims would claim that in the case of their sacred book there is more certainty that the very words of their Prophet were preserved. And doubtless to this is due the overwhelming authority of Al Quran in the minds of the faithful of Islam.

What should be the attitude of the Theosophical student towards revelation? He should treat the scriptures of the world with reverence, remembering their origin, but none of them with submission, remembering that they are transmitted to him by varied channels. He should call to his aid the best scholarship, should gain all the light he can from archaeological and historical researches, and use his best critical judgment in separating the essential truth revealed from all the accretions that may have grown up around it.

If he has developed his higher psychic qualities, he should try to trace and disentangle the ancient from the modern, and search the akashic records for comparison, confirmation, or contradiction of the revelation as it has come into his hands. How immense might be the services of such Theosophical students as they become more numerous and better equipped for this gigantic task. And without this external equipment, much may be done by inner unfoldment. He may unfold within himself his own spiritual powers. He may seek in profound meditation the truth which shines in the revelation beneath many a veil of ignorance and misconstruction. He may so purify his life that his bodies will become translucent to the light of the spirit within him, will illumine the written words.

"The things of God knoweth no man but the Spirit of God" [1 Cor. 2:11]. But that Spirit dwells in every child of man. And as his light shines out, the divine things are revealed to the pure in heart. Until the inner spirit thus responds to the revealed teachings and statements, the Theosophical student must hold his judgment in suspense before the claims of any revelation. It is not true *for him* until he can re-echo it in the voice of his own spirit, his deepest self. Useful and beautiful it may be. Worthy of profoundest study and reverent research are the world's bibles. But until they are affirmed by the spirit within, submission cannot be yielded, lest that should be given to the errors of men which is due only to the Divine Spirit.

What is inspiration? The raising of the normal human faculties by some extraneous influence through grade after grade of intellectual, moral, and spiritual power, up to the point where the extraneous influence may even expel the man from his body and use it for the expression of another individual. Where the new possessor is a Being at a height utterly transcending man, inspiration may pass into revelation. Some may think the word should be restricted to the raising of the powers of the subject from above their normal capacity to the highest point of their possible exercise, short of the expulsion of their owner and his replacement by another individual greater than himself.

The lower grades of inspiration are within the experience of very many. Have you never felt, when listening to a speaker whose knowledge and power transcended your own, that your mental faculties were lifted to a higher level than that to which you could rise unaided? On such occasions, you grasp questions that hitherto have eluded you. You see plainly, where before there had been obscurity. The field of thought becomes illumined, and objects are seen in hitherto undreamed-of relations—you feel that you know. On the following day, you desire to share with a friend the treasures you acquired and you begin to recount the luminous exposition, to describe the great horizons which opened before you. You fail: Where is the light, where the far-off scenes over which your eyes had swept? Your mind has sunk again to its normal level. The inspiration has passed away.

As with the intellectual, so with the moral faculties. You had seen an unknown beauty, had felt an overwhelming admiration for the lofty and the pure: What has become of the warmth, the ardor? Are the cold ashes of the intellectual approval all that remains of the throbbing heart, the passionate delight in the moral ideal? Why does it now look so cold, so gray, so unattractive? You were raised to a higher level than you can reach unassisted. But nonetheless has the moral ideal and its power been shown to you "in the Mount" [Exod. 24:15], and the fact that you have once experienced its all-compelling power will render you more susceptible to it in the future, and the day will come when that which you felt when inspired by another shall become the normal exercise of your own moral faculties.

Coming to higher grades of inspiration, we may know, some of us, what it is to stand in the presence of the Masters, and to feel the marvelous uplift of their presence. There is no need for words, no need for teaching. Their presence is enough. From that presence, we go out again into the ordinary world, to feel the difference of its atmosphere from that of the Holy One. But *we have known*, and the memory remains an abiding power.

Those who have written or spoken under inspiration have been thus uplifted—their own intellectual and moral faculties have thus been stimulated, and raised far above their normal level. It is still they who write or speak, and their own characters and temperaments color what they say, leave their own impress on what they write. But they write and speak far more nobly, far more powerfully than they could do unassisted.

And so we may rise from grade to grade of inspiration until we reach the stage at which the mind and emotions of the man no longer sway his body, but the body is wholly taken possession of and used by One greater than himself. Then it is no longer the man himself who speaks, but "the Spirit of" his "Father who speaketh in" him [Matt. 10:20]. His own limitations are struck away, his own idiosyncrasies vanish, and the inspired utterances flow forth unsullied. Then inspiration may range into revelation.

The process of all this is a very simple one. We know that, by the correlation between changes in consciousness and vibrations of matter, each change in consciousness is accompanied by a vibration of the matter appropriated by the consciousness and forming its body. Each vibration of the matter of a body is accompanied by a change in the embodied consciousness. Either one of the pair may be the initiator—the other ever responds.

When two or more people are together, one more evolved than the other or others, the more evolved person, thinking, desiring, acting, sets up in his own bodies, mental, astral, and physical, a series of vibrations which corresponds to the changes in his consciousness.

These vibrations cause similar vibrations in the mental, astral, and physical matter intervening between himself and the less advanced person or persons present. These vibrations in the intervening matter cause similar vibrations in the neighboring body or bodies. These vibrations are immediately answered by corresponding changes in the embodied consciousness or consciousnesses, and the person or persons concerned, thus placed en rapport with one more advanced, think, desire, act on a higher level than would be possible for them on their own initiative. They are able to understand more keenly, to feel more warmly, to act more nobly than they could do unassisted.

When the stimulus is removed, they gradually sink back to their normal level, but memory is left, and they remember that they "have known." Moreover, it is more easy for them to respond a second time—and so on and on, until they establish themselves on the higher level permanently. Hence the value of companionship with those more advanced than ourselves, of living "in their atmosphere." Words are not necessary. Little speech may pass. But insensibly the subtle body is tuned to a higher key—and only, perhaps, when the companionship is interrupted do the younger become conscious of the change which has thus been brought about by contact with the elder.

Similar results may be brought about by reading the writings of those who are more evolved than we are. A similar series of changes is set up, though less powerfully than by the living presence. Moreover, intent and reverent study may attract the attention of the writer, whether he be in or out of the body, and may draw him to the student, and thus cause the latter to be enveloped in his atmosphere quite as potently as though he were physically present. Hence the value of reading noble literature: we are keyed up to its level for the time, and such reading, steadily persevered in, will lift us to a higher level and establish us thereon. Hence the value of a brief reading before meditation, lifting us into an air more favorable to the work of meditation than we can start from unassisted. Hence the value also of "holy places" for such meditation, places where the atmosphere is literally vibrating at a higher rate than our own. And hence the advice so often given by the instructed to keep, if possible, a room or closet

set apart for meditation, such a place soon gaining an atmosphere purer and subtler than that of the surrounding world. It is of little use for the Theosophical student to be acquainted with these laws if he does not utilize them to his own helping, and to the helping of those around him.

What should be the attitude of the Theosophical student towards the inspired man or the inspired book? He should be receptive, stilling all his normal vibrations so far as is possible, and opening his whole nature to the impact and influx of the waves of vibration that pour forth upon him. But his attitude should be more than receptive: he should gently endeavor to attune himself and to cooperate with the inflowing waves. He should try to strengthen the sympathetic vibrations, so that the accompanying changes in consciousness may be as complete as possible. For this, he must pour out to the inspiring object his love, his trust, his complete confidence and self-surrender, for thus only can he attune his bodies into sympathy with those of the inspirer. He must, for the time, empty himself of his own ideas, his own feelings, his own activities, surrendering himself to reproduce, not to initiate.

As the unruffled lake can mirror the moon and the stars, but as that same lake rippled by a passing breeze can yield only broken reflections, so may the lower being, steadying his mind, calming his desires, and imposing stillness on his activities, reproduce within himself the image of the higher; so may the disciples mirror the Master's mind. And so, also, if his own thoughts spring up, his own desires arise, will he have but broken reflections, dancing lights, that tell him nought.[5]

If you are going to read one of the inspired books of the world—*The Imitation of Christ, The Golden Verses of Pythagoras, Light on the Path, The Voice of the Silence*[6]—it is well to preface the reading with a prayer, if that be your habitual way of raising your consciousness to its highest mood, or with the repetition of a mantra, or the soft chanting of some familiar and beloved rhythm, in order to bring yourself into a sympathetic condition. Then read a phrase, reread, brood over it, savor it mentally, suck out its essence, its life.

Thus shall your subtle body become, to some extent at least, attuned to that of the inspired writer, and repeating his vibrations, shall set up in your consciousness the corresponding changes. Priceless is the value of inspired books: they are steps of a ladder set up between earth and heaven—a veritable Jacob's ladder, on which descend and ascend the angels of God [Gen. 28:12].

There remains a third class of books worthy of the attention of the Theosophical student, but towards which his attitude should be entirely different from those which he adopts towards the revealed and the inspired. These are books containing the observations of students more advanced than himself, observations made by students who are evolving in knowledge of, and in power on, those planes, and have not yet reached the stature of the perfect man.

There are books such as *The Secret Doctrine* and *Esoteric Buddhism*, written by disciples, which are not records of the direct observations of students, but are rather transcriptions of the teachings of Masters, into which errors may creep by misunderstanding of those teachings. H. P. Blavatsky herself told us that there were inevitably errors in *The Secret Doctrine*. And as we have in that wonderful book her own descriptions of the pictures shown to her by her Master, there is an opening for possible errors of observation; these are probably not serious, as she was carefully overlooked and aided during the writing.[7]

These two books stand apart from the bulk of our literature, the Masters having been largely concerned in their production. The books I have in mind are those written by disciples, using their own normal faculties, faculties still in course of evolution: books relating chiefly to the astral, mental, and buddhic planes, to the constitution of man, to the past of individuals, nations, races, and worlds. We are gradually accumulating a large amount of literature of this kind—a literature of observations by students using superphysical faculties. With regard to this, certain things need to be borne in mind.

First: the students in question are in course of evolution, and the faculties of which they make use today, which have become their normal faculties, are more developed and reach higher planes than those which they used ten or fifteen years ago. Hence they see now very much more than they saw then, both in quantity and quality, and this enlarged sight must inevitably give reports differing in fullness from that of the earlier and narrower vision.

Secondly: this greater fullness will change relative proportions and perspective. A thing which seemed imposing and independent when seen alone may become subordinate and comparatively insignificant when seen as a part of a larger whole. It may change form and color, seen with surroundings which become visible only when it is looked at with a higher vision. That which was a globe, sailing through space, to the physical eye, becomes the free end of a continuous body, materially attached to the sun, when seen with superphysical sight. Was it false to describe it a globe? Yes, and no. It was and is a globe on the physical plane, answering to all that is meant by a globe down here. In subtler regions, it is not a globe, but a body, the tip of which is a globe only to gross vision—vision to which its continuation is invisible.[8]

Thirdly: the keener vision detects intermediate stages before unseen, and shows a series of changes between two which, to the less acute sight, were in immediate sequence. Thus, in the earlier observations, it was said that the ultimate physical atom broke up into astral matter. When a similar phenomenon is studied twelve years later, it is seen that the physical atom breaks up into an immense number of inconceivably minute particles, and that these immediately group themselves into forty-nine astral atoms, which may or may not, again, combine into astral molecules.[9]

Again, a whirling wall was mentioned: keener vision sees no wall, but an illusory enclosure, caused by rapid motion, like the fiery circle traced by a whirling fire-tipped stick.[10] So, in the continuous light of gas or electricity, a whirling disk of black and white rays shows gray. Put out the lights, and let the darkness be rent by a lightning flash, the disk hangs motionless, every black and white ray distinct. Which is the true observation? The eye in each case bears true witness to what it *sees*. The different conditions impose upon it different visions.

Other differences also arise, but these may serve as samples. Are, then, books relating to observations useless? They become useless, even mischievous, only when the Theosophical student treats them as revelations or inspirations instead of as observations.

Observation is the basis of scientific knowledge. The correction of earlier observations by later ones is the condition of scientific progress. The student of optics, when confronted with the black-and-white rayed disk, the gray disk, the whirling disk hanging motionless, does not conclude that the conflicting observations make observations useless. He searches for and finds the conditions of light, of the constitution of the eye, which explain the equally true, though contradictory, reports. He submits the observations to renewed experiment and to the scrutiny of reason, until from the contradictions emerges the many-sided truth.

What should be the attitude of the Theosophical student to books of observations? To all such books you must take up the attitude of the scientific student, not of the believer. You must bring to bear upon them a bright intelligence, a keen mind, an eager intellect, a thoughtful and critical reason. You must not accept as final, observations made by other students, even though those students are using faculties which you yourselves have not as yet developed. You should accept them only for what they are—observations liable to modification, to correction, to reviewal. You should hold them with a light grasp, as hypotheses temporarily accepted until confirmed or negated by further observations, including your own. If they illuminate obscurities, if they conduce to sound morality, take them and use them. But never let them become fetters to your mind, jailers of your thought.

Study these books, but do not swallow them. Understand them, but hold your judgment in suspense: These books are useful servants, but dangerous masters. They are to be studied, not worshiped. Make your own opinions; do not borrow those of others. Do not be in such a hurry to know that you accept other people's knowledge, for readymade opinions, like readymade clothes, are neither well-fitting nor becoming.

There is a dangerous tendency in the Theosophical Society to make books of observations authoritative instead of using them as materials for study. We must not add to the number of blind believers who already exist, but to the number of sane and sober students who patiently form their own opinions and educate their own faculties.

Use your own judgment on every observation submitted to you. Examine it as thoroughly as possible. Criticize it as fully as you can. It is a poor service you do us when you turn students into popes, and, parrot-like, repeat as authoritative, statements that you do not know to be true. Moreover, blind belief is the road to equally blind skepticism: You place a student on a pedestal and loudly proclaim him to be a prophet, despite his protests. And then, when you find he has made some mistake, as he warned you was likely, you turn round, pull him down, and trample on him. You belabor him when you should belabor your own blindness, your own stupidity, your own anxiety to believe.

Is it not time that we should cease to be children, and begin to be men and women, realizing the greatness of our opportunities and the smallness of our achievements? Is it not time to offer to truth the homage of study instead of that of blind credulity? Let us ever be ready to correct a mistaken impression or an imperfect observation, to walk with open eyes and mind alert, remembering that the best service to truth is examination. Truth is a sun, shining by its own light. Once seen, it cannot be rejected. "Let truth and falsehood grapple; who ever knew truth put to the worse in a fair encounter?"[11]

Part Four

SCIENCE OF THE SUPERPHYSICAL

Chapter Fourteen

Theosophy as Science (1912)

The old way of study was to state universals, and to descend from them to particulars, and it remains the best way for serious and philosophic students. The modern way is to begin with particulars, and to ascend from them to universals. For the modern reader who has not yet made up his mind to a serious study of a subject, this is the easier road, for it keeps the most difficult part for the last. As this little book is meant for the general reader, I follow this way.

Theosophy accepts the *method* of science—observation, experiment, arrangement of ascertained facts, induction, hypothesis, deduction, verification, assertion of the discovered truth—but immensely increases its *area*. It sees the sum of existence as containing but two factors: life and form; or, as some call them, spirit and matter, others time and space—for spirit is God's motion, while matter is His stillness. Both find their union in Him, since the root of spirit is His life, and the root of matter is the universal aether, the two aspects of the One Eternal, out of space and time.[1]

While ordinary science confines matter to the tangible, Theosophical science extends it through many grades, intangible to the physical, but tangible to the superphysical senses. It has observed that the condition of knowing the physical universe is the possession of a physical body, of which certain parts have been evolved into organs of sense [indriyas]—eyes, ears, et cetera—through which perception of outside objects is possible. And other parts have been evolved into organs of action [karmendriyas]—hands, feet, and the rest—through which contact with outside objects can be obtained. It sees that, in the past, physical evolution has been brought about by the efforts of life to use its nascent powers, and that the struggle to exercise an inborn faculty has slowly shaped matter into an organ through which that faculty can be more fully exercised.

To reverse Buchner's statement: We do not walk because we have legs; we have legs because we wanted to move.[2] We can trace the growth of legs from the temporary pseudopodia of the amoeba, through the development of permanent protrusions from bodies, up to the legs of man—and they were all gradually formed by the efforts of the living creature to move. As W. K. Clifford said of the huge saurians of a past age, "Some *wanted* to fly, and they became birds."[3] The "will to live"—that is, to desire, to think, to act—lies behind all evolution.

The Theosophist carries on the same principle into higher realms, if such exist. And if consciousness is to know any other sphere[4] than the physical, it must have a body of matter belonging to the sphere it wants to investigate—and the body must have senses, developed by the same want [desire] of the life to see, to hear, et cetera. That there should be other spheres, and other bodies through which those spheres can be known, is no more inherently incredible than that there is a physical sphere, and that there are physical bodies through which we know it. The occultist—the student of the workings of the divine mind in nature—asserts that there are such spheres, and that he has, and uses, such bodies.

The following statements—with one exception which will be noted in its place—are made as results of investigations carried on in such spheres by the use of such bodies by the writer and other occultists. We all received the outline from highly developed members of our humanity,[5] and have proved it true, step by step, and have filled in many gaps, by our own researches. We, therefore, feel that we have a right to affirm, on our own firsthand experience—stretching over a period of twenty-three years in one case, and twenty-five in another[6]—that superphysical research is practicable, and is as trustworthy as physical research, and should be carried on in similar ways; that investigators are subject to errors, both in physical and superphysical spheres, and for similar reasons; and that these errors should lead to closer research and not to its discontinuance.

A Table of Correspondences

The following table [diagram 2] presents a view of the spheres related to and including our earth, of the bodies used in investigating them, and of the states of consciousness manifested through them by their owner, the [eternal] man. The eternal man, a fragment of the life of God, is called the monad, a "oneness,"[7] he is verily a son of God, made in His image, and expressing his life in three ways: by the aspect of will, the aspect of wisdom, the aspect of creative activity. He lives in his own sphere, a spark *in* the divine fire, and sends down a ray, a current of his life, which embodies itself in the five spheres of manifestation.[8]

This ray, appropriating an atom of matter from each of the three higher of these spheres,[9] appears as the human spirit [atma-buddhi-manas], reproducing the three aspects of the monad—of will, wisdom, and creative activity—and reveals himself, at a certain stage of evolution, as the human ego, the individualized self. He begins his long journey as a mere seed of life, and, *never losing his identity*, moves through that long journey, unfolding all the powers of the monad that lie hidden within him, as the tree within the seed.

As he conquers his kingdom of matter, his parent monad pours down into him more and more life, and draws from him more and more knowledge of the worlds in which he lives. But the passing into the three highest manifested spheres [atmic, buddhic, manasic] is not enough for gaining full knowledge and full power in our solar system. Two yet remain [kamic, or astral, and physical]—and the process of dipping down into matter goes on.

The spirit strengthens himself for his work by appropriating a molecule of the coarser matter of the lowest sphere he has so far entered, and links on to this an atom from the fourth manifested sphere of denser matter [kamic or astral], and one from the fifth, the lowest, our physical sphere. He is to obtain bodies, formed round these permanently appropriated particles of matter, by which he may be able to know and act upon the five manifested spheres.

We shall see that his lower bodies, forming what is called his personality, are cast off at and after what we call death, and are

Diagram 2[10]

	Spheres	Beings		States of Consciousness	Bodies
Unmanifested	1. Divine (adi or maha-parinirvana)	Logos		Divine triplicity*	....
	2. Monadic (anupadaka or parinirvana)	Human monad		Monadic triplicity† (will, wisdom, activity)	....
Manifested (arupa)	3. Spiritual (nirvanic or atmic)	Man who is	An immortal individuality	Spirit individualized as will (atman)	Atmic
	4. Intuitional (buddhic)	Man who is		Spirit individualized as intuition (atma-buddhi)	Intuitional (buddhic)
	5a. Mental (upper)	Man who is		Spirit individualized as intellect (atma-buddhi-manas)	Causal

Manifested (rupa)	5b. Mental (lower)	Man who has	A mortal personality	Mind (kama-manas)	Mental
	6. Astral or emotional (kamic)	Man who has		Emotions (kama)	Astral
	7. Physical	Man who has		Vitality (prana) a. Energizing vitality–works through etheric double (i.e., linga sharira), composed of four physical ethers b. Automatic vitality–works through dense body (i.e., sthula sharira), composed of solids, liquids, and gases‡	Physical

* The Trinities of religions—the three Persons of Christianity—as manifested in a solar system. They appear three by difference of function, seen from below. The whole solar system may be called the body of the Logos, and the sun His physical body, but they only embody a fragment of Him.

† Man "made in the image of God" [Gen. 1:27]. His aspects, will, wisdom, and activity—or power, knowledge-love, and creativeness—are shown in the embodied reproduction of himself, as will, intuition, and intellect.

‡ Seven subdivisions of matter make up the physical sphere, named from below upwards: solid, liquid, gaseous, etheric, superetheric, subatomic, atomic.

renewed for each successive birth. While the higher, forming his individuality, remain through this long pilgrimage—an important fact as bearing on the possibility of remembering the past. The above facts are tabulated in diagram 2.

It may be asked, "What is the object of this descent into matter? What does the monad gain by it?" Omniscient in his own sphere, he is blinded by matter in the spheres of manifestation, being unable to respond to their vibrations. As a man who cannot swim, flung into deep water, is drowned, but can learn to move freely in it, so with the monad. At the end of his pilgrimage, he will be free of the solar system, able to function in any part of it—to create at will, to move at pleasure. Every power that he unfolds through denser matter, he retains forever under all conditions. The implicit has become explicit, the potential the actual. It is his own will to live in all spheres, and not only in one, that draws him into manifestation.

The Physical Body

The actual unfolding of consciousness is best traced from below, for the physical body is the one which is first organized as its instrument for knowledge, and it unfolds itself by this in the physical world we know. The emotional nature stimulates the glands and ganglia of the physical body, and the mental enthrones itself over the cerebrospinal system, and these proceed with their evolution in the invisible spheres through the stimulus obtained from the physical. We need not dwell on the evolution of the dense physical body, as that may be studied as physical science. Human consciousness is here automatic—the [eternal] man having no longer need to direct physical processes. They go on by habit, the result of long pressure from consciousness.

The finer part of the physical body, the etheric double, permeates the dense, and extends a little beyond it over the whole surface. Its proper sense organs are vortices on its own surface, situated opposite: 1) the top of the head; 2) the point between the eyebrows; 3) the throat; 4) the heart; 5) the spleen; 6) the solar plexus; 7) the base of the spine; 8, 9, and 10 [are located] in the lower part of the pelvic basin. These last are not used, except in black magic.[11]

These vortices—technically called chakras (wheels, from their appearance)—are aroused into activity in the course of occult training, and form a bridge between the physical and astral spheres, so that the latter comes to be included within the activity of the waking consciousness. The health of its dense partner depends on the vitality [prana] in the etheric double, which draws its energy directly from the sun—and, in the part in contact with the spleen, divides this energy into streams, which it conveys to the different organs of the dense body. The surplusage radiates outwards and energizes all living creatures within its range. The very neighborhood of a vigorously healthy person vitalizes, while a weak body draws on all around it for vitality, often seriously depleting those near to it. Physical magnetism, the power of healing, et cetera, are ways in which this surplus vitality may be usefully expended.

Etheric vision—physical vision keener than the normal—may be used for examining minute objects, such as chemical atoms, or for studying such of the nature spirits as use etheric matter for their lowest bodies: fairies, gnomes, brownies, and creatures of that ilk.[12] Very slightly increased tenseness of the nerves, caused by excitement, ill-health, alcohol, may bring these within sight.

The etheric part of the brain plays an active part in dreams, especially in those caused by impressions from outside, or from any internal pressure from the cerebral vessels. Its dreams are usually dramatic, and may embroider any memory of past events, objects, or persons.[13]

In normal healthy persons the etheric part of the physical body does not separate from the dense, but the greater part of it may be driven out by anesthetics, and slips out easily in the case of persons who are mediumistic, often serving as the basis for materializations.

Death is the complete withdrawal [of the etheric double] from its dense counterpart, in conjunction with the consciousness in the higher bodies. It remains with these for a varying interval—usually about thirty-six hours after death—and then is thrown off by the [eternal] man as of no further use. It decays away pari passu with the dense corpse.

Chapter Fourteen

The Emotional or Astral Sphere—Its Worlds and Its Inhabitants

The astral sphere connected with our earth contains (1) two globes with which we need not here concern ourselves; (2) also the astral world and its inhabitants; and (3) the intermediate or desire world, a part of the astral, the inhabitants of which are normally under special conditions.[14] The whole sphere belongs to the state of consciousness which shows itself as feelings, desires, and emotions. These changes in consciousness are accompanied with vibrations in astral matter. And, as astral matter is fine and very rapid in its vibratory motions, the vibrations are visible to astral sight as colors. The passion of anger causes vibrations that yield a flash of scarlet, while a feeling of devotion or love suffuses the astral body with a blue or rosy hue. Each feeling has its appropriate color, because each is accompanied by its own invariable set of vibrations.[15]

The human astral body is, of course, composed of astral matter. And, when accompanying the physical body—which it permeates and beyond which it extends—it appears as a cloud, or as a defined oval, according as its owner is little or much developed. Clearness and brightness of the more delicate colors, increased definiteness of form, and increase of size mark the higher evolution. When the [eternal] man in his higher bodies draws away from the physical—as he does every night in sleep—then the astral body assumes the likeness of the physical. Astral matter being very plastic under the influence of thought, a man appears in the astral world in the likeness of himself—as he sees himself, wearing the clothes of which he thinks. A soldier, slain in battle and appearing in his astral body to a distant friend, will bear his wounds. A drowned man will appear in dripping clothes.

While human beings in the astral world normally wear human forms, the inhabitants of that world who have not had physical bodies—higher fairies, nature spirits connected with the evolution of plant and animal life, and the like—wear bodies that are constantly changing their outlines and sizes. Sportive elementals—as nature spirits are often called—will sometimes take advantage of this plasticity of astral matter to swell themselves up into huge and terrible shapes for the sake of terrifying untrained intruders into their world. Some drugs, such as hashish, bhang,[16] opium, and extreme alcoholic poisoning, so affect the physical nerves as to render them susceptible to astral vibrations—and then the patients catch a glimpse of some inhabitants of the astral world. The horrors which torment a man suffering from delirium tremens are largely due to the sight of the loathsome elementals that gather round places where liquor is sold, and feed on its exhalations, and are attracted round him by the effluvia of his own drink-sodden body.

All feelings of pleasure and pain in the physical body are due to the presence of the interpenetrating astral, and, if this be driven out by anesthetics or mesmerism, feeling disappears from the physical body. In sleep—during which the etheric double does not leave its dense counterpart—the astral can be very quickly recalled by any disturbance of the physical body. But where much of the etheric matter has also been driven out, the bridge of communication [between astral and physical] is broken, and [hypnotic or mesmeric] trance is produced. Under these conditions [which include anesthesia], the dense body can be seriously mutilated without pain supervening. Pain will, however, show itself as soon as the astral body slips again into the physical and "consciousness returns."[17]

It may be said, in passing, that the normal center of human consciousness at the present stage of evolution is in the astral body, from which it works on the physical. "Physical consciousness" is now subconscious—if such a bull may be permitted to an Irishwoman.[18]

The condition of a person during sleep varies with his stage of evolution. The undeveloped man, in his higher bodies, leaving the physical body, hovers round the places with which he is familiar. The average man drifts towards persons to whom he is attracted, but his attention is turned inwards, and he communes with his friends only mentally.[19] At a stage a little higher, his mind is very active and receptive, and can work out problems presented to it more easily than in the physical body—as witness the common sayings "sleep brings counsel," "better sleep on it," and the like. A problem quietly placed in the mind on going to sleep will generally be found answered in the morning.

These people do not all work consciously in the astral world. For this, it is necessary that the attention should be turned outwards, not inwards. Where a man is pure and self-controlled, and shows helpfulness in the physical world, he is often "awakened" in the astral world by a more advanced person. The process consists merely in inducing him to attend to what is going on around him, instead of remaining immersed in thought. His astral body has evolved and has become organized by his mental and moral activities, and he has only to wake up to his astral surroundings.

His helper explains matters to him, and for a time keeps him near him. He shows him that astral matter obeys his thought; that he can move at will and at whatever speed he wishes; that he can walk through rocks, dive into seas, pass through raging fires, step over a precipice and hover in air—always provided that he is fearless and confident. If he loses courage, and only then, he is in danger, and the imagined injury may "repercuss," i.e., show itself on the physical body as a bruise, a scratch, a wound, et cetera.[20]

When he has learned these preliminary lessons, and can see and hear correctly in the astral world, he is set to work to help the "living" and the "dead." He is then what we call "an invisible helper," and spends his night in succoring those in trouble, teaching the ignorant, guiding those who have newly arrived in the astral world through the gateway of death. To these last we must now turn.

The Desire World, or Purgatory

This is the part of the astral world in which conditions are specialized for discarnate human beings—who, unless they have knowledge, are not free in the astral world, but are "the spirits in prison" spoken of by St. Peter [1 Peter 3:19]. They are held prisoners by their desires [kama], and hence the name of *desire world* [Kamaloka] is given to their abode.

We have seen that, at death, the [eternal] man, clothed in his finer bodies, draws himself out of the physical garment worn during earth life—the "coat of skin" [Gen. 3:21] with which "the first man" was clothed after his "fall" into matter, caused by his seizure of "knowledge." "Which things are an allegory," as St. Paul says of the story of Abraham, Sarah, and Hagar [Gal. 4:22–24].[21] Having cast off his coat of skin, the [eternal] man is himself, just as he was while clothed with it, and he "goes to his own place" [Acts 1:25] in the astral world, the place for which he has fitted himself.[22] A rearrangement of the matter of his astral body takes place automatically, unless he has knowledge enough to prevent it.[23]

During the life of the physical body, the astral particles from all the seven astral subdivisions of matter move freely about among themselves, and some of all kinds are always on the surface of the astral body. Sight of the whole astral world depends on the presence on the surface of the astral body of particles drawn from all the seven subdivisions, which answer to our solids, liquids, gases, and the four states of ether.[24]

These particles are not gathered together and fashioned into an organ of vision, like the physical eye. When the [eternal] man turns his attention outwards, he sees "all over him," through all these particles—or through such of them as are in the direction of the object towards which his attention is turned.[25] If the rearrangement of the matter of the astral body takes place, the matter of each subdivision is gathered together, and a series of concentric shells is formed, the densest being outside. Hence the [eternal] man can see only the subdivision of the astral world to which the outermost shell belongs.

The amount of each kind of matter depends on the kind of desires and emotions he has cultivated on earth. If these have been of a low order, the densest astral matter will be very strongly vitalized, and this outermost shell, placing him in touch with the lowest subdivision of the astral world only, will last for a long time. It disintegrates by slow starvation—i.e., by the deprivation of its accustomed satisfactions. Hence a drunkard, a glutton, a sensualist, a man of violent and brutal passions, having strongly vitalized by physical indulgence the densest and coarsest combinations of astral matter, can be conscious of his surroundings only through these, and sees only people like himself, and the worst qualities of those who are of better types. His raging passions can find no satisfaction, because he has lost the physical organs by which he erstwhile gratified them.

Moreover, these passions are much more violent than before. For, during his physical life, most of the force of the astral vibrations was used up in merely setting in motion the heavy physical particles of matter, and only what was left over was felt as pleasure or pain. Hence all passions are pale and weak on earth compared with their violence in the astral world—where, after easily setting in motion the light astral particles, they show the whole remainder of their force as pleasure or pain, as a rapture or an agony inconceivable on earth. This last is what religions call "hell"—and a veritable hell, as to suffering, it is—created by the man for his own dwelling place. But it is only temporary, and might more fitly therefore, for orthodox Christians and Muslims, be called "purgatory."[26] The thick layer of densest matter wears away, and the man loses sight of this sphere of astral life and begins to perceive the next, having learned, by the sad lesson of bitter suffering, that the pleasures he valued on earth are verily "wombs of pain" [Bhagavad Gita 5.22].

The average man does not experience this unfortunate after-death condition, not having drawn into his astral body while on earth much of the densest matter. And such of it as he has is not strongly vitalized, and it cannot hold him. If his interests on earth have all been trivial—a round of office or household drudgery or manual labor, alternating with low, though not vicious, forms of amusement—and he has cared nothing for larger interests (those of the community and the nation), he will find himself shelled in by matter of the sixth subdivision of the astral world, and will be surrounded by the astral counterparts of physical objects, without the power to affect them or to take part in the earth life led among them.[27] He will, therefore, to use a colloquialism, find himself very much bored, and be a prey to an intolerable sense of ennui.

It may be said that this is hard, as most people have to spend their lives in drudgery of some kind. Are they to be bored after death, having drudged before? True. But a little knowledge will prevent this—and for this very reason Theosophy is being spread far and wide. The work which carries on the world need not be drudgery, and to deeply religious people is not drudgery even now. For all useful work is part of the divine activity, and all workers are organs of that activity—

the hands wherewith the Divine Worker accomplishes His work. Production and distribution (agriculture, mining, manufactures, commerce, the pettiest trade) are God's ways of nourishing humanity, and are the means of evolution. When a man, a woman, see their little daily tasks as integral portions of the one great work, they are no longer drudges but coworkers with God. As George Herbert sang,

> A servant in this cause
> Makes drudgery divine:
> Who sweeps a room as for Thy laws
> Makes that and th'action fine.[28]

Those who thus work will find no boredom after death, but fresh and joyous activity. For the rest, they gradually adapt themselves to the new conditions, and are helped to do so, and they find that they are rid of many of the discomforts of earth, and may lead a quite pleasant life. They are in touch with their friends on earth, and find that these are quite companionable during earth's nights, though provokingly indifferent during its days. As Mr. Leadbeater pithily says, "The dead are never for a moment under the impression that they have lost the living," however much the latter lament the loss of the dead they loved.[29]

The man passes on through the sixth, fifth, and fourth subdivisions, enjoying more and more association with those he loves, until he passes into the higher subdivisions—the material heavens of the less instructed religionists of all faiths; the region for art, literature, science, philanthropy, and the large interests of life, followed on earth with some selfishness, and here pursued along the habitual lines and with the use of astral reproductions of physical means and apparatus. These same pursuits, carried on for unselfish motives, lift the [eternal] man into the heaven world, their proper home—and thither also those who followed them more selfishly pass, for when they are weary of them in the astral world, they fall asleep, to wake in heaven.

The astral body has been cast off, shell after shell, and in due time goes back to its elements, like the physical. Some pure and lofty souls pass through the astral world without attending to it, their minds set upon higher things. Others, fully awake, do not allow the matter of their astral bodies to be rearranged, but retain their freedom and perform useful service. Omitting this last class, whose stay in the astral world will depend on other causes, the general rule is that the astral after-death life is long for the undeveloped and short for the well-developed—while the heavenly is long for the latter and short for the former.

The Mental Sphere, Its Worlds and Inhabitants

The mental sphere connected with our earth contains (1) two globes with which we are not now concerned; (2) two worlds, the higher and lower, each with its inhabitants; and (3) a part of the lower placed under special conditions, for the use of discarnate human beings—the heaven world.[30] The whole sphere belongs to the state of consciousness-denominated thought, or mental activity, and its matter answers to the changes in consciousness that are caused by thinking. Its seven subdivisions, though so much finer, again correspond to those of the physical and astral worlds.

And the mental world is, like the physical, divided into two, a lower and an upper—the former consisting of the four denser subdivisions, and the latter of the three subtler. Two bodies belong to it: the mental, composed of combinations of the denser; and the causal, composed of those of the finer. This world is of peculiar interest, not only because man spends here nearly all his time, after the mind is fairly developed, only dipping down into the physical world for brief snatches of mortal life as a bird dives into the sea after a fish, but because it is the meeting place of the higher and the lower consciousnesses.

The immortal individuality [atma-buddhi-manas], descending from above—after the monad [atman] has formed the spirit [atma-buddhi] by sending out his ray—waits in high heaven while the lower bodies are being formed round atoms attached to him, brooding over them through long ages of slow evolution. When they are sufficiently evolved, he flashes down and takes possession of them, to use them for his own evolution.[31]

The habitat of the spirit as intellect [buddhi-manas]—of him "whose nature is knowledge" [Prashna Upanishad 4.9]—is the causal world, the three higher levels of the mental sphere. These give him his body, the causal—the body which remains, ever evolving, throughout his long series of incarnations in denser matter. This world and body are so named because all the causes, the effects of which are seen in the lower worlds, reside in them.

The causal body begins, with the above-named flashing down, as a mere film of matter, egg-shaped, like a shell round the lower bodies formed within it, as the chick in the egg.[32] The delicate network radiates from the permanent atom of the causal body to all parts of this egg-like film, the atom glowing like a brilliant nucleus. With it are associated the permanent atoms of the physical and astral bodies and the permanent molecule-unit of the mental [body].[33] During life, it encloses the whole bodies, and at the death of each, it preserves this permanent germ of each, with all the vibratory powers enshrined within it—the "seed of life" for each successive body. For ages, it is little more than this subtle network and surface, for it can grow only by the higher human activities, by such as arouse in its subtle matter a faint vibratory response. As the personality grows more thoughtful, more unselfish, more engaged in right activities, its harvest for its owner grows richer and richer.

The personalities are like the leaves put forth by a tree. They draw in material from outside, transform it into useful substances, send it down the tree as crude sap, drop off, and wither. The sap is changed into tree food and nourishes the tree, which sends out new leaves to repeat the same cycle. The consciousness in the mental, astral, and physical bodies gathers experience. Casting off the physical and astral bodies as dead leaves, it transmutes these experiences into qualities in the mental body, during its heavenly life. It is indrawn into the causal body with its harvest, casting away the mental body, like the others, and is blended with the spirit, who puts it forth, enriching him with its harvest. It has served the spirit as a hand put forth to take food.

The enriched spirit, the [eternal] man, forms round the old permanent atoms another mental and astral body, capable of manifesting his enhanced qualities. The physical permanent atom is planted, through the father, in the body of the mother, who is to provide the physical body required by the changeless law of cause and effect—and these three lower bodies are nourished and colored by her corresponding bodies. The new personality is thus launched into the mortal world.

While intellect [buddhi-manas] has as its vehicle the causal body, its copy in denser matter, the mind, has the mental body as its instrument. The one has abstract thinking as its activity, the other concrete.

The mind [kama-manas] acquires knowledge by utilizing the sense for observations, its precepts, and by working on these and building them into concepts. Its powers are attention, memory, reasoning by induction and deduction, imagination, and the like.

The intellect *knows*, by the assonance of the outside world with its own nature, and its power is creation, the arrangement of matter into bodies for its own natural products, ideas. When it sends a flash into the lower mind, illuminating its concepts and inspiring its imagination, we call the flash genius.

Both the causal and mental bodies expand enormously in the later stages of evolution, and manifest the most gorgeous radiance of many-colored lights, glowing with intense splendor when comparatively at rest, and sending forth the most dazzling coruscations when in high activity. Both interpenetrate the lower bodies and extend beyond their surface, as has already been stated with regard to the etheric double and the astral body. The parts of all these bodies of finer matter which are outside the dense physical body form collectively the "aura" of the human being, the luminous, colored cloud surrounding his dense body.

The etheric portion of the aura can be seen by Dr. Kilner's apparatus.[34] An ordinary clairvoyant usually sees this and the astral portion. A clairvoyant more highly developed sees the etheric, astral, and mental portions. Few are able to see the portion consisting of the causal body, and fewer still the rare beauty of the intuitional [buddhic], and the dazzling light of the spiritual [atmic] vehicles.

The clarity and delicacy and brilliance of the auric colors, or their opacity, coarseness, and dullness, show the general stage of advancement of the owner. Changes of emotion suffuse the astral portion with transitory colors—as with the rose of love, the blue of devotion, the gray of fear, the brown of brutality, the sickly green of jealousy. The pure yellow of intelligence, the orange of pride, the brilliant green of mental sympathy and alertness, are equally familiar. Striations, bands, streaks, flashes, et cetera, give a multiplicity of forms for study, all expressive of certain qualities in the mental and moral character. The child's aura, again, differs much from that of the adult. But we must pass on, as space is limited.

The mind, working in the mental body, produces results—thoughts—in the astral and physical bodies—in the latter, by using as its instrument the cerebrospinal system. In its own world, it sends out definite "thought forms," thoughts embodied in mental matter, which go forth into the mental world and may incorporate themselves in other mental bodies. Its own vibrations, also, send out undulations in all directions that cause similar vibrations in others.

Comparatively few people, at the present stage of evolution, can function freely in the mental world, clothed only in the higher and the mental bodies, separated from the physical and astral. But those who can do so can tell about its phenomena—an important matter, since heaven[35] is part of the mental world, guarded from all unpleasant intrusions. The inhabitants of the world are the higher ranks of the nature spirits, called, in the East, *Devas*, or "Shining Ones," and by the Christians, Hebrews, and Muslims, angels—the lowest order of angelic intelligences. They are glowing forms with changing shades of exquisite colors, whose language is color, whose motion is melody.

The Heaven World

The heaven portion of the mental world is filled with discarnate human beings who work out into mental and moral powers the good experiences they have garnered in their earthly lives. Here, the religious devotee is seen, rapt in adoring contemplation of the divine form he loved on earth—for God reveals Himself in any form dear to the human heart. Here, the musician fills the air with melodious sounds, cultivating his capacity into higher power. Here, all that love are in close touch with their beloved, and love gains new strength and depth by fullest expression. Here, the artists of form and color work out splendid conceptions in plastic material, responsive to their thought. Here, philanthropists shape great schemes for human helping, architects of plans to be wrought out when they return to earth.

Every high activity followed on earth, every noble thought and aspiration, here grow into flowers—flowers which contain within themselves the seeds which shall later be sown on earth. Knowing this, men may in this world prepare the seeds of experience which shall flower in heaven.

The cultivation of every literary and artistic faculty, of patient and steadfast love, of unselfish service to man, of devotion to God, make a full and rich and fruitful heaven. Those who sow sparingly reap sparingly. While everyone's cup of happiness will be filled to overflowing [there], we make our cups large or small here. The length of our heaven depends on the materials we can carry through death, and these materials are good thoughts and pure emotions. It may stretch to fifteen hundred or two thousand years. It may be but a few centuries—in the very little developed, even less.

When the whole of the experience has been worked up into faculty, the [eternal] man casts off his mental body, and is then truly himself, living in the causal and the two higher bodies. If highly developed, he may live awhile in the higher levels of the mental worlds. Generally, his stay there is very brief—only sufficient to allow him to see his whole past and to glance over his coming life, and he quickly begins to put himself down again, driven by hunger for more experience. The germs of the developed mental faculties are planted in mental matter, to form a new mental body; those of the developed emotional and moral faculties in astral matter, to form a new astral body—and these are the "innate faculties," the "character," which the child brings with him into the world.

The Higher Spheres

The two higher spheres—the intuitional [buddhic], in which the Christ nature unfolds in man, and the spiritual [atmic]—cannot be here fully described. The intuition, the clear insight into the nature of things—that sees the One Self in all and destroys the sense of separateness—

is the faculty of the wisdom-nature: the supreme spiritual *vision*, for which nature has "no veil in all her kingdoms" [*VS* 14]. The spiritual sphere, in which the unity of the human will with the Divine is realized, is the last and highest in the at present manifested system—the monadic and the divine spheres being, as yet, unmanifested.

The wheel of normal human evolution revolves in the three worlds—the physical, the intermediate, and the heavenly. In the first, we gather experience. In the second, we suffer and enjoy according to our life in the first. In the third, we enjoy unalloyed happiness, and transmute experience into faculty, past suffering into power. These we bring back—and thus we grow and evolve, age after age.

Each stage of this aeonian evolution may be studied by quickening the unfolding of the consciousness, and the growth of the bodies belonging to the different worlds. No statement made in this section need be taken on trust—save that about the monad. But the study which enables verification to be fully made is as arduous as that of the highest mathematics or astronomy. A slight development beyond the normal will, however, enable etheric and astral facts to be examined—and such experience may encourage the student to pursue the further task.

Chapter Fifteen

Investigations into the Superphysical (1912)

As evolution steadily carries on the mass of humanity, the crest of its wave must ever be advancing towards new and hitherto unexplored—or only partially explored—regions. Great religious teachers have laid down certain doctrines, far-reaching in their consequences, drawn from a knowledge of superphysical worlds, and their followers have accepted these doctrines on faith, since they were incapable of acquiring for themselves the knowledge of the facts on which they were based. The doctrines of reincarnation and karma, of man's immortality, of the existence of superphysical worlds and their inhabitants—all these recommended themselves to the reason. Anyone of fair intelligence could grasp them, but their claim to acceptance rested more on authority than on proof.

Reincarnation, for instance, may be shown to be the most reasonable hypothesis for man's continual life, but it cannot be demonstrated as a fact—any more than can evolution itself. Karma may be shown to be in harmony with law as we know it, but we can see in our world only a fragment of its huge sweep, insufficient for clear and definite proof. Reason demands data on which to found its judgments, and data in the nonphysical worlds are useless to a mind limited to the workings of the brain and nervous system.

Intuition is sufficient for the person in whom its light is burning, but that light is useful only to its possessor. Intuition in A cannot satisfy the demand of the reason in B for proofs, and no firm edifice can be built on the foundation of another's intuition. Hence, in an age when the concrete mind has grown powerful and little willing to yield to authority, religion has found itself in parlous case. But the progress of evolution is beginning to come to its aid by unfolding in many the powers latent in all—powers which belong to the superphysical worlds and find therein their appropriate field of exercise.

An ever-increasing number of people occupy the crest of the evolutionary wave pouring onwards into the "borderland" and across it. Where a century ago there was a single seer, there are now dozens. Seers trained, half-trained, untrained, are numerous. Sensitives impressed by influences from the superphysical worlds are on the increase. For seventy years, discarnate entities have been offering information through mediums.[1] The "other world" is pressing into this world. Under these circumstances, it is surely desirable that all students should understand something about investigations into the superphysical in order that they may avoid the blind credulity which accepts all, on the one side, and the equally blind incredulity which rejects all, on the other.

Before dealing with investigations, let me make clear my own position with regard to all questions of opinion and belief within the Theosophical Society itself. Some of our members echo the statements of one seer or another, and seem to consider that such a statement ought to preclude further discussion. But no one in the TS has any authority to lay down what people shall think, or not think, on any subject.

We are not in the position of an orthodox church, which has certain definite articles of faith, which imposes certain definite creeds in which all faithful members are bound to believe. The only point which we must accept is universal brotherhood—and, even as to that, we may differ in our definition of it. Outside that, we are at perfect liberty to form our own opinions on every subject. And the reason of that policy is clear and an exceedingly good one.

No intellectual opinion is worth the holding unless it is obtained by the individual effort of the person who holds that opinion. It is far healthier to exercise our intelligence, even if we come to a wrong conclusion and form an inaccurate opinion, than simply, like parrots, to echo what other people say, and so put out of all possibility intellectual development.

In fact, differences of opinion among the members ought to be regarded as safeguards to the Society rather than as menaces—for our one great danger, as HPB recognized, is the danger of getting into a groove, and so becoming fossilized in the forms of belief that many of us hold today. This will make it difficult for people in the future to shake off these forms, and thus will involve posterity in the same troubles which so many of us have experienced with regard to the teachings among which we were born.[2] The Society is intended—always has been intended—to be a living body and not a fossil, and a living body grows and develops, adapting itself to new conditions. And if it be a body which is spiritually alive, it should be gaining continually a deeper and fuller view of truth.

It is absurd for us to pretend, at our present stage of evolution, that we have arrived at the limit of the knowledge which it is possible for men to obtain. It is absurd for us to say that the particular form into which we throw our beliefs at this moment is the form which is to continue forever after us, and to be accepted by those who follow us in time.

All of us who study deeply must be fully aware that our conceptions of truth are continually deepening and widening—that, as we might reasonably expect, we find new avenues opening up before us. And nothing could be more fatal to a Society like ours than to hallmark as true special forms of belief, and then look askance at anyone challenging them, trying to impose these upon those who will come after us. If the Society is to live far into the future, as I believe it will, then we must be prepared to recognize now, quite frankly and freely, that our knowledge is fragmentary, that it is partial, that it is liable to very great modifications as we learn more and understand better—and especially is this true of everything which goes under the name of investigation.

Even if we take a broad truth, like that of reincarnation, which is perennial—even then, it is unwise to insist upon putting it into one particular form, and to treat it as though it could have no other. We ought to recognize that this vital doctrine has been taught in many forms in the past, and is likely to be taught in many other forms in the future. The one important thing to recognize is the evolution of man—the inner man who has continually grown and is capable of attaining perfection. But it is certain that in the course of time we shall gain much knowledge on all subjects that at present we do not possess; and that, even with regard to fundamental truths, there ought to be the fullest discussion, the freest pointing out of weak places in the arguments with which they are supported.

There ought to be a continual attempt to add to the amount of the truth which we already possess. For if one thing becomes clearer than another to those who are opening up in themselves the finer faculties of man, it is that all our conceptions are so immensely below the truth, so much narrower than the truth, that they seem like the mere prattlings of children compared with the arguments of philosophers. Hence it is wise to be humble as well as studious, and always to be willing to hold the form with a comparatively loose hand, while clinging to the essence of that which is inspiring and really nutritious to the spiritual life.

Looking back into the history of the past, no longer blinded by the dust of its conflicts and the whirl of its passions, we can see that the most serious divisions in Christendom arose out of matters beyond human ken, which did not touch the inner realities of the spiritual life, but only the forms into which the various disputants threw their conceptions of matters incomprehensible to them all. Arians and non-Arians disputed furiously as to whether the second Person in the Christian Trinity was of "the same substance as" or of "like substance with" the Father—and the Arians were hunted out of the Church, and persecutions slew their thousands.[3]

The Catholic Church was split in twain and became the Eastern and Western Churches—the Greek and the Roman—on the question whether the third Person, the Holy Spirit, proceeded from the Father, or from the Father and the Son. It is fairly obvious that neither side was in the position to *know* anything about the matter, and that it could make no difference which statement was the nearer to the truth. All that really mattered was that the influence represented under the name of the Holy Spirit should enter the human heart, sanctify and illumine the human life. Whether it came from one Person or from two was unessential to the growth of the spiritual life. Yet for this, that which Christians loved to call the "seamless robe of Christ" was rent in twain.[4]

Among us of the Theosophical Society today, there are very many different opinions as to the nature of the Christ, as to his place in history, as to the proper name to be assigned to him, as to his position in the hierarchy, as to the particular body he used in the past or may use in the future.[5] Again, it is obvious that these questions are beyond the range of the knowledge possessed by most of those inclined to dispute over them. But the only thing which is of vital importance, which really touches the spiritual life, is the existence of a Being who affords us a glimpse of a little more of the divine nature than we should otherwise see, who is to us the supreme teacher, whom we regard with the profoundest reverence—even, perhaps, as an object of worship. None of the differences of opinion touch this intimate, this sacred side—the side which concerns the relation between the disciple and his Lord. The Holy of Holies wherein these meet is far from the tumult and the battle cries of theological strife, and no clash of tongues may penetrate into the silence of that secret sanctuary.

It is vital for each of us that we should realize the ideal of a divine man, that we should see in him an example of what humanity may become, that we should draw from him all the inspiring power of a great ideal, of a perfect example—that we should have an object to which our love and devotion may flow out. That is the important part of the ideal of the Christ. But whether we label him with one name or another, whether we know or do not know his exact nature and his exact place in the great hierarchy of supreme men, divine men, in divinity itself—that is not really so important as some people are inclined to think, when they rush into vehement controversy in support of some half-understood teaching of a favorite leader.

If, in his heart, a man recognizes the supreme teacher, let him give to him the name which to him seems best as expressing what he is to that man's own heart and life. Before these great manifestations of spiritual power to us, who are so far below them all, it is scarcely seemly for us to quarrel as to the special name or special nature of any one of them. To the heart that loves and worships, the name of the object matters but little, for the aspiration of the heart goes upward and brings response—where no response will come in answer to disputes about his nature. The atmosphere of dispute is not one which illumination can pierce. Shall we not learn the lesson contained in the story of the past, and separate our spiritual ideals from the husks of theological definitions? The ideals belong to the eternal, the definitions to time.

Superior-physical investigations may be divided into different classes, according to the vision which is used. The power of perception may be exercised by the consciousness working in the emotional [astral], mental, causal, intuitional [buddhic], or spiritual [atmic] vehicle. If the seer is studying phenomena connected with the astral or mental world—the inhabitants of these worlds, the conditions of purgatory and heaven and the dwellers therein, respectively; thought or desire forms, lower auras, and the like—he will use astral and mental vision, as is convenient. If he can use only his astral body, he cannot see outside that world, and can study only astral phenomena. If he can use the "illusory body"[6]—i.e., the mental body with a temporarily created astral materialization—he will use mental vision, and as much astral as he needs.

If he is studying the past, he will work through the causal. For, though glimpses of past incarnations may be caught on the astral and mental planes—stray pictures thrown or drawn down by special causes—consecutive and voluntary study of the past can be carried out only by the consciousness working in the causal body. The student must not confuse such study with the special activity of the consciousness in the causal body (working by abstract thought, with attention turned inwards not outwards), any more than he [should] confuse the special activity of the consciousness in the mental body (creating thought images and reasoning on them) with the observation of the external phenomena of the mental world, taking place outside his own mental body.

We perceive through the causal body the full picture of the past, and can observe as much detail as we choose. That picture contains a perfect reproduction of the whole past scene, and can be passed quickly or slowly before our gaze, and can be repeated at will. We see not only the causal body, say, of a man, but also his mental, emotional, and physical bodies—and the causal vision of the trained seer includes all, and more than all, the powers of sight exercised on lower levels. Observations on globes of our chain other than the earth are made by going to them in the intuitional [buddhic] vehicle, and shaping any organs required there out of the material of those globes. There are many passages in the Upanishads implying these ideas.[7]

It seems to me that we come down into the physical world in order to make our power of perception definite and precise, by its subdivision into senses through the organs of the senses, and that we then carry the precision and accuracy thus gained back with us to be used by our power of perception when exercised in any of our subtler bodies. It is a fact of experience to every seer who is able to use his causal body freely, with outward-turned attention, that he sees things belonging to all the lower planes—i.e., concrete phenomena. I think the explanation of this lies in the experiences which he has gone through on the lower planes. Previous rounds may also be studied in this way. Observations on the two earlier chains must be made with the spiritual [atmic] vision.[8]

These higher powers of vision, again, include all, and more than all, the powers of sight exercised on lower planes. They do not see vaguely, indefinitely, mistily, but with a clarity and an accuracy beyond all words. As each new power of sight unfolds, the seer is inclined to exclaim: "I never saw before." It is as though the words of the apostle were reversed: "Then I saw through a glass darkly, but now face to face. Then I knew in part, but now I know even as I am known" [1 Cor. 13:12].

It is evident, then, that in considering investigations into the superphysical, we have to deal with various powers of vision, and with an immense range of very varied phenomena. Moreover, as we ascend, the number of seers diminishes, and the reason of the nonseer will be deprived of even the few data for forming a judgment that he could use on lower levels. With regard to those, there being a large number of witnesses, he can compare their testimonies, note where they agree and where they differ.

But with regard to such subjects as past races, rounds, and chains, it seems impossible for those who lack the power to investigate for themselves to exercise any reasonable judgment as to the statements made, for they are thrown back on a mere handful of investigators.

We have available the wonderful series of letters by the Master K. H., systematized by Mr. A. P. Sinnett and published in his invaluable book, *Esoteric Buddhism*, the first in point of time that deals sequentially with these subjects. Then we have H. P. Blavatsky's splendid work, *The Secret Doctrine*, unrivaled in its range. There are the books on Lemuria and Atlantis issued by Mr. Scott-Elliot. There is a little book on Atlantis issued by Mr. Kingsland. There are the researches of Dr. Rudolf Steiner. And there are the records of observations by Mr. Leadbeater and myself, now collected in the book *Man: Whence, How and Whither*. There may, of course, be others which I do not know.[9]

There is, with minor differences, a fair consensus of opinion among all these—with the exception of researches made by Dr. Rudolf Steiner. And the differences in those may be largely due to the fact that he deals with the subject rather from the psychological standpoint than from that of the observation of the succession of external phenomena. Reasoning on ordinary possibilities in the physical world known to all is of very little use in this case. We are in a region where we [i.e., the listed authors] have all described things that are facts or not facts—either they exist or they do not exist. We are not dealing with theories, but with records of observations, or flights of fancy, or a mixture of the two. Hence the need of caution, both in accepting or rejecting—for the time being—the statements made.

The value of W. Kingdon Clifford's arguments on the fourth dimension, based on the higher mathematics, can be estimated only by his mathematical peers.[10] The rest of us cannot judge them, and any opinion we may form is worthless. It is much the same when the nonseer is confronted with the records above-named. Many accept for the time the seer who appeals to them on other grounds—and they accept him, on those grounds, as an *authority*, not being able to judge for themselves. By the exercise of their intuition, or otherwise, they regard one particular person as their teacher, and where reason stops, they believe him or her. That is all right enough. But none of these has any right to impose his own belief in his teacher on anybody else. And it seems fitting that all such should be careful to be moderate in their language, as they are only putting forward opinions which are repetitions of the views of their own respective favorite authorities—and these they are themselves unable to justify by any firsthand knowledge. Whoever the authority may be, he or she is only an individual, who cannot rightly formulate beliefs for others, though fully justified in recording his own.

I am well aware that, in the past, the differences of opinions which have caused great schisms have been—as above pointed out—just those on which the combatants on both sides could have no personal knowledge. But mistakes in the past are signals warning us of pitfalls in the present, and we should profit by them rather than repeat them. It is inevitable that each should form an opinion on the value of the researches made, but none should force his opinion on others. To proclaim one person as an infallible authority on a subject unknown to the proclaimer is to show fanaticism rather than reason. I would ask my own friends not to do this with me.

I do not argue that because, in the higher research, all the students but one agree in the main outlines, therefore the one is wrong. *Athanasius contra mundem* is sometimes right.[11] But let me put a case which suggests caution. Dr. Steiner says, in his *Atlantis and Lemuria*,[12] that at a certain time the history of our earth—at what we call the periods of the early middle third race, when that earth was already largely inhabited—the sun and moon drew gradually away from the earth. We had then three globes, where "till now there had been no material separation" [and] there was a "common globe" composed of what are now sun, earth, and moon. Man's advance from generation by cleavage to generation by sex was accomplished through "the cosmic happenings." Thus the statement appears to refer to matters physical, not allegorical nor mystical.

My own astronomical knowledge is of the smallest, and is entirely secondhand, for I have never made a single astronomical investigation. But my occult research, as well as the teachings of the White Lodge, given through H. P. Blavatsky and A. P. Sinnett, make me deny the above statement—if it be intended to convey a physical fact, and is not merely a symbolical indication of some mental happening. The surface meaning is, in fact, so incredible that one's instinct is to look for another in the case of a writer so justly respected. Moreover, the physical meaning would contradict the whole of the teaching on evolution hitherto put forward in the Society as to chains, rounds, and races; the relation of the lunar to the terrene chain; and so on. This must all be rewritten—and the statements made by the Masters originally, and confirmed by the researches of their disciples afterwards, must be thrown aside. Hence caution is necessary before believing the above statement, though the making of it is quite within the right of any member of the TS.[13]

It is interesting to notice that the matters on which considerable differences of opinion arise are—with the exception of the views of Christ, noted above—matters which do not bear on life and conduct, but on those which, however interesting as knowledge, are outside that which is needed for the guiding of human life. Life and conduct are immensely influenced by a knowledge of the astral and mental worlds—which include purgatory and heaven—of thought and desire forms, of the lower auras, and other matters of that ilk. This great class of superphysical investigations is the class most useful to the ordinary man. The yet more vital teachings of brotherhood, reincarnation, and karma can be taught on intellectual and moral grounds, apart from superphysical research, though they may be aided and reinforced thereby.[14]

The class of superphysical phenomena, then, which is most useful is the one which is most within reach, which a fair number of people can investigate, and on which students are fairly agreed. The differences which arise are differences common to all forms of scientific research, and to these we now turn.

In dealing with superphysical researches—we are in the world of science and not of revelation. There are great truths known to the Masters that none of us are able to reach and to investigate. If any of these are given out by the Masters, people can accept them or not, according to the view they take as to the authority of the source, and the reliability of the transmitter.

But when we are dealing with investigations into other worlds, into the past of our globe, into the various evolutions that have gone on in our solar system; when we are dealing with investigations into races and subraces; when we are concerned in reading the story of the past, whether as applied to the history of humanity or not—on the whole of these things we are not in the region of revelation, we are in the region of research. Exactly the same canons that we apply to research of the ordinary scientific kind, exactly the same caution in accepting results, exactly the same readiness to repeat experiments that have been made, to revise opinions, to recast conclusions that may have been arrived at on insufficient data—the whole of these things which are commonplaces when we are reading about botany or electricity, that we take for granted in all our ordinary scientific studies—the whole of these apply when anyone begins studying the investigations of those who are carrying on researches in a region subtler than that dealt with in the ordinary sciences. They are making experiments. They are relying as much on their own observations, and on comparing those observations with those of others, as must any scientist in the obscurer regions of investigation. They put forward what they have observed, but they do not ask that their statements shall be regarded as part of some great sacred literature, to be looked upon with the utmost reverence and not to be challenged.

Students must get out of this atmosphere altogether, when dealing with people whose senses are merely a little better developed than their own—senses that everybody will be having some time hence. It may be fifty, one hundred, or two hundred years hence, but senses that are in the course of evolution, that all men have to some extent, that many have to a considerable extent. Research becomes mischievous and harmful in its results when the senses used in it are looked upon as some sort of divine gift, instead of as the result of a strenuous forcing process—so that a person possessing them is placed on a pedestal, or treated like a sibyl of ancient days through whom some god was speaking. They are merely senses of a finer and keener kind than the physical, but belonging to the phenomenal world just as much as the physical belong to it. Observations made through them depend for their value on careful attention to the objects observed, and rigid accuracy in reporting that which has been perceived.

Some people may consider that this is a very cold and prosaic way of approaching a subject which is enwrapped to them in glamour and mystery. But when glamour and mystery mean only that they do not understand the question and the methods of investigating it, is it not better to get rid of them? Is it not safer and saner to realize that there is no more mystery and glamour in examining the after-death state with the astral vision than in examining the Tyrol with the physical?—no more, but *also just as much*. For to see a daisy is a thing as wonderful and mysterious as to see an angel, and the dawn and the sunset are as full of glamour to the seeing eye as the shimmer of colors in an aura.

I have said that there is a large class of superphysical phenomena a knowledge of which affects human life and human conduct. To know something of these not only immensely widens our view of life, but the possession of such knowledge is very important in the guidance of our life now. If we understand after-death conditions and their relations to our conduct here, we can so think, desire, and act now, as to ensure favorable conditions then.

Ours is a continuous life, and a knowledge of that which is "beyond the veil" is of vital importance in the sane and rational guidance of our life in this world. Moreover, we are living in these worlds all the time—and an increasingly large number of people are more or less susceptible to the vibrations of the finer matter composing these worlds. It is very satisfactory to find that on these matters there is a consensus of opinion among observers as to the main points, and variations are confined to details. The literature on these is voluminous, both inside and outside the Theosophical Society, and many small variations will be found in statements concerning these phenomena. It will be useful to understand how variations must arise even among fairly developed seers.

There is one great difference between physical and superphysical research—the apparatus used in them respectively. The physical plane scientist, investigating that which escapes his vision by its distance or its minuteness, uses an instrument outside himself—a telescope, a spectroscope, a microscope. The superphysical scientist, under similar conditions, evolves within himself the necessary apparatus.

Intelligence, as M. Bergson points out, works on inorganic matter by means of arrangements of inorganic matter [into instruments], while instinct modifies organic matter into the organ it requires within its own body.[15] In this, occult investigation resembles instinct—in seeking its instruments from the life of the organism, from the consciousness as a whole. Desiring to see, the man creates out of his appropriated matter the organ of vision. He must evolve, by a steady and well-directed exercise of the will, organs which are practically new—and only then can he call on his intelligence to use them as organs of observation in the world from which have been taken the materials for their fabrication.

The occultist has, however, this advantage over his fellow scientist of the physical plane—that the latter must work with instruments which he cannot carry beyond a certain limit of delicacy. Whereas the occultist can continue to create subtler and subtler instruments, right up to the level of the subtlest phenomenon in his solar system. And when he goes beyond the solar system, he can again create instruments suitable to the new conditions.

We must remember that while the senses are being used, it is the [eternal] man himself who is using them, and he is using them from the higher planes. The higher the vehicle in which he is working, the better can he control the observation of the senses going on on the planes below his own. It is the spiritual ego [buddhi-manas], brooded over by the spirit himself [atman], who is the observer, and he puts down his power of perception as senses into the lower bodies, and this power works in their organs of sense. Those organs of sense which work on the lower planes—astral and mental—will be subject to conditions very similar to these working on the physical plane, and these are not difficult to understand.

Let us consider how we see. We say, "I see" or "I observe." But I am inclined to think that very few people analyze the complexity of what seems to them to be the very simple act of sight. In most acts of vision, there is a little real sight and a great deal of memory. What we call "sight" is a complex, compacted of the translation of the impression just made on the retina and the memory of the whole of the past impressions made by the same, or by similar, objects. We are not simply seeing the object with the eye. We have laid up in our memory the images of a number of similar perceptions, and we weld the whole of these into our present perception, and then say, "I see." It is useful to realize this.

If we look at the photograph of a friend, we recognize it. A baby or a dog looks at it and does not relate the flat image on the card to the living father or master whom he knows and loves. We see, for the first time in this life, a number of Spaniards or Indians. We say, "How alike they all are." We confuse them together. They do exactly the same with us. The first thing we see in a number of similar objects is that which they have in common—i.e., their likeness to each other. As we multiply the sense impressions, we gradually notice the differences, their unlikenesses to each other. We distinguish by differences. First, we perceive the common type; then we see the minor distinctions. A shepherd is said to know each of his sheep. We see only a flock.

We really at first see very little of the object of observation, and only as we see it over and over again do we begin to make our perception approximate to the object perceived. As the past experiences of each of us differ widely, we each see each thing differently to a considerable extent. We bring to each new observation a different mass of memories, and these modify the present perception thereof. Hence, apart from mere carelessness, people really see physical objects differently—the greater part of each act of perception being memory, and this being different in each.

Apply all this to observations on the astral plane. The length of time during which the seer has been able to see astrally is an important factor in his accuracy. As he grows more and more accustomed to that world, he will perceive differences more clearly and be less deceived by likenesses. When he meets a new object, he will at once distinguish it from many other objects of a similar type—whereas the new observer will see the likeness and ignore the differences. Accurate observation there, as here, will depend on experience and memory. An account of early observations will err on the side of likeness, and the beginner will note similarities where the more experienced seer observes difference. His view of the astral world will only gradually become more and more detailed and exact.

Next, we must consider the differences between people in this world, as to accuracy, alike, of observation and report—differences which largely arise from differences in the power of paying attention to a thing. The attention of some people is constantly wandering, fluttering like a butterfly from flower to flower, and such people cannot be accurate, either in observing or in recording what they have seen. Not only is accuracy of observation one of the rarest things in the world, but the power of memory, which records exactly what has been seen, varies much in different observers. Inaccuracies are sure to creep into descriptions, unless the observations made are immediately written down.

In fact, inaccuracy is best avoided by having present a second person to write down the record of the observation while the observation is going on. Then the seer can very carefully observe the objects before him, while the scribe can write down the words of description exactly as they fall from his lips. In this way, a mistake in memory will not confuse details, and thus blur the accuracy of the record. For instance, in making the observations now embodied in *Man: Whence, How and Whither*, the two seers observed at the same time, stopping and reexamining any obscure point, discussing with each other—while the objects were being looked at—any difficult matter, while two scribes took down, independently, everything that was said, even to the most ejaculatory sentence.

The higher the vision that is being used, the more useful is it that the seer and scribe should be two different persons. The experienced observer does not need this aid when he is observing the lower planes, which are familiar to him by reiterated observation. He normally lives consciously in the three worlds, and is thoroughly at home in them all. But observations of unfamiliar scenes demand more concentrated attention, and then the aid of a friendly scribe is invaluable.

Another thing which leads to many superficial differences of observation is the difference of interest in the different observers. If an artist, a politician, a student of religion, an artisan, and an idler should visit the same country, hitherto unknown to them, and should send home descriptions of it to their friends, how different would those descriptions be. The artist's reports would lead one to think that the cities consisted of art galleries, studios, concert rooms, and museums, and that art was the chief interest of the nation. The politician would tell of debates, of the strife of parties, of the intrigues of statesmen. The student of religion would draw a picture of church dignitaries discussing theological questions, of conflicting doctrines, of rival sects. The artisan would report conditions of labor, the state of trade, the various crafts practiced, and would show the nation as one huge workshop. The idler would write of theaters and music halls, of dances and dinner parties, of society gossip and dress. Their respective correspondents, if the country were quite new to them, would gain very different ideas about it.

So is it with the many descriptions given by seers of the astral and mental worlds. The personal equation largely colors the observations. The man sees the aspects of life in which he personally feels the keenest interest, and only the thoroughly trained seer gives a fairly unbiased, full, and well-proportioned account.

Again, many descriptions given of the astral world are merely local. People talk of the astral world as though it were about the size of Birmingham or Glasgow, instead of being a world considerably larger than the physical, with an immense variety of peoples and other creatures. Many speak of it as though it could be run over in a few hours, whereas few know a tithe of its varied aspects. Observers look at certain types of people—mostly ordinary discarnate entities—as though nothing else were of interest there, and so gain but a very restricted view.

Suppose that a dweller in a far-off planet were brought here and plunged into a London slum, were taken through its courts and alleys, and shown the lives of its inhabitants. Suppose that, having studied this, he was whisked back again to his distant home, and gave there an account of the "world" which he had seen. His report might be very accurate—as to the slum. But it might give a very false impression of our world.

An instance similar to this may be found in a very interesting little book, entitled *The Grey World.*[16] It describes various very dismal conditions, and describes them well. But comparatively few people will go through these on the other side of death. They belong to the experiences of those only who, clinging strongly to physical life, remain in the etheric double for a considerable time after death, instead of quickly shaking it off and going on into the astral world.

Another difficulty is connected with the nature of astral sight itself. Astral vision differs from the physical not only in that any part of the astral body can be used for seeing with, but also in that the observer sees through everything and round everything—so that objects take on a very different aspect from those of the physical plane, and backs and fronts, insides and outsides are at first much confused. A man's own thought forms appear to him as independent and celestial entities. Astral matter molds itself to his thinking, and he sees a beautiful landscape stretching in front of him, unwitting that it is his own creation. He sees what he expects, for expectation has made images, and these present themselves to him as objects. Recollections of earth picture themselves as astral surroundings, and people with similar ideas live together in scenes collectively constructed. The astral world, to the uninstructed newcomer, is as queer and unlike the reality as is the physical world to the eyes of a newborn baby. Each has to learn the conditions into which he has been plunged.

Here comes in the question of training, which, in the case of those who seek to be taught, differs much with what is called the type, or ray, of the teacher and the pupil. I may be permitted to take, as contrasting examples, Mr. C. W. Leadbeater and myself.[17] Mr. Leadbeater, from the opening of his astral vision, was carefully trained in its use. An older disciple took him in hand, asked him constantly, "What do you see?"—corrected mistakes, explained difficulties, until his observations were accurate and reliable. I was tossed out into the astral world, left to make mistakes, to find them out and correct them, to learn by experience. It is obvious that where training is so different, results will be different.

Which is the better way? Neither, or both. The first way is the better for the training of a teacher. The second is the better for the training for my kind of work. In the long run, each will acquire the powers of the other. These powers are merely obtained in a different order. And if people, instead of quarreling with each other over their differences, would learn to utilize them by cooperating with and supplementing each other, great profit would ensue. One will be best in ascertaining details, the other in discovering broad outlines. More may be done together than either could do independently.

Things change in appearance as the power of vision increases. A globe is seen, and one calls it a globe. Later on, one finds that it is not a globe, but the physical end of a form composed of higher kinds of matter. Down here, the solar system consists of globes rolling in their orbits round a central sun. From a high plane, the solar system looks like a lotus flower, its petals spread in space, its golden center the sun, and the tip of each petal a world. Was one wrong to speak of a world as a globe? No. It is true on the physical plane. But later, one sees things differently.

We see things down here as we might see a picture through holes in a veil which covers it. Through the holes we see patches of color. Remove the veil, and the patches are part of a garment, of a hand, of a face. Alas! Our senses shut out more than they reveal. They are holes in the wall which imprisons our perceptive power. They often deceive us. But such as they are, with all their defects, we must make the best of them. Even talc windows in a wall are better than none.[18]

Moreover, observers, like other people, grow and develop, and observations of today will be much fuller than those of twenty years ago, unless [the observers] have stood still during that period. If they have grown, then they will be using much improved powers, which will enable them to be much more minute and accurate than before. Unless students realize that researches are being made by people who are still growing, they will be upset by all new discoveries.

Superphysical investigations are like the gropings of scientists on the physical plane. The higher senses grow more delicate, just as the scientist manufactures for himself finer apparatus. The records of research should be taken as the work of investigators who have made them as accurate as they can, and who hope to make them fuller and more accurate by and by. We are evolving persons, studying an infinite universe. The worst thing anyone can do is to take our imperfect studies as a "Thus saith the Lord."[19] There are no authorities, absolute and infallible, in the Theosophical Society.

Let me take as an example the investigations made into the atoms by Mr. Leadbeater and myself in 1895 and in 1907–8. In 1895, we said that the ultimate physical atom disintegrated into astral matter. That was what we saw. In 1907–8, using other sight, we found that between the ultimate physical atom and its appearance as astral matter, a whole series of changes intervened—a series of disintegrations into ultimate bubbles in aether, and of integrations back to astral matter.

The case is analogous to the study of an object under the lower and higher powers of a microscope. You look at it through a low power and describe it—say, that you see little separate particles, and that you so describe them in your record of your observation. You put on a higher power. You discover that little threads of matter, too fine to be visible under the lower power, link the particles together into a chain. The first record can hardly be said to be wrong. It recorded accurately what was seen under the low power: the *appearance* presented by the object. All vision can tell only of appearances, and we may always be sure that its records are imperfect. We enlarge our perceptions as we ascend from one plane to another, and gain a completer view of each object.

Only well-trained and experienced seers will avoid the errors which result from looking at facts through a veil of their own thought forms—and this causes further differences. A Roman Catholic untrained seer will find in heaven the Madonna and child, the Christ and the saints. The Hindu will find Sri Krishna and Mahadeva.[20] The Buddhist will sit in rapt contemplation before the Buddha. Angels and *Devas* will be seen crowding round. The mise-en-scene belongs to and varies with the prepossessions of the seer.

What are the facts without the setting? That each man in heaven sees and worships his own object of devotion. And into each such form the One Lord pours something of His life, His love, meeting and welcoming the outpouring of the love of His devotee—for all worship *Him*, though He be wrought into many forms by many hands. Beautiful indeed is it that each man should see in heaven the Divine in the form which attracted his heart while he was on earth, for thus does no man feel a stranger in his Father's house. He is met on the very threshold by the welcoming smile of his Beloved.

The untrained seer of any religion is drawn to those of his own faith, sees their objects of devotion, and thinks that this is all there is of heaven. The trained seer sees them all, and realizes that each makes his own image, and that the image is vivified for him by the one divine life. When he reads the descriptions of heaven in Christian, Buddhist, Hindu books, he recognizes the objects they describe. So he recognizes that which Swedenborg saw, and that which many discarnate entities describe.[21]

The differences do not make him feel that nothing can be known accurately—the effect produced on some by the great diversity of detail. On the contrary, he sees how much of truth there is amid differences of detail, and even that the detail [which is] apparently the most incongruous may give a hint of an overlooked fact to add to his store of knowledge—just as we often learn the most from things with which we the least agree. The things which do not appeal to us—the fact, or the aspect of a fact, which we have not observed—very often supply some particular factor which is distinctly valuable in our intellectual life.

Finally: surely we ought to be strong enough and sensible enough to agree to differ where our minds are made up on any point, and to be ready to listen to views with which we disagree. I disagree on many things with Dr. Rudolf Steiner, but I was the first to draw the attention of the English-reading public to his books, and I opened the *Theosophist* to his articles when it came into my hands. I advised people to read his views *because* they were different from mine. But difference of view does not imply that we wish to ostracize each other, nor that either should drive the other out of the TS. We have broken the yokes from our own necks. We must not make new ones for our descendants to break hereafter.

No one of us possesses the whole truth. Very far are we from the all-round view of those "who have nothing more to learn" in our system.[22] Generations far in the future, ourselves in new bodies will still be extending the limits of the known and pressing on into the unknown. We do not want our limbs to be fettered then by appeals to our present researches, exalted into scriptures, nor to find our opinions canonized into fossils, used as walls to bar our onward progress then.

And do not be too quick to believe. Intuition is a higher faculty than observation, and the intuition of many spiritually-minded people clung to the great truths of religion when the facts discovered by science seemed to prove them false. The facts of nature have not altered, but new aspects of them have been discovered by further observations, and values have been revised—so that intuition is being justified by the progress of the very science which it opposed.

If the intuition of any reader sets itself against any discovery of any investigator, let the former be patient and suspend his judgment. He may be wrong, and may be mistaking prejudice for intuition. If so, he will presently find it out. But *he may be right*—and, while the fact (if it be a fact) must remain true, the view taken of it and of its meaning may be wrong. If so, further knowledge will presently correct the error.

The Theosophical Society cannot be injured by any researches carried on by its members. Its third object justifies them in their work. But it may be injured by the blind zeal of those who pin their faith to any one investigator and denounce all the rest. "Prove all things; hold fast that which is good" [1 Thess. 5:21]. Let us study as strenuously as we can, sift all statements according to our ability, follow peace with all men, and willingly extend to all the same liberty that we claim for ourselves.

Chapter Sixteen

Occultism (1914)

H. P. Blavatsky defined *occultism* as "the study of the divine mind in nature," and it would be difficult to find a nobler definition. All life, all energies, are hidden, and only their effects are patent. The forces by which a jewel is crystallized in the womb of the earth, by which a plant develops from a seed, by which an animal is evolved from a germ, by which a man feels and thinks—all these are occult, hidden from the eyes of men, to be studied by scientists only in the phenomena of growth, of evolution, as these present themselves, while the impelling forces, the nature of "vitality," the invisible, intangible, secret springs of all activities, these remain ever hidden.

Moreover, this admirable definition posits mind behind all the manifestations which we totalize as "nature." It is these manifestations which are woven into that garment by which we see God ("and weave for God the garment thou see'st Him by"). His mind is revealed in natural phenomena, and by the visible, "the invisible things . . . are clearly seen" [Rom. 1:20]. Bruno spoke of natural objects as the divine language. They are the self-expressions of God.[1]

In the divine mind exist the ideas which are to be embodied in a future universe. The world of mind, the "intelligible world," precedes the material world. So taught the Hebrews, so taught the Greeks. And the teaching is confirmed by our everyday experience. We think, before we embody our thought in an action. Ere a man creates a great picture, he must have the idea of the picture in his mind; he "thinks it out" before he paints it on the canvas. It is the world of ideas, the intelligible world, which is the realm explored by the occultist.

He seeks to understand this hidden world, whence flow all outer manifestations; to grasp the ideas which embody themselves in varied forms; to seek the hidden sources of life and to trace their outflow, as the physical scientist seeks and traces physical types and their evolution. He is the scientist of the invisible, as the ordinary scientist is the scientist of the visible—and his methods are scientific. He observes, he experiments, he verifies, he compares—and he is continually enlarging the boundaries of the known.

The occultist and the mystic differ in their methods as well as in their object. The occultist seeks knowledge of God. The mystic seeks union with God. The occultist uses intellect; the mystic, emotion. The occultist watches ideas embodying themselves in phenomena. The mystic unfolds the divine within him that it may expand into the Divinity whose body is a universe.

These sharp-cut definitions are, of course, true only of abstract types. The concrete individuals shade off into each other—and the perfected occultist finally includes the mystic, the perfected mystic finally includes the occultist. But on the way to perfection, the occultist must evolve, pari passu, his consciousness and the successive vehicles in which that consciousness works; while the mystic sinks into the depths of his consciousness, and cares naught for the bodies, which he disregards and abandons.

To borrow two well-known terms: the occultist tends to become the *jivanmukta,* the liberated spirit residing in material bodies; the mystic tends to become the *videhamukta,* the liberated bodiless one.[2] The occultists rise, grade by grade, through the hierarchy. The mystics become the *nirmanakayas,* the reservoir of spirituality, from which are drawn the streams which irrigate the worlds.[3] Blessed, holy, and necessary are both types—the two hands of the one Logos in His helping of His universe.

Bearing in mind H. P. Blavatsky's definition, we can readily see how the more ordinary view of occultism, that it merely means the study of the hidden—without defining the hidden—inevitably grows up. The occultist is to study the divine mind *in nature.* Then he must not only expand his consciousness, so as to enter into the divine mind, but must also evolve his subtle bodies and their senses, in order to contact nature in all the grades of subtlety of her manifestations. This evolution of the subtle senses and the knowledge gained through them of the phenomena of the subtle, or superphysical, worlds of matter—loom large in the eyes of the superficial observer, and he comes to identify occultism with clairvoyance, clairaudience, traveling in the subtle bodies, and the like. It would be as sensible if this same good gentleman identified physical science with its apparatus—its microscopes, telescopes, spectroscopes.

The subtle senses are merely the apparatus of the occultist, they are not occultism. They are the instruments by which he observes the objects which escape the normal physical eye. As the ordinary instruments of science may have flaws in them, and so may distort the physical objects observed, so may the superphysical instruments have flaws in them, and distort the superphysical objects observed. Malobservation with a defective instrument does not vitiate the scientific method, though it may for the moment vitiate particular scientific conclusions. The same is true as regards malobservations with ill-evolved superphysical senses. The occult method is scientific and sound, but for the moment the particular conclusions drawn by the occultist are erroneous. Where then is safety? In repeated observations by many observers—just as in physical science.

Let us examine this a little more closely. A scientific observer finds [that] his observations through his microscope yield him a certain picture. He draws what he sees. Then he puts a higher power on his microscope, and again observes the object. He obtains another picture. He compares the two. He finds that certain parts of the object that he thought were isolated from each other are connected with threads so fine that they were invisible under the lower power. His first observations were accurate, but incomplete. One result of such incompleteness is that every scientific man, in giving pictures of objects as seen through the microscope, notes on them the power of the lens through which he observed them. Again, if a young observer, on comparing his drawings with those made by experts and inserted in the textbooks, finds that he has inserted something not seen in the others, he will test his lens and repeat his observation, taking another object, identical with the first, lest some dust, or hair, or other accidental intruder should have presented itself unbidden for his inspection.

Let us apply this to the student of occultism. He has evolved a power of sight beyond the normal. He observes some etheric object, and puts down his observations. A few years later, having evolved a higher power of sight, he observes the object again, and finds that the two parts of it he thought successive are divided by some intermediate process. I will take an exact instance. Mr. Leadbeater and I in 1895 observed that the ultimate physical atom, being disintegrated, broke up into the coarsest form of astral matter. In 1908, observing the same process again, with a higher power of sight evolved during the intervening years, we saw that the physical atom, on disintegration, ran through a series of further disintegrations, and reintegrated finally into the coarsest form of astral matter. The parallel with the lower and higher powers of the microscope is complete.

Once more: A young observer sees some astral form. He compares it, if he is wise—he is not always wise—with previous observations of older observers, or with statements by great seers in world scriptures. He finds his observation unlike theirs. If he is a serious student, he tries again, making repeated and careful observations, and finds out his mistake. If he is foolish, he proclaims his malobservation as a new discovery.

But, it may be said, people respect the physical scientist, and accept his observations, while they mock at those of the occultist. All the discoveries of new facts were mocked at before the public was ready for them. Was not Bruno burned and Galileo imprisoned for declaring that the earth moved round the sun?[4] Was not Galvani called "the frogs' dancing master" when he laid his finger on the hidden force now called by his name?[5] What matters the mockery of ignorant men to those whose steadfast eyes are seeking to pierce through the veils in which nature shrouds her secrets?

So far as the methods of observation of the material side of nature are concerned, [with] observations carried on by means of improved apparatus—externally manufactured or internally evolved—the methods of physical and of superphysical science are identical. Knowledge is gained by study of the results obtained by predecessors in the same field, and by observations directed to similar phenomena, with a view to verifying or correcting the results.

The evolution of the consciousness which observes through the senses is another matter, and this plays a greater part in occult than in physical science—for consciousness must unfold as higher senses evolve, else would the better tools be useless in the hands of the inefficient workman. But the object of physical and superphysical science alike is the extension of the boundaries of knowledge.

Is this extension desirable or not? If the knowledge be turned to human service, yes; if to the increase of human misery, no. The application of physical science to the destruction of human life is most evil—yet not for that can we seek to block the advance of chemistry. The occultist who knows how to liberate the forces imprisoned in the atom will not place within the hands of the competing nations of the world this means of wholesale destruction. Yet he knows that chemistry is advancing in this direction, and that it must not be hindered in its advance.

As regards the occultists themselves, they are useful or dangerous according to their motives. If they are devoted to the welfare of the worlds, then their rapid evolution is beneficial. If they seek power for their own aggrandizement, then they are dangerous.

The evolution of consciousness is all to the good. For, as that unfolds, the wider view brings the man gradually more and more into unison with the divine will in evolution—and, at a certain point in this expansion, he inevitably recognizes the all-compelling claims of the larger self. But in the lower stages, in the astral and mental worlds, while his self-discipline must be rigid as regards his bodies, pride and selfishness may make him a danger to his fellow men.

The discipline of the senses and the control of the mind are equally necessary, whether the man is aiming at development for service or for individual aggrandizement. He must lead a life of rigid temperance in all things, and he must become master of his thoughts. But if personal ambition rule him, if he seek to gain in order that he may hold, not in order that he may give, then every added power becomes a menace to the world, and he enters the ranks of the Adversary. The occultist must evolve into a Christ or into a Satan—to borrow the Christian terms. For him there is no halfway house.

Safer are the green pastures where the flock may feed at peace than the arid heights, with their crevasses and their precipices, with their shrouding mists and their crashing avalanches. None who has trodden part of the rugged way would seek to induce others to enter on it. But there are some whom an imperious inner force compels; some who cannot rest by the still waters, but must seek to climb the heights.

For such, the way is open—and for them there is no other way which is possible. Only, that they may not add their shattered lives to the "wrecks which strew the path of occultism,"[6] let them gird their loins with strength. Let them don the armor of purity and the helmet of unselfishness. And then let them go forward, in the name of the world's redeemers, with their eyes fixed on the star which shines above them, careless of the stones which gash their bleeding feet.[7]

Notes

Epigraph. Annie Besant, *The Doctrine of the Heart: Extracts from Hindu Letters*, xv.

Introduction

1. These secret teachings are referred to as the Inner Group Teachings, comprised of notes taken by students of HPB's oral teachings; and six ES Instructions—sometimes called E.S.T. Instructions, short for Esoteric (or Eastern) Section (or School) of Theosophy. The ES Instructions were published versions of the oral teachings, three of which were brought out under HPB's supervision, and three posthumously edited by her students, including Annie Besant. As noted, I use the abbreviation ES to refer to HPB's Esoteric School.

2. According to James Morgan Pryse (1859–1942), an American member of HPB's group of personal students in London who was involved in bringing out the posthumously published third volume of HPB's *The Secret Doctrine*, "Mrs. Besant told me that she would pad it [the third volume] out by adding the E.S.T. Instructions, since H.P.B. had told her she might do so." (Quoted in Josephine Ransom, "How *The Secret Doctrine* Was Written," 35.) Another of HPB's students, G. R. S. (George Robert Stowe) Mead (1863–1933) claimed that he was the source of the suggestion to add the Instructions. See *CW* 14:xl.

3. Included in chapter 14, "Theosophy as Science." See pp. 230–31.

4. Annie Besant, *London Lectures*, 111.

5. Ibid., 111–12.

6. Constance Wachtmeister, *H.P.B. and the Present Crisis in the Theosophical Society*, 3–4. William Quan Judge (1851–96) was an Irish-American lawyer and esotericist, one of the original founders of the TS and a close friend

and personal student of HPB. The ellipsis in the quoted letter and all emphasis is original. The parenthetical material is an original footnote. The identity of the person referred to as D in HPB's letter is unknown, though during her lifetime a disciple of the Masters named Djual Khool (various spellings) was sometimes a message bearer for the Masters in the form of astral appearances and letters in his handwriting.

Wachtmeister's pamphlet was published during a spiritual and political crisis in the TS that involved the secession of the American Section from the rest of the TS in 1895. Several of Besant's essays and addresses in the present book refer to this crisis.

7. Bhagavan Das, *Annie Besant and the Changing World*, 41–42. I have omitted two verses in Sanskrit corresponding to the material in quotation marks in the first paragraph. The portion of this sentence following the semicolon corresponds to the second verse, which is from the Mundaka Upanishad (1.2.6). Besant apparently used *Heliodore* as a penname early in her writing career, before joining the TS in 1889.

8. Subsequently reprinted in *Quest: Journal of the Theosophical Society in America* 100 (Spring 2012): 67–73.

9. The year of Leadbeater's birth is controversial. He gave it as 1847, the same year AWB was born. Leadbeater's biographer, Gregory Tillett, argues that it should be 1854. See Tillett, *The Elder Brother: A Biography of Charles Webster Leadbeater*, 16.

10. Charles W. Leadbeater, *A Textbook of Theosophy* (1912), 41.

11. Ibid., reprint, 2007, 51. Italics mine.

12. C. Jinarajadasa, *Occult Investigations: A Description of the Work of Annie Besant and C. W. Leadbeater*, 50. Curuppumullage Jinarajadasa (1875–1953), born in Ceylon (now Sri Lanka), was a student and amanuensis of CWL. He later became president of the TS (1945–53).

13. I omitted the lecture "Psychic and Spiritual Development" (July 13, 1905; Blavatsky Lodge, London) for a similar reason—though delivered at the height of AWB's powers, it covers much the same territory as other selections included here.

14. Sri Prakasa, *Annie Besant as Woman and as Leader*, 78. Sri Prakasa (1890–1971), an Indian politician, was the son of Bhagavan Das.

15. Annie Besant, *The Bhagavadgita: The Lord's Song*.

CHRONOLOGY

1. The sources for this chronology are (1) Annie Besant, *Annie Besant: An Autobiography, with an Additional Survey of Her Life by George S. Arundale, and Biographical Notes Compiled Mainly from Her Own Writings*; (2) Arthur Digby Besant, *The Besant Pedigree*; (3) "A Besant Diary of Principal Events"; (4) C. Jinarajadasa, *The Golden Book of the Theosophical Society 1875-1925*; (5) C. Jinarajadasa, *Occult Investigations*; (6) Arthur H. Nethercot, *The First Five Lives of Annie Besant*; (7) Arthur H. Nethercot, *The Last Four Lives of Annie Besant*; (8) Josephine Ransom, *The Seventy-Fifth Anniversary Book of the Theosophical Society: A Short History of the Society's Growth from 1926–1950*; (9) Josephine Ransom, *A Short History of the Theosophical Society 1875–1938*; and (10) Gertrude M. Williams, *The Passionate Pilgrim: A Life of Annie Besant*.

Chapter One: WHAT THEOSOPHY IS

1. **"Ungrudging love"**: Paul Carus (1852–1919), *The Gospel of Buddha According to Old Records*, 145.
2. **"Overcome the greedy"**: Note the misattribution of the second citation, a teaching of the Buddha.
3. **Great Soul**: Literal translation of Sanskrit *Mahatma*, referring to the highly spiritually evolved Masters of an ancient wisdom tradition who inspired the founding of the TS and provided (in the form of the so-called "Mahatma Letters") many of the core concepts on which HPB's presentation of Theosophy was based. Other synonyms used by Besant in this book include: Adepts, Elder Brothers, Brothers of the Light, Perfect Men; Members of the Great White Lodge (where *white* refers to white magic, not to race). These adepts are opposed by the Brothers of the Shadow, also called the Lords of the Dark Face—otherwise known as Black Magicians, the Black Brotherhood, the Black Lodge (again, without reference to race).
   Messenger: H. P. Blavatsky.
4. **Logos** (Greek: "Word"; plural, Logoi): A term used in Hellenistic philosophy, Gnosticism, and Neoplatonism, as well as Christianity, for a particular aspect of deity or some divine principle. The three aspects of the Logos, as the term is used in Theosophy, are defined in the next selection.

5. **"Loom of Time"**: Johann Wolfgang von Goethe (1749–1832), *Faust* 1.508–509. Translator unknown. First published in "John Paul Friedrich Richter's Review of Madame de Stael's 'Allemagne,'" in *Fraser's Magazine for Town and Country* in February 1830, and popularized by Thomas Carlyle (1795–1881) in *Sartor Resartus*, which appeared in that magazine in serial form, 1833–34. HPB cites these lines in *SD* 1:83.

6. **Sevens in nature**: "The septenary is to be clearly traced in the lunar months, fevers, gestation, etc." (*IGT* 22). In *SD* 2:312n, HPB remarks that Hippocrates (ca. 460–ca. 370 BCE) divided the life of the human being into seven-year periods, noting that children begin to lose their baby teeth at age seven and puberty begins at age fourteen. Elsewhere, HPB indicates that the principle of *atman* (Sanskrit: "spiritual self") awakens "when the child is seven years old, and with it comes the responsibility attaching to a conscious sentient being" (*CW* 10:218). A physician's observation that fevers show seven-day cycles, published in the famous British medical journal the *Lancet* in the 1840s, was noted by HPB in *SD* 2:622n.

7. **Corresponding faculties**: Behind this information on the bodies is one of the core concepts of Theosophy as taught by the Masters and HPB: the seven principles. These principles underlie the structure of our universe, which is considered to be a conscious being (the Logos), as well as that of our individual human consciousness ("the seven principles of man"). Sanskrit words are used to name these seven principles: (1) *sthula sharira*—dense body; (2) *linga sharira*—subtle body or astral double; (3) *prana*—vitality; (4) *kama*—desire; (5) *manas*—mind; (6) *buddhi*—spiritual intelligence; and (7) *atman*—spirit.

   A problem often arises for serious students of Theosophy when trying to reconcile these early teachings with those of Besant and her colleague CWL: the bodies described in the latter do not seem to match up with the seven principles. This confusion has led some people to feel that HPB's Theosophy and that of Besant and Leadbeater are irreconcilable. (See, for example, Geoffrey A. Farthing [1909–2004; http://www.esoteric-philosophy.com/2010/05/life-and-work-of-geoffrey-farthing.html], *The Etheric Double? The Far-Reaching Effects of a False Assumption*.)

   With respect to the seven principles, there are two primary reasons for confusion. First, Besant's published books generally consist of lectures to mixed audiences of members and nonmembers of the TS. She did not want to frighten off prospective members with abstruse Sanskrit terminology, so she used English equivalents. The following passage, relating to one of the ES Instructions and probably written by Besant, expresses just such a policy:

> In speaking to the world and to beginners, it is neither necessary nor useful to be over-particular about words in such a language as English, which is not a scientific one, so long as ideas are expressed so as to be comprehended by such beginners from their standpoint. (*CW* 12:677). (Though this passage is signed by William Q. Judge in the *CW* version, other versions include both his name and Besant's. See Daniel Caldwell, *The Esoteric Papers of Madame Blavatsky*, 587 [cited passage] and 598 [signatures].)

The result of this policy, which Besant practiced for the next forty years, was that HPB's teachings on the seven principles seemed to go underground. Besant apparently assumed that serious students of Theosophy would go directly to HPB's works for such teachings. However, when speaking to members of the TS, she would sometimes use HPB's original Sanskrit terms—a practice in accord with her admonition in the same ES Instruction that HPB "laid great stress on the definite adoption of terms and their systematic use" (*CW* 12:677). Such lectures were rarely collected in book form, though they were sometimes published in Theosophical magazines. This material has all but disappeared from the Theosophical canon since Besant's death, leaving the impression that she supplanted HPB's teachings on the principles with others of her own.

The second reason for confusion about the principles as taught by HPB and by Besant is that Besant was primarily concerned with the subtle bodies. Even serious students of Theosophy sometimes do not grasp the difference between a principle and a body, so when they read Besant's writings on bodies, they appear to be irreconcilable with HPB's teachings on the principles. Yet a passage like that to which the present note is appended demonstrates how careful Besant was to make the distinction.

A body is always a compound of two or more principles. Thus the physical body, as described by Besant in this passage, is a compound of the dense body and the etheric double: sthula sharira and linga sharira (astral double). Besant made the change from astral to etheric because in HPB's voluminous writings the word *astral* was used in so many ways—it could describe any subtle body, plane, or state of consciousness. HPB did sometimes describe the astral double as ethereal (e.g., in her definition of the astral body or double as "the ethereal counterpart of shadow of man or animal" [*TG*, Astral Body]). That word too must not have seemed specific enough to Besant, since any subtle body could be described as ethereal. The term *etheric* arose in connection with Besant's clairvoyant investigations into occult chemistry.

The desire body corresponds to the principles of kama (desire) and prana (vitality). This compound is called *kama-prana* or *prana-kama* in HPB's oral teachings, which Besant was about to publish in 1897 as part of the so-called third volume of *The Secret Doctrine*. Besant would sometimes call this desire body the astral body, though she often stated that she was not happy with the latter term (e.g., Annie Besant, *Man and His Bodies*, 49n).

As Besant notes, the mental body corresponds to "lower mind," which in HPB's writings is called *kama-manas*.

Note that vitality (prana) is listed as a fourth component of our makeup, but is not described or listed as a body. Here it is a pure (uncompounded) principle, as in HPB's teachings.

The next body, called the soul or thinker, is elsewhere identified as the causal body or ego—what HPB calls the *karana sharira* (Sanskrit: "causal body"). It correlates to the higher mind, or buddhi-manas.

Finally, "spirit in its vehicle" corresponds to atma-buddhi, which HPB sometimes called the spiritual monad. The word *vehicle* is a translation of the Sanskrit term *upadhi* (basis). Here the spirit is the seventh principle, atman, and its vehicle is the sixth principle, buddhi. Besant would sometimes call this body the buddhic body. (Incidentally, the word *monad* often causes confusion for readers new to Theosophy who expect it to mean an indivisible whole—yet the spiritual monad seems to have two parts, atman and buddhi. HPB used the word to refer to amalgams of a principle and an upadhi *that function as a unit*. Thus the hyphenated term *atma-buddhi* refers to a monad—as indicated, the *spiritual* monad.)

This notion of an upper principle finding its vehicle in one or more lower principles is the key to the question of how Besant's teachings on the bodies correspond to HPB's teachings on the principles. In fact, a body always consists of a higher principle using one or more lower principles as a vehicle. A vehicle is required for that higher principle to manifest itself and gain experience on a lower plane. Without the principle associated with that lower plane, the higher principle cannot make contact with that plane.

Thus buddhi-manas—the causal body—is the principle of buddhi using manas as a vehicle. kama-manas—the mental body—is the principle of manas using kama as a vehicle. The desire body is kama-prana, the principle of kama using prana as a vehicle. The physical body is kama using linga sharira and sthula sharira as a vehicle.

Note how Besant's simple presentation of the bodies in this piece has expanded in my explanation of the principles that underlie it. Clearly, the readership she was trying to reach to generate interest in Theosophy would have been alienated by such elaboration. She left it to more serious students to work out the consistency of this presentation with HPB's teachings.

Chapter Two: An Introduction to Theosophy

1. **In the East**: Besant is referring to the education of young Indian men under English colonial rule. Discouraged from practicing their own religion and unable to accept Christianity, except perhaps nominally for social advantage, many became atheistic materialists. The situation was spelled out in one of the Mahatma Letters, from which Besant quotes later in this selection (*ML* 475 [Chin]).
2. **Rome**: The Roman Catholic Church, with its seat in Rome: the Vatican.
3. **Rostislav Andreyevich de Fadeyev** (1824–83): HPB's maternal uncle. This letter was published in 1881 in response to journalistic attacks on HPB's character insinuating that she was an impostor.
4. **Peter Alexeyevich von Hahn** (1799–1875): Father of HPB.
   Princess Helene Pavlovna Dolgorukova (1789–1860): Amateur botanist, maternal grandmother of HPB (*CW* 1:xxvi–xxviii; surname variously spelled—I follow de Zirkoff).
   Helene Andreyevna Fadeyev (1814–42): Novelist, mother of HPB.
   Nikifor Vassilyevich Blavatsky (1809–?): Husband of HPB, married in 1849, when she was 18; she left him shortly thereafter. According to Boris de Zirkoff, editor of HPB's *Collected Writings*,

   > All efforts to ascertain the year of N. V. Blavatsky's death have proved fruitless. It is known, however, from a letter written by Nadyezhda A. de Fadeyev [HPB's aunt] to H.P.B. and dated October 1/13, 1877, that he was alive then and living in Poltava. (*CW* 1:xxxv–xxxvii, plus footnote 50; the letter's date reflects Russia's Old and New Style calendars)

   Erivan, Caucasus: At the time of HPB's marriage, a portion of the Russian Empire; now Yerevan, capital of the Republic of Armenia.

19 Avenue Road: Home of AWB, headquarters of the British Section of the TS and location of the meeting rooms of the Blavatsky Lodge from 1889–99.

5. **Nominal office**: Corresponding Secretary.
The *Theosophist*: Periodical founded by HPB and HSO in Bombay, 1879; edited by HSO until his death in 1907, and by AWB 1907–33; still published from the International Headquarters of the TS, Adyar, Chennai, India.
Lucifer: Periodical founded by HPB and Mabel Collins (1851–1927) in London, 1887; edited jointly by HPB and AWB, 1889–91, and by AWB alone, 1891–97; renamed the *Theosophical Review* in 1897 and jointly edited by AWB and G. R. S. Mead until AWB resigned in 1907; folded into the *Theosophist* in 1909.
The *Path*: Periodical founded by William Q. Judge, in New York, 1886, as the organ of the American Section of the TS; published until his death. HPB's articles in these journals are available in *Collected Writings of H. P. Blavatsky* and H. P. Blavatsky, *Theosophical Articles Reprinted from Original Sources*.

6. **Fallibility and mistakes**: HPB wrote,

> No true Theosophist, from the most ignorant up to the most learned, ought to claim infallibility for anything he may say or write upon occult matters. The chief point is to admit that . . . those of us who pretend to teach others more ignorant than ourselves—are all liable to err. Thus mistakes have been made in *Isis Unveiled* . . . and more than one mistake is likely to be found in the present work. This cannot be helped. For a large or even a small work on such abstruse subjects to be entirely exempt from error and blunder, it would have to be written from its first to its last page by a great adept, if not by an Avatara [physical incarnation of a god, e.g., Krishna as an avatar of Vishnu]. (*SD* 2:640)

HPB on not blindly accepting the authority of others, including herself:

> I speak "with absolute certainty" only so far as my own *personal belief* is concerned. Those who have not the *same warrant* for their belief as I have, would be very credulous and foolish to accept it on blind faith. Nor does the writer believe . . . in any "authority" let alone "divine revelation"! (*CW* 11:466)

7. **Henry Steel Olcott**: During the Civil War, HSO was elevated to the rank of colonel in honor of his work as a special investigator charged with

exposing fraudulent use of funds within the War Department in the army and navy. He was also part of a small panel convened to investigate the assassination of President Lincoln.

8. **Eddys' farm**: Homestead in Chittenden, Vermont, where two uneducated brothers, William Eddy (1832–1932) and Horatio Eddy (1844–1922), demonstrated a variety of sensational mediumistic phenomena investigated by HSO and HPB (http://www.answers.com/topic/eddy-brothers). The latter met each other there for the first time on October 14, 1874. For HSO's account of this meeting, see Caldwell, *The Esoteric World of Madame Blavatsky*, 49–53.

9. **TS Sections**: The **TS Adyar**, with headquarters in Adyar, Chennai, India, has numerous branches, lodges, and study groups in forty-eight countries (especially India and the United States) and in several larger geographical regions, such as West Africa and Central America, and a publishing arm called the Theosophical Publishing House with offices in several countries (again, principally India and the United States). See (http://www.ts-adyar.org/node/207; http://www.ts-adyar.org/content/theosophical-publishing-house; http://www.theosophical.org/publications/quest-books?Name=Value).
   The TS Point Loma-Covina, which originated in 1895 when the American Section of the TS under the leadership of William Q. Judge seceded from the Adyar-based TS; with previous headquarters at New York, NY (1895–1900), Point Loma, San Diego, CA (1900–1942), and Covina, CA (1942–51); after a further split in 1951, the organization bearing this name has been headquartered in The Hague, Netherlands (http://en.wikipedia.org/wiki/TheosophicalSocietyPointLoma-Covina; http://www.blavatskyhouse.org/).
   The TS Pasadena, renamed after the 1951 split within the TS Point Loma-Covina group, with current international headquarters in Pasadena, has a presence in eight countries, and a publishing arm called Theosophical University Press (http://www.theosociety.org/pasadena/ts/tsnatsec.htm; http://www.theosociety.org/pasadena/ts/tup-onl.htm).
   The United Lodge of Theosophists (established in 1909), with international headquarters in New York City, has a presence in fourteen countries, with numerous lodges and study groups in India and the United States and a publishing arm called the Theosophy Company (http://www.ult.org/where.html; http://www.ult.org/catalog.html).

10. **Mother of religions**: Besant often used the term *the East* to refer to India, where Hinduism, Jainism, Buddhism, and Sikhism originated.

11. **Chief object of the TS**: This quotation and most subsequent references to letters from the Theosophical Masters first appeared in A. P. Sinnett's *The Occult World*. Besant's original footnotes cite page numbers in this work. Barker, *The Mahatma Letters to A. P. Sinnett in Chronological Sequence*, ed. Vicente Hao Chin, Jr., 2003, collects these letters and many others from the same sources. Throughout this book, I have brought Besant's citations into accordance with this edition. Page numbers are also given for the original edition compiled by A. Trevor Barker.
    The Master KH: One of the sources of the Mahatma Letters, also known as Koot Humi (variously spelled in Theosophical literature).
    Alfred Percy Sinnett (1840–1921): The recipient of many of these letters, at that time a British newspaper editor in India and a personal friend of HPB.
12. **Anglo-Indian**: British citizens living on Indian soil. This Mahatma Letter was written at a time when a Theosophical lodge for Anglo-Indians in Simla was proposed. This lodge was to be run along somewhat different lines than others already in existence throughout the world—in the hope that the Mahatmas would personally educate the members in the development of occult powers.
13. **Yet higher authority**: The Mahachohan: *maha* (Sanskrit: "great"); *chohan* (Tibetan: "lord"). The Mahachohan was the superior of the two Masters primarily responsible for the Mahatma Letters. *Bell ringing* and *cup growing* refer to two of the occult phenomena demonstrated by HPB while living in India and recounted in Sinnett's *Occult World*. The sound of small bells was often heard in HPB's vicinity without an apparent physical source (see, for example, *EW* 164, for a description). Sinnett tells the tale of a picnic in an out-of-the-way location: an unexpected guest arrived, requiring an extra teacup and saucer—and a matching set was produced from beneath the ground under mysterious circumstances (*EW* 146–48).
14. **Lamas**: Tibetan Buddhist priests; here used to refer to high spiritual Masters or Adepts.
15. **Two Great Easterns**: Master KH and Master Morya (Master M), who was the other inspiration for the founding of the TS, as well as a major source of the Mahatma Letters. HPB considered Master M to be her Master.
    Aryan Teachings: The ancient wisdom tradition, or esoteric philosophy, upon which Theosophy is based was said to have originated with a light-skinned race called Aryan (Sanskrit: "Noble") that invaded India

millennia ago—how many millennia (and even whether such an invasion occurred) is a matter of debate among scholars. In Theosophy, the Aryans correspond to a stage in the evolutionary development of humankind called a root race. Seven root races are required for the completion of human evolution on our globe, and the Aryan is the fifth of these root races. People of western European descent belong to the fifth cyclical variation, or subrace, of this fifth root race. Thus the Aryans represent the oldest basis for language, culture, and spiritual development within a certain grand stage of the human evolutionary cycle. This stage is based more on the development of specific aspects of consciousness than on the genetic characteristics that play such an important role in historic and contemporary fascist organizations that have co-opted the word *Aryan*.

16. **Phenomenalism**: Probably not the materialistic philosophy of David Hume (1711–76), but the study of spiritualistic or occult phenomena. The material in brackets was added by Besant.
17. **Other Sage**: The Mahachohan.
18. **"There is no religion higher than truth"**: Motto of the Theosophical Society, HPB's translation of the family motto of the Maharaja of Benares (now Varanasi), originally in Sanskrit: *Satyannasti paro dharmah.*
19. **Eastern School of Theosophy**: Still in existence as the Esoteric School of Theosophy (ES), primarily a training ground for those who wish to dedicate themselves to work on behalf of the Theosophical Society.
20. **Giordano Bruno** (1548–1600): Italian pantheist, astronomer, and mathematician; burned at the stake by the Inquisition for heretical views.
21. **Johann Gottlieb Fichte** (1762–1814): Philosopher of German idealism and the problem of consciousness and subjectivity; influenced by Kant.
    Immanuel Kant (1724–1804): Prussian philosopher of the Enlightenment; author of the monumental and highly influential *Critique of Pure Reason* and other important works in the Western philosophical tradition.
    Arthur Schopenhauer (1788–1860): German pessimistic philosopher, strongly influenced by the teachings of Buddhist philosophy; author of the influential work, *World as Will and Representation.*
    Ralph Waldo Emerson (1803–82): American transcendentalist philosopher, lecturer, essayist, and poet, strongly influenced by Hindu and Buddhist philosophy.
    George Berkeley, Bishop (1685–1753): Irish clergyman and philosopher of idealism, teaching that the universe exists for us only through our perception of it.

Meister Eckhart (Eckhart von Hochheim; ca. 1260–ca. 1327): German theologian, Neoplatonist, and mystic whose Latin writings and German sermons were considered heretical by Catholic authorities; advocate of the virtue of disinterest, a quasi-Buddhistic detachment.
Jakob Boehme (1575–1624): German theologian and nature mystic whose writings were considered heretical by Lutheran authorities; influenced by Paracelsus; early user of the word *theosophic*.
Robert Fludd (1574–1637): Physician, astrologer, mathematician, kabbalist, and metaphysician, influenced by Paracelsus; associated with the development of Rosicrucianism (though not himself a member of the movement).
Thomas Vaughan (1621–66): Welsh clergyman, philosopher, alchemist, and mystic; influenced by Paracelsus; translator from German into English of an important Rosicrucian manifesto first published in 1614; probable author of works written under the name Eugenius Philalethes.
Louis-Claude de Saint-Martin (1743–1803): French philosopher and mystic; proponent (though not the originator) of Martinism, a form of esoteric Christianity; translator of the works of Boehme.
Emanuel Swedenborg (1688–1772): Swedish scientist, philosopher, inventor, and mystic; spent the last twenty-eight years of his life recording visits to heaven and hell and conversations with their inhabitants, including angels, on theological subjects.

22. **Paracelsus** (Philippus Aureolus Theophrastus Bombastus von Hohenheim, 1493–1541): German-Swiss physician, botanist, alchemist, astrologer, and hermeticist; author of scientific treatises and disquisitions on magic.

23. **Jan Baptist Van Helmont** (1580–1644): Flemish physician, physiologist, and chemist, as well as mystic and alchemist; disciple of Paracelsus, founder of pneumatic chemistry and inventor of the term *animal magnetism* (later known as "mesmerism" or "hypnotism").
Greatorex: Nickname of Valentine Greatrakes (1628–83), also called "the Stroker"; born in Ireland, but famous in England for healing by means of animal magnetism.
Franz Anton Mesmer (1734–1815): German physician who developed a theory of animal magnetism based on the reciprocal energetic influence between all beings and objects in the universe; his "mesmeric" techniques created marvelous effects on people, including spontaneous healing.
Jean-Martin Charcot (1825–93): French neurologist and anatomical pathologist, considered to be the founder of modern neurology;

researcher into the relationship between hypnotism and hysteria, pioneer in the clinical use of hypnotism.

Ambroise-August Liebeault (1823–1904): French physician; pioneer in the development of modern hypnotherapy.

24. **Sir William Crookes** (1832–1919): British chemist and physicist; discoverer of the element thallium and pioneer in the study of vacuum tubes and cathode rays; scientific researcher into the phenomena of spiritualism; lifelong member of the TS after joining in 1883.

    Sir Oliver Lodge (1851–1940): British physicist; researcher into electromagnetism; pioneer in wireless telegraphy and the transmission of radio signals; believer in and author on mediumship, spiritualism, and life after death.

25. **Atma-vidya** (Sanskrit): "Knowledge" (or "wisdom") of the "self" (or "soul" or "spirit").

26. **Guidance**: Besant claimed to have direct inner contact with the Masters, so her statement about "guidance strenuously sought and eagerly obeyed" reflects her personal experience, as also HPB's. The Masters themselves declared: "We *advise*—and never *order*. But we *do* influence individuals" (*ML* 271 [Barker]; 134 [Chin]).

27. **Great Breath**: A reference to the traditional Hindu explanation of the origin of the universe as the outbreathing of the creator god Brahma. Similarly, the universe will end at some point in the distant future when Brahma takes in that breath—and the process of exhaling and inhaling universes continues ad infinitum.

28. **Builders**: Also called *cosmocratores* (Greek)—"'Builders of the Universe,' the 'world architects,' or the Creative Forces personified" (*TG*, Cosmocratores).

    Dhyani-Chohans (Sanskrit: "Lords of Light"): "The highest gods, answering to the Roman Catholic Archangels. The divine Intelligences charged with the supervision of Kosmos" (*TG*, Dhyan Chohans).

    Lipikas: "The celestial recorders, the 'Scribes,' those who record every word and deed, said and done by man while on this earth. As occultism teaches, they are the agents of Karma—the retributive Law" (*TG*, Lipikas).

    Planetary spirits: According to HPB,

    > Primarily the rulers or governors of the planets. As our earth has its hierarchy of terrestrial planetary spirits, from the highest to the lowest plane, so has every other heavenly body. In Occultism, however, the term "Planetary Spirit" is generally applied only to the seven highest

hierarchies corresponding to the Christian archangels. These have all passed through a stage of evolution corresponding to the humanity of earth on other worlds, in long past cycles. Our earth, being as yet only in its fourth round, is far too young to have produced high planetary spirits. The highest planetary spirit ruling over any globe is in reality the "Personal God" of that planet and far more truly its "over-ruling providence" than the self-contradictory Infinite Personal Deity of modern Churchianity. (*TG*, Planetary Spirits)

29. **Elementals**: "Invisible Beings—conscious, semi-conscious and entirely senseless—called by a number of names in every country under the sun, and known under the generic name of 'Spirits'" (*CW* 12:187). For further information, see the articles "Elementals" (*CW* 6: 184–201) and "Thoughts on the Elementals" (*CW* 12:187–205). A more complete version of the former, which includes citations from *Isis Unveiled* that have been omitted from the version in Blavatsky's *Collected Writings* 6, may be found in Blavatsky, *Theosophical Articles*, 3:127–63.

30. **Jiva** (Sanskrit: "life"): Sometimes used, as here, to refer to the cosmic life principle, of which prana is a local manifestation on a particular plane or with respect to a particular body; sometimes used to refer to an individual unit of life or consciousness (monad)—in other words, a sentient being.

31. **Sir Benjamin Ward Richardson** (1828–96): British physician and physiologist. His "Theory of a Nervous Ether" is an attempt to explain how the nervous system is affected by pleasure, pain, fatigue, shock, and the introduction of foreign substances such as alcohol or anesthetics based on the notion of a gas (nervous ether) that permeates the system and is set in vibratory motion by such stimuli. This nervous ether may exist in states of high or low tension, the former resulting in excitability and the latter in exhaustion. This theory is discussed at length by HPB in *The Secret Doctrine* 1:531–38.

32. **"God fallen into matter"**: "According to tradition and Occult teaching [Man was] 'a god on earth who had fallen into matter,' or generation" (*SD* 2:261).

    Germinal god: The seed or germ of divinity within us.

33. **Adeptship**: In *The Path of Discipleship*, Besant describes the following schema of spiritual development: preparation, probation, discipleship, initiation (four stages), and adeptship (succeeding the fifth initiation). The lower stage of adeptship mentioned here is presumably associated

with one of the four stages of initiation, perhaps that between the first and second initiations, in which personality is destroyed, along with the feeling of separateness. Personality is associated with the lower manas, so the unification of upper and lower manas described in the present lecture seems to be an alternative way to indicate the destruction of personality—it is absorbed by or dissolved in the upper manas, rather than "killed out," as some earlier Theosophical texts propose (e.g., *LP* 1–3).

34. **Devachan** (Tibetan—should be *dewachen)*: "Land of Bliss."
Devachanic: Anglicized adjectival form of *Devachan*.

35. **Kamaloka** (Sanskrit): Literally, "land (place/plane/planet) of desire."

36. **Form his karma**: See Annie Besant, *Karma*, for a detailed exposition of the relationship between thought forms and karma.

37. **Arhat** (Pali: "noble"): In Theravada (southern) Buddhism, an individual who has achieved enlightenment while still in the body, and is therefore free of the cycle of death and rebirth. For Besant, this evolutionary stage immediately precedes that of becoming a Master and is correlated with the fourth initiation.

38. **Third plane**: Besant is numbering the planes from the highest plane downward, including the two unmanifested planes which she later called divine (first) and monadic (second).

39. **Bare outline**: For more detailed information on the seven principles, see Annie Besant, *The Seven Principles of Man*.

40. **Thus has a master spoken**: This paragraph appears to be a digest of subjects covered in the first letter of Master KH to Allan Octavian Hume (1829–1912; a British civil servant and amateur scientist working in India, also an early member of the TS), alternately enthusiastic and skeptical. This letter includes statements such as the following:

> Now for us poor and unknown philanthropists [i.e., the Masters], no fact of either of those sciences [physical or metaphysical] is interesting except in the degree of its potentiality of *moral* results, and in the ratio of its usefulness to mankind. And what, in its proud isolation, can be more utterly indifferent to every one and everything, or more bound to nothing, but the selfish requisites for its advancement than this materialistic and realistic science of fact? (*ML* 471 [Chin])

Exact experimental Science has nothing to do with morality, virtue, philanthropy, therefore can make no claim upon our help, until it blends itself with the metaphysics. (*ML* 472 [Chin])

Chapter Three: THE LIGHT AND DARK SIDES OF NATURE

1. **Cobra di capella** (Italian): *Cobra di capello*—"serpent of the hood."
2. **Pairs of opposites**: Presumably a reference to the Zoroastrian belief in two opposing principles or godlike beings that have existed since the beginning of time: Ahura Mazda (also called Ohrmazd), the principle of creation; and Aingra Manyu (also called Ahriman), the principle of chaos or destruction.
3. **Brahman** (Sanskrit): The Absolute—the origin of all, including the gods, yet beyond the manifested universe. The act of thinking implies duality: there is a thinker and a thought. Brahman, the Absolute, lies beyond duality and is therefore beyond or without thought.
4. **"Word"**: A cross-cultural reference to John 1:1 ("In the beginning was the Word") and to yogic teachings about mantras as creative and magical words of power.
5. **Positive/negative**: In Besant's time, *positive* had the connotations of active, assertive, aggressive, whereas *negative* had the connotations of inert, passive, resistant.
6. **Manvantara** (Sanskrit): An evolutionary age, of which there are several types. Presumably, Besant means a *planetary* manvantara, a full cycle of seven planetary rounds. Each round consists of development on seven globes of varying degrees of materiality. Furthermore, each round occurs with reference to a different plane of existence and one of the seven principles. We are in the fourth such round, the most material of the seven, concerned with the mastery of the principle of *kama*. Three principles were mastered in earlier rounds—those representing the dense body, the astral double, and *prana*. Because we are midway through the round (on the fourth of its seven globes), the principle of *manas* is becoming increasingly available to us, in the form of kama-manas, or lower mind. manas will be mastered in the fifth round, unless we attempt to accelerate its evolution on a spiritual path such as that

taught in HPB's *The Voice of the Silence*. Only in the sixth and seventh rounds would the two higher planes (buddhic and atmic) and the principles or states of consciousness they represent (*buddhi* and *atman*) become available to humanity at large—though occasionally they may be achieved by individuals who are far in advance of the average level of spiritual development, such as the Buddha. A planetary manvantara is equivalent to 4,320,000,000 years.

7. **Turiyic**: Anglicization of *turiya*, Sanskrit for "the fourth." Four states of consciousness are mentioned in the Mandukya Upanishad (2–7): (1) *vaishvanara*, or ordinary waking consciousness; (2) *taijasa*, the dreaming state; (3) *prajna*, a state of deep sleep, experiencing no separateness, but without awareness of that experience—becoming conscious in this state results in "abiding joy"; and (4) *turiya*, superconsciousness, complete oneness with atman, the self.

   Besant is here counting turiya as the fourth plane, linking vaishvanara with the physical plane, taijasa with the astral or psychic plane (whereon dreams are said to occur); prajna with the mental or heavenly plane (the location of Devachan, a dreamlike state of bliss for the dead), and turiya with the buddhic plane. It could be argued that the definition of turiya in the Mandukya Upanishad would better be represented by the atmic (nirvanic) plane in Besant's chart—and in fact HPB uses the term in that sense. In speaking of the monad as atma-buddhi-manas, she mentions a state in which "the real One Self of man merges *into Brahman*, in cases of high Samadhi (the *Turiya* state), or final Nirvana" (*SD* 1:570).

   The terms *turiya* and *samadhi* (Sanskrit: "ecstasy") are sometimes used interchangeably by writers on yoga. HPB's statement implies there is a low samadhi as well as a high samadhi. If we equate Besant's turiyic plane with the buddhic plane, keeping in mind that the state of bliss associated with this plane is a lower level of samadhi and that the nirvana of the next higher plane is a higher level of the same state, then there is no inconsistency between Besant's teachings about the planes and the Mandukya Upanishad's description of the four states of consciousness.

8. **Psychic plane**: In the contemporaneous manual *Karma*, Besant refers to "the very complicated region indicated by the name psychic plane" (4). Although the term appears in HPB's writings, it seems to have lost currency in Theosophical circles after 1900.

   HPB referred to a lower and a higher psychic plane. The lower psychic plane was the realm of a compound of principles called kama-prana. The upper psychic plane was the realm of a compound familiar to most students of Theosophy: kama-manas, also called lower mind (*IGT* 28–29).

As noted, the result of any compound of principles is a body, or vehicle of consciousness on a particular plane. In Besant's teachings, the compound called *kama-prana* became the astral body and *kama-manas* the mental body. What HPB called the astral body (*linga sharira*) became the etheric double.

The idea of a psychic plane that overlaps the boundary between two other planes is apt to confuse unless we recall HPB's definition of a plane: "As used in Occultism, the term denotes the range or extent of some state of consciousness, or of the perceptive power of a particular set of senses, or the action of a particular force, or the state of matter corresponding to any of the above" (*TG*, Plane).

HPB used the term *psyche* to refer to "the animal, terrestrial Soul; the lower Manas" (*TG*, Psyche). Furthermore, there is a division in the mental plane between *arupa* (formless) levels associated with the upper manas and the *rupa* (with form) levels associated with lower manas. It appears that the upper limit of the psychic plane corresponds with that division.

HPB also makes a distinction between the *personality*, consisting of the "lower quaternary" of four principles (*sthula sharira* or dense body, astral double, prana, and kama), and the *individuality*, consisting of the upper triad (ama-buddhi-manas) (*TG*, Personality). She calls the personality the "animal man" or "animal soul" (e.g., *KT* 91–93) and the individuality the "immortal" or "reincarnating Ego" (e.g., *KT* 101–104).

I suggest that the true meaning of *psyche* or *animal soul* is kama-manas plus kama-prana, or manas-kama-prana (lower mind, desire, and vitality)—just as HPB defines the spiritual soul as having three principles: atma-buddhi-manas. The third element in our makeup is also a triad: the body, consisting of prana-linga-sthula (vitality, astral double, and dense body).

We normally consider our psyche or personality in terms of thoughts and feelings. The notion of animal soul or manas-kama-prana perfectly reflects that self-perception. Considered as a state of consciousness—and in light of HPB's definition of a plane—we are on the psychic plane whenever we operate simultaneously on the basis of thought and feeling. While we are alive, this is practically all the time.

After death, we go through a period of freeing ourselves from the kamic element of our personality, a process with two phases. The first phase involves what HPB calls the *kama-rupa*, a body specially formed after death on the basis of unfulfilled desires from the life just left behind. Once we have burned off those desires in a hell-like or purgatorial state, the kama-rupa dissolves and we pass on to the first phase of Devachan, corresponding to the lower manas, during which we experience a blissful state of living through every idealistic or unselfish plan that was unrealized during our time on earth. We then pass on to a higher level of Devachan corresponding to the ego or individuality before reincarnating once more.

The two lower phases of the afterlife are therefore personality based, and pertain to the lower and upper psychic plane. However, Devachan is also said to be a region in which no evil may enter, whereas on the lower psychic plane we purge ourselves of evil desires. There must then be a dividing line between these two halves of the psychic plane. Besant fixes that line as the boundary between the astral and the mental planes.

Furthermore, there must be another boundary between the Devachan experienced by the lower manas and that experienced by individuals who have developed the higher manas (which according to HPB is the only guarantee of immortality after death—identifying with the individuality as opposed to the personality). For the individual who has developed the individuality rather than the personality, that dividing line represents the boundary between the lower and upper levels of the *mental* plane. For the individual who has developed only the personality, the dividing line lies between the upper psychic plane and the mental plane proper.

This discussion of the psychic plane has attempted to demonstrate the reason it is so "complicated"—and yet also so important to our understanding of ourselves. It refers to the state of consciousness of ordinary, spiritually undeveloped, living individuals who have not gone beyond the personality (animal soul, lower manas) to develop the individuality (human soul, upper manas) and to their experience of the afterlife in consequence of this neglect.

Besant's subsequent teachings about the three worlds (physical, intermediate, and heavenly) served an important function in relation to the psychic plane. Though the concept of three worlds was borrowed from Hinduism, the names of these worlds reflect the description of the afterlife just given. The intermediate world lies between the physical and the heavenly worlds in the same way that the lower and upper psychic planes lie between the physical plane and the arupa (upper mental plane) levels of Devachan. Besant could use these terms to avoid confusing people about the boundaries between planes, and to omit a lengthy explanation of how the astral and mental planes relate to the psychic plane and how the latter relates to the rupa and arupa levels of the mental plane.

9. **Asuras** (Sanskrit): "Anti-gods," so called because they oppose and attempt to overthrow the rule of the gods; sometimes known as titans.
   Mara: (Sanskrit): In Buddhism, the evil demon who tempted the Buddha and whom he had to overcome in order to achieve enlightenment; sometimes associated with the god of death.

10. **Life side / form side**: This statement may represent the first appearance in Theosophical discourse of these terms, representing a distinction carried forward by many later writers. This distinction roughly corresponds to HPB's *noumenon* (life side) and *phenomenon* (form side), in which noumenon—"the true essential nature of being as distinguished from the illusive objects of sense" (*TG*, Noumenon)—represents the nonphysical origin of any physical phenomenon.

11. **With form / formless**: When Besant speaks of worlds with form (rupa), she means those in which the form aspect predominates. When she speaks of formless worlds (arupa), she means those in which the life aspect predominates. As indicated, the dividing line between the rupa and arupa worlds lies in the middle of the mental plane. Thus the more material, less spiritual worlds "below" that line are rupa, and the less material, more spiritual worlds "above" it are arupa.

12. **Royal Institution**: Organization founded in 1799 for the support and promulgation of scientific research. The lecture Besant refers to took place on March 15, 1895. See Sir William Roberts-Austen (1843–1902), "The Rarer Metals and their Alloys."

13. **Stanzas of Dzyan**: An archaic manuscript clairvoyantly perceived by HPB and translated for use as the basis of *The Secret Doctrine*. According to stanzas 7–9, slokas 24–35 (*SD* 2:18–20), the earliest races of humanity were without the mind principle (manas). High spiritual beings called "Sons of Mind" were supposed to incarnate within humanity at a certain evolutionary stage to enable the development of our mind principle. Some of these Sons of Mind balked at the idea and held back. At that time, humanity as a whole was passing through a stage in its evolutionary process of becoming ever more material in which it was mindless and hermaphroditic. The human race then divided into male and female, resulting in reproduction through sexual intercourse. Some humans remained mindless because of the "sin" of the Sons of Mind who held back from incarnating within them. They could not restrain their sexual

urges, resulting in the defilement of their bodies and the production of monsters through intercourse with animals.

Thus, when the Sons of Mind finally began incarnating in human form, they were karmically "punished" for their earlier resistance by having to do so in degraded bodies. Apes were not the precursors of humankind, but among the degenerate offspring of this sin of the "ape-like, intellectually senseless" and "morally irresponsible" early humans (*SD* 1:190).

14. **"A conscious entity becoming consciousness"**: Besant may be glancing at the following passage from a posthumously published paper by HPB:

    > Consciousness *per se*, as understood and explained by Occult philosophy, is the highest quality of the sentient spiritual principle in us, the Divine Soul (or Buddhi) and our Higher Ego, and does not belong to the plane of materiality. After the death of the physical man, if he be an Initiate, it becomes transformed from a human quality into the independent principle itself; **the conscious Ego becoming Consciousness** *per se* without any Ego, in the sense that the latter can no longer be limited or conditioned by the senses, or even by space or time. (*CW* 14:387; emphasis mine)

15. **"The great heresy"**: *Attavada* (Pali): "'The great heresy,' viz. that the Self is separate from the One Self" (Powis Hoult, *A Dictionary of Some Theosophical Terms*, s.v. Attavada). *Atta* is the Pali equivalent of *atman* "self"; *vada* means "view" or "conviction." The Buddha taught *anattavada*, the view that there is no separate, individual reincarnating entity (self or atman), which would make attavada a wrong view—hence, heresy. According to HPB, "the heresies of 'Attavada' (belief in soul or *self*) and that of *Sakkayaditthi* (the delusion of individuality or *personality*, i.e., belief in a "I am" apart from Universal Existence . . .)" are considered by Buddhists to be "'primary delusions,' the direct result of ignorance or Maya" (CW 4:173). HPB also speaks of "the great dire heresy of separateness" (*VS* 9), in the sense of ignoring our interconnectedness with others, which is apparently what Besant refers to here.

16. **Arupa region**: The upper three of seven subplanes in the mental plane, the realm to which the causal body has access, the highest heaven experienced by all human beings during the afterlife, even if briefly, before they reincarnate (though, as noted, the area in which they find themselves, Devachan, is said to be specially protected against incursions of evil).

17. **Deus inversus**: *Daemon est deus inversus* (Latin): "Demon [devil] is God inverted [reversed]." Said to be an old hermetic or kabbalistic axiom. Title of a section of *SD* 1:411–23. Arthur Edward Waite (1857–1942), renowned historian of occultism, notes that the phrase occurs in the writings of Eliphas Levi (pseudonym of Alphonse Louis Constant, 1810–75), who brought the phrase forward from Johann Pistorius, the Younger (1546–1608), author of a work on the Kabbalah published in 1587. See Arthur Edward Waite, *The Mysteries of Magic: A Digest of the Writings of Eliphas Levi*, 120, 126. HPB was deeply familiar with and frequently cited the work of Eliphas Levi.

Chapter Four: Occultism, Semi-Occultism, and Pseudo-Occultism

1. **Returning from India**: Besant had just come back to London on June 20, 1898, after spending ten weeks in India.
2. **Spiritual forces**: This paragraph elaborates the following statement of HPB:

   > It is a law of occult dynamics that "a given amount of energy expended on the spiritual or astral plane is productive of far greater results than the same amount expended on the physical objective plane of existence." (*SD* 1:644)

3. **Occultism**: This succinct definition of occultism does not appear as such in Blavatsky's published writings, though most of its elements do (as in the title of a posthumously published article, "Mind in Nature," *CW* 13:262–69). However, a similar definition is attested in a manuscript attributed to William Q. Judge, another of HPB's personal students: "Occultism has been defined by H. P. Blavatsky to be 'the study of the workings of the Universal Mind'" (*Echoes of the Orient: The Writings of William Quan Judge*, 3:261).
4. **Maya**: Sanskrit: "Illusion."
5. **Future lecture**: A week later, on July 7, 1898, Besant presented a lecture entitled "Emotion, Intellect, and Spirituality" to the Blavatsky Lodge. This lecture was published as a pamphlet by the Theosophical Publishing Society in 1898, reprinted as Adyar Pamphlets, No. 1 (March 1911), and appeared in Besant's *Essays and Addresses*, vol. 1, *Psychology*, 110–45.

6. **Ahamkara** (Sanskrit: "I maker"): In yoga, that aspect of the mind (manas) which creates separation from the self (atman) through establishing and maintaining the illusion of individual identity.

7. **Sheath**: An English translation of the Sanskrit term *kosha*—roughly equivalent to *body*. The Taittiriya Upanishad (2.2–5) describes five such sheaths: *annamayakosha* (the "sheath of food," correlated to the dense physical body or *sthula sharira*), *pranamayakosha* (the "sheath of vitality," correlated to the etheric double, or *linga sharira*), *manomayakosha* (the "sheath of mind," correlated to the mental body—or as here, the "sheath of intellect," i.e., *kama-manas*), *vijnanamayakosha* (the "sheath of knowledge" or "sheath of wisdom," correlated to the causal body, or *buddhi-manas*), and the *anandamayakosha* (the "sheath of bliss," correlated to the buddhic body or *atma-buddhi*). Charts making these correlations clear may be found in Annie Besant, *The Ancient Wisdom*, 194.

8. **Maker of illusions**: "Having become indifferent to the objects of perception, the pupil must seek out the *rajah* [king] of the senses, the Thought-Producer, he who awakes illusion. The Mind is the great Slayer of the Real. Let the Disciple slay the Slayer" (*VS* 1).

9. **Beings**: Besant is referring to a golden age in the evolution of early humanity, comprising the first three of the seven "root races" on our globe: "There were 'gods' on Earth in those days—gods, and not men, as we know them now, says the tradition" (*SD* 1:369). These gods or divine men were the result of highly evolved beings from an earlier creation incarnating in human form: "They may indeed mark a 'special' or extra *creation*, since it is they who, by incarnating themselves within the senseless human shells of the two first Root-Races, and a great portion of the Third Root-Race—create, so to speak, a *new race*: that of thinking, self-conscious and *divine* men" (*SD* 1:457n). These were the legendary divine rishis and kings, who gave way to lesser rulers and teachers, age by age, including those of uneven development subsequently mentioned by Besant.

10. **Force**: Used here in the sense of propagating and accelerating the development of plants in greenhouses, thereby bringing them into bloom out of season. In the same way, the techniques of psychic development referred to here bring human spiritual powers into maturity out of season—meaning ahead of the development of most of humanity, which in the ordinary course of evolution may not achieve them for many thousands of years.

11. **Vedanta** (Sanskrit: "end of the Vedas"): One of the six *darshanas* (Sanskrit: "philosophical views") that have developed in Hinduism, referring specifically to the oldest traditions embodied in the four Vedas (the most ancient and sacred of revealed Hindu scriptures) and the principal Upanishads (later, but still sacred, revealed teachings). Yoga is another of the darshanas.

12. **Prism**: Besant glances at the following passage from HPB, in which the "three-sided prism" probably refers to spirit, soul, and body:

    As the white ray of light is decomposed by the prism into the various colors of the solar spectrum, so the beam of divine truth, in passing through the *three-sided* prism of man's nature, has been broken up into vari-coloured fragments called RELIGIONS. . . . Combined, their aggregate represents one eternal truth; separate, they are but shades of human error and the signs of imperfection. (*IU* 2:639)

13. **Raja (kingly) yoga**: Classical yoga, primarily focusing on meditative practices to achieve higher states of consciousness and self-realization.

14. **Hatha (forceful) yoga**: A more recent innovation, which focuses on mastering the body, including bringing involuntary processes such as breathing and the beating of the heart under the control of the mind. The yoga most widely practiced in the West is a form of hatha yoga, which Besant discusses in the next two paragraphs. Most of the practices Besant rails against in this lecture have fallen out of the Western approach to yoga, though they may still be found in some traditional yoga manuals.

    Hatha yoga is a branch of Tantra, a set of teachings designed to use the physical body as a vehicle for achieving enlightenment. Tantra also includes an infamous "left-hand path"—which Besant subsequently refers to as "those darker schools." The left-hand path involves activities forbidden by traditional yoga (flesh eating, wine drinking, sexual intercourse) in rituals designed to harness sexual energy to achieve higher states of consciousness. Such practices are widely condemned as morally corrupting and spiritually dangerous. In Theosophical literature, the left-hand path is associated with Black Magic and the Brothers of the Shadow.

15. **Apsaras** (Sanskrit: "nymphs"): Sensuous, fairy-like celestial beings, considered a distraction on the spiritual path—an equivalent of the prankish nature spirits discussed in some Theosophical literature.

16. **True spiritual energies**: Besant's statements closely resemble those made in an 1887 interview with HPB (not published until 1900) by Charles Johnston (1867–1931), an Irish Theosophist who married HPB's niece (*EW* 408):

> [The Masters] keep alive the spiritual life of mankind. . . . At certain regular periods, they try to give the world at large a right understanding of spiritual things. One of their number comes forth to teach the masses, and is handed down to tradition as the Founder of a religion. . . . But that is not the only work of the adepts. At much shorter periods, they send forth a messenger to try to teach the world. Such a period comes in the last quarter of each century, and the Theosophical Society represents their work for this epoch. (*CW* 8:401–402)

17. **Force for good**: From "Occultism versus the Occult Arts":

> *True Occultism* or *Theosophy* is the "Great Renunciation of Self," unconditionally and absolutely, in thought as in action. It is Altruism, and it throws him who practises it out of calculation of the ranks of the living altogether. "Not for himself, but for the world, he lives," as soon as he has pledged himself to the work. Much is forgiven during the first years of probation. But, no sooner is he "accepted" than his personality must disappear, and he has to become *a mere beneficent force in Nature*. (*CW* 9:254)

18. **Alphabet of occult knowledge**: In the introductory material to "E.S. Instruction No. III," HPB mentions she "received two letters and a reproof from the Masters" in connection with her work with the Esoteric Section (*CW* 12:582). As HPB examines her conscience for wrongdoing, she makes the following statement:

> In what particular, then, have I failed to do my duty? Simply in this, as I am shown: I have begun to give out Eastern teachings to those who were unacquainted with the Eastern discipline. . . . In short, I have begun to instruct them in *spelling* before I had taught them the *letters* of the Occult alphabet. (*CW* 12:584)

Old precept: From the same Instruction, quoting from a letter of the Masters:

> "There is a very, VERY ancient maxim, far older than the time of the Romans or the Greeks, more ancient than the Egyptians or Chaldeans. It is a maxim all of them (Theosophists) ought to remember and live accordingly. And it is that a sound and pure mind requires a sound and pure body. Bodily purity every adept takes precautions to keep." (*CW* 12:597)

Latch: From *Light on the Path*: Until the "trial initiation of the would-be occultist" has been passed, "he cannot even reach to the latch of the gate which admits to knowledge" (*LP* 31–32).
Occult gateway: From HPB's article "Occultism versus the Occult Arts," which Besant cited earlier in this lecture:

> There are "natural-born magicians"; Mystics and Occultists by birth, and by right of direct inheritance from a series of incarnations and aeons of suffering and failures. These are passion-proof, so to say. No fires of earthly origin can fan into a flame any of their senses or desires; no human voice can find response in their souls, except the great cry of Humanity. These only may be certain of success. But they can be met only far and wide, and they pass through the narrow gates of Occultism because they carry no personal luggage of human transitory sentiments along with them. They have got rid of the feeling of the lower personality, paralyzed thereby the "astral" animal, and the golden, but narrow gate is thrown open before them. Not so with those who have to carry yet for several incarnations the burden of sins committed in previous lives, and even in their present existence. For such, unless they proceed with great caution, the golden gate of Wisdom may get transformed into the wide gate and the broad way "that leadeth unto destruction," and therefore "many be they that enter in thereby" [Matt. 7:13]. This is the Gate of the Occult arts, practised for selfish motives and in the absence of the restraining and beneficent influence of Atma-vidya. (*CW* 9:259–60)

19. **Dangers**: Possibly a reference to the spiritual and political crisis in the TS that developed after HPB's death and climaxed with the secession of the American Section, under Judge's leadership, in 1895. The principle events in this crisis were as follows:

    In May 1891, William Q. Judge came to London from America with Annie Besant, who had been sent there by HPB to address the American Section convention. They were both concerned about HPB's failing health—for good reason, since she died while they were en route.

    In London, Besant began receiving handwritten notes from the Mahatmas in scripts familiar from similar communications received while HPB was alive. Besant rushed to announce to the world in a widely reported lecture that communication had continued with the Mahatmas beyond HPB's death, thereby proving that they were real individuals, not HPB's invention. Meanwhile, rumors reached HSO in India that Judge was drawing attention to recently received Mahatma Letters that some people declared to be suspicious—possibly fraudulent (in the sense that the information contained in them had not come from the Masters) or forgeries (in the sense that they had been written by Judge in the handwriting of the Masters). One such letter was even addressed to HSO.

    Upon hearing of the suspected letters, Besant defended Judge, since they were colleagues in carrying on the work of the ES. Later, when she visited India, HSO placed before her evidence that persuaded her she was deceived by Judge. News of the disputed letters was leaked to the press, which had a field day with Besant and the TS, causing her much personal and public embarrassment. She gathered the evidence together and sent it to Judge, wanting to be fair and to give him a chance to defend himself.

A war of pamphlets by Besant, Judge, and others ensued, culminating in the convening of a judicial committee of TS officers and council members in London to investigate the charges and render judgment. HSO, Besant, and Judge were present. The committee was unable to come to a conclusion, since to do so would commit the TS to acknowledging the reality or unreality of the Masters. The Society's official position was that belief in the Masters was a personal matter and should play no part in the transaction of official TS business. Tensions and agitations continued until the American Section seceded from the larger TS body in 1895, leaving behind only a few lodges and individuals who remained connected with HSO's original organization.

Other issues of procedure and policy involving Judge's status in the TS were also behind the split, including whether Judge was truly vice president of the organization (since he had been appointed rather than elected); whether the true headquarters of the TS was in New York City, where it had been founded in 1875, or in India, where HPB and HSO had transferred it when they left New York for India in 1879; and which of HSO's executive actions in 1892 had validity—his resignation as lifetime president was followed by Judge's election to the presidency and HSO's retraction of his resignation and annulment of the presidential election.

Another area of stress involved Judge's and Besant's shared responsibility as heads of the ES, by order of HPB. Judge was a founding member of the TS, along with HPB and HSO, and had done much to build up the membership of the American Section over twenty years while benefitting from frequent opportunities to learn directly from HPB in person and by correspondence. Besant was a relative parvenu, having just six or seven years work for the organization behind her and only two years of study with HPB. At the climax of the pamphlet wars, Judge accused Besant of having come under the influence of a Black Magician—hence Besant's reference to the dangers of occult study in the present lecture. (Summarized from Ransom, *Short History of the Theosophical Society*, 280–314; and Nethercot, *Last Four Lives*, 26–43, covering events from 1891–95.)

20. **Ark of occultism**: Only consecrated priests were allowed to touch the Ark of the Covenant, containing tablets on which the Ten Commandments were written—anyone else would instantly be struck dead (Num. 4:15–20; 2 Sam. 6:3–7).

21. **"No stain":** Possibly a glance at the following phrase from *Light on the Path*: "It is easy to say, I will not be ambitious: it is not so easy to say, when the Master reads my heart he will find it clean utterly" (*LP* 17).

Chapter Five: The Higher Life

1. **Prayer**: Though it seems consistent with the *bhakti* (Sanskrit: "devotional") yoga tradition of Hinduism, and could conceivably have been uttered by "an ancient devotee," this "prayer" strongly resembles an exhortation from the Methodist theologian Adam Clarke (1760 or 1762–1832), *Holy Bible . . . with a Commentary and Critical Notes*, 3:478n: "Reader, seek the salvation of thy soul as earnestly as the covetous man seeks wealth."

2. **Swami Vivekananda** (1863–1902): One of the first Indian spiritual teachers to come to America. Besant heard him speak at the 1893 World Parliament of Religions in Chicago, which she attended as part of a delegation of speakers sent by the Theosophical Society from London, New York, and India. This story appears in Swami Vivekananda, "Bhakti or Devotion," in *Collected Works of Swami Vivekananda*, 1989, 2:38–53; reprint, 2006, 45. Besant attended a lecture on this subject by Vivekananda at the Blavatsky Lodge in London on July 9, 1896 (Henry S. Olcott, *Old Diary Leaves: The History of the Theosophical Society*, 1935, vol. 6; reprint, 1975, 53).

3. **Probationary path**: The first step in the path to the Masters, as outlined by Besant in *The Path of Discipleship*.

4. **Times of deadness**: For an explanation of how we make spiritual progress during times of depression, see "Spiritual Darkness" in Annie Besant, *The Spiritual Life*, 66–73.

5. **Three aspects of the self**: In Besant's interpretation of the Theosophical concept of the divine trinity that underlies many of the world religions, *will* is a function of the first Logos, *intelligence* (sometimes called "wisdom") is a function of the second Logos, and *activity* is a function of the third Logos. Furthermore, will is the basis of our seventh principle, *atman*; intelligence or wisdom is the basis of our sixth principle, *buddhi*;

and activity is the basis of our fifth principle, *manas*. This is why Besant says, "The self [i.e., the monad or *atma-buddhi-manas*] in man reveals itself in three aspects."

6. **Will and desire**: HPB brought forward this link in the Inner Group Teachings: "Will and desire are the higher and lower aspects of one and the same thing" (*IGT* 5).
7. **Desire nature**: A synonym for our fourth principle, *kama*.
8. **Purification of the Bodies**: Behind Besant's advice in the next several parts of this lecture is a statement by HPB from an article entitled "Lodges of Magic": "Among the indispensable pre-requisites for psychic development, noted in the mystical Manuals of all Eastern religious systems, are a pure place, pure diet, pure companionship, and a pure mind" (*CW* 10:127).
9. **Magnetic**: Commonly used in Theosophical circles at the time of Besant's lecture with reference to what intuitives nowadays would call the "energetic" effects of the aura of a person, place, or group on the objects and people in its vicinity.
10. **Astral matter**: According to Besant, the astral body is made up of the elemental essence ("matter") of the astral plane. This astral essence comes in six grades, one for each lower subplane of the astral plane—and a seventh, more refined and fundamental, called "monadic essence or atomic matter," from which the other six derive. This astral monadic essence resides on the highest subplane of the astral plane. The lowest grade of astral elemental essence, which is the closest to the coarser vibrations of the physical plane, corresponds to base desires of a material nature and the highest grade to lofty desires of a spiritual nature. As the astral body evolves, the lower grades of elemental essence are gradually replaced by the higher grades, making this body less susceptible to the influence of base desires. The distinction between monadic and astral essence is one of the more abstruse points of technical Theosophy. To learn more, see Annie Besant, *A Study in Consciousness*, 43–62.
11. **Desire forms**: Artificial elementals generated by the action of our desires on the matter (elemental essence) of the astral plane.
    Thought forms: Artificial elementals generated by the action of our thoughts on the matter of the mental plane. Desire forms and thought forms are "artificial" in that we have manufactured them ourselves. They are elementals in that, once created, they have a primitive conscious life

of their own. Theosophists often use the term *thought forms* to cover both the astral and the mental varieties of artificial elementals.
Thought body: The mental body.

12. **Laws of Manu**: Besant was probably thinking of 12.10–11, in which control of speech, thoughts, and body are advised—the subject of this portion of her talk. A nearly identical translation of the passage from the Shrimad Bhagavatam by Swami A. C. Bhaktivedanta Prabhupada (1896–1977) may be found at http://www.srimadbhagavatam.org/canto11/chapter8.html: "He who has conquered the tongue, has conquered all."
13. **Worthwhile/true/useful**: Variant of a popular Victorian era Christian teaching on right speech called "The Three Sieves": "Is it true? Is it kind? Is it useful?" Another variant with an additional question appears in New Age spiritual discourse as an "ancient Sufi teaching" called "The Four Gates of Speech."
14. **Triple cord** (also called the sacred thread): A reference to the Hindu coming of age ceremony (Sanskrit: *upanayana*), representing purity of thought, word, and action.

Chapter Six: Methods of Unfoldment

1. **New psychology**: Not Freudian psychology, which was then becoming better known, but that of the coming race or era—the sixth subrace of the fifth root race. This was the last of a six-lecture series entitled "Theosophy and the New Psychology" and published in book form under that title. The previous lectures covered such topics as clairvoyance, clairaudience, and telepathy.
2. **Superconsciousness**: What we might now call "transpersonal" consciousness—literally, beyond the personal levels of consciousness we are familiar with. As the next sentences make clear, Besant is referring to *buddhi-manas* (i.e., the causal body), which she takes to be the cause of genius, as did HPB in articles such as "Genius" (*CW* 12:13–22).
3. **Amongst ourselves**: The series of lectures of which this one forms a part was offered to members of the Theosophical Society in London. Hence this phrase refers to methods of unfoldment being taught at that time within the TS.

4. **Astral centers**: This passage may become clearer if we keep in mind the following editorial note from one of HPB's ES Instructions:

> The centres of sensation, or of internal action, that is of seeing, hearing, smelling, etc.—called *Indriyas* in Eastern systems—are located in the astral man, the physical molecules being only the necessary material agents for receiving impulses from without and transmitting them to the centres." (*CW* 12:661; *IGT* 133)

Indriyas (Sanskrit: "sense organs"): Note that what HPB calls the *astral man* is the equivalent of what Besant calls the astral "body," vehicle of the principle of kama. HPB uses the term *astral double* to refer to the principle of *linga sharira*, which Besant calls the "etheric double," the vehicle of the principle of *prana*. Some writers on Theosophy have criticized Besant for making these changes (e.g., Geoffrey Farthing, as noted). In this case, Besant was probably hoping to prevent confusion in readers of HPB's works over the distinctions between astral body, astral man, and HPB's usage of the word *astral* to refer to a variety of nonphysical phenomena.

HPB and Besant are both referring to traditional Indian teachings about the linga sharira. Georg Feuerstein, a contemporary yoga authority, further clarifies by saying that "the gross body in itself is thought to be insentient. It becomes animated when it is linked with the *linga-sharira*," which includes "the sensory potentials" (i.e., the *indriyas*). (Georg Feuerstein, *The Encyclopedia of Yoga and Tantra*, s.v. Linga-Sharira)

Thus we have physical senses, which become animated when linked with these sensory potentials in the etheric double (resulting in a sensation), but are only registered in our brain when the corresponding organs in the astral body are operational (resulting in a feeling) and can only be recognized and directed by our consciousness when the organs of the mental body are likewise operational (resulting in a thought or a memory). For Besant's own description of how the centers in the various bodies interact see *Seven Principles*, 16–17.

5. **American literature**: Besant was probably referring to the work of American New Thought writer William Walker Atkinson (1862–1932). Beginning in 1903, Atkinson purveyed yoga teachings under the pseudonym Yogi Ramacharaka, including *The Science of Breath* (1903), *Fourteen Lessons in Yogi Philosophy and Oriental Occultism* (1903), *Advanced Course in Yogi Philosophy and Oriental Occultism* (1904), and *Hatha Yoga, or The Yogi Philosophy of Physical Well-Being* (1904).

6. **Indian and Westerner**: Besant had spent considerable time living in India and traveling throughout the subcontinent during the ten years between her first visit in December 1893 and the delivery of this lecture in summer 1904. Her statements in this paragraph might have been true of some portion of the Indian population at that time. Yet she was speaking to a primarily English audience in London, so they may also imply colonial stereotyping: the unworldly Indian versus the worldly Westerner.

7. **Attributes of matter**: The three *gunas* (Sanskrit): *sattva* (which Besant calls "rhythm"), *rajas* ("mobility"), and *tamas* ("inertia"). According to yogic thought, all matter is made up of combinations of these three qualities. The dietary system that involves the three gunas comes under the heading of *Ayurveda*, a body of ancient healing practices that originated in India.

8. **Mental body organs**: The chakras of the mental body. Charles W. Leadbeater writes,

   > In each of our vehicles there are certain force-centers which in Sanskrit are called chakras—a word which signifies a wheel or revolving disc. These are points of connection at which force flows from one vehicle to another." (*The Inner Life*, 196)

   For information sensed in the mental body chakras to be registered in the physical brain, these chakras must be linked to the astral body chakras and thence to the etheric double chakras, which are linked to the brain—thus the importance of developing the astral body chakras from the mental body chakras.

9. **"Nearer than hands and feet"**: From "The Higher Pantheism," by the British Victorian Poet Laureate Alfred Lord Tennyson (1809–92).

Chapter Seven: THE REALITY OF THE INVISIBLE AND THE ACTUALITY OF THE UNSEEN WORLDS

1. **Alexander Bain** (1818–1903): Scottish professor of philosophy at Aberdeen University, educational reformer, and early writer on the science of psychology. The notion that our beliefs affect our conduct is a cornerstone of Bain's philosophy: "The difference between mere conceiving or imagining, with or without strong feeling, and belief, is

acting, or being prepared to act, when occasion arises" (Alexander Bain, *Mental and Moral Science: A Compendium of Psychology and Ethics*, 372).

2. **Egypt**: The doctrine Besant cites can be traced to the Hermetica—esoteric texts written in Greek, attributed by some scholars to the 2nd and 3rd centuries CE (http://en.wikipedia.org/wiki/Hermetica). These texts named their author as Hermes Trismegistus (Thrice-Great Hermes), who was identified with the ancient Egyptian god Thoth. Hermes and Thoth both were gods of writing (http://en.wikipedia.org/wiki/HermesTrismegistus). HPB believed the Hermetica originated in ancient Egypt (see, for example, *CW* 13:231–33).
   India: Probably a reference to the myth of Vishnu's dream, in which the god floats in the waters of endless space on the back of the many-headed serpent Shesha. A lotus flower containing the phenomenal universe sprouts from his navel, representing the world as his dream—or, as Besant puts it, a passing divine idea.

3. **Adam Kadmon**: In the Kabbalah, the celestial or heavenly man, said to be the archetype upon which the phenomenal universe is based, as well as the form of the individual human being.
   Talmud: "'If thou wilt know the invisible, open thine eye wide on the visible,' says a Talmudic axiom" (*SD* 2:118). Probably from Isaac Myer, *Qabbalah: The Philosophical Writings of Solomon Ben Yehudah Ibn Gebirol or Avicebron and their connection with the Hebrew Qabbalah and Sepher ha-Zohar, etc.*, 109.
   Philo Judaeus (ca. 20 BCE–50 CE): Jewish theologian of Alexandria. Besant is probably referring to a citation in *Isis Unveiled* 1:56: "'The incorporeal world then was already completed, having its seat in the Divine Reason,' says Philo." The original source continues: "and the world, perceptible by the external senses, was made on the model of it" (Philo, *De opificio mundi* [*The Creation of the World*] 10; in Charles Duke Yonge, *The Works of Philo Judaeus, the Contemporary of Josephus*, 9).

4. **Pythagoras of Samos** (ca. 570–ca. 495 BCE): "Ionian Greek Philosopher, mathematician, and founder of the religious movement called Pythagoreanism" (http://en.wikipedia.org/wiki/Pythagoras).
   Plato (ca. 428/427–ca. 348/347 BCE): Greek philosopher, student of Socrates (ca. 469–399 BCE), author of the Platonic Dialogues, foundational texts of Western philosophy (http://www.newworldencyclopedia.org/entry/Plato; http://www.newworldencyclopedia.org/entry/Socrates).
   The following summary of the Platonic philosophy of creation from Isaac Preston Cory's *Ancient Fragments . . . with an Introductory*

Dissertation and an Inquiry into the Philosophy and Trinity of the Ancients, a work cited frequently by HPB, fills in some gaps in Besant's condensed summary. After declaring that "The doctrines of Plato differ only in refinement" from those of Pythagoras (hence Besant's statement, "And so with Plato"), Cory continues:

> God and Matter, two originally independent principles, are held to be, as it were, the extremities of that chain of being which composes the universe. Subordinate to the God, we have the Intelligible world of Ideas or the Forms. . . . When the Deity or Demiurgus thought proper to compose the world, he looked to this ideal world as the exemplar, in whose likeness he constructed his new work. He impressed the disordered material Chaos with the Forms, and rendered the world a living animal, after the pattern of its ideal prototype, consisting of a soul endued with Intellect, and of a body of which all beings comprehended in it, Gods Men Animals or material species, are but the concrete individuals, of which the abstract ideas unalterably subsist in the intelligible world. (xlvi–xlvii)

The following statement from *Isis Unveiled* supports Besant's reference to the universal mind: "Pythagoras taught his disciples that God is the universal *mind* diffused through all things" (*IU* 1:131).

5. **Thou art That**: *Tat tvam asi* (Sanskrit), one of the "great sayings" (Sanskrit: *Mahavakya*) of Hinduism, a constant refrain in Chandogya Upanishad 6.8–16.

6. **Consciousness veiled in matter**: Behind this passage is the following teaching from *The Secret Doctrine*:

> Metaphysically and esoterically there is but One Element in nature, and at the root of it is the Deity; and the so-called seven elements, of which five have already manifested and asserted their existence, are the garment, the veil, of that deity; direct from the essence whereof comes Man, whether physically, psychically, mentally or spiritually considered. (*SD* 1:460)

The elements concerned here are earth, water, fire, air, and ether. They are linked with the five manifested planes, which Besant calls physical, astral, mental, buddhic, and nirvanic or atmic. If we take each element as a symbol of its associated plane, then the body made up of that element—which allows us to perceive or move within its own plane—is a garment or veil placed over the God or Spirit within us. Thus HPB hints at the physical body, the astral (psychic) body, the mental body, and the buddhic or spiritual body (i.e., *atma-buddhi*).

7. **Garments**: The following passage from Besant's *A Study in Consciousness* ties together the ideas expressed in this and the preceding paragraph of Besant's lecture:

    [The monad—the god or spirit within us] will evolve his consciousness on these [the five manifested planes] by taking from each plane some of its matter, veiling himself in this matter and forming it into a sheath by which he can come into contact with that plane, gradually organising this sheath of matter into a body capable of functioning on its own plane as an expression of himself, receiving vibrations from the plane and transmitting them to him, receiving vibrations from him and transmitting them to the plane. As he veils himself in the matter of each successive plane he shuts away some of his consciousness, that of it which is too subtle for receiving or setting up vibrations in the matter of that plane. (40)

    According to Besant, "consciousness on any plane means the power of answering to the vibrations of that particular plane" (ibid., 39–40). Thus the increase of illusion inherent in each step of the monad's descent into matter is a result of two things: (1) having yet to evolve consciousness on each plane (through organizing sheaths into bodies); and (2) this shutting away of "higher" portions of itself that cannot respond to the matter of a particular plane.

8. **Life and life vehicles**: the distinction between life, which is eternal and immortal, and form (life vehicles or bodies), which is impermanent and perishing.

9. **Plunge**: "We plunge into the depths of our own being in quest of something which consciousness may have treasured up beneath it, but at the bottom of all things we find it awaiting us, 'a gem of purest ray supreme'" (see Austin Phelps, *The New Birth, or the Work of the Holy Spirit*, 130).
    Austin Phelps (1820–90): American Congregationalist minister and president of the Andover Theological Seminary at the time *New Birth* was published. The book is about religious or spiritual conversion, a subject of interest to Besant throughout her life.

10. **Spiritual world**: Besant often uses *world* as a synonym for *plane* and *spiritual* for the principle of buddhi. Thus the "spiritual world" would be the plane of buddhi. According to HPB, immortality in the afterlife is only possible to the person who has linked the principle of manas with that of buddhi during life. Such a person would be free of the three worlds in which the personality operates: the physical world (or plane),

the intermediate world (Kamaloka or the astral plane), and the heavenly world (Devachan or the mental plane).

11. **Brahma-vidya** (Sanskrit: "knowledge of God"): Used as a synonym for *Theosophy* (Greek: "knowledge of God"). *Gnosis* (Greek: "knowledge") has the connotation of hidden wisdom or knowledge of spiritual truth.

12. **Proof of the existence of God**: This passage and a similar one on p. 76 derive from a lecture of 1893, "India, Her Past and Her Future," (*Essays and Addresses*, vol. 4: *India*, 30–32), in which Besant cites Brihadaranyaka Upanishad 3.7.23 and 4.4.18, 20, 22; Mandukya Upanishad 7; and Katha Upanishad 2.20, 23 (all based on translations by Roer).

13. **Reflex action of prayer**: A subject of debate during the nineteenth century—the scientific materialists arguing that the only effect of prayer was to calm the mind of the person praying.

14. **Animals and men**: Besant may have based this statement on passages like these from *The Secret Doctrine*:

    > In the animals every principle is paralyzed, and in a foetus-like state, save the second (vital) and the third (the astral), and the rudiments of the fourth (Kama, which is desire, instinct) whose intensity and development varies and changes with the species. (*SD* 2:255)
    >
    > Up to the Fourth Round, and even to the later part of the Third Race in this Round, *Man* . . . is, so far, only an animal intellectually. It is only in the actual *midway* Round that he develops in himself entirely the fourth principle as a fit vehicle for the fifth. (*SD* 2:161–62)

    According to HPB, we are presently at that midway point—on the fourth globe of the fourth round in the fifth of seven root races (that associated with *manas*, the fifth principle).

Chapter Eight: OCCULTISM AND OCCULT TRAINING

1. **Hebrews**: In a diagram in *The Secret Doctrine*, HPB lists the four worlds described in the Kabbalah in descending order along the spirit/matter continuum as follows: (1) archetypal; (2) intellectual or creative; (3) substantial or formative; and (4) physical or material. In a note to this diagram, she explains,

    > The word "Archetypal" must not be taken here in the sense that the Platonists gave to it, i.e., the world as it existed in the Mind of the Deity;

> but in that of a world made as a first model, to be followed and improved upon by the worlds which succeed it physically—though deteriorating in purity. (*SD* 1:200n)

By "world of mind," Besant is probably referring to the intellectual or creative world, though the physical world could serve as "a gross and rough reproduction" of any of the first three worlds. Her choice of words hints that she equates the mental plane with the intellectual or creative world.

Hindus and Buddhists: For the Hindus, Brahman (the Absolute) is the Supreme. According to HPB, "the true Buddhist, recognising no 'personal god,' nor any 'Father' and '*Creator* of Heaven and Earth,' still believes in an *absolute consciousness*, 'Adi-Buddhi'" (*SD* 1:635).

Theosophy: Compare this passage from *The Secret Doctrine*:

> The whole Kosmos is guided, controlled, and animated by almost endless series of Hierarchies of sentient Beings, each having a mission to perform, and who—whether we give to them one name or another, and call them Dhyani-Chohans or Angels—are "messengers" [literal meaning of the word *angel*] in the sense only that they are the agents of Karmic and Cosmic Laws. They vary infinitely in their respective degrees of consciousness and intelligence. (*SD* 1:274–75)

Two of these degrees are represented by the terms Besant uses here: *architects* (sometimes called watchers by HPB) and *builders*. "The 'Builders' are a class called Cosmocratores, or the invisible but intelligent Masons, who fashion matter according to the ideal plan ready for them in that which we call Divine and Cosmic Ideation" (*CW* 10:341; *TBL* 49).

In *The Secret Doctrine*, HPB states that "there are three chief groups of Builders" (*SD* 1:127). The function of the first group is that of the "invisible but intelligent Masons" described above. "The Second group of the Builders is the Architect of our planetary chain exclusively; and the third, the progenitor of our humanity" (*SD* 1:128). Furthermore, "as the work of each Round is said to be apportioned to a different group of so-called 'Creators' or 'Architects,' so is that of every globe; *i.e.*, it is under the supervision and guidance of special 'Builders' and 'Watchers'—the various Dhyani-Chohans" (*SD* 1:233).

2. **Logos**: The divine mind, the originator or conceptual creator of our physical planet plus its associated nonphysical planes, as well as several other closely related planets (often called globes in Theosophical literature), not all of which exist on our physical plane. The evolution of humanity takes place within this so-called "solar system" (not to be confused with

the solar system defined by current astronomical thinking), whose sun is the physical plane representative of the Logos.

Planetary Logoi: Nonphysical beings (also called *Dhyani-Chohans*), roughly equivalent to Christian archangels, who are responsible for overseeing the material creation and maintenance of our evolutionary system, including seven "sacred" planets of which the seven planets of traditional astrology (Sun, Moon, Mercury, Venus, Mars, Jupiter, Saturn) are said to be symbols. Each represents a particular department of the work of creation, as well as one of the seven principles. The Planetary Logoi are sometimes called architects or watchers by HPB.

Rulers of the elements: Nonphysical beings who are responsible for overseeing the building of our solar system from elements traditionally described in esoteric teachings as earth, water, fire, air, and ether (also called *akasha*, Sanskrit for "radiance"). These are what HPB calls the builders. Besant and Leadbeater sometimes use the Sanskrit term *Devarajas* ("Rulers of the Gods," or "Shining Ones") for these beings.

Note that Besant is describing what HPB called the five planes of the manifested kosmos—the so-called macrocosmic planes. Our entire evolution as physical and spiritual beings is contained within the lowest of these macrocosmic planes. Each macrocosmic plane has seven subplanes—and these are the more familiar seven planes of our evolutionary system.

Following HPB's application of the hermetic principle, "As above, so below," Besant indicates that the association of the five elements with the five manifested macrocosmic planes carries into its subplanes. Thus our physical plane is associated with the element earth, our astral plane with water, our mental plane with fire, our buddhic plane with air, and our nirvanic or atmic plane with ether or akasha. Furthermore, each of these seven microcosmic planes has seven subplanes that are associated with the same elements in the same order.

The placement of fire before air may reflect the Greek origin of the Latin word *aether*, "air"; *aithein*, to "kindle" or "blaze"—in which case the order of the elements reflects a continuum of increasing immateriality: earth, water, ether as fire, ether as air, and ether as akasha. This continuum plays an important role in the occult chemistry investigations of Besant and Leadbeater.

3. **Subelements**: In their clairvoyant investigations into occult chemistry, Besant and Leadbeater further identified the seven subplanes of the physical plane with seven states of matter: solid (earth), liquid (water),

gas (here identified with fire), and four ethers. Originally, Besant and Leadbeater simply supplied these ethers with Roman numerals (Ethers I–IV). Thus she says here that the *first* ether corresponds with air, the *second* with "the divine flame." Later, these labels for the subplanes of the physical plane were further particularized as follows: (1) solid; (2) liquid; (3) gaseous; (4) etheric (*akashic*); (5) super-etheric (super-akashic); (6) subatomic; (7) atomic. (The latter two terms have different meanings than those we associate with them from contemporary science.)

In one of her ES Instructions, HPB lists the *tattvas* (Sanskrit: "thatness," i.e., realities), calling them "forces of nature" (*CW* 12:605), in an order similar to Besant's: (1) "solid or earthly substance"; (2) "watery or liquid substance"; (3) the "luminous plane of our atmosphere" (hence Besant's correspondence to fire—the Sanskrit word here is *tejas*, which can mean "fire," "heat," or "luminosity"); (4) "the aerial plane where substance is gaseous" (corresponding to Besant's element of air—her "first ether"); (5) akasha or ether (Besant's "second ether," the "divine flame"); and two unmanifested tattvas, which HPB calls *anupadaka* (Sanskrit: "parentless") and *adi* (Sanskrit: "primordial") (*CW* 12:612). However, in a subsequent ES Instruction, HPB gave out a chart that listed the elements in the following order, perhaps reflecting ancient Greek teachings on the subject: earth, water, air, fire, ether, divine flame, akasha (Diagram V, *CW* 12, between pp. 660–61). In the present lecture, Besant appears to have adopted the terms and order for the elements assigned to the tattvas in the one ES Instruction and folded in a term from the diagram in the other.

For a helpful visual representation of the elements in their relationship to the microcosmic planes and subplanes, see Besant, *A Study in Consciousness*, 20.

4. **Kosmos**: The following note (probably by Besant) to "E.S. Instruction No. IV" indicates the reason for this spelling:

> "Kosmos" (spelt with a K) was used by H.P.B. in the sense of the Manvantaric manifestation as a whole; she often applies the adjective 'cosmic' (with a *c*) to phenomena of the Solar System, and speaks of that system as the Cosmos, and the Universe. (*CW* 12:656)

5. **Mastering the theory**: On this subject, HPB stated,

> No one should go into occultism or even touch it before he is perfectly acquainted with his own powers, and that he knows how to commensurate it with his actions. And this he can do only by deeply studying the

philosophy of Occultism before entering upon the *practical* training. Otherwise, as sure as fate—He will fall into black magic. (*CW* 10:226)

6. **Rightly understood**: Besant refers to teachings by HPB on the nature of evil in *The Secret Doctrine* (e.g., the sections entitled "Daemon Est Deus Inversus" in vol. 1 and "On the Myth of the Fallen Angels in Its Various Aspects" in vol. 2) and essays such as "The Origin of Evil" (*CW* 8:110–25); and to related teachings of her own in lectures such as "The Light and Dark Sides of Nature," included in this volume, and "The Use of Evil" in *The Spiritual Life*, 100–18.

7. **Purification, virtue, noble thinking and living**: These subjects are dealt with extensively in the series of lectures published in Besant's *In the Outer Court*.

8. **No one will help another**: Besant is referring to a passage in Leadbeater's *Invisible Helpers* (i.e., those who are able to function in full consciousness on the astral plane):

    Sometimes a man gradually rouses himself out of this condition [of being completely wrapped up in his own dreams]—wakes up to the astral world around him, as it were; but more often he remains in that state until someone who is already active there takes him in hand and wakens him. This is, however, not a responsibility to be lightly undertaken, for while it is comparatively easy thus to wake a man up on the astral plane, it is practically impossible, except by a most undesirable exercise of mesmeric influence, to put him to sleep again. So that before a member of the band of workers will thus awaken a dreamer, he must fully satisfy himself that the man's disposition is such that he will make good use of the additional powers that will then be put into his hands, and also that his knowledge and his courage are sufficient to make it reasonably certain that no harm will come to him as a result of the action. (Charles W. Leadbeater, *Invisible Helpers*, 51–52)

9. **Feelings and thoughts as living beings**: Two passages from the Mahatma Letters stand behind this paragraph:

    Every thought of man upon being evolved passes into the inner world and becomes an active entity by associating itself—coalescing, we might term it—with an elemental; that is to say with one of the semi-intelligent forces of the kingdoms. It survives as an active intelligence, a creature of the mind's begetting, for a longer or shorter period proportionate with the original intensity of the cerebral action which generated it. Thus, a good thought is perpetuated as an active beneficent power; an evil one as a maleficent demon. And so man is continually peopling his current in

> space with a world of his own, crowded with the offspring of his fancies, desires, impulses, and passions, a current which reacts upon any sensitive or nervous organisation which comes in contact with it in proportion to its dynamic intensity. (*ML* 472 [Chin])
>
> Remembering thoughts are things—have tenacity, coherence, and life,—that they are real entities—the rest will become plain. Disembodied [i.e., out of body on some higher plane]—the creator is attracted naturally to its creation and creatures; sucked in—by the Maelstrom dug out by his own hands. (*ML* 49 [Barker]; 66 [Chin])

10. **Inspiration from above**: The following passage from *The Doctrine of the Heart* amplifies Besant's remarks on learning to distinguish the voice of a Master from others to which the student of occultism may be exposed:

> Two points I want to make clear: (1) that untrained psychics always run the risk of putting forward things really said by the enemy as injunctions from the Master; and (2) that the Master says nothing that the intellect of His audience cannot grasp, and against which their moral sense revolts. The Master's words, however much they may be opposed to one's previous thoughts, never fail to bring the most absolute conviction, alike to the intellect and to the moral sense of the person addressed. They come like a revelation, rectifying an error which becomes at once apparent; they stream down like a column of light dispelling the gloom; they make no claim on credulity or blind faith. (46–47)

11. **Elemental essence**: Theosophy teaches that consciousness evolves from mineral to plant to animal to human. But this is only a portion of its evolution along what commentators on *The Secret Doctrine* call the "ladder of life." There are three stages before the mineral stage and three after the human stage, for a total of ten stages. The three earliest stages are called the elemental kingdoms. These kingdoms are comprised of evolving elemental essence. The first kingdom corresponds to the matter of the upper mental plane, including that of our causal body. The second kingdom corresponds to the matter of the lower mental plane, including thought forms and our mental body. The third kingdom corresponds to the matter of the astral plane, including desire forms and our astral body. Any being on the astral plane will have a body made up of the elemental essence of the third kingdom, including the Devas—and so with the other two kingdoms. The final three stages are superhuman and are called the Dhyani-Chohanic kingdoms.

    Elemental essence evolves by becoming ever more material, "dropping down" (involution) through the three elemental kingdoms until it reaches the mineral stage. Up to this point, the process is driven by what Besant calls, in the next paragraph, a "downward-coming wave of the life of the Logos." At the mineral stage, this wave turns around and begins rising up (evolution) back toward spirit, propelled by the monad's desire to return to oneness with its source, the "divine flame" of which it is a spark. This process creates a dynamic tension between our consciousness and our bodies. Our consciousness is on the evolutionary path toward spirit, but our bodies are on the involutionary path toward matter.

By the time this lecture was delivered (1904), Leadbeater had treated the subject of elemental essence in relation to our mental and astral bodies in several books, including *The Astral Plane* (1895); *The Devachanic Plane* (1896); and *The Other Side of Death, Scientifically Examined by Clairvoyant Observation and Carefully Described* (1903).

For more information on the Ladder of Life, see Geoffrey A. Barborka, *The Divine Plan: Written in the Form of a Commentary on H. P. Blavatsky's Secret Doctrine*, 57–59.

12. **Threshold of liberation**: In the Besant/Leadbeater tradition as taught when this piece was published (1907), this initiation is the fifth of five. It allows the properly prepared candidate to move from discipleship to adeptship or mastery. At the time this lecture was delivered, these steps were laid out only in Besant's *The Path of Discipleship* and Leadbeater's *Invisible Helpers* (1896). A more expanded exposition came later, in Leadbeater's *The Masters and the Path* (1925).

13. **Beings that deceive**: CWL's *The Astral Plane* and *The Devachanic Plane* deal with the following problematic astral entities: (1) undifferentiated elemental essence responding to our thoughts; (2) artificial elementals (thought or desire forms) generated by ourselves or others; (3) shells of the deceased (i.e., their decaying astral bodies, whose intelligence has moved on to a higher plane) that have been vitalized by nature spirits or elementals; (4) nature spirits, which are capable of casting a glamour over us and deceiving us by illusion; (5) pupils of Black Magicians; and (6) Black Magicians themselves.

14. **Drops downward**: i.e., from the buddhic plane of unity to the maya "illusion" of the lower planes of separateness.

Chapter Nine: The Conditions of Occult Research

1. **Old rules**: Besant may be referring to the list of rules provided by HPB for the ES, presumably based on the teachings of the Masters. They included the following:

   > The use of wine, spirits, liquors of any kind, or any narcotic or intoxicating drug, is strictly prohibited. If indulged in, all progress is hindered, and the efforts of teacher and pupil alike are rendered useless. All such substances have a directly pernicious action upon the brain, and especially upon the "third eye," or *pineal gland*. . . .
   >
   > The moderate use of tobacco is not prohibited, for it is not an intoxicant; but its abuse, like that of everything else—even pure water or bread—is prejudicial.
   >
   > As to diet: The eating of meat is not prohibited, but if the student can maintain health on vegetables or fish, such diet is recommended. The eating of meat strengthens the passional nature, and the desire to acquire possessions, and therefore increases the difficulty of the struggle with the lower nature. (*CW* 12:496)

   Concerning tobacco, we should keep in mind that in HPB's time cigarettes, for example, were hand rolled from loose and presumably unadulterated tobacco. Much of today's tobacco has been adulterated to increase its addictive tendencies, which would likely render its use "prejudicial."

2. **Spirillae** (Latin, plural of *spirillis*: "spiral"). The concept of spirillae first appears in Theosophical literature with the publication of Besant's and Leadbeater's 1895 investigations into occult chemistry as an article by Annie Besant in *Lucifer* 17 (November 1895): 211–15. It did not originate in the teachings of HPB, but rather in an earlier spiritualist explanation of scientific enigmas such as the nature of heat, electricity, light, color, and magnetism, *The Principles of Light and Color* by Dr. Edwin Dwight Babbitt (1828–1905; http://research.borderlands.com/wiki/EdwinD.Babbitt).

   Besant and Leadbeater claimed to have discovered the "ultimate physical atom" through their clairvoyant investigations. By this term, they meant the basic building blocks of matter on the physical-plane end of the spirit/matter continuum. This ultimate physical atom existed in seven modifications of increasing materiality, one for each subplane of the physical plane. It was not to be confused with the atoms of contemporary science, which represented one way in which matter on the lowest subplanes of the physical plane could be viewed—those associated with solids, liquids, and gases.

The diagram of this ultimate physical atom published in the three editions of Besant and Leadbeater's *Occult Chemistry* (1908, 1919, and 1951) and in other Theosophical works occurs in a slightly different form in Babbitt's book (see p. 102). It appears that Besant and Leadbeater took this diagram, which they fully attributed, as an already established "scientific" (or at least clairvoyantly deduced) starting point for their explorations. They then refined what Babbitt wrote and drew by bringing it within the purview of Theosophy. A comparison of the two presentations to see what Besant and Leadbeater added and left out of Babbitt's explanation—though out of place here—might be a worthwhile endeavor.

A later description of this diagram by Leadbeater will suffice for a diagram:

> When you look at a physical ultimate atom with etheric sight you first of all see that it resembles a wire cage; then, looking more closely, you find that each wire is made up of a finer coil, and that in all there are seven sets of such spirillae. One of these spirillae is developed into activity in each round of evolution, so, as we are now in the fourth round of our earth chain incarnation, there are only four spirillae in activity at present in the majority of atoms. In each round a new set will be developed, so that in the seventh round the entire seven spirillae will be active; the atoms will therefore be better atoms in the seventh round than they are now, and the people who will live in that round will therefore find it far easier than people do to-day to respond to inner things and to live the higher life. (Charles W. Leadbeater, *Talks on the Path of Occultism*, vol. 2: *The Voice of the Silence*, 378)

HPB's Theosophy posits seven rounds of a planetary chain as one periodical unit (*manvantara*) of evolution within our system of learning and growth. The planetary chain consists of seven globes. The first three globes represent increasing degrees of materiality during a process of involution of spirit into matter, the fourth represents the turning point of deepest entrenchment of spirit in matter, and the final three globes represent increasing degrees of spirituality during a process of evolution from matter back to spirit. All degrees of consciousness participating in this system will pass from planet to planet and round to round, until they have experienced every form or expression of *being* allowable within the system.

Furthermore, each round represents the development of one of the seven principles, not only in the matter of that round, but also in the perceptual abilities of the most advanced form of consciousness passing through that round—humanity. The fourth spirillis of our round represents the principle of *kama,* which will be fully unfolded by the end of this round.

This notion of the spirillae of the physical permanent atom may originate in one of the Stanzas of Dzyan (5.4), which relates *fohat* to spirals: "Fohat traces spiral lines to unite the sixth to the seventh" (*SD* 1:118), which is to say that it links *atman* (the seventh principle, pure spirit) to *buddhi* (the sixth principle, as *upadhi* for the seventh).

HPB defines *fohat* as

> the "bridge" by which the "Ideas" existing in the "Divine Thought" are impressed on Cosmic substance as the "Laws of Nature." Fohat is thus the dynamic energy of Cosmic Ideation; or, regarded from the other side, it is the intelligent medium, the guiding power of all manifestation, the "Thought Divine" transmitted and made manifest through the Dhyani-Chohans, the Architects of the visible World. Thus from Spirit, or Cosmic Ideation, comes our consciousness; from Cosmic Substance the several vehicles in which that consciousness is individualized and attains to self—or reflective—consciousness; while Fohat, in its various manifestations, is the mysterious link between Mind and Matter, the animating principle electrifying every atom into life. (*SD* 1:16)

Remembering that an upadhi is always more material than the principle it carries, we may perhaps assume that fohat operates in the same way at other levels of being. Working in spirals, it unites each principle (spirit, or some more spiritual substance) with its upadhi (matter, or some more material substance).

The ultimate atoms of Besant and Leadbeater, which operate as the fundamental building blocks of every plane, are in a sense spirit/matter units. They represent increasingly material modifications of the primordial matter that HPB calls *mulaprakriti* (Sanskrit: "root substance"). As spirit/matter units, they would each link a higher principle to a lower, more material upadhi. Furthermore, HPB says that "an atom may be compared to (and is for the Occultist) the seventh principle of a body, or rather of a molecule" (*CW* 10:370–71; *TBL* 109).

Keeping in mind the difference in usage between current scientific definitions of these terms and those of HPB, the molecule is clearly a *compound* body (i.e., an upadhi) for the atom. Hence fohat could be said to link them—and a clairvoyant able to perceive the action of fohat would perhaps see the spiral lines as Besant and Leadbeater's spirillae.

3. **Astral sense centers**: A posthumously published ES Instruction attributed to HPB states,

> The Kama [fourth principle] during life does not form a Body which can be separated from the physical Body. It is intermolecular, answering molecule for molecule to the physical Body, and inseparable from it molecularly. Thus it is a form yet not a form; a form within the physical Body, but incapable of being projected outward as a form. This is the Inner, or Astral Man, in whom are located the centres of sensation, the psychic senses, and on whose intermolecular *rapport* with the physical Body, all sensation and purposive action depend. (*CW* 12:708; *IGT* 189; the latter indicates in a footnote that the source is unknown.)

As noted, the centers of sensation are the nonphysical *indriyas*, which Besant here calls the "sense centers" of the astral body. These sense centers produce the *cognitive* experience of seeing, hearing, smelling, tasting, and touching on the physical plane. The *psychic centers* are the chakras, which elsewhere Besant calls the "organs" of the astral body. When developed, these psychic centers allow for *astral* vision and hearing. Besant's mention of the building up of the *physical* sense organs refers to the *karmendriyas* (Sanskrit: "organs of action"), which she identifies with the sources of sense data in the physical body: eyes, ears, nose, tongue, hands, and skin.

The distinction between sense centers and sense organs is important. A sense center is an operative but undeveloped chakra, providing a faculty of perception on a *lower* plane. A sense organ is a fully developed chakra, providing perception on the *same* plane. Thus the astral sense centers enable perception on the physical plane, whereas the astral sense organs provide perception on the astral plane. All of us have the former. Only those who have a fully developed astral body—including all of its sense organs or chakras—have the latter.

For a technical explanation of such differences, see Besant's *A Study in Consciousness*, 111–40.

4. **Ways of observing**: The distinction seems to be between clairvoyant observation from within a state of ordinary waking consciousness (in which "the physical observation is alive") and from within a state of fully conscious trance (in which the eyes may remain open while astral

sight is employed). Presumably, in the latter case, physical observation is toned down ("you try to shut out the outer world"), but not eliminated.

This passage, along with the next two paragraphs, can be properly understood only by keeping in mind Besant's model of astral vision. This model stipulates that the physical senses have their origin in astral sense centers, as noted, and that astral vision does not mean the activation of the astral equivalent of physical sight. Astral vision is an experience of the whole astral body taking in sense impressions of the astral plane while the brain interprets these impressions in terms of images associated with physical sight. For this to occur, the astral sense impressions must first be registered by the astral body and then activate the astral sight center, which translates these impressions in visual terms that are passed on to the physical brain. Thus the astral body and the physical body are both engaged in the experience of astral vision.

Implied in this model of astral vision are several potentially faulty states, each of which Besant discusses in this lecture. First, the physical brain (or physical observation) is completely cut out of the loop as in deep sleep or trance, in which case sense impressions may be registered in the astral body but are not recalled upon retuning to ordinary waking consciousness. Second, the astral sense centers that stand behind the physical senses are only partially developed, in which case impressions registered by the astral body come through but without being interpreted properly by the physical brain, resulting in inaccuracies or difficulties in articulating what was perceived. Third, the astral sense centers are fully developed and physical observation is "alive" but tends to impose overly material interpretations onto impressions taken in by the astral body, resulting in perceptions of heavenly streets paved with gold, and so on.

Besant also implies in the present passage that there is a set of ideal conditions for the functioning of astral vision: (1) sense stimulation from the physical environment is reduced by choice of a quiet location in which to work; (2) the focus of consciousness is turned away from the outer world by means of trance; and (3) physical observation is kept "alive" by allowing the eyes to remain open. If the astral vehicle and the astral sense centers are sufficiently developed, there should be a smooth flow of impressions into the astral body, which are translated by the astral sense centers in terms of visual images that are passed on to the physical brain and verbalized. A notetaker is present to record the results. This ideal set of conditions is what Besant means by the phrase "using the consciousness along two or three lines at the same time."

5. **Box Hill**: A village in Surrey, about 20 miles southwest of London. The conditions under which these investigations took place in 1895 were described in a letter of Leadbeater published in the *Theosophist* under the title "Dr. Besant's First Use of Clairvoyance."

6. **Whirling between the eyes**: In some esoteric literature, such sensations are said to indicate the opening of the third eye, often identified with the sixth chakra, which is located between the eyebrows. This opening allows for the development and use of clairvoyant vision.

7. **Subdivision of the atom**: The process Besant describes was hinted at by HPB. As noted, an atom is "the seventh principle of a body, or rather of a molecule." HPB continues:

   > The physical or chemical molecule is composed of an infinity of finer molecules and these in their turn of innumerable and still finer molecules. Take for instance a molecule of iron and so resolve it that it becomes non-molecular; it is then, at once transformed into one of its seven principles, *viz.*, its astral body; the seventh of these is the atom. The analogy between a molecule of iron, before it is broken up, and this same molecule after resolution, is the same as that between a physical body before and after death. The principles remain *minus* the body. Of course this is occult alchemy, not modern chemistry. (*CW* 10:370–71; *TBL* 109)

   Besant and Leadbeater's ultimate atom is what HPB describes as the seventh principle of a molecule. A molecule, here, is compound (principle plus upadhi); whereas an atom (principle only) is not. The implication of what HPB says is that all matter on a particular plane is compound, but can be resolved into the principle that corresponds to that plane. When this has been accomplished, we have the fundamental building block of matter on that plane, the ultimate atom. Besant and Leadbeater's clairvoyant investigations took this idea one step further by hypothesizing that an attempt to divide the ultimate atom of a particular plane would lead us to the compound matter of the next higher plane. In a sense, what we have here is a psychic equivalent of nuclear fission that separates principles from their upadhis.

8. **Scientific proof**: At the time these statements were made (1905), the first edition of Besant and Leadbeater's *Occult Chemistry* (1908) had not yet been released, nor had the second round of clairvoyant investigations upon which it was based occurred (1907). However, the original 1895 article on "Occult Chemistry" had just been republished in pamphlet form (London: Theosophical Publishing Society, 1905). This early work

was based on the notion that the atom, once thought to be indivisible, was made up of smaller particles. During the ten years between the publication of article and pamphlet, the electron was named and some of its properties described—a fact which Besant and Leadbeater might have seen as a corroboration of their clairvoyant investigations.

Chapter Ten: PSYCHISM AND SPIRITUALITY

1. **Ordinary biology**: This passage is influenced by the Lamarckian theory of evolution, named for Jean-Baptiste Lamarck (1744–1829). Adherents of evolutionary theories originating with Darwin tend to discredit Lamarck, but there were Western scientists in the nineteenth century who took his ideas seriously. The following passage from Besant's *The Evolution of Life and Form* makes her argument clearer:

   If we take, for a moment, a swift survey of the evolution of forms, we shall find that the building of organs follows the exercise of life functions. In the earliest forms, there are no organs, but the functions of life are present and active. The creature breathes and assimilates, circulation goes on. But there are no organs for digestion, no organs for breathing, no organs for circulation. The whole body does everything. But as evolution proceeds, and definite organs are formed in the physical body, in the nervous system, and as later, in the astral body, chakras or astral centers of sensation are formed—as this goes on, we find a more specialized being developed with definite organs. Always, the organ comes after the function, and through the organ the function expresses itself more and more perfectly. That is a fundamental principle. And do not forget that in this you are on what is thought the safer ground of Western science. You do not find an organ appearing before the development of its function. You always find the life impulse first, and then the molding of the matter into a shape which enables that impulse to express itself more perfectly. (146–47)

2. **Devourers**: In *The Secret Doctrine*, HPB quotes an occult commentary that describes the element of fire:

   Fire alone is ONE, on the plane of the One Reality; on that of manifested, hence illusive, being, its particles are fiery lives which live and have their being at the expense of every other life that they consume. Therefore they are named the DEVOURERS." (*SD* 1:249–50)

Furthermore, "the white corpuscles are the scavengers, 'Devourers'" (*IGT* 71). This seems to be the specific teaching to which Besant was referring.

3. **Ethers of the brain**: Probably a reference to Babbitt's *Principles of Light and Color*, in which this phrase appears several times. In part, the book offers a spiritualistic explanation of clairvoyance, mental healing, and other psychic abilities on the basis of mesmerism, using terms such as *animal, vital, psychic, mental,* and *spiritual ethers.* These ethers are apparently nonphysical, information carrying, wavelike energies which our inner senses may receive and transmit, often through the eyes and hands, resulting in influences of various kinds on different levels of our being and that of others.

   Besant may also be referring to her occult chemistry investigations with Leadbeater, which correlated the physical body to the solids, liquids, and gases of the three lowest subplanes of the physical plane and the etheric double to the remaining four etheric states—or ethers. This double is said to overlay the physical body, as the nonphysical model for the latter. In this capacity, it could perhaps act as a transmitter of information from the higher bodies to the physical brain.

   The intriguing notion that imaginative, creative, or artistic abilities are functions or products of ethers working in the brain likely came from Babbitt. See, for example, Babbitt's chapter "Chromo-Mentalism" (446–533), in which the ethers of the brain are discussed, including their effects on intuition, genius, and clairvoyance—especially the handy summary of these discussions on 527–29.

4. **Society for Psychical Research (SPR)**: Organization founded in London in 1882 (and still in existence) for the scientific and historical investigation of phenomena associated with mediumship, hypnotism and mesmerism, thought transference (telepathy), hauntings, and so on. The TS and the SPR were on uneasy terms as a result of an SPR investigation of HPB in India in 1885, which concluded negatively—and, many thought, unfairly. HPB liked to poke fun at the SPR, calling it the "Spookical Research Society" (e.g., in her interview with Charles Johnston, *CW* 8:393; *EW* 321).

5. **Sheaths or bodies**: Although it may seem here and elsewhere that Besant uses these terms interchangeably, for her there is an important distinction between them. A *sheath* is an unorganized nonphysical body. When we operate in ordinary waking consciousness on the physical plane, the mental sheath provides *most* of us (at humanity's current level of

development) with the faculty of thought; and the astral sheath provides *all* of us with the faculty of feeling. To perceive on the astral or mental plane, we need an astral or mental *body*. Few of us have organized these bodies to that degree, though the methods Besant suggests throughout this book may allow us to do so. To move freely on the astral or mental plane in full consciousness, we need a fully developed astral or mental body, which Besant sometimes refers to as a "vehicle of consciousness." Only souls who are well advanced on the path of spiritual attainment have developed their astral or mental body to such a degree. The following passage from Besant's *A Study in Consciousness* makes these distinctions clear:

> In the East, they speak of the astral and mental vehicles of consciousness, when acting in relation to the physical, as *koshas*, or sheaths, and use the term *sharira*, or body, for a form capable of independent action in the visible and invisible worlds. (119)

Pure reason: *Buddhi-manas*, i.e., the causal body—that which is "next above" the mental body.

6. **Siddhis** (Sanskrit: "accomplishments"): Used in yoga to describe various spiritual powers that develop in connection with certain meditation practices (what Besant would call psychism in the terms of this lecture); considered by many traditional yoga authorities to be distractions on the path of spiritual liberation.
7. **Pagan book**: The verse cited has no reference to a pagan book—but its continuation does: "And [God] hath made of one blood all nations of men for to dwell on all the face of the earth. . . . *For in him we live, and move, and have our being*; as certain also of your own poets have said, *For we are also his offspring*" (Acts 17:26, 28). The two phrases I have italicized are said to originate in the works of the pagan poets Aratus of Soli (ca. 315/310–240 BCE) and Epimenides (7th or 6th century BCE), hence Besant's reference to a "Christian book" quoting from a "pagan book." The first phrase was in frequent use by Besant, Leadbeater, and other Theosophists of their time.
8. **Stature of Christ**: A glance at Ephesians 4:13: "Till we all come in the unity of the faith, and of the knowledge of the Son of God, unto a perfect man, unto the measure of the stature of the fulness of Christ."
9. **Olive Schreiner** (1855–1920): South African writer, free-thinker, and antiwar activist. The story is "I Thought I Stood" from *Dreams*, 125–29.

Chapter Eleven: COMMUNICATION BETWEEN DIFFERENT WORLDS

1. **Spiritualistic**: The primary distinction between Spiritualistic and Theosophical methods of obtaining clairvoyant information or communications from discarnate beings is that the latter is accomplished as an act of will in full consciousness and allows for contact with the highest and most reliable sources of information, whereas the former is passive and requires a deep trance state in which the medium is unconscious of the nature of what transpires and who is using the body to communicate. HPB considered the spiritualistic method to be unreliable, as to the information received, and dangerous to the body of the medium (e.g., in "Are Chelas Mediums?" [*CW* 6:223–27]). The "changing age" reflects the emergence of the sixth subrace of the fifth root race, within which the principle of *buddhi* (spiritual intuition) will be more developed than presently.

2. **Spiritual body**: The highest appropriations of matter mentioned here involve the buddhic and atmic (nirvanic) bodies, said to be available only to masters and their initiated disciples. Besant lumps these two bodies together under the term *spiritual body* when addressing beginning students of Theosophy (e.g., in the charts at the end of Besant's *Seven Principles*). She addresses more advanced students with the terms *buddhic body* or *atmic (nirvanic) body*. Some readers see inconsistencies in Besant's books as a result of not recognizing which audience she was trying to reach.

3. **Sphere**: Besant is borrowing an ancient cosmological model in which there are several concentric spheres surrounding the earth, each named after one of the planets, including the moon. HPB sometimes spoke of a sublunary sphere, which Besant equates here with the astral plane. The physical distance to the moon is a scientifically and mathematically known fact, and the earth's atmosphere gets increasingly thinner across that distance, as if by analogy with the astral plane's increasingly subtle matter. Yet we should probably not take Besant's statement about the size of the astral plane literally. Just as the subtle bodies are distributed around the physical body in concentric layers, from least to most subtle, so with the layers of our planetary aura—the planes or spheres.

4. **Far future time**: Besant is describing conditions in the fifth round. Rare individuals in our fourth round have so accelerated their evolution that

they are developing along fifth-round lines. Plato and Confucius are said to have been among these "fifth-rounders" (*ML* 85 [Barker]; 176 [Chin]). A planetary round involves the development of seven root races on each of seven globes that occupy planes of various degrees of density. See Barborka, *The Divine Plan*, for a lucid explanation of the evolution of humanity through races, globes, and rounds.

5. **M. Jourdain**: The main character in *Le Bourgeois gentilhomme* by Moliere (Jean Baptiste Poquelin; 1622–73). He learns to his amazement during a philosophy lesson on the distinction between poetry and prose that he has been speaking prose all his life (2.6).

6. **Marconi message**: A communication sent by wireless telegraphy, named after Guglielmo Marconi (1874–1937), the inventor who first tapped the commercial potential of radio transmission.

7. **Perfect instruments**: Compare the following passage from Besant's *Man and His Bodies*:

   > The consciousness of the Master stretches itself out in any direction in which he sends it, assimilates itself with any point to which he directs it, knows anything which he wills to know; and all this in order that he may help perfectly, that there may be nothing that he cannot feel, nothing that he cannot foster, nothing that he cannot strengthen, nothing that he cannot aid in its evolution. To him the world is one vast evolving whole, and his place in it is that of a helper of evolution. He is able to identify himself with any step, and at that step to give the aid that is needed. (165–66)

8. **Expenditure of energy**: The following passage from HPB explains several points in this article—not only the issue of why higher beings will use the least amount of force necessary to communicate with us, but also the reasons for the "difficulty and danger" of such communications and the problems entailed in the "letting loose of forces not usually employed on the physical plane." Furthermore, this passage provides a rationale for Besant's later remarks on the law of action and reaction (referred to here as compensation or karma) and the "destructive results on those around her" of phenomena worked by HPB:

   > The production of phenomena is not possible without either the aid or disturbance of elementals. Each phenomenon entails the expenditure of great force, and also brings on a correspondingly great disturbance in the elemental world, which disturbance is beyond the limit natural to ordinary human life. It then follows that, as soon as the phenomenon

is completed, the disturbance occasioned begins to be compensated for. The elementals are in greatly excited motion, and precipitate themselves in various directions. They are not able to affect those who are protected. But they are able, or rather it is possible for them, to enter into the sphere of unprotected persons, and especially those persons who are engaged in the study of occultism. And then they become agents in concentrating the karma of those persons, producing troubles and disasters often, or other difficulties which otherwise might have been so spread over a period of time as to be not counted more than the ordinary vicissitudes of life. This will go to explain the meaning of the statement that an Adept will not do a phenomenon unless he sees the desire in the mind of another lower or higher Adept or student; for then there is a sympathetic relation established, and also a tacit acceptance of the consequences which may ensue. It will also help to understand the peculiar reluctance often of some persons, who can perform phenomena, to produce them in cases where we may think their production would be beneficial; and also why they are never done in order to compass worldly ends, as is natural for worldly people to suppose might be done,—such as procuring money, transferring objects, influencing minds, and so on. (*CW* 9:111–12)

9. **Free of ferment and decay**: I.e., no alcoholic beverages or meat (flesh).

10. **Vestal virgins, or sibyls**: This information was more likely a product of CWL's and AWB's clairvoyant investigations than of historical research in the conventional sense. See Annie Besant and Charles W. Leadbeater, *The Lives of Alcyone: A Clairvoyant Investigation of the Lives throughout the Ages of a Large Band of Servers*, 2:660–61, for a clairvoyantly perceived past life involving adept communication through vestal virgins.

    CWL believed he had met Pythagoras in a past life and become a student of one of his students. See Leadbeater, *How Theosophy Came to Me*, 1–4; also Besant and Leadbeater, *The Lives of Alcyone*, 2:689–90.

    CWL and AWB began investigating the past lives of the young J. Krishnamurti (1895–1986; nicknamed Alcyone) shortly after CWL discovered him on the beach at Adyar in April 1909. These lifetimes were probed in reverse order "as history was investigated backwards" (Tillett, *Elder Brother*, 119). The resulting material was then rearranged chronologically—thus the earliest investigations appeared toward the end of this massive work.

    CWL also believed that his Master in the present life, KH, had been Pythagoras in that past life (Leadbeater, *The Inner Life*, 8). Besant's statement about "more lives than one" may indicate that CWL was acting as a channel for KH in the manner described here.

11. **William Thomas Stead** (1849–1912): English writer on spiritualism, friend of Besant, editor for several years of the *Pall Mall Gazette*; responsible for passing *The Secret Doctrine* to Besant to review after it was first published (Nethercot, *First Five Lives*, 285); author of *Letters from Julia, or Light from the Borderland: A Series of Messages as to the Life Beyond the Grave . . .* (1897). Stead died in the sinking of the *Titanic*.
    Miss Julia Ames (no reliable biographical information): Supposedly, a young American journalist whom Stead briefly met in the 1890s and who died shortly thereafter. Stead then began receiving communications from her via automatic writing (http://en.wikipedia.org/wiki/WilliamThomasStead).
    Julia's Bureau: A daily seance circle founded by Stead in 1909. It was made up of several carefully selected intuitives who met each morning under the guidance of Stead's spirit contact Julia for the purposes of answering queries about the afterlife and comforting the bereaved (ibid.).

12. **Mediumistic phenomena**: The childhood abilities Besant attributes to HPB are mentioned in one of HPB's letters:

    > I proved to [HSO] that all that mediums could do through spirits others could do at will without any spirits at all; that bells and thought-reading, raps and physical phenomena, could be achieved by anyone who had a faculty of acting in his physical body through the organs of his astral body; and I had that faculty ever since I was four years old, as all my family know. I could make furniture move and objects fly apparently, and my astral arms that supported them remained invisible; all this ever before I knew even of Masters. (H. P. Blavatsky, "Letters of HPB to Dr. Hartmann [1885–86]")

    In the words of a Mahatma, if Besant had "used the word 'Seer' instead of 'medium' the idea would have been rendered more correctly, for a man becomes rarely an adept without being born a natural Seer" (*ML* 42 [Barker]; 61 [Chin]). The difference between a medium and a seer is that the latter does consciously what the former does unconsciously. Much of HPB's teaching on the "powers latent in man" hinged on this distinction.

13. **Two hundred years**: Close readers of *The Mahatma Letters* may wonder at this statement, since Master KH wrote, "After nearly a century of fruitless search, our chiefs had to avail themselves of the only opportunity to send out a European body upon European soil to serve as a connecting link between that country and our own" (*ML* 203 [Barker]; 79 [Chin]). The clue appears in a lecture given by Besant in London shortly after

she was elected president of the TS, "The Relation of the Masters to the Theosophical Society":

The Masters taught that during the last quarter of every century a messenger was sent by them to provide an impetus to the spiritual evolution of humanity. According to Besant, HPB had been sent as such a messenger not only at the end of the nineteenth century, but also at the end of the eighteenth, during the French Revolution, having come from "a noble Austrian family"—and had failed on that earlier occasion. By implication, the last successful messenger must have appeared at the end of the seventeenth century, two hundred years before the founding of the TS. Besant did not say who the latter messenger was, nor did she provide a source for the information on this earlier incarnation of HPB (Besant, *London Lectures*, 124–25).

14. ***Old Diary Leaves***: HSO's six-volume memoir of meeting HPB, the founding of the TS, and the early history of the organization from 1874–98, which ran for many years as a serial in the *Theosophist.* The first three volumes were released during HSO's lifetime and the remaining three posthumously. The relevant passage is reprinted in Caldwell, *Esoteric World,* 76–83. See also *Esoteric World,* 94–95, for a letter of HSO that also describes this effect. Geoffrey A. Barborka, in *H. P. Blavatsky, Tibet and Tulku,* goes into great detail on HPB's work as a channel for the Masters, using the Tibetan word *tulku* (signifying a temporary or permanent transfer of intelligent awareness from an advanced spiritual being, living or dead, to a living human, often undertaken through meditation or conscious trance) to distinguish it from unconscious trance mediumship used to communicate with the unexceptional dead.

15. **Mayavi rupa** (Sanskrit: "body of illusion"): Besant explains the *mayavi rupa* as follows:

> When a man passes out of the physical body he may use the astral, but so long as he is functioning in that he is limited to the astral world. It is possible, however, for him to use the mind body—that of the lower manas—in order to pass into the mental region, and in this he can also range the astral and physical planes without let or hindrance. The body thus used is often called the *mayavi rupa,* or body of illusion, and it is the mind body rearranged, so to speak, for separate activity.
>
> The man fashions his mind body into the likeness of himself, shapes it into his own image and likeness, and is then in this temporary and artificial body free to traverse the three planes at will and rise superior to ordinary human limitations. (*Man and His Bodies,* 119–20)

16. **Olcott**: HSO described his first encounter with Master M in New York in 1877 in *Old Diary Leaves*. (See *EW* 97–99 for the relevant passage.)
Fontainebleau: Besant narrated her first encounter with Master M in the summer of 1889 in "In the Twilight," an unsigned, irregular feature in the *Theosophist*. Each installment dealt with personally experienced occult adventures and their explication. The participants in these twilight colloquies at Adyar were given epithets. Besant's was "the Vagrant," because of her incessant lectures tours around the world:

> Soon after I joined the Society, it happened that I was in England at a time when HPB was in Fontainebleau, France, where *The Voice of the Silence* was written. She wrote me to go over and join her, which I did with joy. She was living in a delightful old house out in the country, and I was put in a bedroom near hers, a door connecting the two. One night, I awoke suddenly owing to an extraordinary feeling that there was in the room. The air was all throbbing, and it seemed as if an electric machine was playing there; the whole room was electric. I was so astonished (for it was my first experience of the kind) that I sat up in bed, wondering what on earth could be happening. It was quite dark, and in those days I was not a bit clairvoyant. At the foot of the bed, a luminous figure appeared, and stood there from half a minute to a minute. It was the figure of a very tall man, and I thought, from pictures I had seen, it was HPB's Master. Near him was another figure, more faintly luminous, which I could not clearly distinguish. The brilliant figure stood quite still, looking at me, and I was so utterly astounded that I sat perfectly still, simply looking at him; I did not even think of saluting him. So I remained motionless, and then gradually the figure vanished. Next day I told HPB what had happened, and she replied: "Yes, Master came to see me in the night, and went into your room to have a look at you." This was my first experience of seeing a Master; it must have been clearly a case of materialization, for as I have said, I was not in the least clairvoyant at the time. ("In the Twilight," *Theosophist* 31 [May 1910]: 1098)

17. **Leadbeater**: CWL recounted several encounters with the Masters in the mid-1880s—when traveling with HPB from England to India in 1884 and subsequently at Adyar after HPB returned permanently to Europe in 1885—in *How Theosophy Came to Me*, 79–80, 116–17, 143–47, 149–53.
Damodar K. Mavalankar (1857–85?): Brahmin who joined the TS in 1879 against the wishes of his family and thereby became an outcaste. Worked in the *Theosophist* office in Adyar; went on a journey to visit the Masters in the Himalayas in 1885 and never returned; recorded many narratives

of his astral and physical contacts with the Masters (*EW* 139–40, 142–43, 215–16, 228–29).

Pandit Bhavani Shankar (1859–1936): Met HPB and HSO shortly after they first landed in Bombay; joined and worked for the TS for many years. was reported as having seen Master Morya in Bombay while with a group that included Damodar in January 1882 (Ransom, *Short History of the Theosophical Society*, 165). His own account of an astral manifestation of Master Morya appears in Caldwell, *Esoteric World*, 236–37.

Grandhi Soobiah Chetty (1858–1946): Member of the TS since 1882, when the founders were in India; superintendent at the Adyar International Headquarters of the TS; claimed to have seen Master Morya in 1874, which HPB believed to have been impossible, but which was later corroborated in a communication from the Master (*EW* 209–210).

18. **Law of action and reaction**: An interpretation of the law of karma on the basis of Newton's third law of motion. The most direct statement of this law appears in "Conversations on Occultism with H.P.B.": "There is a law that if a White Magician uses his occult power an equal amount of power may be used by the Black one" (*CW* 10:270).

19. **Physical health**: Besant is citing the first of HPB's seven rules of chelaship, each of which bears consideration in connection with the subject of psychic and spiritual development:

> 1. Perfect physical health; 2. Absolute mental and physical purity; 3. Unselfishness of purpose; universal charity; pity for all animate beings; 4. Truthfulness and unswerving faith in the law of Karma . . . ; 5. A courage undaunted in every emergency, even by peril to life; 6. An intuitional perception of one's being the vehicle of the . . . Divine Atman (Spirit); 7. Calm indifference for, but a just appreciation of everything that constitutes the objective and transitory world, in its relation with, and to, the invisible regions. (*CW* 4:608)

HPB's sister attested to the negative effects of producing occult phenomena on HPB's health:

> Truth compels me to say that H. P. Blavatsky was very reluctant to satisfy idle curiosity. She has her own way of looking very contemptuously at any physical phenomena, hates to waste her powers in a profitless manner, and was, moreover, at the time quite ill. Every phenomenon produced *at her will* invariably costs her several days of sickness.
>
> I say "at her will," for phenomena, independent of her, took place far more frequently in their midst [i.e., members of the TS] than those produced by

> herself. She attributes them to that mysterious being whom they all call their "Master." Such manifestations of forces (to us) unknown leave her unhurt. (A. P. Sinnett, *Incidents in the Life of Madame Blavatsky: Compiled from Information Supplied by Her Relatives and Friends*, 207-208)

The following passage from the Mahatma Letters also speaks of the toll taken on HPB by these phenomena:

> Thus, while fathering upon us all manner of foolish, often clumsy and suspected phenomena, she has most undeniably been helping us in many instances, saving us sometimes as much as two-thirds of the power used, and when [we] remonstrated—for often we are unable to prevent her doing it on her end of the line—answering that she had no need of it, and that her only joy was to be of some use to us. And thus she kept on killing herself inch by inch, ready to give—for our benefit and glory, as she thought—her life-blood drop by drop, and yet invariably denying before witnesses that she had anything to do with it. (*ML* 312–13 [Barker]; 296 [Chin])

20. **Friend's thought form**: Former child prodigy violinist, one-time member of the TS, and later authority on Indian music, Maud MacCarthy (1882–1967) testified to one of these visitations in "In the Twilight":

> I saw our President [AWB] once towards the close of a recital I was giving in Melbourne. Some way down the hall there was an empty patch, and there, right in the middle, so that there could be no mistaking her for somebody else, she sat in her white dress looking up at me. I was somewhat surprised, and looked away that I might not be distracted from what I was doing; when I looked again, she was gone. ("In the Twilight," *Theosophist* 30 [July 1909]: 504–505; MacCarthy is "the Fiddler.")

21. **"Speak in English"**: In a letter, HPB explained: "Two or three times, perhaps more, letters were precipitated in *my presence* by a Chela who could not speak English and who took ideas and expressions out of my head." H. P. Blavatsky, *Theosophical Articles*, 2:511.

Furthermore, in another letter, HPB indicated how she was taught by her Master across the language barrier between them:

> To make it clear with Master I also used English, which whether bad or good was the same for Him as he does not speak it but understands every word I say out of my head; and I am made to understand Him—how I could never tell or explain if I were killed but I do. (*ML* 478 [Barker]; 454 [Chin])

The process is explained in detail in HPB's interview with Charles Johnston (see *CW* 8:397–98; *EW* 322–23).

22. **Brother of the Shadow**: This passage reflects Besant's controversial views on the secession of the American Section of the TS under the leadership of William Q. Judge in 1895. As noted, her side of the dispute accused Judge of having forged several Mahatma Letters (thus having acted under the influence of a Brother of the Shadow). Judge's side offered a counter-accusation that Besant had come too much under the influence of her then Indian guru, Gyanendra Nath Chakravarti (1861–1936; Gregory John Tillett, *Charles Webster Leadbeater, 1854–1934: A Biographical Study*, 973 [chap. 6 n6]). It was hinted that the charismatic Chakravarti—and AWB herself—was a Black Magician or acting under the influence of such (Nethercot, *Last Four Lives*, 38–39).

    On this basis, it would be easy to discount this "one other possibility that should not be omitted." Yet, according to the Mahatma Letters, something similar had occurred in 1886, involving an American medium, journalist, and bestselling author by the name of Laura Carter Holloway Langford (1843–1930; http://tennesseeencyclopedia.net/entry.php?rec=1623). She had become active in the London Lodge of the TS and collaborated on the trance dictation of a book on the early history of human evolution. Sinnett at first had believed her to be a possible mouthpiece for Master KH—though this was denied by the Master himself. Several Mahatma Letters commented on her training and failure as a *chela*.

    The following letter was written by HPB to Sinnett—but one of the Masters seems to have taken it over midstream to comment on the situation with Holloway:

    > The first bomb-shell from the Dug-pa [Brothers of the Shadow] world came from America [i.e., Holloway]; you welcomed and warmed it in your own breast, you drove the writer of this [HPB] more than once to the verge of despair, your thorough-going, sincere earnestness, your devotion to truth and the "Masters" having been made powerless for the time being, for discerning the real truth, for sensing that which was left unsaid for it could not be said and thus leaving the widest margin for suspicion. The latter was not unfounded. The Dugpa [*sic*] element triumphed fully at one time—why? because you believe in one [Holloway] who was sent by the opposing powers for the destruction of the Society and permitted to act as she and others did by the "higher powers," as you call them, whose duty it was not to interfere in the great probation save at the last moment. *ML* 484 [Barker]; 459 [Chin])

23. **Smaller bodies**: These statements are unfair to the many individuals in organizations such as the TS Point Loma, the TS Pasadena, and the

United Lodge of Theosophists, who honored HPB's teachings about the importance of establishing a nucleus of universal brotherhood (the first object of the TS since its inception) with dedication and self-sacrificing service. For decades following the publication of Besant's derogatory remarks, these Theosophical organizations produced much worthwhile literature.

They have kept the original editions of HPB's works in print, brought out the writings of William Q. Judge, and cultivated new voices, such as those of Gottfried de Purucker (1874–1942), an erudite and cogent explicator of all aspects of occultism; Geoffrey A. Barborka (1897–1982; http://blavatskyarchives.com/barborkabib.htm), author of *The Divine Plan*, an illuminating commentary on *The Secret Doctrine*; and Boris de Zirkoff (1902–81), editor of *The Collected Writings of H. P. Blavatsky* and a grand-nephew of HPB.

24. **Adyar manifestations**: As noted, one purpose of this essay was to explain the validity of controversial appearances of the Masters who had founded the TS at the International Headquarters in Adyar as HSO lay dying in early 1907. These apparitions, which Besant called the "Adyar manifestations," were said to be witnessed by HSO, Besant, and a few others tending to the dying man. Their alleged purpose was to communicate the Masters' choice of Besant as HSO's successor in the role of president of the TS. This claim (made by HSO and bruited by Besant) caused an uproar in the TS worldwide, since the organization's bylaws specified that after HSO's death, the next president would be nominated for election, not appointed. For one version of the Adyar manifestations, see Ransom, *Short History of the Theosophical Society*, 366–70. For a contrasting, nonpartisan view, see Nethercot, *Last Four Lives*, 99–106.

    Besant *was* elected president by a wide margin. But in some quarters, the question of the validity of the Adyar manifestations remained in the air, especially because Besant announced after her election that communication with, and guidance of the TS by, the Masters had been reestablished—despite HPB's memorandum of a conversation with Master KH, believed to have been written in 1888, that "the Society has liberated itself from our grasp and influence and we have let it go" (*LMW* 2:59). Besant's claims remain controversial to this day among the various groups that trace their origins to HPB's teachings and the purposes for which the TS was founded.

25. **Lord of the Burning Ground**: Shiva, with reference to the Hindu practice of cremating the dead and Shiva's function in the Hindu *trimurti* ("trinity") as the destroying/renewing aspect of godhead.

26. **Open door**: A reference to what HPB called the "great psychic and spiritual change now taking place in the realm of the human Soul." This change, she continued,

> began towards the very commencement of the now slowly vanishing last quarter of our [19th] century, and will end—so says a mystic prophecy—either for the weal or the woe of civilized humanity with the present cycle which will close in 1897. (*CW* 12:1)

Furthermore, during this period, "there will be a large rent made in the Veil of Nature, and materialistic science will receive a deathblow" (*SD* 1:612). On another occasion, HPB wrote:

> Those who will not have reached a certain point of psychic and spiritual development, or that point from which begins the cycle of adeptship, by that day [December 31, 1899]—those will advance no further than the knowledge already acquired . . . and the sluggards will have to renounce every chance of advancement in their present incarnation—until the year 1975. (*CW* 12:492)

To HPB's personal students, such as Besant and Judge, the notion of the open door meant establishing inner communication with the Masters. As Judge explained HPB's teachings on the matter,

> Up to 1897 the door is open to anyone who has the courage, the force, and the virtue to TRY, so that he can go in and make a communication with the Lodge which shall not be broken at all when the cycle ends. But at the striking of the hour the door will shut, and not all your pleadings and cryings will open it to you. Those who have made the connection will have their own door open, but the public general door will be closed. (Judge, *Echoes of the Orient*, 2:10)

According to Judge, the closed door after 1900 was necessary because, as HPB explained,

> Were the public effort to go on any longer than that, a reaction would set in very similar to indigestion. Time must be given for assimilation, or the "dark shadow which follows all innovations" (paraphrase of *ML* 1 [Barker]; 2 [Chin]) would crush the soul of man. (Ibid., 9–10)

Though written during the period of the open door, the Mahatma Letters recount many instances of the "doubt, suspicion, and fear" aroused whenever they were made public. The Mahatmas often intimated that communications would be withheld if such reactions continued. As noted, a letter of 1888 indicated that the Masters had let go of the TS, thus marking the date when communication was suspended. One final letter was received by Besant in 1900, nearly a decade after HPB's death (*LMW* 1:123–24)—and this may be an example of what she meant by the phrase "save when absolutely necessary."

Yet, in the opening statement of this paragraph, Besant implied that some type of communication with the Masters had been maintained but was not "permitted to be made public." This is in accord with Judge's statement that already established communication with the Masters would continue after the door had closed.

In making public the Adyar manifestations, Besant risked—and brought down upon herself—the turmoil that had accompanied previous communications from the Masters. This is also in accord with Judge's prediction of the public reaction of spiritual indigestion.

In the next paragraph, Besant explains why such turmoil develops: If we believe in and practice the psychic and spiritual skills required to establish contact with high spiritual beings such as the Masters, then manifestations of their guidance and influence on our lives may become normal to us and fully understandable in others. If we only accept them theoretically, they may seem abnormal and frightening. Thus Besant's essay attempts not only to educate those who may not understand the nature of communication between worlds, but also to provide some guidelines for how TS members should behave on both sides of the line between the experiencers and the nonexperiencers of such communications.

Besant continued to educate people about the possibility of communication between the worlds well beyond 1897. Did she simply ignore the fact that the door was closed? Perhaps. But it seems more likely that her motive was humanitarian and egalitarian. Even if direct communication with the Masters would thereafter be a rare achievement, whatever work the world did as a result of her teachings on the organization and development of the bodies might benefit humanity, whether during the subsequent seventy-five years or in future generations and lifetimes.

27. **Peril**: A crisis of leadership and vision often occurs in spiritual and religious organizations when the founders pass on. Yet Besant believed herself to be in communication with the Masters under whose impetus

the TS was founded. In her view, there was no guarantee that anyone else who might be elected president could make such a claim and continue to guide the TS with the support of the Masters. If another president had been elected, she might have retained her status as head of the Esoteric School—and that would have been the "minority" left to "carry on the work" of the Masters. Yet, it is doubtful that the TS would have "perished as an organization," especially since smaller groups based on HPB's teachings were continuing in America under other leadership.

Besant's politicized rhetoric here was likely intended to prevent another secession, such as that of the American Section nearly twenty years earlier. That secession resulted in part from a dispute about the genuineness—i.e., "truth and importance"—of communications from the Masters. Besant's position was to reject these communications and accuse William Q. Judge of forgery. Others were now accusing her of having invented the Adyar manifestations.

I am indebted to Pablo Sender for pointing out that the 1888 Mahatma Letter indicating that the TS "has liberated itself from our grasp" continues with the statement that "it is now a soulless corpse, a machine run so far well enough, but which will fall to pieces when he [HSO] is gone" (*LMW* 2:59–60). Sender sensibly argues that this is the peril facing the TS to which Besant refers in connection with her election as president.

28. **Explosive compound**: Considering Besant's career as president of the TS from the distance of eighty-five years, this statement seems both ironic and prophetic. She certainly was adept at mixing explosive combinations of beliefs and then having to deal with the collateral damage to herself and the TS (as in the case of her presenting Krishnamurti as the World Teacher, which resulted in the secession of the German Section in 1913). But, as she admits a few sentences later, "the laws of nature do not change because we are ignorant of them, and if we make a mistake, however conscientiously, we shall suffer as we strike against the law."

29. **Warning**: "We never regard a friendly warning as a 'threat'" (*ML* 222 [Barker]; 89 [Chin]).

30. **Coming Race**: In 1909, Besant was campaigning throughout the world with the message that members of the TS were the heralds or forerunners of the New Age that would be ushered in by the sixth subrace (on a small scale, in several hundred years) and by the sixth root race (on a large scale, in many thousands of years). As noted in the introduction, HPB herself promoted this notion in her 1891 "Letter to the Fifth Annual Convention of the American Section of the TS" (*CW* 13:173). Either

development could be considered the "crest of the wave of normally advancing humanity" mentioned earlier in Besant's essay.

31. **Master builders**: This closing, with its glance at 1 Corinthians 3:10, may seem like a grandiose rhetorical flourish, but Besant means what she says literally. Knowledge without love is the *kama-manas* of our fifth subrace of the fifth root race, manifesting itself as scientific materialism. The love that turns knowledge into wisdom is a characteristic of the sixth subrace of the fifth root race and of the sixth root race, both of which involve the expression and evolution of buddhi.

    The TS would become the master builders of this coming race to the extent that its members had developed their subtle bodies along the lines Besant sketches here—including the possibility of communication with the Masters and becoming their servants in the cause of accelerated evolution. Buddhi would develop naturally in anyone who put the first object of the TS into practice—since the development of a nucleus of universal brotherhood would break down the sense of separateness characteristic of kama-manas (our developmental level as fourth-rounders in the fifth subrace of the fifth root race) and lead to the experience of unity represented by buddhi and the development of buddhi-manas (which begins to show itself increasingly in the sixth subrace). Besant's teachings on psychic and spiritual development should be understood as playing a part in the realization of this broad, visionary, humanitarian aim.

Chapter Twelve: THE LARGER CONSCIOUSNESS AND ITS VALUE

1. **Lectures**: This was the concluding lecture of an eight-lecture series entitled "The Changing World," delivered in London during the summer of 1909.
2. **Anatomy**: The only way to make the "anatomical" portion of this lecture clear is to lay out the relations between the terms as we might a mathematical problem. The following information is drawn from an article by Annie Besant, "Instinct and Intuition." I have added the names of the principles to make clear the links between Besant's English and HPB's Sanskrit terms.

We start with the threefold division of the human being into spirit, soul, and body, then subdivide each of these divisions into their principles:

- **Spirit** is the human monad (*atma-buddhi-manas*).
- **Soul** is lower mind (*kama-manas*) plus emotion-passion (*kama-prana*)—what HPB called the psychic, animal, or terrestrial soul (*TG*, Psyche). Note that this group also forms a triad: manas-kama-prana.
- **Body** is vitality (*prana-linga*) plus automatism (*linga-sthula*). Here we have our third triad: prana-linga-sthula. (The title of the article from which this schema is drawn makes clear that automatism is Besant's word for instinct. In a chart in from HPB's ES Instructions, the "plane of instinct" is linked with the "astral image," another name for *linga sharira* [*CW* 12: diagram V, between 660 and 661; *IGT* 54]).

Then we determine how each principle is embodied:

- **Atman** (which Besant also calls spirit) is clothed in a will-body (relating it to the first Logos)—in other contexts this body is called atmic or nirvanic.
- **Atma-buddhi** (which Besant calls intuition) is clothed in a wisdom-body (relating it to the second Logos) or a bliss-body (relating it to the *anandamayakosha*)—in other contexts this body is called buddhic.
- **Buddhi-manas** (higher mind, which Besant calls intellect) is clothed in a causal- or creative-body (relating it to the third Logos).
- **Kama-manas** (lower mind) is clothed in a mental- or thought-body.
- **Kama-prana** (emotion-passion) is clothed in a desire- or sensation-body—in other contexts called the astral body. Note that the word *passion* implies kama (emotion) vitalized by prana. Also, the term *sensation-body* reminds us that the seat of sensations is in the astral body.
- **Prana-linga** (vitality) is clothed in an etheric or vital-body—in other contexts called the etheric double.
- **Linga-sthula** (automatism) is clothed in the dense- or action-body (i.e., the physical body).

Finally, we note how the higher principles are reflected by the lower, with the reflecting point being the division between the upper (*arupa*) and lower (*rupa*) mental planes, or between higher and lower manas, thus:

- The **will** of atman is reflected by the automatism of the physical plane and body—hence the term *action-body* for the physical body.
- The **wisdom** of buddhi is reflected by the emotion-passion of the astral plane and desire-body (implying that the higher emotion of love—free of passion—leads upward to the unity consciousness or compassionate wisdom of buddhi, a point Besant makes in the present lecture).
- The **activity** of manas (intellect) is reflected by the lower mental plane and thought-body.

3. **Triple nature of the spirit**: This statement is based on one of HPB's Inner Group Teachings: "Atma-Buddhi-Manas [the monad] in man correspond to the three Logoi in Kosmos" (*IGT* 38).
4. **Mind, emotion, desire**: In the schema of note 2 for this selection, what Besant here calls "desire" would there be "passion." The implication is that there is a continuum between a higher kama (emotion, love) and a lower kama (desire, passion), perhaps represented by kama-prana—desire infused by vitality. Thus, in the context of this lecture, it could be said that will becomes desire when consciousness is turned toward "objects in the lower world" and motivated to seek them out by vitality.
5. **Spiritual and natural bodies**: Note that Besant has switched from speaking about principles to speaking about the bodies that clothe them. Thus her "spiritual body" corresponds to the individuality or causal body. Her "natural body" corresponds to the personality or mental body plus astral body—called "subtle" because neither is material in the purely physical sense. The other subdivision of the natural body is the dense physical body.
6. **"We are told"**: Though there are resonances in this paragraph and the preceding one with principles from *The Secret Doctrine* (e.g., from the Proem, including the three fundamental propositions, and from the section entitled "Summing Up," both in vol. 1), the source for the connection between changes of vibration and changes of consciousness appears to be the Vishnu Purana (1.2). Besant's discussion of this passage in *The Evolution of Life and Form* (25–28) makes the origin of the

concept explicit. For a more developed presentation, see Besant, *A Study in Consciousness*, 29–32.

7. **Veritable science**: "See *The Science of the Emotions* by Bhagavan Das" [original footnote].

8. **The other two senses**: Seven senses are mentioned in Mundaka Upanishad 2.1.8. In one of her ES Instructions, HPB speaks of "our seven physical senses (two of which are still unknown to profane science)" (*CW* 12: 532). Elsewhere, she states: "Owing to our having reached only the Fifth Race and being (so far as Science is able to ascertain) endowed with only five senses, the two remaining senses that are still latent in man can have their existence proven only on phenomenal evidence, which to the materialist is no evidence at all" (*CW* 12:610). Furthermore,

> as to the 6th sense of this, our race [the 5th race of the 4th round], it has hardly sprouted above the soil of its materiality. It is highly unreasonable, therefore, to expect for the men of the 5th to sense the nature and essence of that which will be fully *sensed* and perceived but by the 6th—let alone the 7th race—*i.e.*, to enjoy the legitimate outgrowth of the evolution and endowments of the future races with only the help of our present limited senses. The exceptions to this quasi universal rule have been hitherto found only in some rare cases of constitutional, abnormally precocious individual evolutions; or, in such, where by early training and special methods, reaching the stage of the 5th rounders, some men in addition to the natural gift of the latter have fully developed (by certain occult methods) their sixth, and in still rarer cases their seventh, sense. (*CW* 5:144)

In a note to the ES Instructions by one of HPB's students, we find the following further elucidation: "To the five senses at present the property of mankind two more on this globe are to be added. The sixth sense is the psychic sense of colour. The seventh is that of spiritual sound" (Caldwell, *Esoteric Papers*, 472). Based on the diagrams of vibrational rates of colors and sounds supplied in this note (ibid., 472–73), it appears that the sixth and seventh senses will extend our range of perception into presently unavailable vibrational rates of each. From Besant's mention of ether here, it seems that she relates these two new physical senses to the etheric subplanes of the physical plane.

Nineteenth-century scientists developed a number of ether theories to explain the properties of light and gravity based on an analogy to sound waves, which require a medium like air or water to propagate. Seemingly immaterial and undetectable, ether was supposed to permeate all matter and space. Use of the term has fallen out of favor in present day theorizing about the nature of the universe.

One challenge of deciphering Besant's use of the word *ether* is that its meaning can change with the context. Sometimes, as with HPB's writings, it refers to classical explanations of the nature of matter by Greek philosophers (earth-water-fire-air-ether). At other times, it is linked with mesmerism and spiritualistic or occult explanations of the nature of the universe and the working of the senses (e.g., the ethers of the eye or brain, meaning their receptivity to light or other electromagnetic or occult influences). When explaining clairvoyantly perceived information about the atom, Besant uses the term *ether* to refer to the upper subplanes of the physical plane. When relating all three of the above usages to contemporary science, she calls in supposedly obsolete (but at one time respectable) scientific theories. The following passage from *The Secret Doctrine* demonstrates how these usages are related to one another:

> "Chaos" is called senseless by the ancients, because it represented and contained in itself (Chaos and Space being synonymous) all the Elements in their rudimentary, undifferentiated State. They made of Ether, the fifth element, the synthesis of the other four; for the Aether of the Greek philosophers is not its dregs—of which indeed they knew more than science does now—which are rightly enough supposed to act as an agent for many forces that manifest on Earth. Their Aether was the Akasa of the Hindus; the Ether accepted in physics is but one of its subdivisions, on our plane,—the Astral Light of the Kabbalists with all its evil as well as good effects. (*SD* 1:342–43)

The phrase *its dregs* is explained in *Transactions of the Blavatsky Lodge*: "the *Astral Light* is simply the dregs of *Akasa*," i.e., "the storehouse of all human and especially psychic iniquities" (*CW* 10:251; *TBL* 65).

9. **A few Sundays ago**: In "The Coming Race" (June 20, 1909), published, with the present lecture, in Annie Besant, *The Changing World and Lectures to Theosophical Students*, 103–31.

10. **Frederic William Henry Myers** (1843–1901): One of the founders of the Society for Psychical Research, and author of *The Human Personality and Its Survival of Bodily Death* (New York: Longmans, Green, 1903).

11. **Pseudo-occult books**: William Walker Atkinson's works touched on all the subjects Besant mentions, including, as noted, his writings on yoga under the pseudonym Yogi Ramacharaka. Besant's exasperation is understandable: Atkinson's magazine *Advanced Thought* and his

publishing company of the same name were housed in the Fine Arts Building, 410 S. Michigan Avenue, Chicago, IL—where the American Section of the TS and its publishing arm the Theosophical Book Concern were located during the first decade of the twentieth century. To make matters worse, after 1910, Atkinson began repackaging many of Leadbeater's teachings under the pseudonym Swami Panchadasi.

12. **Bringing fuel for the fire of sacrifice**: A traditional approach to the guru in the Upanishads (e.g., Mundaka Upanishad 1.2.12).

Chapter Thirteen: REVELATION, INSPIRATION, OBSERVATION

1. **"Lived and died a Hindu"**: "*Buddhism*, p. 116" [original footnote]. T.W. Rhys Davids, *Buddhism: Its History and Literature*.
   Thomas William Rhys Davids (1843–1922) was a British scholar specializing in the translation and explication of the large canon of Buddhist texts in the Pali language—the basis of Theravada Buddhism—widely considered those closest to what the Buddha actually taught.

2. **"Do not believe in a thing"**: "*Kalama Sutta* of the *Anguttara Nikaya*" [original footnote].
   Kalama Sutta (Pali): Teaching to the Kalama Clan.
   Anguttara Nikaya (Pali): Numbered Discourses, one of five subdivisions of the Sutta Pitaka ("Basket of Teachings"), itself one of three divisions of the Pali Canon of Theravada Buddhism.
   This is the translation cited in Henry. S. Olcott, *Buddhist Catechism*, 44.

3. **Avatara** (Sanskrit): Incarnation of a god, as Rama and Krishna were incarnations of the god Vishnu.

4. **Akashic records**: *Akasha* is defined by HPB as "the subtle, supersensuous spiritual essence which pervades all space" (*TG*, Akasa). Theosophical writers sometimes refer to akasha and the astral light, one of its lower (i.e., more material) subdivisions, as "Nature's picture gallery" and "Nature's memory" because within it are recorded all events that transpire in the physical and superphysical universe—hence the term Besant employs here: *akashic records*. According to HPB, "All things that ever were, that are, or that will be, having their record upon the astral light, or tablet of

the unseen universe, the initiated adept, by using the vision of his own spirit, can know all that has been known or can be known" (*IU* 2:588).

5. **Unruffled lake**: Behind this passage stands the following citation of a letter from HPB's Master in an ES Instruction: *"Before the pupil can be taught, he must learn how to conduct himself as regards the world, his teacher, the sacred science, and his* Inner self," the letter adds, quoting the Eastern aphorism that *"the ruffled water-surface reflects naught but broken images"* (*CW* 12:584).

6. ***The Imitation of Christ (De Imitatione Christi)***: A fifteenth-century devotional text attributed to Thomas a Kempis (ca. 1380–1471).
The Golden Verses of Pythagoras: A set of 71 lines ("verses") written in Greek in dactylic hexameter, attributed Pythagoras, and offering spiritual instruction along moral and ethical lines.

7. ***Esoteric Buddhism***: Early compilation and interpretation by A. P. Sinnett of the teachings of Masters KH and M, based on their letters to him. The book was a bestseller in the late nineteenth century and was in its sixth edition at the time of HPB's death. It was once considered a fundamental Theosophical text (despite HPB's reservations about it). It was supplanted by Barker's *The Mahatma Letters to A. P. Sinnett*.
Overlooked and aided: For corroboration of these claims of how *The Secret Doctrine* was written, see Caldwell, *Esoteric World*, 299.

8. **Globe**: This obscure passage may refer to CWL and AWB's clairvoyant investigations of August 23, 1896, during which our solar system was perceived from the buddhic plane as a many-petalled lotus flower. A sketchy mention of these perceptions appears in C. Jinarajadasa, "Investigations into Early Rounds," 731. Besant first reported them in a lecture to the Blavatsky Lodge in 1898, notes of which were not published until 1910. See "A Note on Our Solar System (As Given in *The Secret Doctrine*)", 197–200. A more complete transcript appeared under the title "Our Planetary Chain" in 1928. Similar imagery appears in a number of CWL's writings. The following excerpt from his *The Inner Life* makes Besant's reference in the present lecture more intelligible:

   > The man using the sight of the fourth dimension may observe that the planets which are isolated in our three dimensions are all the time joined in another way which we cannot yet see; and from the point of view of that higher sight these globes are but the points of petals which are part of one great flower. And the glowing heart of that flower throws up a central pistil which appears to us as the sun. (97–99)

9. **Forty-nine astral atoms**: "Each physical atom is represented by forty-nine [seven times seven] astral atoms, each astral atom by forty-nine mental atoms, and each mental atom by forty-nine of those on the buddhic plane" (Annie Besant and Charles W. Leadbeater, *Occult Chemistry: Clairvoyant Observations on the Chemical Elements*, 1919, 2nd ed., appendix, iii).

10. **Whirling wall**: This phrase refers to the original 1895 occult chemistry investigations, which were subsequently corrected by further observations in 1907. See Besant and Leadbeater, *Occult Chemistry: Clairvoyant Observations* (1919), 11, 22.
Whirling fire-tipped stick: Ibid., 12.

11. **"Let truth and falsehood grapple"**: Paraphrased from John Milton (1608–74), *Areopagitica: A Speech for the Liberty of Unlicensed Printing, to the Parliament of England* (1644), in John Milton, *The Complete English Poems*, 613. The original has the phrase *free and open* instead of Besant's *fair*.

Chapter Fourteen: THEOSOPHY AS SCIENCE

1. **Aether** (Greek): The fifth element, corresponding to the substance of the heavenly spheres, used here in the sense that HPB often did, as a synonym for *akasha*.

2. **Ludwig Buchner** (1824–99): Physician and materialist philosopher, author of *Kraft und Stoff* (*Force and Matter*). Besant is referring to the following passage:

   > Eyes were not bestowed upon us in order that we might see with them, any more than we have received feet in order that we may walk with them. Rather do we see and walk because we have eyes and feet. The function is not the origin, but the result of the organ. Sight did not exist before the eye, nor speech before the tongue, but the reverse. (Ludwig Buchner, *Force and Matter, or Principles of the Natural Order of the Universe . . . A Popular Exposition*, 177)

3. **They became birds"**: Besant probably means Thomas Henry Huxley (1825–95), English scientist, comparative anatomist, paleontologist, supporter and popularizer of Darwinism, first proponent of the theory that birds evolved from dinosaurs—and, incidentally, inventor of the term *agnostic*. For Clifford, see chapter 15, note 10 (p. 362).

4. **Sphere**: "I use the word 'sphere' to indicate the whole extent of matter belonging to a definite type, i.e., built of atoms of one sort [physical atoms, astral atoms, mental atoms, etc.]. There may be several worlds in a sphere; thus the heaven world is in the mental sphere. The word plane has been used in this sense, but it is found that people do not readily grasp its meaning" [original footnote].

5. **Outline**: Presumably, *Esoteric Buddhism* and *The Secret Doctrine*. Besant's *The Ancient Wisdom* was her own version of that outline.

6. **Firsthand experience**: A contemporary article by Besant, "The Growth of the TS," makes clear that Besant herself is meant by the reference to twenty-three years (p. 506)—and Leadbeater is probably meant by the reference to twenty-five years. In this article, Besant dates the development of her clairvoyance back to when she joined the TS in 1889 and came under the tutelage of HPB (p. 500)—despite an article cited earlier entitled "Dr. Besant's First Use of Clairvoyance," which implied a date of 1895.

   Elsewhere, Besant tells the following story of an interaction with HPB that supports her claim:

   > I remember once saying to HPB in my early days: "I am not in the least clairvoyant." She said: "You are exceedingly clairvoyant." I did not like to contradict her, as she was a difficult person to contradict. Besides, one preferred to think over a thing that she said, that did not strike one at first as very helpful. And so I quietly waited, and she said: "How do you finish up your sentence when you are speaking?" I said: "I see two or three different endings before my eyes, and I choose the one that seems most musical." She said: "That is clairvoyance—to see a thing that is not physically visible; to be able to look at and choose among a number of things that you thus see, is a form of clairvoyance." What one sees is a form which does not belong to the physical body, but to the mental body. Your mental body sees it and sends it down to the physical brain. (Annie Besant, *Brahmavidya: Divine Wisdom*, 67)

   If Besant's clairvoyance dates back to 1889, then CWL's must have developed two years earlier, in 1887. However, CWL provides the date of 1885 for his clairvoyant training (Charles W. Leadbeater, *Messages from the Unseen*, 46).

7. **The eternal man**: "This is the statement, including what is said farther on about the monad, noted above as not having been verified by the writer's own observation. This highest self is only made manifest to such

as we are on rare occasions in a great downflow of dazzling light: in his own nature, in his own world, he is beyond the reach of any vision yet attained by any of us. Yet what we call our life is his, since he is the highest self in each of us, 'the hidden god'—as the Egyptians used to say" [original footnote].

"The hidden god": The Egyptian god Amun (various spellings) was known as "the hidden one" (http://www.newworldencyclopedia.org/entry/Amun).

8. **Spark in the divine fire**: A common metaphor for the monad in Theosophical literature. In *The Secret Doctrine,* HPB speaks of monads as "the immortal sparks reflecting the universal divine flame" (*SD* 1:275).
   Sends down a ray: A common Theosophical metaphor for the process by which a principle on a higher plane takes on an *upadhi* or body on a lower plane—as in this statement by HPB, in which she describes the lower ego (*kama-manas*) in terms of the higher ego (*buddhi-manas*) as "a Ray of the latter falling into Matter, that is to say animating man and making of him a thinking, rational being on this plane" (*CW* 6:205). In Besant's essay, the phrase applies to the monad on the second unmanifested plane (which she calls *anupadaka* or monadic) as it acquires the upadhis necessary on the five manifested planes for embodiment on the last of these, the physical plane.

9. **Permanent atom**: Not a concept found in HPB's Theosophy—at least in this form. In *The Mahatma Letters,* Master M states that the human being "starts downward as a simply spiritual entity—an unconscious seventh principle . . . with the germs of the other six principles lying latent and dormant in him" (*ML* 75 [Barker]; 122 [Chin]). The permanent atoms are these germs (in the sense of seeds), but perceived clairvoyantly, as material realities, instead of conceptually, as ideas or metaphors.

   To explore the connection between AWB's and CWL's teachings on the permanent atoms and HPB's Theosophy, we must consider three questions: Why are the germs of the principles called atoms? Why are they called permanent? What functions described in HPB's Theosophy correspond to the functions assigned to them by AWB and CWL?

   It appears that the permanent atoms are a specialized form of what HPB calls "life atoms." Life is here an expression of the principle of *prana* (when it refers to the life force that animates an individual or unit of consciousness) or *jiva* (when it refers to the universal life force). According to HPB,

> *Jiva* or *Prana* is quite distinct from the atoms it animates. The latter belong to the lowest or grossest state of matter—the *objectively* conditioned; the former—to its highest state: that state which the uninitiated, ignorant of its nature, would call the "objectively finite," but which, to avoid any future misunderstanding, we may, perhaps, be permitted to call the *Subjectively Eternal*. (*CW* 5:111)

The highest state of matter is called "subjectively eternal" because it is not only conditioned, as a part of the manifested universe, but also conscious, as an expression of spirit. Thus a life atom is what I earlier described as a spirit/matter unit—but *animated*. HPB makes a distinction between animated and dormant life atoms:

> We regard and call in our occult phraseology those atoms that are moved by Kinetic energy as "life-atoms," while those that are for the time being passive, containing but *invisible* potential energy, we call "sleeping atoms," regarding at the same time these two forms of energy as produced by the one and same force, or life. (*CW* 5:113)

A life atom or spirit/matter unit is animated when involved in gathering experience, as during the active expression of an individual's life on the physical plane. After death, some life atoms transmigrate into other forms (though, as we shall see, they reassemble themselves when that individual prepares to reincarnate). Others, according to AWB and CWL, no longer gather experience during the afterlife, but are withdrawn into the causal body—the permanent atoms. These would represent dormant life atoms. Other kinds of dormancy of life atoms are conceivable, such as when a planet, chain, solar system, or larger unit of creation goes into the quiescent state that HPB calls *pralaya* (Sanskrit: "dissolution").

HPB sums up the relationship between life and atom in the term *life atom* as follows:

> The "Jiva," or life principle which animates man, beast, plant or even a mineral, certainly *is* "a form of force indestructible," since this force is the one life, or *anima mundi*, the universal living soul, and that the various modes in which the various objective things appear to us in nature in their atomic aggregations, such as minerals, plants, animals, &c., are all the different forms or states in which this force manifests itself. (*CW* 5:112)

AWB and CWL developed the idea that there must be an "atomic aggregation" among these "various modes" that represents what HPB calls root matter: the truest or most fundamental expression of matter and spirit on each plane. This is the spirit/matter unit that AWB and

CWL call the ultimate atom. When this spirit/matter unit is animated by jiva, it may become a permanent atom.

Elsewhere, AWB and CWL speak of the third Logos as a *life wave*, a metaphor for the force of jiva just described. At the beginning of creation, this life wave enters the manifested universe and begins to animate the dormant atoms it encounters there. The result is HPB's life atoms.

The atoms that the life wave first animates are the ultimate atoms (root matter) of each plane. Furthermore, each life wave is made up of monads. Thus, when a human monad encounters the manifested universe, it picks up or "appropriates" a life atom from the atomic (highest) subplane of each plane. This permanent atom becomes the core, seed, or germ of the body or bodies that operate on each plane.

These bodies will develop more fully from matter of the lower subplanes of each plane, representing the veiling of consciousness in matter. Since the permanent or ultimate atom is an expression of *atman*, it is a manifestation of god consciousness on each plane, as modified by the principle represented by that plane. During the evolutionary process, the veiling of matter must be stripped away so that the god consciousness represented by each permanent atom is revealed. The method is the gathering of experience that applies to, or can be contained within, any ultimate atom: the purest, most refined expression of the principle of a particular plane—that worthy of the atman or god consciousness within each ultimate atom. Thus are the germs of each principle mentioned by Master M redeemed from latency or dormancy through making the seventh principle fully conscious—the process often mentioned in Theosophical literature in which "Man becomes a God" (e.g., *SD* 2:186).

Now, what makes the permanent atoms permanent? HPB says that after death, "The Man's lower 'principles' are disintegrated in time and are used by Nature again for the formation of new human principles" (*SD* 1:173). Further, she states that

> (*a*) the life-atoms of our (*Prana*) life-principle are never entirely lost when a man dies. That the atoms best impregnated with the life-principle (an independent, eternal, conscious factor) are partially transmitted from father to son by heredity, and partially are drawn once more together and become the animating principle of the new body in every new incarnation of the Monads. Because (*b*), as the *individual* Soul is ever the same, so are the atoms of the lower principles (body, its astral, or *life-double*, etc.), drawn as they are by affinity and Karmic law always to the same individuality in a series of various bodies. (*SD* 2: 671–72)

Notice that HPB says, "the atoms *best* impregnated with the life principle." These would be the permanent atoms of AWB and CWL. They are the "best" in that they represent the atman or seventh principle of each atom: an appropriated ultimate atom from each manifested plane. The life atoms of the lower subplanes in which our consciousness is veiled may also be attracted to us and re-form the bodies for our next life. These would represent our evolutionary stage in that lifetime—the veiling we must dissolve to achieve god consciousness on each plane, as represented by the ultimate atom.

What functions do the permanent atoms perform? To answer this question, we must refer to HPB's concept of karmic tendencies, or *skandhas* (Sanskrit: "attributes"; see *KT* 77–78, 129). These tendencies are acquired through our thoughts, emotions, and actions in each life. They become the karmic causes driving our experience in the next life. According to HPB, no suffering or evil tendencies may accompany us into the blissful rest of the Devachan phase of the afterlife, which we experience in connection with the causal body. Hence these tendencies wait, so to speak, beyond the door of that level of being and are drawn to us once again when we leave it behind in the process of reincarnation (*KT* 154, 161): "Karma, with its army of Skandhas, waits at the threshold of Devachan, whence the *Ego* re-emerges to assume a new incarnation" (*KT* 141).

According to AWB and CWL, the permanent atom of each body stores everything we have learned in that body during life—not only the skandhas, but also the faculties for thinking in the mental body, feeling in the astral body, and action in the physical body. Such learning is present in these permanent atoms as tendencies for them to replicate or resist certain vibrations of thought, feeling, or action that were set up in our past lives.

We carry with us the tendencies (veiling) we need to clear up from life to life, but we also carry the faculties we need to develop and refine from our first manifestation as human monads within an evolutionary *manvantara* to our last, hence the permanence of the permanent atoms. They are thus withdrawn into the causal body during the Devachan period of the afterlife rather than left behind at the door, though the skandhas within them remain temporarily latent (as dormant life atoms). At the point of reincarnation, they become the rallying point and guiding mechanism for forming a new mental, astral, and physical body, which includes not only our faculties and skandhas, but also the life atoms of our previous bodies with their own tendencies to vibrate or resist vibration in certain ways, thus locking us in to the karmic tendencies of that life. This army of life atoms is what waits for us beyond the door of Devachan in each new life.

Though some Theosophical commentators reject the notion of the permanent atoms as neo-Theosophy, we have seen that it is implied by several strands within HPB's Theosophy. One further teaching ties these ideas together:

At various widely separated points in her work, HPB speaks of a divine or cosmic monad, a spiritual monad, a human monad, a soul monad, an astral monad, and a physical monad. In *CW* 12: 531, Boris de Zirkoff provides a diagram that systematizes these monads as follows:

- atman: the *spiritual-divine* monad (equivalent of divine or cosmic monad)
- atma-buddhi: the *spiritual* monad
- buddhi-manas: the *intellectual* monad (equivalent of human monad, when the latter term refers to the soul)
- kama-manas: the *psychic* monad (equivalent of astral monad or astral soul)
- kama-prana: the *beast* monad (equivalent of animal soul)
- prana-linga-sthula: the *astro-physical* monad (equivalent of physical monad)

Each of these monads is made up of a higher, more spiritual principle plus a lower, more material upadhi that allows that principle to manifest itself on a particular plane. Principle plus upadhi act as a unit on that plane, hence each plane has a monad. Whether perceived as an animated life atom (HPB), or as an ultimate atom appropriated by the spiritual-divine monad when it enters the manifested universe, the mental permanent atom appears to be equivalent to the intellectual monad, the astral permanent atom to the psychic monad, and the physical permanent atom to the astro-physical monad. (But note that Besant uses the phrase *mental permanent molecule-unit* rather than mental permanent atom, for reasons explained in note 33 for this selection, below.)

10. **Diagram 2**: A parenthetical note below the original diagram stated: "The student may find the Sanskrit terms useful, as they have been much employed in Theosophical literature, and the above are my own English equivalents." I have moved the terms listed in this note into the diagram itself.

Mahaparinirvana (Sanskrit: "Great [plane] beyond nirvana"): Besant claims in her parenthetical note that this term and the next were in use by the Buddhists for describing the two unmanifested planes. The term probably comes from the title of a Mahayana Buddhist text, the Mahaparinirvana Sutra, which discusses higher degrees of nirvana.
Parinirvana (Sanskrit: "beyond nirvana"): This term appears in HPB's *Theosophical Glossary*, defined as follows: "Absolute *Non-Being*, which is equivalent to absolute *Being* or 'Be-ness,' the state reached by the human Monad at the end of the great cycle" (*TG*, Paranirvana). It is probable that this definition is what gave rise to Besant's calling the second unmanifested plane the monadic plane. In Buddhism, *parinirvana* also refers to the state of nirvana achieved by Gautama Buddha at the death of his physical body.

11. **Vortices**: Besant lists the chakras in descending order—what she calls the first is more usually the seventh. In some Theosophical books, the order and names of the chakras differ from those given in ancient Tantric systems and in modern New Age versions. In the original Tantric teachings, all the chakras are located along a vertical line that corresponds to the spinal column. In the modern system, they are numbered in ascending order from the base of the tailbone to the crown of the head. There is no spleen chakra in either the ancient or the modern system—it would be outside the vertical alignment of the other chakras. The chakra in the area of the solar plexus is given as the second in the Theosophical system, whereas it is the third in the modern system. The second chakra in the traditional and the modern system is associated with the genital area and is apparently classified in the Theosophical system as one of those "used in black magic."

    These changes may be traced to HPB's ES Instructions, in which she speaks of seven "Master Chakras" (also called "centers of action") in the head, each of which controls one of the seven nerve plexuses in the body (*CW* 12:619–20). A diagram in "E.S. Instruction No. I" shows that these seven master chakras are associated with the seven principles. Furthermore, there are three remaining centers of action in the "lower functional organs," which HPB says are only used in Black Magic (*CW* 12, Diagram 1, between pp. 524 and 525).

    The relationship of the spleen to the chakra system is explained in "E.S. Instruction No. V," a posthumously published compilation of notes of Inner Group meetings with HPB:

The Spleen corresponds to the Linga-Sharira, and serves as its dwelling-place, in which it lies curled up. As the Linga-Sharira is the reservoir of life for the Body, the medium and vehicle of Prana, the Spleen acts as the centre of Prana in the Body, from which the life is pumped out and circulated. It is consequently a very delicate organ, though the physical Spleen is only the cover for the real Spleen. (*CW* 12: 699) (See *IGT* 177–78 for indications of the sources [or lack thereof] for these statements in the extant transcripts of Inner Group meetings.)

HPB sometimes lists *linga sharira* and prana as the second and third principles, respectively, and sometimes as the third and second—which perhaps explains why some later Theosophical books relate the spleen to the second chakra (e.g., Leadbeater, *The Chakras*, 12) and others to the third (e.g., Leadbeater, *The Inner Life*, 196).

HPB notes that "no two authorities up to the present day agree as to the real location in the body of the Chakras" (*CW* 12:621). The same thing seems to be true of their number. One traditional Tantric source identifies no fewer than fifty-six chakras by name. (Arthur Avalon [Sir John Woodroffe], *The Serpent Power: The Secrets of Tantric and Shaktic Yoga*, 152). HPB herself mentions seven "principal plexuses in the body," as well as "forty-two minor ones to which Physiology refuses that name," for a total of forty-nine (seven times seven) (*CW* 12:619). With so many variations in teachings about the chakras to consider, we would do well to acknowledge that each system may serve a valid purpose and function and to be cautious about comparing one to another.

12. **Nature spirits**: For further information, see Charles W. Leadbeater, *The Hidden Side of Things*, 76–112. Besant may have intended this passage to serve as indirect advance notice of this book's publication.

13. **Dreams**: "See the many cases given in du Prel's *Philosophy of Mysticism*" [original footnote].
Baron Carl du Prel (1839–99): Early psychic investigator and theorizer who researched spiritualism, mediumistic phenomena, trance, dreams, and animal magnetism (i.e., hypnotism). Originally in German, *The Philosophy of Mysticism* was first published in English in 1889.

14. **Globes**: Usual descriptions of the astral plane, as in Leadbeater's 1895 book on the subject, focus so exclusively on the fate of the dead that we are apt to forget about its other contents. Here Besant provides a comprehensive view. The two globes on the astral plane precede and follow ours in the planetary chain and are usually designated Globes B and F (ours is Globe D; Globe C is Mars and Globe E is Mercury—all

on the physical plane). Note the distinction Besant makes between the *astral world*, for the living, and the *intermediate world* or *desire world* (i.e., Kamaloka), for the dead.

15. **Astral colors**: These associations of colors with expressions of emotion on the astral plane are illustrated in Annie Besant and Charles W. Leadbeater, *Thought-Forms,* and Charles W. Leadbeater, *Man Visible and Invisible.* The latter also includes illustrations of the astral body, the mental body, and the aura, subsequently discussed by Besant.

16. **Bhang** (Sanskrit): A narcotic in use in Besant's time in India—leaves and twigs of the hemp plant that were chewed, smoked, or infused as tea for their intoxicating effect. The word is currently used as a synonym for marijuana, the use of which may also provide terrifying glimpses of the astral world and its denizens.

17. **Feeling disappears**: Besant is drawing our attention here to two cases in which the physical body will be insensitive to pain: (1) the astral body has been withdrawn; or (2) the etheric double has been largely withdrawn (complete withdrawal would mean death). The implication is that the astral body can travel away from the physical body, as when we dream, and the etheric double stays with and in a sense protects the physical, sending the astral body a message to return if the physical body is disturbed or in danger. Anesthesia and hypnotic or mesmeric trance may either drive out the astral body or cause a withdrawal of most of the etheric double that acts as a connecting link, or bridge, between the physical body and the centers of sensation in the astral body. In either case, the body may experience pain, but the pain will not register in consciousness. Thus Besant explains not only the rationale of anesthesia in surgery but also that of experiments in hypnotism in which a hypnotized subject is impervious to pain.

    Besant recounts a personal experience of anesthesia that involves the second case described above:

    > If you once take out part of the etheric double, you are in a terrible muddle. You may be as conscious as you like, but you are in a fog. I experienced that only once, under the influence of laughing-gas, when a tooth was taken out, and I will never do it again. The gas drives out the etheric double, producing trance in that way. In the case of anesthetics the etheric double is driven out, and you float about in it. In my case, I dimly saw my body on the chair and the dentist, but as if I were looking through a dense fog. The fog was my own etheric double. It was a very disagreeable experience, and having dislocated myself in this way, I

could not get right for days. I went in and out of my body repeatedly to try to fit myself in. ("In the Twilight," *Theosophist* 34 [May 1913]: 279)

18. **Bull**: An Irish bull is an unintentionally contradictory or incongruous statement (i.e., calling the physical consciousness subconscious). A bull is also an edict, as in a Papal bull—a specially signed and sealed letter issued by the pope, often dealing with doctrinal matters affecting the governance and membership of the Roman Catholic Church. Though Besant was born in London, three of her grandparents were Irish. This passage loses some of its irony without the historical context. American newspapers were fond of calling Besant the "high priestess of Theosophy" during her lecture tours, especially after her election to the presidency of the TS (e.g., *Los Angeles Herald*, vol. 34, no. 356 [September 22, 1907], http://cdnc.ucr.edu/cdnc/cgi-bin/cdnc?a=d&d=LAH19070922.2.102.19&cl=CL2.1907.09&srpos=0&dliv=none&st=1&e=-------en-Logical-20--1----boggs-CHAPTER---1887).

19. **Communes with his friends**: Two possible interpretations of this vague statement suggest themselves: (1) communication takes place in dreams with our friends, perhaps at the mental body level, but because of our only "average" level of development in the astral body, we cannot bring it through to the physical brain and therefore do not remember it; or (2) we communicate with our friends in dreams only if we are sufficiently mentally alert to do so—otherwise, we may be drawn to them in our astral body but are too self-absorbed to notice and interact with them, seeing only our own thoughts about or projections onto them. It may be that by "communes with his friends mentally only," Besant meant "communes with his friends *as thought forms* only." The following note by Besant (first published in the *Theosophical Review* in 1899, and therefore based on AWB and CWL's clairvoyant investigations of Devachan in previous years) seems to support this view:

    We never know in the three lower worlds [physical, astral, mental] more than the thought form we create of our friend. How much of our friend animates that thought form depends on two things—his own stage of development and our power of response to him. The more of him we can answer to, the more of him will vitalize our thought form. But till we reach the buddhic plane [i.e., until we identify ourselves with buddhi-manas], we cannot know him as he is. Any number of thought forms [in the lower worlds] may be vitalized by an Ego [i.e., buddhi-manas], as rays of one sun may illumine many vases; as much of his life as the form can contain and transmit shines through it. It has been observed in Devachan that an ego embodied on earth may be working actively in thought forms inhabiting the "closed worlds" of many inhabitants of Devachan. (Bhagavan Das and Annie Besant, *Mystic Experiences: Tales of Yoga and Vedanta from the Yogavasishtha*, 63n)

The inhabitants of Devachan are protected from outside influences, hence their worlds are said to be "closed." For further details about how people "embodied on earth" may work within the thought forms of deceased loved ones in Devachan, see Leadbeater, *The Devachanic Plane*, 58–62.

20. **Rocks/seas/fires/air**: Besant describes what CWL called the tests of earth, water, fire, and air (Leadbeater, *Invisible Helpers*, 194–95).
"Repercuss": Henry S. Olcott defines repercussion as follows: "the reacting upon one's physical body of a blow, stab, or other injury, inflicted upon the [astral] Double while it is projected and moving about as a separate entity" (*Old Diary Leaves*, 1:388). In an installment of "In the Twilight," Besant related a personal experience of repercussion, probably from the 1890s:

> It occurred to me once in my early days, when in an astral adventure I saw a mast about to fall on me. I thought to myself: "That will come right across me." The next moment, I remembered that it would not hurt me if it did. But the result of that momentary thought was a repercussion. The next morning I had a great blue bruise on my leg when I awoke. The vibration in the astral body causes a similar vibration in the physical body. Hence the bruise. (*Theosophist* 34 [May 1913], 277)

21. **"Fall" into matter**: It could be said that the entire second volume of *The Secret Doctrine*, entitled *Anthropogenesis* (Greek: The origins of humankind) is dedicated to the explication of this allegory of the "Fall of Man" as described in the second and third chapters of Genesis—and coyly hinted at here, in Besant's highlighting of certain keywords with quotation marks.

22. **"His own place"**: Peter was writing about Judas Iscariot, who went "to his own place" after hanging himself in shame for having betrayed Jesus to the Romans. Some commentators assume that Peter is referring to hell.

23. **Rearrangement**: Besant describes what CWL called the formation of the desire elemental—his term for what the Mahatmas and HPB called the *kama-rupa* (desire body). For further information on the desire elemental, see CWL's *The Astral Plane*, where the rearrangement of the astral body is described (50–52, 57–59); and his exhaustive treatment of the subject in

The Other Side of Death Scientifically Examined by Clairvoyant Investigation and Carefully Described (184–205). The knowledge of how to prevent this rearrangement is gained in the process of becoming fully conscious on the astral plane as an invisible helper during life.

24. **Seven subdivisions**: The seven subplanes of the astral plane are analogous to ("answer to") the seven subplanes of the physical plane: the lower subplanes are more dense, like our solids, liquids, and gases; the upper subplanes are more subtle, like the four ethers. It may go too far to say that the lowest subplanes of the astral plane correspond to the astral equivalent of solids, liquids, and gases. However, it may not be incorrect to say (according to another of Besant's labeling schemes) that these subplanes correspond to the astral versions of earth, water, fire, air, and ether. In this scheme, the three higher subplanes are named superetheric, subatomic, and atomic—the last to indicate the connection of the highest subplane (usually numbered the first) to the root matter or ultimate atom of the astral plane. The series duplicates itself yet again in the subtler matter of the mental plane.

25. **Astral sight**: "Newcomers in the astral world always look through the astral simulacra of eyes, because accustomed to turn their attention outwards in that way, just as they move their legs for walking. Both are unnecessary" [original footnote].

26. **Purgatory**: "Both these religions, while ordinarily speaking of hell as everlasting, have passages in their scriptures which contradict the idea. The New Testament speaks of a time when 'God shall be all in all' [1 Cor. 15:28], and Al Quran declares: 'All things shall perish save His Face' [28:88; 55:26–27]" [original footnote].

27. **Sixth subdivision**: The least material or "uppermost" subplane is counted as the first. The hell or purgatory previously described would be the "lowest," most material subplane (seventh subdivision) of that world—its purgatory. See Leadbeater, *The Astral Plane*, 53–56, for further information on these subplanes.

28. **George Herbert** (1593–1633): British poet and clergyman. From his poem "The Elixir."

29. **Mr. Leadbeater**: *Textbook* (2007), 92.

30. **Worlds**: Note the distinction between mental *sphere*, referring to the whole plane, and its two *worlds*, referring to the upper mental plane (home of the causal body or buddhi-manas) and the lower mental plane (home of

the mental body or kama-manas). The two globes are Globes A and G of our planetary chain, located in the lower mental sphere. Also note the use of the term *heavenly world* for that aspect of the afterlife situated on the lower mental plane. This is Devachan, in which, according to HPB, we experience "a period of rest and bliss . . . with an utter temporary oblivion of all the miseries and sorrows of life" as "the reward for all the undeserved miseries of life." Furthermore, "that which prompted man to sin, namely his terrestrial passionate nature can have no room in it"—which is why Besant says it has been "placed under special conditions" (*CW* 7:180 and note).

31. **Long ages of slow evolution**: Our progression through the mineral, vegetable, and animal stages of evolution until the moment of individualization occurs. The physical body begins to evolve during the mineral stage, the astral during the vegetable stage, and the mental during the animal stage (Besant, *A Study in Consciousness*, 87–88).

32. **Film of matter, egg-shaped**: Besant is describing what HPB called the auric body, envelope, or egg—the *hiranyagarbha* (Sanskrit: "golden egg"): A concept introduced in her ES Instructions as one of the seven principles, though not previously mentioned "on account of its being so sacred" (*CW* 12:526). The filmy quality of the auric envelope is defined in a comparative chart of the "'Principles' and 'Aspects'" as follows: "The substratum of the Aura around man is the universally diffused primordial and pure akasha, the first film on the boundless and shoreless expanse of Jiva, the immutable Root of all" (*CW* 12:607). Jiva is used here in the sense of "Life, as the Absolute" (*TG*, Jiva). Thus the "first film" represents the first differentiation of matter in the manifested universe—which is no doubt why Besant refers to it here as a film of matter. The association of the auric envelope with the causal body occurs in the Inner Group Teachings: "This envelope is the receptacle of all Karmic causes and photographs all things like a sensitive plate" (*IGT* 6–7). Thus the causal body or auric envelope, being made of akasha, is an individual's akashic record.

33. **Permanent molecule-unit**: This is the equivalent of the permanent atoms in the other bodies. There are two bodies on the mental plane. The causal body has a permanent atom made up of an ultimate atom of mental matter from the highest subplane of the mental plane. Thus the mental body, which deals only with the lower and denser levels of the mental plane, cannot have its own permanent atom. Notice the use of the word *molecule* to indicate that the mental unit is a compound rather

than a fundamental (atomic) aspect of matter and consciousness. In the later writings of CWL and AWB, it is more usual to see this component of ourselves referred to simply as the *mental unit*. It is the core around which the mental body forms and the storage place for the experience of our personality during life (especially our mental experience). The function of the mental unit resembles that of the *antahkaranah* (Sanskrit: "inner instrument") in HPB's Theosophy:

> The *path* or bridge between the Higher and the Lower Manas, the divine *Ego*, and the *personal* Soul of man. It serves as a medium of communication between the two, and conveys from the Lower to the Higher Ego all those personal impressions and thoughts of men which can, by their nature, be assimilated and stored by the undying Entity, and be thus made immortal with it, these being the only elements of the evanescent *Personality* that survive death and time. (*TG*, Antahkarana)

34. **Dr. Walter John Kilner** (1847–1920): A British medical doctor who experimented with specially prepared optical filters (dyed glass plates used as screens—hence Besant's mention of apparatus) to view the aura around the body and to observe its characteristics in health and disease. He claimed to pursue these investigations without reference to occultism or clairvoyance, hoping to discover a means whereby anyone could perceive the aura. The results of his studies were published in *The Human Atmosphere; or The Aura Made Visible by the Aid of Chemical Screens*.

35. **Heaven**: "Called in the older Theosophical books Devachan, or Sukhavati" [original footnote].
    Sukhavati (Sanskrit: "Land of Bliss"): In Mahayana Buddhism, the Western Paradise (also called the Pure Land) of Amitabha Buddha (the Buddha of Infinite Light). One object of spiritual practice of certain Buddhist sects is to be reborn in that paradise after death as a means of circumventing the ceaseless round of reincarnation in lower worlds, including the earth.

Chapter Fifteen: INVESTIGATIONS INTO THE SUPERPHYSICAL

1. **Seventy years**: This essay was first published in 1912. The first trances of the American medium Andrew Jackson Davis (1826–1910), who was a

powerful influence on the development of spiritualism, occurred seventy years earlier, in 1843 (http://www.andrewjacksondavis.com).

2. **The teachings among which we were born**: Besant was perhaps thinking of this passage from Blavatsky's *The Key to Theosophy*:

   > Every such attempt as the Theosophical Society has hitherto ended in failure, because, sooner or later, it has degenerated into a sect, set up hard-and-fast dogmas of its own, and so lost by imperceptible degrees that vitality which living truth alone can impart. You must remember that all our members have been bred and born in some creed or religion, that all are more or less of their generation both physically and mentally, and consequently that their judgment is but too likely to be warped and unconsciously biassed by some or all of these influences. If, then, they cannot be freed from such inherent bias, or at least taught to recognise it instantly and so avoid being led away by it, the result can only be that the Society will drift off on to some sandbank of thought or another, and there remain a stranded carcass to moulder and die. (*KT* 305)

3. **Arians**: Those who believed in teachings attributed to Arius of Alexandria (ca. 250/256–336 CE)—"that Christ is a created and human being, inferior to God the Father, though a grand and noble man, a true adept versed in all the divine mysteries" (*TG*, Arian). After the First Council of Nicaea (325 CE), such teachings were condemned as heretical, resulting in a century-long conflict between believers on both sides, replete with politically and religiously motivated condemnations, exiles, and slaughter (http://en.wikipedia.org/wiki/Arianism).

4. **Robe of Christ**: A reference to John 19:23, which mentions the robe Jesus was wearing when captured and imprisoned by Roman soldiers, who divided up his clothing among themselves. Used here as a metaphor for the undivided Church, which was rent by the schism between the Roman Catholic and Eastern Orthodox Churches in the 11th century.

5. **Different opinions**: This is a partial list of ideas about the Christ promoted by various members of the TS during the thirty-five years between its founding and the publication of this essay:

   - "The nature of the Christ": AWB and CWL claimed that during the ministry of the man Jesus, he was overshadowed by the consciousness of the "World Teacher" (a translation of the Sanskrit term *Jagatguru*), sometimes identified with Maitreya, the Bodhisattva who some Buddhist sects believe will incarnate as the successor of Gautama Buddha (who is often called "the *former* World Teacher" by AWB and CWL).

- "His place in history": G. R. S. Mead, at one time a secretary of HPB, published a book speculating on whether Jesus lived a century earlier than the date currently assigned to his life. HPB dropped hints to that effect (*CW* 4:603) and Mead followed them up by posing questions to AWB and CWL during clairvoyant investigations in 1897–98 (Jinarajadasa, *Occult Investigations*, 34–40). See Mead, *Did Jesus Live 100 BC? . . . Being a Contribution to the Study of Christian Origins.*
- "The proper name to be assigned to him": HPB wrote an article about whether the epithet *Christ* originated in the Greek word *chrestos* (good man) or *christos* (anointed). See "The Esoteric Character of the Gospels," *CW* 8:172–217. Besant could also be referring to her own teachings about the identity of Christ, Krishna, and Maitreya.
- "His position in the hierarchy": AWB and CWL taught that, in what they called the "occult hierarchy" that guides the evolution of our planet, there were two primary roles, that of the ruler and that of the teacher. Christ was the teacher (often called the World Teacher).
- "The particular body He used in the past or may use in the future": the Christ, as World Teacher, was said to have used the body of Jesus, who was at that time (100 BCE) only an initiated disciple. Jesus (*not* the Christ) was then reborn about the year 1 CE as Apollonius of Tyana (and became a Master). The Christ, however, was said to have incarnated previously as the Hindu Krishna, an avatar of the god Vishnu, and to be preparing to reincarnate as the next avatar of Vishnu, called the Kalki Avatara. J. Krishnamurti was trained by Besant and Leadbeater to be the next vehicle of the Christ as World Teacher, as Jesus was said to have been such a vehicle.

The sources for Besant's and Leadbeater's gradually developing views are too numerous and scattered to cite conveniently here. Despite their oddness when stated baldly, and their subsequent rejection by several segments of the TS that broke away in protest of these views, Besant's logic in presenting them is compelling—e.g., in *How a World Teacher Comes, as Seen by Ancient and Modern Psychology*, some of which can be traced back to HPB's posthumously published papers, especially those grouped together under the heading of "The Mystery of the Buddha" (*CW* 14:370–453).

Perhaps Besant's controversial views on the World Teacher could be rehabilitated by reconsidering the notion of *Jagatguru* as an enlightenment principle instead of as a semi-personalized consciousness (e.g., the Christ Consciousness) or a specific enlightened being (e.g., Bodhisattva Maitreya). Such a principle would correspond to HPB's *atman*, and the various overshadowings and incarnations cited by Besant would simply be instances of this principle's operation, without implying identity of soul or personality, as we usually think of these terms. It is shocking to Hindu and to Christian religious sensibilities to hear that Christ was Krishna reincarnated. Yet it is intriguing to consider that a nonpersonal cosmic enlightenment principle representing the highest level of divinity achievable in human form—i.e., atman—could be working through a historical Krishna or Christ.

6. **"Illusory body"**: "The *mayavi rupa*" [original footnote].

7. **Upanishads**: "Without senses, enjoying sense objects' [Bhagavad Gita 13.14]. 'Without eyes, he sees, without ears he hears,' etc. [Shvetashvatara Upanishad 3.19]. 'He is the seer, the hearer, the knower' [Brihadaranyaka Upanishad 3.8.11]" [original footnote].

8. **Earlier chains**: A reference to clairvoyant investigations of the earliest history of our evolutionary scheme, consisting of the first two planetary *manvantaras* (also called chains). See Annie Besant and Charles W. Leadbeater, *Man: Whence, How and Whither: A Record of Clairvoyant Investigation*, 19–32.

9. **William Scott-Elliot** (1848–1919): *The Story of Atlantis: A Geographical, Historical, and Ethnological Sketch Illustrated by Four Maps of the World's Configuration at Different Periods*; and *The Lost Lemuria, with Two Maps Showing the Distribution of Land Areas at Different Periods*; reissued together as *The Story of Atlantis and the Lost Lemuria, with Six Maps*. According to Joscelyn Godwin, Scott-Elliot was an aristocratic Scotsman, the tenth laird of Arkleton. (*Atlantis and the Cycles of Time: Prophecies, Traditions, and Occult Revelations*, 89) Scott-Elliot was also part of the London Lodge of the TS. CWL provided at least the maps for his books, if not also the clairvoyant content. (Godwin's biographical information on Scott-Elliott differs radically from that provided at http://en.wikipedia.org/wiki/WilliamScott-Elliot.)

William Kingsland (1855–1936): *A Child's Story of Atlantis*. Kingsland, an electrical engineer, was one of HPB's original students in England, elected president of the Blavatsky Lodge in 1889. According to Godwin, this book was actually dictated "by angels" to a child in a Theosophical family and edited for publication by Kingsland (ibid., 96).
Dr. Rudolph Steiner (1861–1925): *The Submerged Continents of Atlantis and Lemuria: Their History and Civilization, Being Chapters from the Akashic Records*. Austrian philosopher, mystic, and authority on the writings of Goethe and Nietzsche, Steiner met Besant in London at a TS convention in 1902. He was at that time the head of the German Section of the TS. Ten years later, a rift developed between him and Besant over their different interpretations of the second coming of Christ (in particular over her advocacy of J. Krishnamurti as the future vehicle of the World Teacher, whom she identified with Christ). This ideological rift resulted in the secession of the German Section from the International TS and its reconstitution as the Anthroposophical Society in 1913. Besant's critical mention of Steiner's work in this article and her references to the Arian controversy and the schism between the Roman Catholic and Eastern Orthodox Churches were signs of the strain engendered within the TS by the impending secession of the German Section.

Besant neglected to mention one other important early work in the genre of clairvoyant investigations of prehistory by members of the TS—*Man: Fragments of Forgotten History by Two Chelas*. The two chelas were Mohini Mohun Chatterji (1858–1926; Godwin, *Atlantis*, 73–74) and Mrs. Laura C. Holloway (later Langford). Chatterji was an attorney and early member of the TS in India. As noted, Mrs. Holloway was an American author and medium. HPB at first supported this collaborative project and later expressed serious reservations about it. The book was not in print at the time Besant's article was written, which may explain why she did not refer to it.

10. **William Kingdon Clifford** (1845–79): British mathematician and philosopher, known for his anticipation of Einstein's Theory of Relativity and for his rationalistic attacks on the blind faith of religious dogmatism. Besant is probably referring to Clifford's work on mathematical expressions of the curvature of space, which contributed to notions of the fourth dimension that were under discussion at the time this essay was written.

11. ***Athanasius contra mundem*** (Latin: "Athanasius against the world"): Nickname of St. Athanasius of Alexandria (ca. 296/298–373 CE),

considered an early father of the church in both Roman Catholicism and Greek Orthodoxy. The nickname arose due to his dogged opposition to Arianism, which he maintained even against powerful Arian bishops and emperors.

12. ***Atlantis and Lemuria***: The page number provided in a footnote in the original article and the pamphlet reprint is incorrect. The passage under discussion from Steiner's book, *Submerged Continents*, appears on pp. 188–89 (see http://babel.hathitrust.org/cgi/pt?id=nyp.33433087381061).

13. **Caution is necessary**: Besant's summary is adequate and unbiased. Steiner was writing about the period when "the astral, or Desire, body,—known as 'kama' in Theosophical literature,—was united with terrestrial man, and the objects of the senses became objects capable of being desired; man was thus bound through his desire body to earthly existence (ibid., 187–88).

    The key to Besant's objection to this passage lies in the clause "if it be intended to convey a physical fact, and is not merely a symbolical indication of some mental happening." The same objection could be raised to much of what she and CWL published in *Man: Whence, How, and Whither*—especially since so many of the book's clairvoyant revelations run counter to the paleontological, anthropological, and archaeological discoveries of the century following its publication.

    Steiner's information may be valid somehow—if not on our physical, fourth round, fourth globe planet, then on the astral planet represented by some earlier globe or round. In the same way, Besant and Leadbeater's observations may apply to some evolutionary stage of some round or globe, not necessarily the ones we are involved with at the moment. Or Besant and Leadbeater's observations, as well as Steiner's, may be merely mental and symbolic. Whatever the case, Besant's principles for evaluating clairvoyant information should be applied just as much to her own as to Steiner's, whether or not it seems to be more obviously aligned with the evolutionary schema laid down by the Masters and HPB.

    Lunar Chain: The planetary manvanatara that preceded ours, associated with the moon. Ours is the earth or terrene chain.

14. **Superphysical phenomena**: The three classifications of teachings implied in this paragraph bear deeper consideration. Some Theosophists argue that because the "vital teachings of brotherhood, reincarnation, and karma can be taught on intellectual and moral grounds, superphysical investigation isn't needed. The TS's first object of forming "a nucleus of the universal brotherhood of humanity" is enough to justify its existence.

In the case of the second classification of teachings, those that "influence life and conduct" through an understanding of the workings of the astral and mental worlds, superphysical investigation may be justified by the extent to which a knowledge of life after death, for example, affects how we think about ourselves and behave toward others. Theosophists who think along these lines might consider the third object of the TS, "to investigate unexplained laws of nature and the powers latent in man," worth pursuing as a form of service to humanity and (as Besant notes) a means of reinforcing the teachings about brotherhood, reincarnation, and karma.

In the case of the third classification of teachings—matters "which, however interesting as knowledge, are outside that which is needed for the guiding of human life"—superphysical investigation might not be of much value, especially if it leads to "considerable differences of opinion," schisms, and other unbrotherly behavior. Arguably, the contents of books such as those on Atlantis or Lemuria—even *Man: Whence, How and Whither*—might fall into this category. This statement is not meant to denigrate the perennial interest in such books or in the superphysical investigation that has gone into them. But it is meant to point out one reason some Theosophists might feel cautious about devoting time and energy to the third object of the TS or encouraging others to do so. Actively *discouraging* others to do so, however, would violate the all-important value of freedom of belief within the TS. As Besant puts it here, "the only point which we must accept is universal brotherhood—and, even as to that, we may differ in our definition of it. Outside that, we are at perfect liberty to form our own opinions on every subject" (247).

15. **Henri Bergson** (1859–1941): French philosopher. Besant is probably referring to the following passage from *Creative Evolution*:

> [Psychical activity] has the choice between two modes of acting on the material world: it can either effect this action *directly* by creating an *organized* instrument to work with [instinct]; or else it can effect it *indirectly* through an organism which, instead of possessing the required instrument naturally, will itself construct it by fashioning inorganic matter [intelligence]. (Henri Bergson, *Creative Evolution*, 142)

The words *organic* and *inorganic* are used here and in Besant's paraphrase in the less familiar sense of "organized" and "disorganized" (rather than the usual sense of "alive" and "not alive"). Bergson's point is that instinct organizes the body of a plant or an animal into the instrument required to perform a certain task and that intelligence fashions disorganized matter into an instrument or tool that extends the abilities of the body to perform a task it is not naturally (i.e., organically) equipped to perform.

16. **The Grey World:** novel by Evelyn Underhill (1875–1941), an English Pacifist writer famous for her penetrating explorations of mysticism. The novel details the inner life of a man who dies as a child in an impoverished family in the London slums and is quickly reborn into a middle-class family with spiritually stifling Edwardian values. Yet he retains haunting, even terrifying, memories of the spiritual emptiness of his existence in the "grey world" between lives.

    Besant and Leadbeater adopted the notion of the grey world as a description of the afterdeath fate of individuals who clung to the etheric double and were not able to move on to the astral realm. For Underhill, presence in the grey world indicated that the soul's capacity for spiritual love and compassion for suffering humanity had been insufficiently developed—a characteristic of Besant and Leadbeater's description of the astral plane, especially its lower levels.

17. **Ray**: Besant is referring to the Theosophical notion of the seven rays, each of which defines a particular function of the soul and temperament of the personality. CWL was said to represent the second ray of wisdom, hence Besant's reference to him as a teacher. Besant claimed to represent the first ray of leadership, of which her presidency of the TS and later political work on behalf of home rule for India were expressions. This is what she means by the reference to "my kind of work" in the next paragraph. For further information about the rays, see Ernest Wood, *The Seven Rays: A Theosophical Handbook*.

18. **Talc windows**: In Besant's time, a thin sheet of muscovite mica used as a window, somewhat inferior to glass in transparency and often tinted. Talc and mica are different minerals, yet the use of the word *talc* for muscovite mica was once common enough to make it the first definition of the word in the 2nd ed. of Webster's *New International Dictionary of the English Language* (1940). This usage has since disappeared. The current term for such windows is *isinglass*.

19. **Thus saith the Lord**: Common refrain in the Bible, here used metaphorically to refer to an indisputable article of faith.

20. **Mahadeva** (Sanskrit: "Great god"): Shiva.

21. **[Emanuel] Swedenborg**: The Swedish mystic's most famous book is *Heaven and Its Wonders and Hell: Drawn from Things Heard and Seen* (1758), originally written in Latin. Usually called *Heaven and Hell*, the book describes Swedenborg's visionary visits to various destinations in the afterlife and conversations with the angels, devils, and humans encountered there—hence Besant's reference to discarnates. In one of the ES Instructions, HPB makes a cautionary reference to Swedenborg:

> Remember that with our physical senses alone at our command, none of us can hope to reach beyond gross matter. We can do so only through one or another of our seven *spiritual* senses, either by training, or if one is a born seer. Yet even a clairvoyant possessed of such faculties, if not an Adept, no matter how honest and sincere he may be, will, through his ignorance of the truths of Occult Science, be led by the visions he sees in the Astral Light only to mistake for God or Angels the denizens of those spheres of which he may occasionally catch a glimpse—as witness Swedenborg and others. (*CW* 12:528)

22. **"Who have nothing more to learn"**: Translation of the Pali term *asekha* ("nonlearner"), associated in the Besant/Leadbeater tradition with the fifth initiation that makes an individual a Master.

Chapter Sixteen: OCCULTISM

1. **Divine language / self-expressions of God**: These phrases condense and summarize statements such as the following from Bruno's "Valedictory Oration to the Professors and Audience at Wittenberg University" (1588):

> Wisdom is apparent in the shape and body of all things; it calls upon man with a thousand voices, and in all parts of the earth. For all things—the stars, animals, all bodies, and their adornment—are living voices of wisdom, the token and work of God. They manifest the most high Providence, and in them, as in a book, are written the wisdom, power, and bounty of God. For the invisible being of God is perceived and recognized by that which he has created. (I. Frith, *The Life of Giordano Bruno, the Nolan*, 182–83)

2. **Jivanmukta** (Sanskrit): An individual who has achieved liberation while living—and has thus retained the bodies.
Videhamukta (Sanskrit): An individual who has achieved liberation at death—and has thus let go of the bodies.

3. **Nirmanakayas** (Sanskrit): "The *Bodhisattvas* [enlightened beings] or late Adepts, who having reached Nirvana and liberation from rebirth, renounce it voluntarily in order to remain invisibly amidst the world to help poor ignorant humanity within the lines permitted by Karma" (*CW* 12:31). Besant is referring particularly to this passage from *The Voice of the Silence*:

   > The "Guardian Wall" or the "Wall of Protection." It is taught that the accumulated efforts of long generations of Yogis, Saints and Adepts, especially of the Nirmanakayas—have created, so to say, a wall of protection around mankind, which wall shields mankind invisibly from still worse evils." (94n)

4. **[Giordano] Bruno**: Burned at the stake by the Inquisition for heretical views, including not only the heliocentric model of the solar system but also the idea of multiple worlds and stellar systems.
   Galileo Galilei (1564–1642): Astronomer, mathematician, and philosopher, famous for his telescopic observations of the solar system and his advocacy of the heliocentric model of it, for which he was tried by the Inquisition and acquitted on the basis of recantation.

5. **Luigi Galvani** (1737–98): Bolognese physician, comparative anatomist, and discoverer of the relationship between electricity and stimulation of the nervous system, through experiments on frogs. The following quotation is attributed to him: "I am attacked by two very opposite sects—the scientists and the know-nothings. Both laugh at me—calling me 'the frogs' dancing-master.' Yet I know that I have discovered one of the greatest forces in nature" (in William Crookes, *Investigations in the Phenomena of Spiritualism*, 21).

6. **Wrecks**: Probably a reference to the following statement of HPB, as reported by CWL:

   > "Ah! you Europeans," she said, "you think you are going to enter upon the path of occultism and pass triumphantly through all its troubles; you little know what is before you; you have not counted the wrecks by the wayside as I have. The Indians know what to expect, and they have already passed through tests and trials such as have never entered into your wildest dreams; but you, poor feeble things, what can you do?" (Leadbeater, *How Theosophy Came to Me*, 74)

7. **Star**: HPB sometimes referred to the monad as a star (e.g. *SD* 1:572–73). However, this may also be a veiled reference to the Order of the Star in the East (OSE), a Theosophical organization founded in 1911 under

Besant's sponsorship to promote the notion that "Alcyone" (a star in the constellation of the Pleiades—the alias or "star name" of J. Krishnamurti, at that time sixteen years old) was to become the vehicle of the World Teacher and usher in a new golden age. From that point until 1929, when Krishnamurti dissolved the OSE and renounced his role as World Teacher, the word Star (capitalized) in AWB's and CWL's writings often referred to him.

We might think of the star in Besant's analogy in terms of any higher being (such as a Theosophical Master) acting as an inner or outer teacher and guide to whom we have devoted ourselves in growth, learning, and service of humanity—or even in terms of the Logos itself. The following passage in one of HPB's ES Instructions seems to hint as much (note the parallels to Besant's imagery of star and rocky path):

> "If Sun [adept] thou canst not be, then be the humble Planet [chela]," says the *Book of the Golden Precepts* [*VS* 36]. And if even that is beyond our reach, then let us at least endeavor to keep within the ray of some lesser star [initiate], so that its silvery light may penetrate the murky darkness, through which the stony path of life trends onward; for without this divine radiance one risks losing more than he imagines. (*CW* 12:625)

Sources

What Theosophy Is. Pamphlet, Theosophical Tracts 4a, also containing "An Epitome of Theosophy" by Alexander Fullerton. 16 pp. London: Theosophical Publishing Society, n.d. Bound with 25 other pamphlets from the 1890s, mostly by AWB, with title on spine: *Theosophical Essays*. An approximate date of publication may be surmised from the last page, where *Man and His Bodies* (1896) is listed for sale and *The Ancient Wisdom* (1897) is described as "in preparation."

An Introduction to Theosophy. Pamphlet. 32 pp. London: Theosophical Publishing Society, 1896. In *Theosophical Essays*.

The Light and Dark Sides of Nature. Lecture of June 12, 1895: Blavatsky Lodge, London. *Lucifer* 19 (October–November 1896): 114–20; 177–85. Collected in *Essays and Addresses*, vol. 3: *Evolution and Occultism*, 210–38. London: Theosophical Publishing Society, 1913. Reprinted in Olcott Manual, No. 9, *True, Semi-, and Pseudo-Occultism*, 29–53. Wheaton, IL: Theosophical Press, 1941. This selection drawn from *Essays and Addresses*.

Occultism, Semi-Occultism, and Pseudo-Occultism. Lecture of June 30, 1898: Blavatsky Lodge, London. Pamphlet. 23 pp. London: Theosophical Publishing Society, 1898. Reprinted as Adyar Pamphlets, No. 19. 27 pp. Adyar, Madras, India: Theosophist Office, November 1912. Collected in *Essays and Addresses*, vol. 3: *Evolution and Occultism*, 180–209. London: Theosophical Publishing Society, 1912. Also appeared in Olcott Manual, No. 9, with title *True, Semi-, and Pseudo-Occultism*, 3–28. Wheaton, IL: Theosophical Press, 1941. Reprinted again under original title. 17 pp. Adyar, Madras, TPH, 1994. This selection drawn from *Essays and Addresses*.

The Higher Life. The *Theosophist* (Hollywood) 51 (January 1930): 395–402. For one year, the *Theosophist* was published from two locations with different editors and contents. The *Theosophist* (Adyar) was published in India, edited by AWB. The *Theosophist* (Hollywood) was published in America, edited by Marie Hotchener (1865–1945). The January issue of the *Theosophist* (Hollywood) had the same volume number as that of the *Theosophist* (Adyar), but the February and later issues of the Hollywood journal were renumbered as vol. 1. The present lecture was preceded by an editorial note:

> Unrevised notes of a lecture given in 1902. It was sent to the Assistant Editor [Hotchener] by the widow of a deceased American Theosophist who heard it. We are not sure whether it has ever been published or not, but prefer to give our readers the benefit of the doubt because it is so full of valuable teaching.

Assuming the date is correct, the auditor must have heard the lecture in England or India, since AWB was not in North America in 1902. She gave an unpublished lecture entitled "Laws of the Higher Life" on September 6, 1902, at the Northern Federation Conference, Harrogate, England, and a series of three lectures, published in book form as *The Laws of the Higher Life*, in December 1902 in Benares for the Indian Section Convention. The present lecture does not resemble the published ones.

The Lecture Bureau of the American Section advertised the availability of typed transcripts of a lecture called "Laws of the Higher Life" in the *Theosophic Messenger* from 1903–8. It seems likely that the present lecture was a transcript of that given at Harrogate and the version published in the *Hollywood Theosophist* was from one of these typed manuscripts. I have retained the original editorial subheadings.

Methods of Unfoldment. Lecture of June 26, 1904: Small Queen's Hall, London. In *Theosophy and the New Psychology*, 105–24. London: Theosophical Publishing Society, 1904.

The Reality of the Invisible and the Actuality of the Unseen Worlds. First published in the *Theosophical Review* 36 (August 1905): 489–98. Subsequently released as Adyar Pamphlets, No. 40. 16 pp. Adyar, Madras, India: Theosophical Publishing House, April 1914. Reprinted 1921. This selection drawn from the reprint.

Occultism and Occult Training. Lecture of June 20, 1904: Concertgebouw, Amsterdam. In *Transactions of the First Annual Congress of the Federation of European Sections of the Theosophical Society, Amsterdam, June 19–21, 1904,* edited by Johan van Manen, 389–98. Amsterdam: Council of the Federation, 1906.

The Conditions of Occult Research. Lecture of July 9, 1905: Empress Rooms, Kensington, England. In *Transactions of the Second Annual Congress of the Federation of European Sections of the Theosophical Society, July 6–10, 1905, London,* 435–44. London: Council of the Federation, 1907. Reprinted posthumously in the *Theosophist* 68 (February–March 1947): 293–300; 361–68.

Psychism and Spirituality. Lecture of June 16, 1907: Small Queen's Hall, London. In *London Lectures, 1907,* 3–26. London: Theosophical Publishing Society, 1907.

Communication between Different Worlds. First published in the *Theosophist* 31 (November–December 1909): 223–33; 365–74. Subsequently released as Adyar Pamphlets, No. 30. 32 pp. Adyar, Madras, India: Theosophical Publishing House, August 1913. Possibly based on lectures of 1907: "Communication between Different Planes" (June 7: Harrogate, England), "Varieties of Communication between Different Planes of Consciousness" (July 13: Birmingham, England), and "The Nature, Methods, and Laws of Intercommunication between the Worlds" (September 28: Philadelphia, PA).

The Larger Consciousness and Its Value. Lecture of July 11, 1909: Large Queen's Hall, London. In *The Changing World and*

Lectures to Theosophical Students, 155–80. London: Theosophical Publishing Society, 1909.

Revelation, Inspiration, Observation. Lecture of July 4, 1909: British Convention of the TS, St. James's Hall, London. First published as "The Theosophical Student in Face of Revelation, Inspiration, and Observation" in *The Changing World,* 317–33. Reprinted as pamphlet with title *Revelation, Inspiration, Observation: An Approach to Them for Theosophical Students*. 16 pp. London: Theosophical Publishing House, 1948. This selection drawn from *The Changing World.*

Theosophy as Science. Section 1 of *Theosophy,* 21–42. London: T. C. & E. C. Jack, 1912. I have omitted the final paragraphs, under the heading "Religious Ceremonies and Rites," as not relevant to this book.

Investigations into the Superphysical. First published in the *Theosophist* 33 (August–September 1912): 743–57; 893–909. Subsequently released as Adyar Pamphlets, No. 36. 33 pp. Adyar, Madras, India: Theosophical Publishing House, December 1913. Reprinted 1919. This selection drawn from the reprint. The original article appeared with the following note:

> This paper is the amplified substance of part of a lecture delivered in several places in England, Scotland, and also in Paris in the spring of the present year [1912]. It was reported in each case, and I have written the paper with the help of these reports.

This lecture, "Variations in Clairvoyant Observations," was given as follows: February 24 (Manchester), February 28 (London), March 12 (Glasgow), March 14 (Edinburgh), and April 5 (Paris).

Occultism. First published in the *Theosophist* 35 (March 1914): 863–70. Subsequently released as Adyar Pamphlets, No. 97. 8 pp. Adyar, Madras, India: Theosophical Publishing House, January 1919. This selection drawn from the latter.

Bibliography of Works Cited

Avalon, Arthur (Sir John Woodroffe). *The Serpent Power: The Secrets of Tantric and Shaktic Yoga*. 1919. 7th ed. Reprint with Sanskrit text omitted, New York, NY: Dover, 1974.

Babbitt, Edwin Dwight. *The Principles of Light and Color, Including among Other Things: The Harmonic Laws of the Universe; the Etherio-Atomic Philosophy of Force; Chromo Chemistry; Chromo Therapeutics; and the General Philosophy of the Fine Forces; Together with Numerous Discoveries and Practical Applications*. 1878. 2nd ed. East Orange, NJ: College of Finer Forces, 1896. http://books.google.com/books?id=ABYQAAAAYAAJ.

Bain, Alexander. *Mental and Moral Science: A Compendium of Psychology and Ethics*. London: Longman, Greens, 1868. http://babel.hathitrust.org/cgi/pt?id=hvd.32044048284228.

Barborka, Geoffrey A. *The Divine Plan: Written in the Form of a Commentary on H. P. Blavatsky's Secret Doctrine*. 1961. 2nd ed. Reprint, Adyar, Chennai, India: Theosophical Publishing House, 2002.

———. *H. P. Blavatsky, Tibet and Tulku*. 1966. Reprint, Adyar, Madras, India: Theosophical Publishing House, 1986.

Barker, A. Trevor, comp. *The Mahatma Letters to A. P. Sinnett from the Mahatmas M. and K.H.* 1924. 2nd ed. Facsimile. Reprint, Pasadena, CA: Theosophical University Press, 1992.

———. *The Mahatma Letters to A. P. Sinnett from the Mahatmas M. and K.H. in Chronological Sequence*. Edited by Vicente Hao Chin, Jr. Adyar, Chennai, India: Theosophical Publishing House, 2003.

Bergson, Henri. *Creative Evolution*. Translated by Arthur Mitchell. New York: Henry Holt, 1911. http://babel.hathitrust.org/cgi/pt?id=loc.ark:/13960/t03x93b05.

Besant, Annie. *The Ancient Wisdom*. 1897. Reprint, Adyar, Chennai, India: Theosophical Publishing House, 2001.

———. *Annie Besant: An Autobiography, with an Additional Survey of Her Life by George S. Arundale, and Biographical Notes Compiled Mainly from Her Own Writings*. Adyar, Madras, India: Theosophical Publishing House, 1939.

———. *The Bhagavadgita: The Lord's Song*. 1895. 2nd ed. 1953. Reprint, Adyar, Chennai, India: Theosophical Publishing House, 2005.

———. *Brahmavidya: Divine Wisdom*. 1923. 2nd ed. Adyar, India: Theosophical Publishing House, 1927.

———. *The Changing World and Lectures to Theosophical Students*. London: Theosophical Publishing Society, 1909.

———. *The Doctrine of the Heart: Extracts from Hindu Letters*. 1899. Reprint, Adyar, Chennai, India: Theosophical Publishing House, 2003.

———. *Essays and Addresses*. 4 vols. London: Theosophical Publishing Society, 1911–13.

———. *The Evolution of Life and Form*. 1899. 2nd ed. Benares, India: Theosophical Publishing Society, 1905.

———. "The Growth of the TS." *Theosophist* 33 (July 1912): 497–510.

———. *How a World Teacher Comes, as Seen by Ancient and Modern Psychology*. London: Theosophical Publishing House, 1926.

———. *In the Outer Court*. 1895. 2nd ed. Adyar, Chennai, India: Theosophical Publishing House, 2007.

———. "Instinct and Intuition." *Bibby's Annual* 7 (1912): 27.

———. *Karma*. 1895. Reprint, Adyar, Madras, India: Theosophical Publishing House, 2011.

———. *The Laws of the Higher Life*. 1903. Reprint, Adyar, Chennai, India: Theosophical Publishing House: 2006.

———. *London Lectures, 1907*. London: Theosophical Publishing Society, 1907.

———. *Man and His Bodies*. 1896. 2nd ed. Reprint, Adyar, Chennai, India: Theosophical Publishing House, 2008.

———. *Man's Life in This and Other Worlds*. Adyar, Madras, India: Theosophical Publishing House, 1913.

———. *Man's Life in Three Worlds: A Booklet for Beginners*. 1919. Reprint, Chicago, IL: Theosophical Press, 1923.

———. "A Note on Our Solar System (As Given in *The Secret Doctrine*)." *Adyar Bulletin* 3 (July 1910): 197–200.

———. "Occult Chemistry." *Lucifer* 17 (November 1895): 211–15.

———. *Occult Chemistry*. London: Theosophical Publishing Society, 1905. Reprint of 1895 *Lucifer* article.

———. "Occultism and Occult Training." *Quest: Journal of the Theosophical Society in America* 100 (Spring 2012): 67–73.

———. "Occultism in Daily Life." *Theosophist* (Hollywood) 1 (November 1930): 932–37.

———. "Our Planetary Chain." *Theosophist* 49 (August–September 1928): 623–31; 727–32.

———. *The Path of Discipleship*. 1896. Reprint, Adyar, Chennai, India: Theosophical Publishing House, 2002.

———"Psychic and Spiritual Development." *Adyar Bulletin* 6:47–56 (February 1913). (Also published as Adyar Pamphlet, No. 64. Adyar, Madras, India: Theosophical Publishing House, April 1916.)

———. *The Seven Principles of Man*. 1892. Rev. ed. Reprint, Adyar, Madras: Theosophical Publishing House, 2008.

———. *The Spiritual Life*. 1912. Rev. ed. Wheaton, IL: Quest Books, 1991. (Originally published as *Essays and Addresses*, vol. 2)

———. *A Study in Consciousness*. 1904. 2nd ed. Adyar, Chennai, India: Theosophical Publishing House, 1999.

———. *Theosophy and the New Psychology*. London: Theosophical Publishing Society, 1904.

Besant, Annie and C. W. Leadbeater. *The Lives of Alcyone: A Clairvoyant Investigation of the Lives throughout the Ages of a Large Band of Servers*. 2 vols. Adyar, Madras, India: Theosophical Publishing House, 1924.

———. *Man: Whence, How and Whither. A Record of Clairvoyant Investigation*. 1913. 5th ed. Abridged. Adyar, Madras, India: Theosophical Publishing House, 1971.

———. *Occult Chemistry: Clairvoyant Observations on the Chemical Elements*. Adyar, Madras, India: Theosophist Office, 1908. 2nd ed. London: Theosophical Publishing House, 1919. 3rd ed. Adyar, Madras, India: Theosophical Publishing House, 1951.

———. *Talks on the Path of Occultism*. 3 vols. 1926. Reprint, Adyar, Chennai, India: Theosophical Publishing House, 2004.

———. *Thought-Forms*. 1905. Abridged. Wheaton, IL: Quest Books, 1999.

Besant, Arthur Digby. *The Besant Pedigree*. London: Besant and Co., 1930.

"A Besant Diary of Principal Events." *Theosophist* 69: 84–88 (October 1947).

Bhagavan Das. *Annie Besant and the Changing World*. Adyar Pamphlets, nos. 190–91. Adyar, Madras, India: Theosophical Publishing House: October–November 1934. http://hpb.narod.ru/BesantAndChangingWorldBD.html.

———. *The Science of the Emotions*. London: Theosophical Publishing Society, 1900.

Bhagavan Das (trans.) and Annie Besant. *Mystic Experiences: Tales of Yoga and Vedanta from the Yogavasishtha, with Notes by Annie Besant*. 1927. Reprint, Varanasi, India: The Indian Bookshop, 1988.

Blavatsky, H. P. *Collected Writings*. 15 vols. Edited by Boris de Zirkoff. Wheaton, IL: Theosophical Publishing House, 1950–91.

———. *Isis Unveiled*. 2 vols. *Collected Writings*. Revised and corrected 1st ed. of 1877. Edited by Boris de Zirkoff. Wheaton, IL: Theosophical Publishing House, 1972.

———. *The Key to Theosophy*. Facsimile of 1st ed. of 1889, with glossary from 2nd ed. and a new index. Pasadena, CA: Theosophical University Press, 2007.

———. "Letters of HPB to Dr. Hartmann (1885–86)." *Path* 10 (March 1896): 366–73. http://books.google.com/books?id=NAkpAAAAYAAJ.

———. *The Secret Doctrine*. 3 vols. *Collected Writings*, 1888. Edited by Boris de Zirkoff. 1979. Reprint, Wheaton, IL: Theosophical Publishing House, 1987.

———. *Theosophical Articles Reprinted from Original Sources.* 3 vols. Los Angeles: Theosophy Co., 1981.

———. *The Theosophical Glossary.* Facsimile of 1st ed. of 1892. Los Angeles: Theosophy Co., 1973.

———. *Transactions of the Blavatsky Lodge of the Theosophical Society: Discussions on the Stanzas of the First Volume of The Secret Doctrine.* Los Angeles: Theosophy Co., 1923.

———. *The Voice of the Silence, being Extracts from the Book of the Golden Precepts.* Facsimile of 1st ed. of 1889. 2nd ed. 1992. Reprint, Wheaton: IL: Quest Books, 1997.

Buchner, Ludwig. *Force and Matter, or Principles of the Natural Order of the Universe, with a System of Morality Based thereon: A Popular Exposition.* 1855. 4th English ed. from 15th German ed. London: Asher, 1884. http://babel.hathitrust.org/cgi/pt?id=mdp.39015022387321.

Caldwell, Daniel. *The Esoteric Papers of Madame Blavatsky.* Whitefish, MT: Kessinger, 2004.

———. *The Esoteric World of Madame Blavatsky: Insights into the Life of a Modern Sphinx.* Wheaton, IL: Quest Books, 2000.

Carus, Paul. *The Gospel of Buddha According to Old Records.* 1894. 5th ed. Chicago: Open Court, 1897. http://babel.hathitrust.org/cgi/pt?id=mdp.39015008473244.

Clarke, Adam. *Holy Bible . . . with a Commentary and Critical Notes.* 6 vols. 1810–25. Reprint, New York: Emory & Waugh, 1833. http://babel.hathitrust.org/cgi/pt?id=nnc1. 0043207677. URL for vol. 3.

Collins, Mabel. *Light on the Path and Through the Gates of Gold.* Pasadena, CA: Theosophical University Press, 1997.

Cory, Isaac Preston. *Ancient Fragments of the Phoenician, Chaldean, Egyptian, Tyrian, Carthaginian, Indian, Persian, and Other Writers; with an Introductory Dissertation and an Inquiry into the Philosophy and Trinity of the Ancients*. 1828. 2nd ed. London: William Pickering, 1832. http://babel.hathitrust.org/cgi/pt?id=hvd.32044038414439.

Crookes, William. *Investigations in the Phenomena of Spiritualism*. London: J. Burns, 1874. http://babel.hathitrust.org/cgi/pt?id=mdp.39015035035982.

Farthing, Geoffrey A. *The Etheric Double? The Far-Reaching Effects of a False Assumption*. Privately printed. June 1995. http://www.katinkahesselink.net/metaphys/etheric.htm.

Feuerstein, Georg. *The Encyclopedia of Yoga and Tantra*. 1997. Revised and expanded. Boston, MA: Shambhala, 2011.

Frith, I. *The Life of Giordano Bruno, the Nolan*. London, Trubner, 1887. http://babel.hathitrust.org/cgi/pt?id=mdp.39015026092638.

Godwin, Joscelyn. *Atlantis and the Cycles of Time: Prophecies, Traditions, and Occult Revelations*. Rochester, VT: Inner Traditions, 2011.

Hoult, Powis. *A Dictionary of Some Theosophical Terms*. London: Theosophical Publishing Society, 1910.

"In the Twilight." *Theosophist* 30 (July 1909): 504–508.

———.*Theosophist* 31 (May 1910): 1098–1100.

———.*Theosophist* 34 (May 1913): 277–80.

Jinarajadasa, C. *The Golden Book of the Theosophical Society 1875–1925*. Adyar, Madras, India: Theosophical Publishing House, 1925.

———. "Investigations into Early Rounds." *Theosophist* 32 (August–September 1911): 724–37; 871–89.

———. *Letters from the Masters of the Wisdom*. First Series. 1919. 6th ed. Adyar, Madras, India: Theosophical Publishing House, 1988.

———. *Letters from the Masters of the Wisdom*. Second Series. 1925. Reprint, Adyar, Madras, India: Theosophical Publishing House, 2002.

———. *Occult Investigations: A Description of the Work of Annie Besant and C. W. Leadbeater*. Adyar, Madras, India: Theosophical Publishing House, 1938.

"John Paul Friedrich Richter's Review of Madame de Stael's 'Allemagne.'" *Fraser's Magazine for Town and Country* 1 (February 1830): 28–37. http://babel.hathitrust.org/cgi/pt?id=inu.30000080778487.

Judge, William Q. *Echoes of the Orient: The Writings of William Quan Judge*. Edited by Dara Eklund. 4 vols. 1975–93. 2nd rev. ed. Pasadena, CA: Theosophical University Press, 2009–2011. Vol. 2: http://www.theosociety.org/pasadena/wqj-echoes/EchoesOrient2-WQJ.pdf. Vol. 3: http://www.theosociety.org/pasadena/wqj-echoes/EchoesOrient3-WQJ.pdf.

Kilner, Walter J. *Human Atmosphere, or The Aura Made Visible by the Aid of Chemical Screens*. London: Rebmann, 1911.

Kingsland, William. *A Child's Story of Atlantis*. London: Theosophical Publishing Society, 1908.

Leadbeater, C. W. *The Astral Plane*. 1895. Rev. ed. Reprint, Adyar, Chennai, India: Theosophical Publishing House, 2010.

———. *The Chakras*. 1927. Reprint, Wheaton, IL: Quest Books, 2001.

———. *The Devachanic Plane, or The Heaven World: Its Characteristics and Inhabitants*. 1896. Reprint, Adyar, Madras, India: Theosophical Publishing House, 1987.

———. "Dr. Besant's First Use of Clairvoyance." *Theosophist* 54 (October 1932): 11–13.

———. *How Theosophy Came to Me*. 1930. Reprint, Adyar, Madras, India: Theosophical Publishing House, 2001.

———. *The Hidden Side of Things*. 1913. 3rd ed. Adyar, Madras, Chennai: Theosophical Publishing House, 1999.

———. *The Inner Life*. 2 vols. 1910–11. Abridged ed. in 1 vol. Wheaton, IL: Quest Books, 1978.

———. *Invisible Helpers*. 1896. 2nd ed. Revised and enlarged. 1928. Reprint, Adyar, Madras, India: Theosophical Publishing House, 2007.

———. *Man Visible and Invisible*. 1902. Abridged. Wheaton, IL: Quest Books, 2000.

———. *The Masters and the Path*. 1925. 2nd ed. Abridged. 1983. Reprint, Adyar, Chennai, India: Theosophical Publishing House, 2002.

———. *Messages from the Unseen*. Adyar, Madras, India: Theosophical Publishing House, 1931.

———. *The Other Side of Death, Scientifically Examined by Clairvoyant Investigation and Carefully Described*. 1903. 3rd ed. Adyar, Madras, India: Theosophical Publishing House, 1954.

———. *A Textbook of Theosophy*. Adyar, Madras, India: Theosophist Office, 1912. (Also reprint, Adyar, Chennai, India: Theosophical Publishing House, 2007.)

Mead, G. R. S. *Did Jesus Live 100 BC? An Enquiry into the Talmud Jesus Stories, the Toldoth Jeschu, and Some Curious Statements of Epiphanius, Being a Contribution to the Study of Christian Origins*. London: Theosophical Publishing Society, 1903.

Milton, John. *The Complete English Poems*. Edited by John Campbell. New York, NY: Knopf, 1992.

Myer, Isaac. *Qabbalah: The Philosophical Writings of Solomon Ben Yehudah Ibn Gebirol or Avicebron and their connection with the Hebrew Qabbalah and Sepher ha-Zohar, etc.* Philadelphia, PA: printed by author, 1888. http://books.google.com/books?id=ojTIOf8LCIgC.

Nethercot, Arthur H. *The First Five Lives of Annie Besant*. Chicago, IL: University of Chicago Press, 1960.

———. *The Last Four Lives of Annie Besant*. Chicago, IL: Chicago University Press, 1963.

Olcott, H. S. *Buddhist Catechism*. 1881. 42nd ed. Adyar, Madras, India: Theosophist Office, 1908. http://archive.org/details/abuddhistcatechi0000olcouoft

———. *Old Diary Leaves: The History of the Theosophical Society*. 6 vols. 1895–1935. 2nd ed. Reprint, Adyar, Madras, India: Theosophical Publishing House, 1972–75.

Phelps, Austin. *The New Birth, or the Work of the Holy Spirit*. Boston: Gould & Lincoln, 1867. http://books.google.com/books?id=q8AMAAAAIAAJ.

Prakasa, Sri. *Annie Besant as Woman and as Leader*. 1940. 3rd ed. Bombay: Bharatiya Vidya Bhavan, 1962.

Prel, Carl, Baron du. *The Philosophy of Mysticism*. Translated by C. C. Massey. London: Redway, 1889.

Ransom, Josephine. "How *The Secret Doctrine* Was Written." In H. P. Blavatsky, *The Secret Doctrine*. 6 vols. 5th ed. 1:18–36. Adyar, Madras, India: Theosophical Publishing House, 1971.

———. *The Seventy-Fifth Anniversary Book of the Theosophical Society: A Short History of the Society's Growth from 1926–1950*. Adyar, Madras, India: Theosophical Publishing House, 1950.

———. *A Short History of the Theosophical Society (1875–1938)*. 1938. Reprint, Adyar, Chennai, India: Theosophical Publishing House, 1989.

Rhys Davids, T. W. *Buddhism: Its History and Literature*. 1896. 2nd ed. London: Putnam, 1904. http://babel.hathitrust.org/cgi/pt?id=uva.x030125760.

Richardson, Sir Benjamin Ward. "Theory of a Nervous Ether." *Popular Science Review*, 10 (1871): 379–87. http://babel.hathitrust.org/cgi/pt?id=uc1.b3080913.

Roberts-Austen, Sir William. "The Rarer Metals and their Alloys." *Nature* 52, no. 1331 (May 2, 1895): 14–18; no. 1332 (May 9, 1895): 39–41. http://babel.hathitrust.org/cgi/pt?id=uva.x001518370.

Schreiner, Olive. *Dreams*. 1890. 2nd ed. London: T. Fisher Unwin, 1891. http://books.google.com/books?id=3tQOAAAAIAAJ.

Scott-Elliot, William. *The Lost Lemuria, with Two Maps Showing the Distribution of Land Areas at Different Periods*. London: Theosophical Publishing Society, 1904.

———. *The Story of Atlantis: A Geographical, Historical, and Ethnological Sketch Illustrated by Four Maps of the World's Configuration at Different Periods*. London: Theosophical Publishing Society, 1896.

———. *The Story of Atlantis and the Lost Lemuria, with Six Maps*. London: Theosophical Publishing Society, 1925.

Sinnett, A. P. *Esoteric Buddhism*. 1883. 8th ed. London: Theosophical Publishing Society, 1911.

———. *Incidents in the Life of Madame Blavatsky: Compiled from Information Supplied by Her Relatives and Friends*. 1886. 2nd ed. London: Theosophical Publishing Society, 1913.

———. *The Occult World*. London: Trubner, 1881.

Spierenburg, Henk J. *The Inner Group Teachings of H. P. Blavatsky to Her Personal Pupils (1890–91)*. 1985. 2nd ed. San Diego, CA: Point Loma Publications, 1995.

Stead, William Thomas. *Letters from Julia, or Light from the Borderland: A Series of Messages as to the Life beyond the Grave Received by Automatic Writing from One Who Has Gone Before.* London: Richards, 1897. (Later editions: *After Death, or Letters from Julia: A Personal Narrative.*)

Steiner, Rudolf. *The Submerged Continents of Atlantis and Lemuria: Their History and Civilization, Being Chapters from the Akashic Records.* Translated by Max Gysi. Chicago: Rajput Press, 1911. http://babel.hathitrust.org/cgi/pt?id=nyp.33433087381061.

Swedenborg, Emanuel. *Heaven and Hell.* Translated by George Dole. West Chester, PA: Swedenborg Foundation, 2000.

Tillett, Gregory John. *Charles Webster Leadbeater, 1854–1934: A Biographical Study*. Online edition. 2008. http://leadbeater.org/tillettcwlnotes.htm.

———. *The Elder Brother: A Biography of Charles Webster Leadbeater.* London: Routledge & Kegan Paul, 1982.

Two Chelas [Mohini Mohun Chatterji and Laura C. Holloway]. *Man: Fragments of Forgotten History*. London: Reeves & Turner, 1885.

Underhill, Evelyn. *The Grey World.* London: William Heinemann, 1904. http://babel.hathitrust.org/cgi/pt?id=uc2.ark:/13960/t3028qk8h.

Vivekananda, Swami. *Complete Works of Swami Vivekananda.* 8 vols. 1985–89. Subsidized edition, reprint, Kolkata, India: Advaita Ashrama, 2006.

Wachtmeister, Constance. *H.P.B and the Present Crisis in the Theosophical Society*. London: privately printed, 1895. http://blavatskyarchives.com/theosophypdfs/wachtmeisterhpbandthepresentcrisis1895.pdf

Waite, Arthur Edward. *The Mysteries of Magic: A Digest of the Writings of Eliphas Levi.* 1886. 2nd ed. Revised and enlarged. 1896. Reprint, Secaucus, NJ: University Books, 1974.

Williams, Gertrude M. *The Passionate Pilgrim: A Life of Annie Besant.* London: John Hamilton, 1931.

Wood, Ernest. *The Seven Rays: A Theosophical Handbook.* 1925. Reprint, Wheaton, IL: Quest Books, 1984.

Yonge, Charles Duke. *The Works of Philo Judaeus, the Contemporary of Josephus.* 4 vols. New York: Henry G. Bohn, 1854–55. http://babel.hathitrust.org/cgi/pt?id=hvd.32044023336332. URL for vol. 1.

Index